Patrick Weller AO is a graduate of Oxford and the Australian National University. He has been professor of politics at Griffith University since 1984 and is now in the School of Government and International Relations. His areas of research are Australian politics and comparative institutions. He is author of *First Among Equals* (1985), *Malcolm Fraser Prime Minister* (1989), *Australia's Mandarins* (2001), *Cabinet Government on Australia* (2009), and co-author of *Westminster Compared* (2009), *Inside the World Bank* (2009) and *Learning to be a Minister* (2010). He is currently writing a comparative study of prime ministers in Westminster systems.

KEVIN RUDD
TWICE PRIME MINISTER

PATRICK WELLER

MELBOURNE UNIVERSITY PRESS
An imprint of Melbourne University Publishing Limited
11–15 Argyle Place South, Carlton, Victoria 3053, Australia
mup-info@unimelb.edu.au
www.mup.com.au

First published 2014
Text © Patrick Weller, 2014
Design and typography © Melbourne University Publishing Limited, 2014

This book is copyright. Apart from any use permitted under the *Copyright Act 1968* and subsequent amendments, no part may be reproduced, stored in a retrieval system or transmitted by any means or process whatsoever without the prior written permission of the publishers.

Every attempt has been made to locate the copyright holders for material quoted in this book. Any person or organisation that may have been overlooked or misattributed may contact the publisher.

Text design by Phil Campbell
Cover design by Phil Campbell
Typeset by J&M Typesetting
Printed in Australia by McPherson's Printing Group

National Library of Australia Cataloguing-in-Publication entry

Weller, Patrick, 1944–.

Kevin Rudd : twice prime minister / Patrick Weller.

9780522857481 (paperback)
9780522867329 (ebook)

Includes index.

Rudd, Kevin, 1957 – .
Prime ministers—Australia—Biography.
Politicians—Australia—Biography.
Australia—Politics and government—21st century.

994.07092

CONTENTS

Preface		vii
Part I–The Beginning		
1	A Queensland Boy	3
2	Calligraphy and Christianity	21
3	Diplomat to China	35
4	Politics in Queensland	48
5	A Political Initiation: from Candidate to Backbencher	68
6	Stalking Downer, Surviving Latham	86
7	Winning the Leadership	102
8	Models, Ideas and Beliefs	118
9	To Victory	129
Part II–Governing		
10	Taking Over	147
11	Reaching Out	160
12	Punching above Our Weight	171
13	Facing the Global Crises	185
14	A Week in the Office	204
15	A Time for Questions	215
16	Playing on the International Stage	227
17	Resetting Priorities: Climate Change	244
Part III–Struggling		
18	Challenges	267
19	The Coup	285
20	How Rudd Governed	300

| 21 | Limbo | 337 |
| 22 | Going Down Fighting | 356 |

Notes	373
Acknowledgements	384
Index	386

PREFACE

27 June 2013. Kevin Rudd was sworn in as Prime Minister of Australia for the second time. Three years after he had been driven from office in a sudden coup, the Labor Party re-elected him as leader and he replaced Julia Gillard as prime minister. But this event was very different from his first election in December 2007.

Then, there had been hope and expectation: a new prime minister and a new government. The swearing in of the Rudd government was a changing of the guard. The Howard era was over. The new ministers were young, ambitious and optimistic. As their families mingled at Government House, as new faces took the oath of office, observers commented that here was a two-term, maybe even a three-term government that would change Australian society. At its head was a triumphant Kevin Rudd, riding a wave of public support that was to last for the next two years. Smiling, promising, articulate, young, forward-looking and often droll, his image found its reflection in the ever-popular cartoon character Tintin.

Early on, many of Rudd's ministers likewise seemed to shine, to emerge from the anonymity of Opposition with the competence to manage the affairs of government. Australia survived the Global Financial Crisis in a way that made other countries curious and envious. There were few initial scandals: the government would not lose its first minister until eighteen months had passed. The polls indicated support for the prime minister and the government, as leaders of the Opposition fell by the wayside, discarded by their parties before having the chance to fight an election.

But then, at the first sign of trouble in the polls, the Labor Party removed Rudd in a coup of which most of his ministers were unaware. The government never recovered. After the coup came minority government, division and constant internecine warfare. The government languished in the polls with a level of support that suggested the next federal election result would be the worst in Labor's history—an annihilation. Massive defeats in state elections in New South Wales and Queensland were harbingers of what the Labor Party could expect. And so Labor, seemingly through gritted teeth, returned to Rudd as its last hope, if not of winning then at least of saving the seats of the many who saw only electoral oblivion ahead.

It was a very different Kevin Rudd who returned to office in June 2013. It had to be. In 2007 he had been a fresh face, a new image: the convivial, Mandarin-speaking nerd who seemed so different from past leaders and who for the past year had been introducing himself to the people of Australia. He offered a series of ambitious plans for the country while arguing that he was cautious and conservative in economic management. In the election campaign he foreswore big spending: 'This madness has to stop' was his response to Prime Minister Howard's new electoral commitments.

In 2013 Kevin Rudd retained some of his popularity but none of his novelty. After his term as prime minister, he had been foreign minister for eighteen months and was then on the backbench for another fifteen. But essentially, all that time, regardless of whether he'd been planning his comeback (which he often had) or was merely being himself, he had been the alternative to Julia Gillard. His colleagues had done their best to besmirch his reputation, in the hope that he would be so damaged that he could never again be credible as prime minister. They'd sullied his standing. But they had not undermined his popularity. If the parliamentary caucus had preferred Gillard the three previous times they'd had a choice, the people had preferred Rudd. Eventually, the caucus too turned to him, by 57 votes to 45.

The cause was tough. He had two, perhaps three months before an election. The Opposition could say nothing derogatory about him that his colleagues had not already said. There was a series of policy bombs to defuse. Rudd himself might still have had the drive, the self-belief that had allowed him to survive three years of denigration and personal vitriol, but he could not be the Tintin of 2007, the optimistic, cheerful face of the future. The second term was to be a grim battle from day to day as hope of victory soon vanished, and the only real issue was whether the seats of the next generation of Labor leaders could be saved. It was to be 'nasty, brutish and short'.

The Rudd governments may get short shrift from historians. Like so many past Labor governments, internal battles and bitterness made re-election in 2013 unlikely. However, this political death was arguably less dramatic than that of some of its predecessors: the Hughes and Scullin Labor governments disintegrated, brought down by dissidents; the Whitlam government was sacked by the governor-general after more than a year of internal discord, including the loss of a deputy prime minister/treasurer, a speaker and other senior ministers. The second Rudd government just subsided into defeat, too divided, too tarnished, too disliked to seriously claim that it could be trusted for another term.

Yet Rudd himself remains an unusual case: the son of a poor Queensland dairy farmer; a party member without a faction who twice rose to lead a bitterly factionalised Labor; the only federal Labor leader to win a majority since Paul Keating in 1993; only the fifth leader in 115 years to win an election that took Labor from the

Opposition to the Treasury benches; and only the second prime minister since 1914 to be sworn in for a second time—the other was Sir Robert Menzies, which is rare company indeed. This book tells the story of how Rudd achieved all that, how he rose to become, and work as, Prime Minister of Australia.

★ ★ ★

The prime ministership is a job. It is not quite like any other, but it is a job nonetheless, and the position creates expectations. Some responsibilities come with the appointment: determining governmental arrangements, running Cabinet, making parliamentary appearances, representing Australia internationally. Other activities are determined by the priorities of the individual prime ministers—policy areas, media appearances, public speeches—or sometimes by external pressures, be they financial crises, bushfires or boat people. So prime ministers in part choose what they do, and in part are required by tradition and circumstance to react to the initiatives of others. There are some things that only prime ministers can do, and others that can be delegated to ministers or actors. These are choices for prime ministers, choices that will determine how their government is run. They are seldom appreciated in public.

Much of the process of governing has to be done in private. As an iceberg shows only one-tenth of its mass above water, so the public only sees a small part of the efforts that prime ministers must apply to the job. Announcements that appear to have been scripted on the back of an envelope are often the outcomes of extensive internal discussions and calculations. No other job in the country makes such relentless demands in terms of the range of skills needed, the variety of topics to be addressed, the constancy of the pressure. It alone undergoes intrusive round-the-clock media interest and the forensic scrutiny of every word and action. It takes particular personalities to thrive in this climate of tension.

Many may aspire to be prime minister; every first-year politics class at university will have one or two such dreamers. Some take the first steps along the route. A few attain a high status in political parties. Fewer still get to parliament, where the rivalry may be more obvious, the ambitions more naked. Even leadership of a party is no guarantee of the top job; eight of the Australian Labor Party's eighteen leaders were never prime minister. Only twenty-eight people so far have become prime minister and three of those were caretakers, sworn in for a few days while parties chose new leaders. Only four people have been prime minister and then resumed office after another incumbent has held the job. People rarely become prime minister by accident; it is almost always the result of a long, dedicated journey, one of gaining experience, winning support, developing a profile, honing skills, and invariably working with a high level of ruthlessness. And this is coupled with a degree of *fortuna*—being in the right place at the right time, when circumstances are propitious, when enemies are in disarray. Leaders shape their times, but they also respond to them. Those that finally make it then have to use the opportunity to react to emerging threats and to make their mark on the nation in the form that *they* want.

Prime ministers do not live in a bubble. They live in a movable network of relationships. They must constantly work with others who shape their attitudes, guide their thinking and offer both examples and cautionary tales. Some of those supporters promote their careers deliberately, some by chance, perhaps through gritted teeth.

This book seeks to explain how one person came to the job and sought to meet its demands, lost the job, then won it back again and had to work in very different circumstances to the first time. It does not try to provide a detailed account of everything in Kevin Rudd's life, nor to explore all the opinions about each stage of his career. It does not seek to sit in judgement on the policies that he introduced, nor ask whether he should have adopted alternative strategies or done things differently. It does try to identify what made him the man he is, how in his early career we can see the personality that became prime minister, and how those characteristics shaped his terms in office.

★ ★ ★

This book has a broken history. It was at first intended to be an interim report: to explain how Rudd came to office and how he worked as prime minister in his first two years in power. I finished writing it in early 2010, soon after the international climate change conference in Copenhagen, but before many of the early signs that Rudd was in some trouble began to emerge. In the next few months, the book went through the normal stages of editing and indexing, even as the picture of a supremely confident Rudd began to be tarnished. It was due to go to the printer on 24 June 2010—the day Rudd lost his prime ministership. The book was put on ice.

For the next three years, I waited for the moment when I could confidently believe that Rudd's career was over, so that I would not again have the book stalled by some sudden event, such as a comeback. I continued to interview Rudd, even after he resigned as foreign minister in February 2012. It was as well I waited. I was on a bus travelling from Geneva to Grenoble in June 2013 as the SMSes began to flow, providing details of the leadership joust taking place. When Rudd finally announced he would leave parliament that November, I returned to the book, inevitably changing much that had been written (hindsight has advantages!), and extending the story to the completion of his Australian career. My interest was in Rudd as prime minister, in understanding the how and why of the prime minister's task, so I paid little attention to his time as foreign minister, even though it deserves consideration in its own right.

This interrupted history has two impacts. First, much of the writing and some of the interviewing was done in 2009. I talked to some of those who were to become Rudd's greatest critics and gained their approval to include quotations from their interviews in the text. They backed Rudd strongly then, his prospects appearing to be good, and I have not tried to change this perception in revising the text—that is what they said then, and I have assumed it was sincere. Nor have I sought to detract attention from the energy and enthusiasm with which Rudd approached many policy areas, or the interaction he had with the public, even if some of the initiatives were not fruitful. The chapters in Part II deal with the issues that were seen as important at the time, and the initiatives that the prime minister regarded as significant.

The second, related point is that those chapters were not initially written with the benefit of hindsight. Since June 2010, everything, and I mean everything, has been interpreted through the lens of the Gillard coup. Many have sought to justify how they behaved then by later raising issues and complaints that they never expressed at the time.

Looking back on those events after he left politics, Lindsay Tanner, the former Minister for Finance, wrote:

> When regimes are deposed by radical and extraordinary means the new rulers invariably demonise those who have been unseated in order to justify the enormity of their own behavior. You can even see this in the way historians are still unraveling the web of Tudor propaganda that painted a grotesque caricature of Richard III in order to justify Henry Tudor's seizure of the British crown in 1485 ...
>
> Removing a first term elected prime minister by a caucus vote, ostensibly because of his management style, is such an

extreme thing to do that those involved have found it necessary to enormously exaggerate the deficiencies in Kevin Rudd's leadership. There were some deficiencies, it's true ... The critical question, though, is whether they justified a leadership ambush of the kind that occurred on 23 June 2010.

He thought the move unwarranted; others disagree. But he is right about the strategy: Rudd's critics condemned him, first in private and then, when that did not work, in public.

As for fifty years I have been fascinated by the story of Richard III, whose reputation was so unfairly damned, first by Thomas More and then Shakespeare (great play, lousy history), Tanner's comparison resonated with me. The constantly recirculated stories and gossip about Rudd reflect a desire to demonise him, to blame him for all the failings of recent Labor governments, whether he was in or out of office at the time. These stories are different from the accounts given in 2009, and that is worth remembering. What changed so dramatically? The criticisms are often coloured by where the sources stood in 2010 and/or what they thought of later events. Some who backed him in 2010 attacked him vigorously later; many returned to him in 2013, even if out of desperation. All of these retrospective accounts, whether in favour or critical of Rudd, must be seen through that lens. There are an increasing number of such stories, though, fortunately for Rudd, none of the authors have the prestige of a Thomas More or the genius of a Shakespeare.

★ ★ ★

This book is not an authorised biography. I was not required to gain consent for what I wrote. Nor has Kevin Rudd read what I have written, in 2010 or in 2014. However, the project was undertaken with the cooperation of Rudd. Readers should therefore know how and in what circumstances the book was written.

I have known Kevin Rudd for twenty years. After the 2007 election, I inquired whether it would be possible to develop a project in which I talked to him intermittently to explore how, over time, his role as prime minister changed. It was intended to be something like *The Clinton Tapes*, a project undertaken in Washington by Taylor Branch, who talked to President Clinton on an irregular basis and only published his account of the process in 2009. The benefit was that he could provide a series of contemporaneous images, rather than one story given at the end of Clinton's presidency. I suggested, in similar terms, that nothing should be published until Rudd's term was over, whether that be three, five or ten years. That proposal morphed into this biography, initially an account of how he came to be prime minister and how he approached the job in the first two years, very much the learning period. Circumstances then made it an account of his two terms as prime minister.

The Prime Minister's Office facilitated access. I talked to Kevin Rudd on six occasions, in six different locations, while he was prime minister. I talked to him another three times before he returned to the job and a further three times after he left politics. I talked to ministers, Rudd's staff and those of other ministers, as well as public servants, journalists and a number of international figures throughout 2008 and 2009. With co-author Ann Tiernan, I also talked to ministers and departmental secretaries for our book *Learning to Be a Minister*, which was published in 2010. The interviews were mostly taped, with the agreement that, if any comment were to be attributed directly, I would go back for approval to use the precise words. Otherwise, all comments could be used without attribution.

I also spent four separate weeks, between December 2008 and December 2009, in the Prime Minister's Office, mostly sitting and observing the comings and goings. On occasion I was able to sit in on meetings of the prime minister with staff, civil servants, delegations or other ministers. I could walk in and out of the general office area without impediment. I could watch the sudden changes of atmosphere, the swings of mood. I also attended a number of prime ministerial visits to hospitals, formal openings and other public occasions, to see him at work. One minister described my position as 'embedded', to use a term usually applied to journalists in arenas of war. It was less than that, but much greater than academics are usually able to achieve.

Of course, being there at all made me well aware of the meetings that I could not attend, and of how much else was going on. I had access to Rudd's schedules, the daily programs of meetings from week to week. I became aware, despite having written for more than thirty years about prime ministers, ministers and public service mandarins, and more generally about Cabinet, of how much more there was to know. Just being there was both a privilege and an eye-opener. If the public knows about 10 per cent of what prime ministers do, perhaps I can now assist in shedding some light on another 20 to 30 per cent of the process of governing, and on the challenges and frustrations, the pressures and pleasures, that all prime ministers face. I suspect that the remaining percentage of the governing process within the Prime Minister's Office will never be available to anyone but the practitioners. Where there are no written records, only those in the room can tell the stories—their memories will differ, their recall will be selective, their accounts will diverge, their motives will be different and their accuracy will be contested. Two people may have genuinely different accounts of the same conversation, albeit ones that serve their own interests. Interviews therefore have their deficiencies, but until we can check them against the official records, they remain the best source we have. All such accounts, however, can provide at best interim conclusions.

Preface

Writing from this position provided me with great benefits. It allowed me to see my subject in action, to watch as events unfolded, to see at times how a prime minister tackles issues and contemplates events as they arise. Of course, tensions can also arise from this. The observance of things as they happen provides an unusual lens. Seeing the world from the unique viewpoint of the Prime Minister's Office inevitably affects a writer's perspective. Yet it should be possible to describe and explain what was done, why certain decisions were made, without either endorsing them or accepting that they were the only options.

That is what I have sought to do. This book may have been written from close to the throne, but it is not an official view. It has been an interesting ride, sometimes dispiriting, always fascinating.

Patrick Weller
Griffith University, Brisbane
May 2014

PART I

THE BEGINNING

1
A QUEENSLAND BOY

One hundred kilometres north of Brisbane, and 15 kilometres inland, Nambour used to sit astride the Bruce Highway when it still wove through towns and villages, before the bypasses. Nambour is the regional centre of local government and industry, the hub for all the little towns scattered along the railway from Brisbane to Gympie. In 1961 its population was 5336, but it was a centre of social activity. It used to hold sugar festivals and debutante balls. Timber was the dominant industry; Methodism was the establishment religion. The town was founded in the 1860s by immigrants from the eastern counties of England. Their severe approach to work, alcohol and dancing reflected the culture of the town: hard work, optimism, a communal drive and evangelism. It also provided a flip side: the young could feel 'stifled by its proprieties, snobbishness and low horizons ... the town's claustrophobia was tangible'. It was one of those towns that could provide kids with opportunities to develop skills and confidence as they grew up, but no future outside the local industries. In the 1960s and 1970s there was no local university. The bright kids left.

Kevin Rudd was born at Selangor Hospital in Nambour on 21 September 1957. His father, Bert, was a returned soldier, and a descendant of two convict families. One was that of a young convict girl, Mary Wade, who survived the rigours of the Second Fleet to start a dynasty and watch it multiply until her own death in 1859. The other was that of the twice-deported Thomas Rudd; he served one sentence, returned to England, and was then convicted and transported a second time. Bert was born in Uranquinty, in southern New South Wales, in 1918, one of a large railway family of nine children. He left school young and was a labourer, just twenty years old, when war broke out in 1939. He enlisted and served in the Engineers in Palestine, North Africa and Borneo. After the war he decided to join an old army mate cutting cane in Nambour. Like many returned servicemen, he did not talk much about the war. But, as he once told his children, when you have seen your friends blown up or shot in the back, you never forget.

Kevin's mother, Margaret De Vere, was born in 1921, one of seven, and raised in the Nambour district. Her oldest brother served as a councillor in the Maroochy Shire, eventually becoming chairman. Her youngest brother was chairman of Gympie Shire. She too had been affected by the tragedy of war. For three years she had exchanged letters with her first love, George Parkinson, whom she had met while training to be a nurse in Brisbane. He had joined the army as a private, fought around the world and was commissioned in the field. He was killed at Buna on the north coast of the Papua New Guinean mainland. After she died, her family found that she had kept his letters all her life. Margaret nursed in Brisbane during the war and then returned to Nambour to work at the Selangor Hospital, where she was a ward sister.

Bert and Margaret met after the war and married in September 1948. Initially, Bert worked a banana plantation at Yandina Creek, on flat land that seemed a long way from any town. They lived in an old deserted schoolhouse that needed extensive renovation. There was no power, and a clay kitchen floor. The only telephone was a party line.

Their first three children were born while they lived there: Malcolm in 1949, daughter Loree in 1950 and Greg in 1954.

In 1956 they moved to a small dairy farm of around 100 hectares some 17 kilometres north of Nambour near the town of Eumundi, with a population (in 1961) of 399. Bert did not own the farm and shared the profits with the landlord. For the family, the new property, though small, offered greater comfort and the freedom to roam, a pleasant change from Yandina Creek, where the isolation seemed complete. From the top of the paddock they could see the town, comfortably within walking distance. And the house had electricity; with a flick of a switch they could have light.

A year later Kevin was born. The first eleven years of his life were, in many respects, like those of so many Queensland country boys. They were a combination of living, riding and working around the farm. He was born with bow legs. In those days, rather than let them straighten naturally, the doctors attempted to rectify the problem. When Kevin was about three, his legs were encased in plaster for some months. He was restricted in movement; that required patience. When the plaster was removed he had to learn to walk again.

His sister, Loree, described him as a pleasant child, always smiling, always finding ways to relate to other members of the family. As the youngest, he was initially the centre of attention. Loree was seven when he was born and enjoyed playing with him; neither of her brothers was prepared to contemplate playing with a girl, unless it was cricket in the yard. Brother Greg was mischievous and physical; he was a fan of wrestling on television and enjoyed trying the holds he saw on his younger brother. Loree recalls Kevin coming away from games with Greg with bruised shoulders, but then heading out again to re-enter the fray. He could not be restrained and was persistent even then.

To the north, the farm backed onto the North Arm of the Maroochy River, so there were about 5 kilometres of creek to explore.

The Beginning

Life was bike riding and sometimes horse riding, playing 'ping-pong' on the dinner table, draughts and cards, or cricket outdoors, climbing trees, building cubbyhouses, and going on long walks around the farm. Work on the farm involved everyone at different times. Learning to leg-rope the cows, lay out their feed and assist with milking them were regular occurrences, as were planting and picking vegetables and fruit, feeding hens, gathering eggs, opening and closing gates to paddocks, and playing with the dog and cat. They listened to radio serials and news, and on TV watched *The Mickey Mouse Club* and later *Bandstand*, *The George Wallace Show* and *The Benny Hill Show*. Movies included those with Jeanette McDonald and Nelson Eddy, Zorro and John Wayne. Wood chopping, emptying the scrap bucket, plucking a beheaded chicken and burning the rubbish were among the less-favoured chores.

Farming was hard work. Bert had to milk the cows twice a day, and each time it took three to four hours. Sometimes the children would assist with bringing in the cows, distributing the feed, placing or removing suction caps on teats, and cleaning the yard or dairy. Although the youngest, Kevin would be there, sometimes assisting and sometimes making castles in the feed box.

Unlike some of their contemporaries, the children were never kept away from school because there was a crisis on the farm or their help was needed for other purposes. Education was regarded as vital. The kids went to Eumundi state school, which was run by Mr and Mrs Kelly. It was organised into four classrooms, each covering two grades. As Loree notes:

> At the age of five, Kevin walked with us to school. By that stage, as we were getting older, we used to catch the milk carrier. The milk carrier used to come and pick up cans and we would load them into the back from the dairy. When it was coming up to

the house to head off, we were waiting out the front, it would stop and let us climb in the back with the cans and you would just hang on, on the way to school.

There were assumptions that the children would follow their father onto the land. 'You have to decide', his father once told Kevin, 'what your future is going to be. Will it be dairy or wheat?' That was the prospect ahead.

From an early age, Kevin showed interest in the wider world. Loree recalls that the older kids may have noticed their father was reading the paper, but Kevin would ask about what he was reading. 'When I was very young', says Kevin, 'I'd sit on his knee while he read the Queensland "bushman's bible" *Country Life*. That's how I learned to read actually. He'd read aloud and I'd find the words. I think that's how I learned about the Cuban Missile crisis'.

Kevin recalls his father taking him on camping trips, and being taught bush craft, but he was often out or busy on the farm, so Kevin did not see it as a 'really close relationship'. To his older children Bert was a cheerful larrikin, unpretentious, and not so careful with money, thinking it was there to spend. He could be incisive and intelligent, although the lack of opportunity in country New South Wales had precluded any further education. He was popular, good company, with a sense of humour. He encouraged and supported his children. He was also a Mason.

Margaret's Catholicism defined her. She had been brought up by a stoic, hardworking and iron-willed mother who had been frustrated by her husband's profligacy with the proceeds of the pub he owned. Margaret, in turn, demanded of her children a tight observance that the older three at least found difficult to accept without question. They would be required to recite the rosary while Bert was in the next room watching Disney. Greg had no doubt where he preferred to be. Calls to attend church could echo across the farm as the kids were summoned home.

There was tension between Bert and Margaret. They were constrained by the different perceptions of the proper roles for men and women of the era, and frustrated by the isolation on the farm. They had fallen in love, but found living together all the time much harder. Bert's laconic style clashed with Margaret's rigid and risk-averse approach; her life was founded on her faith, a faith that allowed her to endure any problems and struggles. Both parents loved their children and found common interest in their development. They stayed together but often found it easier to work apart. Bert ran the farm and became active in the community. He was one of the founders of the local indoor bowls club.

Initially Kevin and Greg shared a room, with Greg in the upper bunk, Kevin in the lower. Greg's untidiness could annoy his younger brother, who even then was neat and organised. Greg says:

> I have this perfect picture of him. I walked in one night and he was standing at the chest of drawers very tense and annoyed, so tense he was almost shaking, and he said, 'Is it so hard to pick up those socks and put them in the drawer?' I'll never forget that. I probably said, 'Yeah, it is'. I still enjoy getting a rise out of him now.

The tension between the parents made life at home hard for the older siblings; one by one they sought to leave. Malcolm joined the army at fifteen; he wanted to get away from the farm. As he was a bright kid doing well at school, his high school headmaster tried to persuade him to stay until he finished Year 12, but Malcolm wanted his own life and chose to go to the Army Apprentice School in Victoria; his parents, somewhat reluctantly, signed the forms. Malcolm served in Vietnam.

Loree chose to go to boarding school in Gympie when she was fifteen, in part because she felt caught in the tensions between her parents and did not want to take sides. Nor did she want to be burdened with confidences. When she left school at seventeen, she decided, to her parents' horror, to enter a convent in Brisbane, rather than take up a place at teachers' college. She spent the six months before the entry date nursing at the Mater Hospital in Brisbane.

Greg was given the choice of going to the local high school and helping on the farm, becoming a weekday boarder and helping on the farm at weekends, or going to board in Brisbane. He chose boarding at Marist Brothers in Brisbane; he wanted to get right away from the milking and from his mother's religious demands.

In the 1967–68 Christmas break, the family went on its one great family holiday. The destination was Malcolm's passing-out parade in the Mornington Peninsula in Victoria. They towed an erratically behaving caravan from Eumundi first to Sydney and the Taronga Park Zoo and then on to Canberra and its War Memorial. They stopped to visit Bert's family at Uranquinty before dropping the caravan and continuing to Melbourne. After the formal parade they ventured to the mansions of Toorak, where Bert took his family to meet John Buchan, businessman and Liberal Party stalwart. In the army, Bert had been Buchan's driver in the Middle East and they had remained in contact thereafter. It was Kevin's first trip to the country's great cities and centres of government.

In 1968, only Kevin was at home with his parents. He was aware of the tensions, the occasional distance between his parents and then the reconciliations. If the atmosphere got too oppressive, he would ride out on his pony and spend the day exploring the creek bed that bordered the farm. Kevin was close to his mother. She passed on her interests in politics, sport, newspapers and the radio. She encouraged his reading, and his curiosity. He began to learn the piano, which his father was unsure was a proper activity for a boy.

Then, on 14 December 1968, the predictable world of Kevin's childhood collapsed. Bert had been to an indoor bowls function in

Brisbane with his friends. They chose to stay overnight. Faced with the need to milk the cows in the morning, Bert decided to drive back. On the way he ran off the road. The family was woken by a phone call in the early hours of the morning. Bert was in hospital in Brisbane. Over the next two months, the family visited him in hospital, Loree from the Brisbane convent, Greg from the local boarding school, Margaret and Kevin making the long journey down from Eumundi. Over six weeks his condition varied; he was expected to recover. Then Bert contracted septicaemia in hospital. Margaret stayed in Brisbane and Kevin went back to school. Bert died on 12 February 1969. He was just fifty years old. Malcolm, on compassionate leave from the army, picked Kevin up from school and had to break the news. Kevin was eleven and without a father.

He was also without a home. As a share farmer, Bert did not own the house in which the family lived. While he was in hospital, neighbours had assisted in keeping the farm working. Even though Margaret Rudd may have been able to farm the land, she was never given the opportunity. A new tenant was needed; the Rudds had to leave and Margaret had to earn a living. They were gone within a few weeks.

The next two years were hard. The family had no settled home. Initially, Margaret chose to return to nursing, but she had not nursed for twenty years and her qualifications were outdated. She moved to Scarborough in northern Brisbane to work in a nursing home. Kevin spent the next few weeks staying with neighbours, and continued to go to Eumundi Primary until the end of the term. The families were pleasant and friendly, but the eleven-year-old missed his mother. When she came to visit, he was suddenly asked, in front of the family he was staying with, whether he wanted to come to Scarborough. Of course, he agreed.

So Kevin found himself shifting school and living, initially with just his mother, in a small flat. His older brother Greg had been boarding at Marist Brothers Ashgrove; he joined Kevin at Scarborough and at the De LaSalle Catholic school there, but hated the claustrophobic atmosphere where his mother was grieving, he was grieving and Kevin was grieving. Greg could not accept his mother's view that their plight was all the will of God. He fled back to Marist Brothers Ashgrove, where arrangements were made to cover his fees. Kevin was at a new school and had few friends. At the end of each school day he walked down to his mother's workplace and waited in her office, often for hours, until she got off duty. It was a lonely time.

Margaret knew she needed to retrain at the Mater Hospital in Brisbane. In the way of the time, that meant that she had to live in the nurses' quarters. She gave up the flat, moved to Brisbane and sent Kevin to join Greg at Marist Brothers Ashgrove. He hated it: the regimentation, the authority, the brutality and the learning by rote are the characteristics he remembers most. In the traditional mode, the Marist Brothers were tough and craved sporting heroes. Kevin was not robust or good at, or particularly interested in, sport except cricket, where he toiled ineffectively as a wicketkeeper in a lower grade.

Holidays were almost worse. In the 1969–70 Christmas break, his mother rented a small flat under the house of some friends in Nambour for the summer. It was cramped with Margaret and her two younger sons there. When Loree decided to leave the convent and join them, it became claustrophobic. Greg moved out to the Marcoola surf club and slept there in a fibro bunkhouse.

When the summer lease expired, they had nowhere to call home. They drove from one relative to another, spending a few nights with each. Once when they arrived to find the relatives out, Kevin, Loree and their mother had to sleep in the car. It was not a common occurrence, but the memory and the sense of helplessness linger. It was, in terms Kevin later used, 'bleak charity'. Unhappy at school, disrupted at home, reliant on the goodwill of relatives, moving from place to place for two years: these were memories that were to remain with Kevin and shape his approach to life: 'What I think it did for me was it made me feel this thing very deeply and emotionally: that this sort of thing should not happen to anybody'.

Then some stability returned. Margaret finished her training. The insurance company paid out on Bert's small insurance; it had been in dispute because of missed payments while he was in hospital. It was not much, but it allowed her to buy a small house in Princess Street in Nambour, a house in which she lived for the rest of her life. It is a small, typical Queensland house, built on the slope above a road: a kitchen and living area, three bedrooms clustered at one end, with an enclosed verandah at the front, and raised off the ground with room for a car underneath. Loree remembers:

> The house was very Spartan and there was lino on the floor and one TV in the corner. There was very, very little furniture. In Kevin's room there was a single bed, a single desk, which was Greg's desk, a tiny little desk, and a bookcase.

Margaret was able to return to the nearby Selangor Hospital to resume life as Sister Rudd. It gave Kevin a stable home, a settled location and the ability to develop a circle of friends. It also ensured a close and devoted relationship between mother and son. In the next year or so it provided a place to display the Hansards that Kevin ordered and which were delivered regularly. Loree says he was still young when he started reading Hansards:

> He was very interested in the parliamentary process and he understood how laws were made and how they [were] put together and the process of change. Even as a teenager at school, you could see him thinking about how you would implement

change and what you would need to get things done through government channels. He was thinking of government as a vehicle for change, even as a young person ... Whether that influence came from my mother and my father or whether he just listened more, I don't know.

He went to Nambour High School, a school of which he is proud, for the last three years of his secondary education from 1972 to 1974. The school has expanded over the years, gradually filling its site alongside the main road through the town; at that time it was the Bruce Highway, which now bypasses the town. In the 1970s it was a lively school, often with bright young teachers in their first year out of teachers' college before they were sent to the country for their service there. Nambour High has developed a public profile since, for the future Prime Minister Rudd, Treasurer Wayne Swan, Minister for Ageing Justine Elliot and one of the prime minister's press secretaries, Fiona Sugden, were all educated there between the 1970s and the 1990s. There were others, too, suggesting the school was able to inculcate in some of its kids the drive to do well (and in the process, to leave Nambour). Rudd and Swan never met there, even though they were only two years apart.

Loree had left the convent after her father died. While Kevin was at Marist Brothers, she went to teachers' college and completed her teacher training. Under the terms of her bond, she was allowed to teach near home for a year, so she joined Kevin and his mother in Nambour and taught at Nambour state school, which is on the same site as Nambour High School. She and Kevin walked to school together in the morning and often back in the afternoon. Loree remembers: 'Sometimes after school he'd come over to my classroom as I was tidying up and give me various hints on how to improve my teaching, as only little brothers can do'. The next year, she left

Nambour to teach in Weipa and then went to Dimbulah on the Atherton Tableland.

Kevin flourished in the new environment. Stability and good teaching allowed his curiosity to flourish. Loree watched her young brother grow:

> I would describe Kevin as like a plant that you have kind of got in this really clay soil, not going anywhere, not growing, not dying. It is just sitting there. Then suddenly it is put in fertile soil and it has got the sun and the rain and water. That is Kevin this year in Nambour. That is really what I saw before my eyes. He was so organised. He had all his subjects. He loved them. He loved his teachers. He loved going to school. He loved—and he would watch—*Monty Python* was on TV at that time and *Aunty Jack* was on. I mean I used to look at them and think, 'What are you laughing at Kevin?', and he would just chuckle, chuckle, chuckle.

He was quickly into the new challenges. He was articulate, informed and inquisitive; he played cricket for the Yandina Creek C team.

Nambour encouraged debating, and Kevin was part of the A team. His close friend Fiona Callander was part of the B team. They used to develop strategies and practise down the road from the Callander farm at the house of history teacher Fae Barber. She provided the chocolate cake; when they won they gave her a brooch inscribed: 'Fae Barber, gastronomically yours, the 1974 debaters'.

Kevin entered a national public-speaking competition run by the Jaycees. He liked to talk about social justice. He won the Nambour competition, then the Capricornia final at Biloela, and finally the state final in Brisbane. He had to fly to Perth to contest the national championship. He did not win. The teacher who taught him public speaking, Ron Derrick, said: 'No-one could teach Kevin, we were only able to guide him and he did the rest'. At the Inter School Christian fellowship, he agreed to debate a local Salvation Army girl about the reality of Christianity. Kevin was the sceptic, the doubter. They attracted the largest crowd of the year.

He enjoyed the theatre and participated in drama, remembering in particular Beryl Muspratt:

> She was really good at bringing young country kids out of themselves ... It was a great gift and much under-acknowledged and under-appreciated ... It's people's ability to identify the talents and draw them out and be the encouragers and then the enablers. So, there were school productions and there was Young People's Theatre which was different and ran after school. I was active in that with the Callander girls.

He performed in a Molière production, *Le Medecin Malgre lui*, translated as the Mock Doctor, after school. At school he played the Minister for Pleasure and Pastimes in Julian Slade's musical *Salad Days*. He developed a presence, a confidence and a style. Nambour High School may have liked its sporting heroes, such as Wayne Swan a year or so earlier, but it gave opportunities for the debaters and the actors to flourish. Kevin grabbed the opportunity.

Above all, he found the intellectual challenge of history and English to his liking. In his final year he was taught English and Ancient History by Fae Barber, then a 39-year-old who had just arrived from Sydney (and whom he once introduced as 'my *Ancient History* teacher'). She later described the process: 'I prepared a lesson and Kevin prepared a lesson and we proceeded by a Socratic method'. In 1974 they studied Robert Bolt's play *A Man for All Seasons*. (The same year, another Year 12 student, far away in Victoria, was reading *A Man for All Seasons* and, as a consequence, decided to drop his plans to do medicine and to enrol in a law degree. Peter Costello was 'fascinated by the interplay of law, morality, conscience and politics'.) Kevin wanted to explore further; he wanted to know more about a person who was prepared to stand up for his principles, even to the point of death. When he won a school prize, a book token, Barber took him down to Brisbane to spend it. He bought a number of books on ancient history and donated them to the school, because he had felt the lack of books there. While there, he also bought a present for Barber: a copy of Thomas More's *Utopia*. It was inscribed: 'To Mrs Barber "In memory of a yearlong battle with ignorance"—to perpetuate the ambiguity'. ('I never really understood whether he was talking about him or me', quipped Barber.) It was unsigned. Thomas More, courtier, administrator, historian, Tudor apologist and finally a martyr of conscience, was an interesting choice for a seventeen-year-old. She gave him Adam Smith's *The Wealth of Nations*.

His other twin interests developed simultaneously. He had been fascinated by China since he was ten, when his mother gave him a book on archaeology. China in the early 1970s was only gradually opening to the West. It had been wracked by the Cultural Revolution, of which there were few details. Then ping-pong diplomacy—the invitation to a table-tennis team to visit and play—was followed by Gough Whitlam's visit in 1971. Whitlam was condemned by the desperate McMahon government for his softness on communism, only to have the Liberal attack undermined a week later by the announcement that Henry Kissinger had been on a visit to Beijing.

The Whitlam visit had an impact on the young Rudd, who wrote to him: 'Dear Mr Whitlam, I am fifteen years old. I am a student at Nambour High School. I want to become an Australian diplomat. What should I do?'

Whitlam wrote back: 'You really should go to university and the study of a foreign language would be useful'. Chinese did not appear in the Nambour High School or Queensland curriculum.

The other part of his education came from school friends, or rather the parents of school friends. The Rudd household was not especially party political. Bert's attitudes had been those of a typical small landholder and returned serviceman: Country Party in his attitudes, but supportive rather than active. Nambour was the electorate of Frank Nicklin, the Country Party premier, and the Country Party was the only force in town. His mother may have voted for the Democratic Labor Party. Politics was never a strongly argued subject around the table.

Kevin's national and international political insights came from elsewhere. One of his closest friends from the debating team was Fiona Callander. Her father, Bob Callander, was a journalist who had worked around the world; he had seen the impact of war and poverty. Then he decided he wanted a quieter life and left the Sydney suburb of Beecroft to grow pineapples in Wombye. Callander brought a more cosmopolitan perspective to the quiet hinterland; he talked widely and often about subjects that crossed the spectrum. Kevin lapped it up:

> Bob was the first person I ever met with anything to do with the Labor Party ... Nambour in the 1970s was not exactly the centre for international socialism. I found it fascinating watching Gough on television on one hand and being able to talk to somebody on a pineapple farm in Nambour who had met all these people and could tell me some of the texture of what these national luminaries were really like ... He brought politics alive in my mind and also the world alive in my mind. In those days to meet somebody in Nambour who had worked in London, was a journalist, travelled extensively in Europe, said to me that there was an exciting pulsating world out there and, secondly, national political life was not simply something on television. It was something made up of real human beings, people of flesh and blood and this bloke had walked among them.

Buoyed by Callander's insights, Kevin attended meetings of Young Labor in Nambour while the Whitlam government went from triumph in 1972 to that narrow 1974 victory: 'I remember sitting through a very long harangue from Senator George Georges with myself, one other bloke and a dog, literally'. Politics was growing in his mind.

Callander was not the only model. Bert's wartime commanding officer, John Buchan, had been one of the three founders of the community organisation Apex Clubs. He was a friend of Sir Robert Menzies, as well as president of the Victorian Liberal Party from 1958 to 1962, and treasurer from 1963 to 1967. He was a classic member of the Victorian establishment. But he was far more than that. Kevin recalls:

> John Buchan had this great sense of perfectly Edwardian noblesse oblige, a sense of personal responsibility towards the people with whom he worked or who had worked for him. When my father died he therefore maintained correspondence with me through until I was elected to parliament and then he died.

During his high-school years, Kevin used to visit and sometimes stay with the Buchans during summer; like many Victorians they had an apartment on the Gold Coast. He thought the Buchans were disappointed when he eventually joined 'the other side', but they remained in close contact. Buchan died aged eighty-nine, just after Rudd was elected to parliament; Rudd attended his funeral in Melbourne and then continued to visit his widow.

His enduring friendships with two such different men reflect Kevin's ability to relate across the generations, classes and professions. He was as comfortable in the Callander's Nambour farmhouse as in the Buchan's Gold Coast penthouse. He listened to their experiences and they, in turn, found it worthwhile to invest time and interest, both then and over the next twenty years, in this seventeen-year-old Queenslander from a poor and disrupted family.

Kevin was dux of the school, a straight-A student, when he left at the end of 1974. Nambour High had provided the environment for his talents to flourish at a time when he had the stability and growing maturity to take advantage of the opportunities it offered. The teaching had been good, the staff often friendly and supportive. He applied for entry to the Arts/Law degree at the University of Queensland and was awarded a place.

For the boy from Nambour, provincial towns, whether Nambour or Cairns,

> are just large enough to have a critical mass of culture, public entertainment and the arts, usually through theatre, usually through local performances, usually through local debating societies, going back to the great School of Arts tradition of the turn of the previous century. They are large enough to have that, but small enough whereby kids with ability could achieve and be recognised and rewarded for their achievement. If you were so encouraged by being locally successful, it gave you a huge amount of confidence to do other things ... A lot of folk have come out of those towns which have a pronounced civic culture, a pronounced local culture which is not just about sport ... [It] esteemed academic achievement, esteemed cultural achievement; but at what I would describe as a sufficiently modest scale that you could with some ability achieve well. I think kids growing up in large cities with huge schools don't have that.

Nambour might have provided the stability and inspiration, but it was not going to be a significant part of Kevin's future. Yet his connections were not forgotten. 'I'm Kevin and I'm from Queensland' became a neat self-deprecating line. The place still has a pull. He remembered those who had helped him. When Ron Derrick was sick, he received a note of good wishes. When Bob Callander was dying of cancer, Rudd visited the hospital and talked to him for hours.

Rudd returned when he could to visit his mother; his children were a joy to their grandmother. By 2001 Margaret was eighty and in ill health. Loree returned to the Nambour house she had left over twenty-five years before. She got a job in the local hospital and lived with her mother until she died in 2004. She is still there. She campaigned locally. She recalls knocking on a door just after the Scores strip club scandal had been revealed. When she said she was campaigning for the Labor Party, but without revealing who she was, the householder laughed. 'Hey, go Ruddy, he likes the nudies just like we do', he chortled.

Loree contrasts her reaction to events to those of Kevin:

> We all know families where they ... go through similar things but one out of the group somehow has something within him that chooses a path that says, 'I'm going to fix things', whereas the rest of us say, 'Well, that's life'. Kevin's that one in our family.

The family ties stayed close and devoted. Loree admired the brother who took control, and watched that small boy who became prime minister with the amused interest of the big sister. And he remembered her. On her birthday in 2009 he rang twice. Since she was out both times, he sang 'Happy Birthday' to the answering service.

2

CALLIGRAPHY AND CHRISTIANITY

As dux of the school, Kevin had the full range of university options. The expectation was that he would go to the University of Queensland. To his mother's consternation, he turned down a place in Arts/Law and chose to take a break for a year, to relieve the pressure of hard work and settle on what he might want to do. Initially, he stayed in Nambour and worked in a cafe that now displays a plaque commemorating the fact that a future prime minister once served at the tables there. Then he chose to head off south, first to Brisbane, where he was a barman at the Paddington Hotel. For a non-drinking country boy not yet of legal drinking age, it was a rough introduction to a tough pub. By the time he left, 'I could hold four pots in the left hand and get the head right in each of them'.

He moved further south to Sydney, where he initially stayed with Bert's sister and, through Bob Callander's connections, worked in Grace Brothers, Roselands. He was the spruiker who introduced the displays that were put on stage for the entertainment of the shoppers. Then he struck out on his own. Looking at the noticeboards at the University of Sydney, he found a room to let in a house in Albion

Street, Surry Hills and shared there with one guy and 'three very attractive female lawyers' who were in the fifth year of their degree. It was, he said, 'kind of fun' for the first time living in a house with a group of young sophisticates. He could have a drink, talk about politics, be away from family and just grow up. He found a job as a ward cleaner at Canterbury Hospital that paid much better than his last job. He was cleaning a floor on 11 November 1975 when he heard of the sacking of the Whitlam government:

> I was just shocked, that that could happen. I didn't take to the streets or anything like that. I just remember leaning on my mop saying, 'How on earth did that happen?' I think, even as a kid, I got the impression about how a sense of crisis could be both constructed and manufactured. Constructed by political play obviously by Fraser, manufactured by a broader media environment at the time which had reached the decision to bring Whitlam down as well.

He registered to vote for the first time in an election in the inner-Sydney electorate.

Kevin spent these months in Sydney looking for meaning and faith. He visited a new church each week, just to discover their beliefs and approach. He went to

> the Wesley Centre Mission because I lived in the middle of town. I used to go to St Michael's Anglican Church—it was virtually next door to where we were living in Albion Street in Surry Hills—the Scots Presbyterian Church in the middle of Sydney, the Pitt Street Congregational Church, which is now Pitt Street Uniting, St Michael's Surry Hills. It was my habit just to wander around, sit up the back and have a listen. So I think it was [at] Pitt Street Congregational Church that I ran into the Freckletons.

When the pastor asked any visitors to identify themselves, Kevin said he came from Nambour. At the end of the service, a pastor from a different church, Frank Freckleton, also a visitor, came to say hello. His wife was the sister of a Nambour teacher, so Kevin got to know the Freckletons. Their daughter had just finished a degree at the Australian National University (ANU) and was able to tell Kevin about the university. She had also been a resident at Burgmann College on the campus. Kevin says:

> I hadn't decided then where I was going to university; from memory I had deferred a position at University of Queensland. I may have already applied to the University of Sydney—I'm not sure—and then I applied to the ANU. I was trying to make up my mind whether to do Arts/Law or Asian Studies/Law or Asian Studies and then Law. So it was the debate in my mind at the time.

He sought information and in late 1975 he applied for Burgmann at the ANU. Acting as his referee, Frank Freckleton described Kevin as 'courteous, willing to work and with a happy disposition'; he was also 'ambitious'. His school deputy praised his intellect and also concluded he was a 'mature and responsible young man'.

Kevin had been brought up a Catholic, his mother's faith. He had attended mass with her as a matter of course:

> We went to church at the local Catholic church in Eumundi. And every second Saturday we'd be rounded up to go to catechism. Mum would bellow out of the window of the farmhouse across the flats, 'It's time for catechism', as Greg and I would disappear into the distance. But she had a habit of being able to round you up pretty quickly and get you there.

Catholic school religion was no more than 'you would tend to observe as an eleven- to thirteen-year-old attending a Catholic boarding school: mass three mornings a week and regular prayers in the classroom. But no particular spark of personal faith'.

Kevin began to have doubts about the more doctrinaire characteristics of Catholicism while he was working in Sydney. During that year, he recalls, he 'did a lot of reading and a lot of reflection about the great "whys" of life'.

> Part of the reason for not going straight to university was to sort a few things out in my head rather than embark on a career path or some academic path without understanding some foundational questions as to 'What's it all about ... at least for me'. And so sometime in the last quarter of that year, I think, I made an adult decision that I was a believer. But that came after a solid year's reflection.

In February 1976 Kevin moved to Canberra and the ANU. He lived at Burgmann College, interdenominational and freewheeling. It had only opened a few years before. One of its founding students was the party-loving Peter Garrett. A year or so later Nick Minchin arrived. The student body included the riotous, the studious, the religious and all kinds between. The college had both a chapel and a bar.

Kevin enrolled in the Faculty of Asian Studies. The ANU had a number of advantages. It was small. It had expertise in Chinese language and literature. And it was a long way from Queensland.

When Kevin went to the ANU, he was a Christian rather than an advocate of any church. He points out that:

> I knew enough about church history to understand how they emerged, how the Reformation occurred and how the various

revolts within the Reformation subsequently occurred. But I think there is only one essential question and that is, 'Based on the evidence that you're presented, do you believe or not in the existence of God?'

It was, he argues, a consequence of reflection, and says:

the proofs available to me were no more remarkable than were available to people who have reflected on these things over the centuries; no more persuasive or unpersuasive depending on who is reflecting on them. But that's the conclusion I've reached and it's a conclusion that I've subsequently been comfortable with.

At the time, there was a college padre of an evangelical bent. He encouraged the students to think about their role and future in life. That was already Kevin's inclination:

For me it was a question of reflecting on the claims of the church, neither Catholic nor Protestant but the church, about the existence of God and the life of Jesus of Nazareth; and reflecting further whether I accepted—as a matter of faith and reason—that those claims were true. And having reached that conclusion, only one proposition emerges from that: How then do you lead your life? For me it provides a form of moral compass in the broadest sense. However flawed your life might turn out to be, at least you have a sense of your fundamental bearings.

The first breakfast in orientation week turned out to be critical to his life. Kevin sat down opposite Thérèse Rein. He introduced himself. She retorted: 'You know, I think you are the first Kevin I've ever met'. Rudd recalls thinking: 'What a marvellously snotty thing to say'. She thought it was just a truthful comment with no hidden meaning. Later in the week, as she recalls:

> Kevin and I were walking back in the same direction [from a Student Christian Movement meeting] and he said, 'You live at Burgmann College, don't you?' I said, 'I do', because [I'd met this] whirlwind of people, and he said, 'I do too so why don't we walk back together?' And he said, 'Do you want a cup of tea?' … so we had tea in his room with the door open.

Thérèse had come to the ANU from Melbourne. Her father had been in the RAAF in the war and had injured his back in a plane crash. After the war he was eventually confined to a wheelchair. He used his returned service rights to undertake a degree in aeronautical engineering. He worked in Adelaide and then in Farnborough in the UK. He was an archer in the Australian team in the Stoke Mandeville Games, the precursor of the Paralympics. When he returned to Australia, he became a driving force in developing disabled athletics.

Thérèse was born in Adelaide, the first child in the family. When she was in high school, the family moved to Melbourne and she completed her secondary education at Firbank, a private girls school. Thérèse expected to go to the University of Melbourne, but the ANU had an early entry scheme for outstanding students, so she applied and was accepted; it was just insurance. Then her father was in another terrible accident. He was driving home from work along St Kilda Road. A drunk driver travelling in the other direction at more than 150 kilometres per hour lost control of his vehicle. The car hit the median strip, flipped in the air and landed on the roof of Thérèse's father's car, trapping him inside. The drunk driver was killed and Thérèse's father badly injured. The next months were a blur as the family regularly travelled over to the Heidelberg Hospital. Thérèse's matriculation exams came and went; she did poorly. She did not get into Melbourne and, although she could have gone to Monash, the family thought it might be useful for her to go to the ANU. Besides, they thought they might all be moving to Canberra soon, a shift that did not eventuate. Thérèse was therefore at Burgmann for that meeting of minds.

Thérèse was fascinated by Kevin's aspirations and his social conscience. He explains why he wanted to study Chinese:

> Australia's recognised China. America's recognised China. China is huge and growing. It's to our immediate north. The next century is going to be the China century and it's really important for Australia that we have people who not only speak the language but understand the history and culture of the Chinese people because our future lies there.

They talked about education and politics. This person, she recalls thinking when they met, should go into politics; this person should be prime minister.

From that first meeting, Kevin and Thérèse's lives intersected regularly. They were part of the same group and they fought on and off for the next two years, not personally but about ideas. Both had separate interests, Kevin in the activities of the Asian Studies students, including the production of Chinese opera, while Thérèse liked bush dancing. When Thérèse contracted glandular fever in the first year and was so tired she could not get out of bed, it was Kevin who came to check on her. He collected food from the dining room, brought it up to her and ensured she ate it. He was a solicitous friend.

On 17 October 1977, towards the end of her second year, Thérèse was walking back to her room when Kevin fell in step beside her. She remembers vividly:

I was walking back to my room and he was walking in that direction. That wasn't the direction of his room, and I said, 'Where are you going?' He said, 'I'm going to see someone'. So he kept walking. I said, 'Well who are you going to see?' He said, 'I'm going to see someone'. So we're walking along and he's still with me. Well we're running out of corridor here, because my room was one off the end of the corridor, and I said, 'Oh, so you're going to see Kathy'. He said, 'I'm going to see someone'. So I went to my room, I said 'Goodnight, have a nice night', and went into my room and shut the door. Then there was this knock on the door and I went to the door and opened it and I said, 'Weren't they home?' He said, 'No, I'm coming to see you'. I laughed and I said, 'Well that's nice'. He said, 'I thought we should go out'. I said, 'We've just been out'. He said, 'No, together'. I said, 'What now? It's really late'. Anyway, so he asked me out.

That combination of playfulness and seriousness was typical. Thereafter they were regarded as a couple. She was nineteen, he was twenty.

Kevin was never interested in campus politics. He was not a student activist, even as the campus, just across the lake from Parliament House, fumed at the perceived illegitimacy of the new Fraser government that had so easily won the federal election in December 1975. Organised politics was not yet for him. The challenges were more personal.

University friend Harry Barber was already at Burgmann College when Kevin Rudd arrived. But the link to Kevin was not only Burgmann but also the Evangelical Union:

> The EU connected us across the years and across disciplines in the way that the football club does, or the hockey team. University is not much of a deal if you're only meeting the people you're studying with and that was the sort of thing I was trying to avoid.

Thérèse remembers Harry as 'having a great sense of humour, being very kind, very warm. He kind of reminded me of Pooh Bear at the time'. He too was searching for understanding. Harry would wrap himself up in an old greatcoat and set out with Kevin before breakfast, into the mist and fog that often blanketed Lake Burley Griffin, to talk about religion, about God, about all those things that are of concern to the young as they search for meaning. These walks were described as perambulatory prayer meetings, two young men wanting to know what to believe. Harry recalls: 'We were both serious people and we wanted a meaningful context for things and we wanted to make a difference for the good'.

As students, they were not into practical outcomes; they were trying to work out where they were and how they might make real contributions in the future. Their interest could readily be distinguished from the partygoers' and the politicians'. No-one, said one colleague, would ever have any doubts about which group Kevin belonged to.

Christian theology was combined with Chinese studies. Kevin was the secretary of the Evangelical Union at the ANU. The EU was the link that brought together people from different disciplines and backgrounds. There, as Kevin says, they all explored the choices:

> The standard readings: on the right you all read John Stott ... the modern father of English evangelical Anglicanism. And at the other, slightly lefty, end of the evangelical spectrum you had Bonhoeffer's *Letters from Prison* and *The Cost of Discipleship*. So you had John Stott's basic Christianity at one end and C.S. Lewis up the middle, mere Christianity, and over to the left Dietrich Bonhoeffer: muscular Christianity. I am a great fan of Lewis's Christian apologetics.

As ever for students, the way forward becomes an accident of timing and opportunity. Kevin regarded himself, in those first years at university, as quite a conservative Christian. In the third year of university he was responsible for organising the university mission and had to identify an evangelist to invite to the campus:

> Someone recommended a Baptist. I listened to this guy for three days. It was unapologetic Bonhoeffer social gospel: 'Get active in politics'. I'm the guy that got this guy, seeing the words 'Baptist' and thinking 'that is safe'. This guy provides a marvellous set of apologetics about it being impossible to be a person of faith unless you are active in social justice through the political process.

He found the challenge confronting:

> I have actually not quite got there yet. I'm probably twenty to twenty-one years of age and so this has an effect on me—this is the year before I head off to Taiwan and my transition into social justice–Christianity—in the sense that it is quite right for a person who has formed Christian views to be able to be concerned about human rights. I began subscribing to an American journal called *Asia Watch*, which was monitoring human rights, not just in China but elsewhere.

The serious students did not just talk about religion. When they discussed social problems, Harry remembers Kevin saying: 'When I'm prime minister …' It was not so often that it became routine, but nor was it just the once either. Whether it was already an ambition seems less clear; to Rudd it was a figure of speech, a way of identifying what needed to be fixed, what was 'Right and Important, with capital letters', as Harry describes them.

Kevin took to his study of Chinese with dedication. Harry watched with admiration: 'He had this big fat dictionary that was as high as it was wide but Kevin just loved it, he went to it like Pooh to his honey pot, he'd just lick off another layer'. He may not have been the most brilliant linguist, but he worked consistently and hard. Thérèse says:

> he did this wonderful unit called Chinese Calligraphy and Painting; they had to actually practise the characters; this is very Zen; you sit there with an ink stone and you grind it and then you mix the ink with the brush and the water. It's very harmonising; you think about the meaning of the character that you're writing. One of the most wonderful characters was done by the younger brother of the last emperor; this single big character on a scroll we saw in Beijing was the character for a tiger, and the energy, the strength, the elegance and the power of the way the character was drawn conveyed the tiger.

For his second long vacation, Kevin decided to see a bit more of Australia. After Christmas at Nambour, he hitchhiked up the Queensland coast. He visited Loree, then did some teaching on the Atherton Tableland, and revelled in the independence.

At the end of his third year, he decided he needed to improve his skill in the Chinese language and to go overseas. He applied for a grant from Beijing, but failed, perhaps the first failure in his career. Instead, he won a scholarship to cover his basic costs in Taiwan. He might have been lucky. In Beijing he would then have been restricted to the compound for foreign students. Although Taiwan was still an authoritarian regime run by the Kuomintang (KMT, the Chinese Nationalist Party), there were few restrictions on private lives. As long as people did not take political action, they were free to say whatever they wanted in private. It was far easier to chat to the local people, to make personal friends, to get to know families and thereby to develop language skills.

The scholarship was useful, but not enough. Kevin and Thérèse decided to stay in Canberra over the break. Thérèse had finished her degree and applied for a job in the public service; she duly got the job—and found it excruciatingly boring and pointless. Kevin took a number of jobs, including cleaning the house of journalist Laurie Oakes, to raise funds for Taiwan.

The months in Taiwan in 1979 were Kevin's first experience overseas:

> I stayed in a fantastic place called the Republic of China Recover the Mainland Anti-Communist International Youth Activity Centre (中华民国反共复国国际青年活动中心). I lived there and studied at a very good teaching academy which was the Mandarin Training Centre at the Taiwan Normal University … effectively the tradition of normal universities is to train teachers; this one had a Mandarin training centre within it.
>
> We were all foreigners but most were overseas Chinese from elsewhere, a number of Japanese, a number of Chinese who didn't speak Mandarin, who spoke Cantonese or whatever. A small number of barbarians—a few Brits, the odd American and I think one or two Australians. So yes, it was really good for my Chinese. I had to earn some money so I used to teach English on the side as well.

The visit was also a political education. Kevin's time there saw the Kaohsiung Incident, the beginning of the end of the KMT regime. Kaohsiung is the town in the south of the island that saw the birth of the Taiwanese democratic movement. Watching the suppression of dissenters ensured that he 'had no misty-eyed view of authoritarianism'. Propaganda was everywhere, Kevin recalls:

> I always remember my favourite paper was called 中央日报, the *Central News*, which I only discovered later was the official organ of the KMT. I didn't think they had official organs in those days.

I thought they had them in PRC. In those wonderful days the articles would refer to the Chinese leadership as a bandit regime. Literally every time it mentioned the regime in Beijing they were called the Communist Bandit Regime (共匪). So in the 中央日报, referring to Deng Xiaoping, they use to call him Deng Fei (邓矮匪), the communist bandit Deng or Deng Ai Fei (邓匪), which would be Stumpy, Communist Bandit Deng. It was wonderfully propagandistic. And across the Taipei Railway Station [a sign] was always in huge neon lights, 反共复国, 'Oppose the communists; Recover the mainland'.

While in Taipei, Kevin had been given a transcript of the trial of Wei Jingsheng, a dissident who had edited a series of periodicals critical of the government in 1978 and 1979, for which he was arrested and tried (Wei would subsequently spend the next twenty years in prison before leaving China for the United States). Kevin decided that he wanted to write his honours thesis on Wei. It was an unusual choice in a department where most theses took an historical subject. He asked Sinologist Pierre Ryckmans to be his supervisor.

Ryckmans saw Kevin as a conscientious, mature and dedicated student: he was respectful, polite and tidy; he came to every meeting well prepared for any discussion and was business-like in his dealings. Ryckmans said in 2006 that he 'was very surprised and impressed to learn from recent profiles in the press that his early years were marked by hardship and poverty'. He had assumed that Kevin was a product of a privileged private school education.

Over the next year Kevin produced a detailed and scholarly thesis. The first part was an analysis of the concept of human rights in Chinese history. He argued that there was no classic Chinese term for the concept and that, where it was used, its main application referred to the right of expression, not some liberal democratic interpretation. He then provided a brief history of the demands for human rights across the centuries and, in more detail, the debate that had developed in the People's Republic of China since 1949. He analysed the forces that led to the poster campaign of 1978 and 1979 and to the growing repression of the regime in the face of specific criticism that named the guilty parties.

The most detailed section of the thesis was an exposition of the work of Wei Jingsheng in the journal he edited, *Tansuo*, variously translated as 'Exploration', 'Investigation' or 'Inquiry'. Six editions of *Tansuo* were produced, but only four under Wei's editorship before he was arrested. *Tansuo*, Kevin argued, rejected any notion of an ideological norm and also rejected political orthodoxy. Since Wei was the only one of those pushing for human rights to be put on trial, his case deserved particular attention. Kevin proposed that Wei was arguing for a relativist understanding of the truth—he attacked Marxism and Maoism as antithetical to democracy; he believed that the pluralism in the natural order must find expression in a diversity of opinion.

The second half of the thesis was a translation of the transcript of Wei's trial. It illustrated the power of the state and the frailty of the system of justice in China in 1979. For an honours thesis, it was an impressive and thoughtful study. Kevin was given a first-class honours degree.

The choice of the topic is instructive, and so was his asking Ryckmans, known to be critical of the regime and with expertise in the work of dissidents, to act as supervisor. He chose to work on a contemporary topic for which sources were hard to find and sensitivities were raw, where many scholars had strong and divergent views. He wrote about a topic that left no illusions about the power of the state and the use of its authority to crush opposition. It ensured that human rights in China would never be out of his mind.

In 1980, at the same time he graduated from the ANU, Kevin joined the Australian Labor Party.

3

DIPLOMAT TO CHINA

In 1980, Kevin applied for entry to the Department of Foreign Affairs (DFA). The department had traditionally been seen as part of the establishment, a bastion of private school alumni. The selection process included a cocktail party in which the social poise of candidates could be assessed. In the 1960s it would have been rare for a product of country Queensland to pass the tests. Kevin felt that he was an outsider in such a race; others thought he was just the sort of person the department was looking for: well educated, an expert on China, and a Mandarin speaker. As a colleague explains: 'By the time he got in, background was really not an issue. You still had to speak and write good English. You probably didn't drop your "h"s and drop your "g"s and get in'. The department was trying to extend its reach, to include a wider social representation, and the new generation of diplomats had lost some of the cultural cringe of trying to be British. Nevertheless, remnants of the old style still surfaced during the interview process.

Kevin attended the traditional cocktail party, always seen as a trial for those less accustomed to the mores of the eastern-suburbs social set. It was held in the house of the departmental secretary, Peter Henderson, Robert Menzies's son-in-law. Kevin watched as some of his competitors dug themselves into oblivion, not knowing that the secretary of the department was actually the person who ran it. He found himself cornered, in front of a blazing fire, by a crusty deputy secretary.

'What do you think of 1975?' he was asked.

Kevin responded: 'It is very simple. My views are not my views, they are simply statements of fact—it was unconstitutional'. Pressed, he repeated the point.

'Oh', said the deputy, 'so you would have preferred a banana republic?'

To which he said, 'No, just a democratic state'.

In retrospect, Kevin thought the deputy liked having someone stand up to him and thereafter they had a positive, if lively, working relationship. Kevin was 'flabbergasted' when he was selected. He joined the department in 1981. A year later, after a period as a graduate trainee, he was appointed to Sweden. As he put it: 'Ah, the universal wisdom of foreign ministries. You know something about China? Sweden's the place for you. It'll broaden you'.

It became a rush. Thérèse had stayed in Canberra for a masters thesis in psychology while Kevin completed his degree and went through the training year at DFA. She submitted her thesis the same week that they were married, in November 1981. They left the day after the wedding for a brief honeymoon at Waikiki Beach in Honolulu, in transit to Stockholm. Kevin says:

> We arrived at Stockholm on the twenty-third of November in the most ferocious snowstorm I'd ever seen. But then I'd never seen a snowstorm in my life. I didn't have an overcoat. It's minus fifteen and it's snowing. I looked at Thérèse and said: 'This is another planet'.

There were benefits from the posting for the development of Kevin as a diplomat. The ambassador, William Flanagan, was coasting to retirement. The posting was remote and unlikely to receive attention from Canberra. Since the embassy was small, the staff had to become familiar with all the activities of a mission, whether reporting on the politics or fulfilling consular duties to assist wayward Australian tourists. In the way of diplomats, Kevin had to gain knowledge of some significant but esoteric topics. He was required to become a generalist, to relate to a wide range of groups. Kevin organised an Australian film festival in Stockholm and was the Australian representative at the first international conference on the depletion of the ozone levels, held in Stockholm in 1982.

In his second year there he was also given responsibility for covering Norway. He wrote a detailed report on the Soviet gas pipeline to Western Europe and the issues of energy security for Europe. The report attracted attention in Canberra because of the range of contacts and the quality of the analysis. One reaction noted:

> He wrote with elegance, and revealed incredibly good insights from such a young man. He made excellent contacts and he was thorough, thoughtful and professional—some say he is so committed that it's difficult to discern the real person beneath. My feeling is that some people really are totally committed not just to their work but to excellence in all they do.

It was an apprenticeship in the field.

Sweden also provided an insight into other models of government and allowed Thérèse and Kevin to live in new circumstances. Sweden was then a social democrat's ideal model, where governments worked in corporatist mode. By contrast, the two visited Thatcher's England on holiday, where they were joined by their mothers. The four of them visited the Lake District, the Cotswolds and Oxford, Kent and then London, all crammed in the one car.

In their second year in Sweden, they moved out of Stockholm to live on a small farm. As Thérèse recalls: 'You just put your skis on and go. In summer I learned to windsurf'. It was, in contrast to later times, a quiet if useful educational interlude. It had not been intended to be so. Thérèse had wanted to undertake a degree and then work, but the length of the degree had been extended and the diplomatic exchange arrangements to allow diplomatic partners to find a job had not been negotiated by the ambassador, who insisted that Thérèse Rein was Mrs Rudd and believed that women should not work.

Kevin and Thérèse spent two years in Sweden. They returned to Canberra in time for the birth of their first child, Jessica, in December 1983. They had time to show her off to the grandparents, buy a house and then head off to Hong Kong. China called. The embassy wanted a person who was fluent in Mandarin, and Kevin was selected as second secretary. First he spent six months in Hong Kong at the Chinese University to do a refresher course in Chinese. While he was there, he made a brief visit to the embassy. He chose to go by train from Hong Kong to Guangzhou and thence by rail for two days to Beijing. It was a long trip, and an unusual route at that time. The decision reflected a self-confidence and self-assuredness. He was willing to travel in a way that exposed him and his language skills. How better to see China than via a long train journey on his own, rather than from the red carpet as an arriving diplomat?

The experience is still vivid for Kevin. China had been at the centre of his life for more than a decade: as a source of fascination, as a language to be studied, as a political system to be analysed, as a set of beliefs to be understood. Now, for the first time, he was actually there. He travelled in a four-berth sleeper and shared the compartment with three others, including an officer of the People's Liberation Army

(PLA) in uniform. Conversation was limited. The PLA officer spoke little English and Kevin still felt some inhibitions about the fluency of his Mandarin. His greatest fascination was watching the country unfold through the window of the train:

> Here I am, I am 25 years old … and I am finally going to the country whose language and history I have studied for most of my adult life. My first impression of China was sitting on a train for two days from Canton to Beijing, and never once looking out the window without seeing people … dressed still in a Mao suit of one description or another.

He arrived at Beijing Central Railway Station with a sense of excitement and history:

> It was very much an old-fashioned way to arrive in Peking for the first time, to have taken the train from one end of the country to the other. I quite liked that, and then to be met at Beijing, at the old Peking Railway Station. The embassy met me and then we went for a drive through Peking, through Tiananmen Square. I thought, ha, this is where it has all happened.

The Beijing of 1984 was a city not yet transformed into the megalopolis of today. The hutongs and courtyards were still common, even if many residents had moved to the blocks of architecturally identical flats. Kevin recalls:

> There was only one building more than six storeys and that was the Civic Building that was outside the old city walls and it was twenty storeys. It is still there. Changan Street had not changed since the communists had bulldozed the city walls in the '50s. So

it was a low-set city with practically no cars. I drove everywhere. I had to worry about mowing people down on bicycles. The other thing to worry about was horse-drawn vehicles because they are all over the place and I think the only road they were kept away from was Changan itself, but every back street was full of horse carts of one description or another and in the outer parts there were still camel trains. That was old Beijing.

The three years that he spent in Beijing were years of rapid change as China began to open up. Kevin and his family lived in enclosed diplomatic quarters. It was an enclave of relative comfort, but still infested by rats. Kevin has recalled sitting on the edge of a bed with a bat in hand, waiting to fend them off. That was a stark reminder of the world he now lived in. Besides taking care of Jessica, Thérèse spent the time in China organising the talented diplomatic wives, who included archaeologists, historians and anthropologists, into carefully planned excursions around Beijing.

Kevin, like all diplomats, had his travel restricted to within a 50-kilometre radius of Beijing, unless permission was granted to go elsewhere. The one place he and Thérèse could go for recreation was the single road out to the Great Wall and the Ming tombs. There were signs along the way on the side roads saying 'No foreigners beyond this point' in several languages. Occasionally, they would be able to go to the holiday resort in the old German concession of Quihuangdao, where the embassy maintained some flats, which had not seen a coat of paint since the revolution and were drab at best. Only gradually were these restrictions lifted during the 1980s.

Consequently, the embassy staff tended to intermingle primarily with each other and with other expatriates. When they went to the Ming tombs for a family picnic, they played cricket on the marble paths. In winter they played on the ice at the Summer Palace. Kevin even played for the embassy team in games near the Temple of Heaven, by repute winning one game with 'one of the least distinguished leg-byes of all time'. It was a socially and sometimes geographically enclosed existence.

There were still limitations on the degree to which diplomats were able to socialise with Chinese citizens. Dinners had to be officially approved, so they tended to be at the official residencies. Occasionally some gem of information might be dropped, but the events remained somewhat stiff. Each diplomat would have a range of contacts that they had to manage with care. Colleagues reported (albeit anonymously) that Kevin 'maintained contact with them in a very sensible, non-risk type of way and at times reported quite significant bits of information that they passed on to him, conveyed to him orally, at least'. Gradually, the rigid demarcations were relaxed over Kevin's period in Beijing, but he recalls that he did not really make friends until he started to go back to China in the 1990s. Discussions and meetings could still be a little forced and uptight, but the country did, over the next decade, become less of a closed society.

The economy was starting to open up. When Kevin arrived, supplies of food were not always readily available. In winter there were no fresh vegetables, so everyone kept stacks of frozen white cabbages on their windowsills. When someone was sent to Hong Kong to collect the diplomatic mail, they would return with suitcases of lettuces. Then Deng Xiaoping allowed the people in the country to sell their excess produce—by the mid-1980s, stalls had begun to appear on Beijing's streets, selling fruit and vegetables, and the 'lettuce run' became unnecessary. Nevertheless, the process of finding, buying and cooking food could be exhausting, so in their last year in China, Thérèse got a job in the office of the *Washington Post* so that they could hire a cook who could take over the chores. By 1986, Beijing was seen as a 'city of cranes' as buildings sprang up.

The Beginning

For Kevin the politics were fascinating, and understanding it was his responsibility. Even while the economic controls were being relaxed, China was experiencing a debate between Deng Xiaoping and his opponents about the speed and even the reality of modernisation. The debate, Kevin remembers, had gone from

> the decision in the early 1980s to establish the special economic zones through ... to '84 when I arrived. They had a special party of congress on, in part, the total reform of the economic system. Through that whole period leading up to '84 and again from '84 to '89, the intensity and internal debate was about what the liberalisation of the economy meant in terms of domestic economic reform and what was called then the outside world. 'Do we need internal reform the way the outside world had gone?' It was quite intense.

But the debate was held in private, within the limits of the Chinese Communist Party and government. One diplomat recalls that 'every article in every publication had been carefully vetted by the propaganda officials for its appropriate political correctness'.

Kevin learned to read the newspapers with the skill of a Beijing resident adept at deciphering the messages between the lines, to identify what was actually happening and what the consequences might be. The great challenge was to understand the political debates going on behind closed doors. He would talk to people in the Chinese academies, always with a minder in tow, and try to appreciate the import of any hints that might be provided.

Kevin had to be a practical Sinologist, not only interpreting what was happening but also extracting the implications for trade or other political terms. With Australia beginning to build up its economic links with China, the government needed to understand its internal politics. Kevin recalls:

It was classic Chinese tea leaves. We had to read all the fault lines of this in the interstices of the Chinese media, and we gatherers, embassy 'internalists' as we were called, from the Western diplomatic missions, usually [met] on a weekly basis to analyse the press together for the previous week and what was actually happening, why did this commentary appear, what was it intending to say and did you notice the change in the line from that phrase to this phrase. Did you notice that X had been saying this and Y hasn't been?

Occasionally you would have foreign visitors who would then get a further personal insight as to what was happening. And one of the marvellous insights in those days used to be from the French, those French Communist Party connections, so we all loved those days when ancient French Coms would arrive in town.

Deng Xiaoping had been a student in Paris fifty years before.

He used to know the whole crew and then they would catch up with their old mates and then we would get the debrief from the French Embassy about what had actually gone on, to the point I remember having a debrief from the French internalist ... He was an excellent Chinese Com analyst. He gave us a rendition from one of these meetings about who would be confirmed in new positions of leadership following the 1985 conference of the party and who would be retiring. I wrote a memorandum, as you did in those days, to Canberra ... and then ran through it all. And then it was absolutely right, so I was made to look terribly terribly intelligent by virtue of the fact that I just got out on the grog with the French First Secretary.

Inevitably, there were long debates within the embassy about the meaning of the things observed. Kevin would put a draft of a report on the table for discussion and he impressed colleagues with the force of his logic. There were no flights of fancy; it was all grounded. His ordered approach reminded a colleague of 'those Chinese cabinets for Chinese medicines; they all have a little label on the front and there are forty-seven or forty-eight drawers and each one has got its place and everything is filed away'.

Kevin, like all the diplomats, had to service the flood of visitors too. As China began to open up, so interest burgeoned. The embassy sometimes felt like a travel agency. Because of Kevin's knowledge, many wanted to benefit from his insights. Stories abound of his performances there. Some emphasise his competitiveness. Once, when asked to brief Prime Minister Bob Hawke, he reputedly told a colleague the prime minister wanted a few dot points, but then he developed a detailed five-page brief. His ambassador cut him off when the prime minister started to get restless. Others tell of more amusing moments. When he acted as interpreter for then ambassador Ross Garnaut and was required to translate the comment that the two countries were experiencing a period of unprecedented closeness, his rendition was met with laughter. He had suggested that 'China and Australia are currently experiencing fantastic simultaneous orgasms'. He thereafter left the official interpreting to the professionals.

Kevin's career seemed mapped out. His immediate boss was David Irvine, who followed the path that Kevin might have pursued had he chosen to continue in DFA, a path that would have taken him across a number of countries, to appointments as ambassador to large nations, such as Indonesia and China, in and out of advisory and management positions within the department and possibly into areas of intelligence. Irvine was Kevin's superior in China and a textbook example of a career diplomat.

Was this image of David Irvine also the image of Kevin Rudd? Kevin was seen by colleagues as focused and ambitious, but ambitious within the realms of a diplomatic career. Colleagues in Beijing did not regard him as being overtly political, even if he generally had 'a young Labor view of the world, not a silly young Labor view'. One visitor was met at the airport by Kevin and they talked on the way back to the embassy. The visitor later commented to one of Kevin's senior officers that he had been impressed. 'Yes', responded the officer, 'we'll both be working for him one day'. (He was right, although he meant as secretary of DFA, not as prime minister!).

Others were impressed too. Author Linda Jaivin, herself a resident of and expert on China, said that 'it was pretty evident to me that Kevin was the clueiest person' when it came to analysing Chinese politics. In 2003, Greg Sheridan wrote about the time he was *The Australian* correspondent in Beijing. When visiting Beijing, it was traditional for journalists as a group to be provided with briefings by the embassy. When Sheridan asked for a briefing on human rights, he was offered a private one in which he was met by Kevin:

> What was surprising was that the embassy entrusted such a delicate matter to so junior an officer ... even then he was regarded as one of the most brilliant of the young foreign service officers. His briefing on human rights displayed a formidable knowledge of Chinese politics, an almost perfect blend of confidence and discretion, a nuanced apologia of Australia's essentially do-nothing approach to the subject.

For Kevin, human rights remained an area of great concern. Towards the end of his stint in Beijing, he wrote a report on human rights in China. It was realistic and critical of the regime. He felt it was ignored, or at least that the Australian government did not do what he wanted it to do. The ambassador thought the government had an appropriate policy towards human rights in China.

Kevin was getting frustrated:

> After I came out to the embassy in Beijing, DFA put me into the Policy Planning Branch. The job was to do 'over the horizon' think pieces. I was given the Rise of Gorbachev and Implications for Soviet Political Change in East Asia. I produced probably a 25-page document over about two to three months; this was before it was clear where Gorbachev was going and in those days he delivered his speech at Vladivostok. It went up to Hayden and then I waited for several weeks for it to come back. At the end of this piece there was a tick and the words 'Good Work'. I didn't think it was insulting, I just thought it was folly, absolute folly, to spend two to three months of analytical work to come to the conclusion that it added up to nothing in terms of real action.

It was part of the push factors that were to get him looking elsewhere: 'I was finding myself in a situation where, to use the term I used a lot of the time, we are being paid to be intellectual pervs on the world, rather than actors in the world'.

When he rang his brother Greg in 1988 to talk about prospects in Queensland, the frustration showed. According to Greg—and rephrased with his adjectival vernacular—Kevin said:

> One thing I have learned so far. I have written briefs. I have read briefs. And I have co-authored briefs. Some were average and some were pertinent. But what I have discovered is that that is not good enough, because at the end of the line you have either got dickhead politicians or average politicians and the occasional good politician who actually interprets and enacts the brief. So I have got to be at the decision end; otherwise what is the point of it all? What is the point of having a lot of good ideas if you are

handing those ideas to people when you just can't trust that they (a) either understand them properly or (b) enact them properly.

He wanted to expand his experience, so he applied for and was selected as the next representative of the Office of National Assessments in London.

Over the next few years, Kevin was twice promoted in absentia. In the Department of Foreign Affairs and Trade (or DFAT, as the DFA was renamed in mid-1987), it is possible to apply for generic promotion to a higher grade. Even without working there for a few years, Kevin became a member of the Senior Executive Service. He kept his options open, but his views on the limitations of a DFAT career were hardening.

4

POLITICS IN QUEENSLAND

In the late 1980s, Queensland was in a state of transition, or rather a state of anxiety. For thirty years the National Party had dominated politics, bolstered by an electoral gerrymander, a supine Liberal coalition partner and an incompetent Labor Opposition. After the coalition collapsed in 1985 and the Nationals won a majority in their own right, the government became less tolerant and less responsive; the image of 'the deep north' presented a picture of folksy populist politics and educational backwardness. Its arrogant use of power led to an emerging opposition that still lacked coherence or a voice. Then the ABC broadcast a *Four Corners* episode called 'The Moonlight State', which documented police corruption and political acquiescence. The premier was away in Disneyland; his deputy, seeking a reputation for political decisiveness, established an inquiry to test the ABC's claims and appointed Tony Fitzgerald, then only slightly known, to chair it. Over the next eighteen months, the political landscape was shaken as the Fitzgerald Inquiry uncovered sleaze and political decay. In August 1987 the National Party removed its long-surviving premier, Joh Bjelke-Petersen, from office, but its reputation sank even as his successor struggled to improve its image.

In its thirty-two years as the Opposition, Labor had tried a number of leaders, mostly trade unionists in their fifties. The party seemed resigned to life as the Opposition. No-one could recall the former days of glory when Labor had governed for all but two years of the period from 1915 to 1957. Then, starting in 1983 after federal intervention, a group of young, tertiary-educated party members became determined to end the long wilderness period. In 1987 they elected Wayne Goss to the party leadership. He was thirty-seven, a lawyer with experience in legal aid and the Aboriginal legal services. He had a sharp brain, intellectual discipline, a preparedness to work hard and driving ambition. He was not only able to surround himself with a new Labor elite, but he also motivated some of the smarter members of the older cliques to work harder.

Goss needed a principal private secretary to assist with the reinvigoration of Opposition policy and tactics; he advertised the position in the *Courier-Mail* and the national press. On the day that the advertisement appeared, Kevin Rudd was in Brisbane as part of DFAT's recruitment drive. The department used to send comparatively recent graduates to explain why the next cohort of bright young students should put their names down for the highly competitive process. As the bus from the city turned into Sir Fred Schonell Drive and entered the final stretch to the University of Queensland, Rudd read the advertisement. It piqued his interest. He felt a challenge; in part he wanted to assist in ridding Queensland of the National Party government. The frustration in DFAT provided the push. Now there was also a pull: 'I wanted to see if I could work in a political office. I wanted to see if I had it within me to go into politics myself, whether that was the right space for me to be in'.

He had earlier written to Minister of Defence Kim Beazley's office seeking a position on the staff there, but to no avail. A position with Goss would finally give him the opportunity to try his hand at something different—the practical reality of politics.

The Beginning

He talked to his brother about Labor's prospects. Then he applied to Goss, whom he had never met—one of around eighty people who did so. Goss shortlisted five and interviewed all of them himself. He made an appointment to interview Rudd in Canberra when, as Opposition leader, Goss was invited to the opening of the new Parliament House. They talked for two hours. Goss noted later: 'What I liked about Kevin was that he showed discipline, a new perspective and a similar analysis to myself in terms of the challenges confronting Labor after thirty-two years in Opposition'.

Rudd, in turn, thought Goss 'was very fixed, focused, determined—he had one objective, which was to pull off the impossible'. For Rudd, it was a big jump. Labor had not won office for over three decades. The Fitzgerald Inquiry had not yet revealed to the public some of the practices of the National government. Goss was untried. Almost no-one thought Labor could win. History makes it look like a wise move, but at the time it was a massive leap in the dark.

Goss wanted to hire Rudd, but first Rudd had to get leave from DFAT. His request raised eyebrows. DFAT staff had gone to work for state premiers, but an Opposition leader was a new slant. Besides, they had almost never come back, so as an exchange scheme it was not seen as successful. Nevertheless, his request was granted, with some reluctance.

Rudd arrived in Brisbane in June 1988. Goss immediately tested him. Rudd had said that he wanted to have Sundays off, but Goss was in the middle of planning a mid-term campaign. 'We were going to have a run-through on the Sunday, so I phoned Kevin on the Saturday and said he should come into work on the Sunday—it would give him a quick overview of the starting pin of the mid-term campaign'.

The response was immediate. As Goss recalled, 'while he liked Sundays with the family, getting the job done was crucial and if that meant working through the night or on a Sunday you knew you could rely on him. He had discipline'. It was scarcely a lesson that had to be taught. On almost the first night, he started work after dinner

His brother Greg, with whom he was staying, asked what he was doing.

Rudd replied, 'Writing housing policy'.

Greg asked, 'What do you know about housing policy?'

'Not much, but I have got to learn.'

From the beginning, the Labor campaign was organised around an inner three: Goss, Rudd and campaign manager Wayne Swan. Rudd and Swan started in the same town; their lives intersected at regular intervals; and they became two of the three most important ministers in a Labor government. Like Rudd, Swan was a Nambour boy, born in 1954. His father owned a service station in town. At Nambour High School, two years ahead of Rudd, Swan was a sports star: captain of the football team, a surfer. The two never met there. As Rudd told their old school during the 2007 election campaign, 'Wayne was very very cool; I was very very not'.

Goss and Swan worked closely together. When Rudd arrived, Swan was the person who introduced him to the local networks, particularly within the Labor Party. The three of them drove the campaign; it was focused and disciplined. Rudd assisted on policy and Swan on tactics, but the demarcations were never absolute. At times, everyone did anything that needed to be done.

For eighteen months after Rudd arrived, most Queensland eyes were on the Fitzgerald Inquiry. Fitzgerald proved far more independent and energetic than the state Cabinet had wanted. The investigations went beyond the police to implicate ministers, and even argued that the system of government, with its weighted electoral system ensuring the constant re-election of the Nationals, allowed the corruption to flourish. In mid-1989, just a few months before the election, Fitzgerald published his report. It was a damning indictment of the government, from the iniquities of the gerrymander to the practices of the police. The National Party premier promised to implement it 'lock, stock and barrel' and was soon overthrown by his party. The government was ripe for defeat.

The Labor Party in turn had to persuade the electorate that it was worthy of being elected, and that, however shambolic the government, Goss could be trusted. So while the government floundered, the Labor troika of Goss, Rudd and Swan began to sell the Labor leader.

Rudd also built contacts within Queensland. He had not lived there for fifteen years and had never worked in Brisbane. He made a list of the leading businesses and made contact with them. Many had never talked to Labor politicians before. By the time of the election, he had a Rolodex full of names and a good idea of how they interacted. He paid special attention to the media and the health worlds.

During the election campaign, Rudd left nothing to chance. The whiteboard in his office contained a schedule of policy announcements. As the election neared, it became more and more detailed. The schedules initially covered months, then weeks. In the last month, the whiteboard listed a daily menu. The emphasis was on maintaining the party's discipline and painting a picture of financial responsibility; Goss and Rudd had to persuade voters that electing them was not a risk, that they could be trusted. Goss released a series of policy papers. One such paper, 'Making Government Work', was presented in a full university lecture hall, covered by television cameras. It was delivered in the middle of the day and reported in the evening news bulletins. It was, declared an editorial in the *Courier-Mail*, an indication the Labor Party was ready to govern.

The election was tense. After thirty years it was hard to believe that Labor was about to win. The Treasury had written a briefing for an incoming Labor government. Only after the election did Rudd pick it up and say: 'Now I can read it'. To do so any earlier would have been tempting fate, taking the electors for granted. But considerable thought had gone into the transition that began on Sunday, 3 December, a day after the result. In the end, Goss won the 1989 election quite easily.

Rudd remained at this time an almost unknown figure. An edited account of the election, published in 1991, contains not a single reference to him. Even the chapter on the Labor Party, written by Swan, does not refer to his contribution. The emphasis was on Goss, and properly so, because he, more than anyone else, was responsible for bringing Labor back to power after so long in the wilderness.

Goss convened a transition-to-government team that met for the first time on that Sunday afternoon after the election. He faced an immediate test. He wanted to change the structure of the public service. When he was told it could be done but would take six months, he dictated the legal advice to illustrate it could be done immediately. And it was—just two days later. That set the tone for the government.

Unlike all the Labor ministers, Rudd had actually been in government, albeit at a fairly junior level in the Commonwealth service. So Tom Burns, the voice of Labor tradition in the new Cabinet, quipped, 'Well Ruddy, you're the only one that's worked in a government around here. What are we going to do?'

Over the next week, the government departments were reduced from twenty-eight to eighteen, chief executives were shuffled to fit the departments and the Cabinet was sworn in. The ministers were those who had been in the Shadow Cabinet, some of whom were survivors of the earlier decimations of the Labor Party during the long period of National hegemony. None had ministerial experience; a few soon struggled.

Goss was a tough taskmaster. He emphasised the need for discipline, not just to win office, but to govern successfully. On one occasion when he was away, two of his senior ministers allowed a

Question Time to degenerate into a shouting match; he called them in to dress them down. That was not the image he wanted to create.

He was demanding of his staff. He wanted advice that was clear and comprehensive. Even if the Fitzgerald Inquiry report had effectively given the government much of its legal and administrative agenda, questions remained about how they might be implemented. The government was both in a hurry and concerned that it would not frighten what it saw as conservative voters.

By choice and necessity, the government was run from the centre. Goss liked to work systematically through a series of routines. He had a philosophy of 'no surprises'. He did not need to know everything, but he needed to be aware if something was about to blow up in the media. He wanted a process that allowed the premier

> to set broad objectives, in Cabinet, in speeches, through lots of telephone calls. You try to develop a culture, an attitude within government. You try to signal to people those individual policy issues which are so important that they should come to me. This is one way of ensuring compliance in policy. I have a personal interest in some issues and may pick up on some smaller issues as a way of giving a signal or to see if the policy is being implemented on the ground.

One means was through a more systematic Cabinet process. The first decision of the Goss government was the approval of a new Cabinet handbook that established a routine for the drafting and circulation of Cabinet submissions in a form that allowed ministers to understand clearly what the Cabinet was to approve. The idea, Goss told his ministers, was to ensure that ministers, not public servants, made the decisions. So Goss wanted 'good coordination and control'. Goss was also concerned that the Premier's Office did not become 'too removed and too hands-off', leading to the criticism that no-one was in control. Goss was meticulous, disciplined and hardworking. He expected others to be the same. He took a lawyer's logic to issues. He was prepared to listen to his advisers, but could also be decisive when he made up his mind. He trusted an inner core of ministers on whom he relied in the most sensitive portfolios.

Initially, much of the working of the central process relied on the Premier's Office, and thus on Rudd. The Premier's Department that Goss had inherited had little policy capacity; the Office had to fill the gap. In his role as Principal Policy Adviser (later called the Principal Private Secretary; PPS) to the premier, Rudd wanted to bring order and direction to the working of the centre of government. Logic, neatness and thoroughness were the guiding principles. He argued that leaders' offices had two functions:

> Providing a source of advice alternative to that deriving from the premier's or the prime minister's own department; and

> Providing a mechanism for the co-ordination of policy advice and activities across the ministerial offices

To serve that end, the Premier's Office established a Policy Unit, with half a dozen advisers whose responsibilities covered all the activities of government.

Rudd was not the only close adviser. Peter Coaldrake became the chair of the new Public Sector Management Commission (PSMC), whose remit was to review the structure and working of all departments. At Goss's request, Glyn Davis took three years' leave from Griffith University, initially to be one of the three commissioners of the PSMC, and later to work with Rudd in the Office of Cabinet. John Mickel was private secretary and acted as liaison with the ALP and the backbenchers. Dennis Atkins was media director. These were all strong personalities who played their roles across government. Rudd, Coaldrake and Davis joined Goss, Burns and Treasurer Keith de Lacy on the Machinery of Government (MOG) Committee that reviewed the reports of the PSMC (and led to the idiom that people had been 'mogged').

Goss sat at the centre, in charge. The premier had to be fully briefed on everything that might come across his desk. So Rudd 'standardised all advice flowing into the Premier's Office, from details of forthcoming events to "topical issue briefs" which kept the premier advised on topics likely to arise in media conferences or parliament'.

The premier's suite sits on the top floor of the Executive Building at 100 George Street. At one end, overlooking the river, is the office of the director-general of the Department of the Premier. At the other is the premier's office, with a view of the city (by one account, the former premier preferred the view of working cranes to a sedate river). Rudd's office was a small room in the premier's suite, giving him immediate, unimpeded access when he wanted.

Rudd understood that ministerial advisers had different perspectives from those of officials and sought to explain the differences. They had to be aware of the possible political impact of a policy proposal, on the ministry, the party, the community and the media; they needed to ensure it was compatible with the proposals of other ministers and with the government's long-term strategy.

The PPS sat at the centre of the administrative circle and was responsible for making the system work. One adviser explained, 'Goss doesn't see himself as the ringmaster—others around him are responsible for the ring mastering'. That usually meant his principal adviser, who

> saw all correspondence going in and out of the Premier's in-tray, attended all important meetings where a political presence was

required, discussed leadership with the party leadership and talked constantly with the media side of the Premier's Office. The PPS worked in an office adjoining the Premier's room, had to be there when the Premier started in the morning, remain available all day then work back to attend to office arrangements, approve schedules and deal with a stream of supplicants seeking the Premier's time.

There was an additional responsibility: 'When the premier exercised coordination by taking decisions, implementation fell to the Principal Private Secretary'. Rudd became the bearer of bad news. Those not prepared to criticise the premier attacked his chief lieutenant.

The purpose was to support a premier who was determined to run a tight ship. Aware that the government was seen as inexperienced, Goss was wanted to chair a disciplined Cabinet. He did not want a government 'freewheeling out of control' and needed to curb the impatience of new ministers. Adviser Michael Stephenson noted:

> During the first term there was suspicion about our highly centralised system. Ministerial offices thought we were interfering and we were. In the first year they weren't widely consulted. We were trying to bed down a new government ... over time there has been a change in relationships. The politics of fear only works for a time.

Rudd's colleagues justified the adversarial approach as necessary; they had to ensure there were no surprises and to identify where the problems might be: 'Sometimes the style has to be abrupt, but we march to a different drum up here because the premier has to look after eighteen portfolios'.

The circumstances perhaps demanded unusual action. There had been no change of government for thirty-two years. The public service was used to a National Party agenda and was as unaccustomed to new initiatives as the Labor government. Some decisions perhaps exacerbated the problems. Reshuffled heads of department needed to take charge of reconstituted departments and were faced with the prospect of a review of their operations by the PSMC. The combination of change and new government made many uncomfortable and suspicious. A small group of department heads who had not been given positions were sent to the 'Government Research Unit' (the abbreviation of GRU was not an accident and it quickly became known as the 'Gulag') until the government decided how it could use them or whether they would resign. It was not a wise decision because it not only provided an easy target for criticism but allowed the heads constant reinforcement of each other's grievances. The GRU was not maintained for long, though the legend survived for much longer. These were lessons that Rudd took on board.

On hearing bad news, or while insisting on better service to the premier, Rudd could also be abrupt, impatient and demanding. He terrified some of those he dealt with. He thought there was no time for the injured egos of those who provided work of poor quality. The Queensland public service was nowhere near the standard of DFAT, one of Canberra's premier departments. He found it frustrating and was not slow to say so. He gained the sobriquet of Dr Death. From whom it came is uncertain. Some say it was ministers who saw their Cabinet submissions sent back because they did not satisfy the Cabinet rules. Others credit it to public servants who feared that a summons to meet Rudd was a precursor to disastrous news. Still others credited the Opposition with inventing the term, but thought they muddled Rudd, who did not have a doctorate, with Coaldrake, who did. Regardless, Tom Burns and Coaldrake used to welcome Rudd with a cheery 'Hello, Death'. He was teased by his colleagues and at times almost bore the term with pride. It stuck.

Yet the support the private office delivered was not enough. Dissatisfied with the quality of advice he was receiving, Goss was determined to improve it. He always regarded the 'backroom' as essential to political success. Although the government had immediately created a Policy Coordination Division within the Premier's Department, Goss wanted a better service, one that was able to pull together the strings of policy across the government. Rudd had spoken to Gary Sturgess, the head of the Cabinet Office serving the Liberal Premier of New South Wales, Nick Greiner, and Goss decided to create a Queensland Office of Cabinet. He announced it would have functions of consultation, advice, monitoring implementation, identifying cross-portfolio issues, undertaking special projects for the premier, advising on forward programs and managing the Cabinet process. The position of director-general was advertised nationally but no-one was too surprised when the selection committee recommended Rudd to the premier.

Rudd went back into bureaucrat mode, driving a policy agenda. Davis, then policy officer, recalls:

> We had a Cabinet Office retreat soon after the new organisation was established, and I recall a room full of people at some impossible hour after midnight as the new Director-General drove us through a comprehensive list of policy topics and operational issues. He was making absolutely sure we had identified every priority and assigned responsibility so it was always clear who was managing what. This level of thoroughness is the difference between being good at a task and being outstanding. Kevin Rudd was determined to run the best policy shop in the nation, and did so from the day he took on the challenge.

In introducing the Office of Cabinet a few days after it was formally commissioned on 1 July 1991, Rudd explained what it was about. Policy, he asserted, 'can be defined as the consistent, codified and publicly articulated response by government to problems arising within the jurisdiction of that government and problems which exhibit common or similar characteristics'. If government behaviour is to be truly consistent, therefore, policy coordination is essential so that there is 'consistency of policy development, articulation and implementation across the whole of government so that the part intelligently reflects and contributes to the whole'. The function of the office was to serve Cabinet through its minister, the premier. It should articulate the policy objectives, not seek control over day-to-day operations. It would, Rudd argued,

> seek co-ordination by testing specific proposals against a set of policy objectives and principles determined by Cabinet. Its advice to the premier will be couched with an eye to policy consistency. It will also, however, be concerned about the achievement of policy objectives as this too is part of the brief which Cabinet has given it.

For the next three years, Rudd played a central role as the principal official adviser to Goss, with the benefit of an office of around 100 staff supporting him. The Office of Cabinet was high profile and politically contentious; the Opposition accused it of being a home for Labor apparatchiks. Rudd was attacked as being the 'de facto deputy premier'. At times, the staff could be abrupt, demanding reactions from senior officers in other departments with a vigour that upset those used to more respect to seniority in its own right.

Rudd explains his own perception. He was mission oriented, driven by a desire to get things done, rather than drift. Once it was determined what should be done in terms that were properly defensible, then the purpose was to do it: 'At that point I become what some have described as driven but not driven for the sake, the aimless point, of being driven. I am driven because of a conclusion about a particular [issue]'.

Goss recalls:

> I think some ministers did not like him. Some public servants did not like him, even if they respected his ability and the agenda. Kevin and I were very disciplined and if you're going to drive that big agenda you've got to hold people to account. Sometimes Kevin did it on my behalf, sometimes he did it on his behalf. I've got no doubt that sometimes he went too far, but that's the price you pay if you're trying to get from A to Z.

In Cabinet, Goss would test the ideas of ministers, questioning their assumptions and plans, always with the benefit of Cabinet Office briefings. He sometimes terrified ministers. That did not make the staff of the Office of Cabinet popular when they demanded information and action on behalf of the premier.

Others felt that Rudd's single-minded focus could cause difficulties. Says his close colleague, media director Dennis Atkins:

> The one enduring criticism I've got of Kevin is that he would expect from senior public servants endless hard work and just being there all day. But he'd do it without really having much concern for their feelings or the fact that it was Sunday. He'd call people in and have them waiting for hours and then, say, 'Oh look, I haven't got time to see you now. I'll see you tomorrow'. It is the sort of thing he did far too often.

Rudd assumed everyone had his work ethic and wanted to achieve what he did. His sense of time (or rather the lack of it) created frustration. He would keep people waiting long after the designated time for an appointment, seen by some as an exercise of power. His colleagues thought up different ways of dealing with it: one arranged to put a cup of his favourite coffee on his spot when the meeting was scheduled to start. If he was not on time, it got cold. Another used to go back to his office; when rung to be asked why he was not here, he responded that Rudd wasn't there so why should he be. Others merely had to wait. At the same time, Rudd was careful about any misuse of government funds, and scrupulous about unnecessary expenditure. His idea of a Christmas party, quipped Peter Coaldrake, was to provide cheese to go with the Jatz.

Rudd ranged across the activities of government. He sat beside the premier and deputy premier in the annual Cabinet budget committee as ministers and their chief executives were questioned on their proposals. His requests were seen as peremptory. But as long as he and Goss were on the same wavelength, he was effective. He could be deeply focused. If he chose to work on a new area, he would delegate all the routine business to others and then immerse himself for weeks. He relentlessly dedicated 80 per cent or more of his time to the topic, until he was master of the brief.

The Mabo and native title cases, for example, were seen as too complex to be left to a line department. Rudd brought together a team from across government: constitutional lawyers, engineers and land title experts. One observer said he could 'talk about twenty-seven different kinds of land tenure and how the different leases worked'. He would read, debate, argue and question until he was able to convince himself that he knew what he was talking about and what the policy implications might be. Others may have disagreed wildly with what the government chose to do, but he did not want to be trumped on basic knowledge. The issue became particularly controversial when Aboriginal leaders like Noel Pearson complained that the government in general, and Rudd in particular, were not serious in their proposals.

Inevitably, the Office of Cabinet became most involved in those areas of policy in which the premier had a personal interest or where the issues crossed departmental boundaries. Goss recalls that drought relief was one of those. The government put together a drought-relief taskforce, then they

> approached a number of rural industry leaders and said that we could either run the normal drought-relief program or we could bring them 'in the tent'. We made it plain that we would outline details of programs—including costings—but would accept advice from them on how programs could be improved. They responded in a positive way and we delivered a much better program as a consequence. Kevin ran that program.

Ian Macfarlane, later a minister in the Howard government, was one of those who participated and maintained the confidences. Rudd also played a key role, Goss argues, in a ten-year hospital rebuilding program, which was designed to look a decade ahead to overcome past neglect.

The government was constantly in a bind. There was pent-up enthusiasm for reform, reflected in the agenda proposed by the PSMC and the two commissions established on the recommendation of the Fitzgerald Inquiry report, the Electoral and Administrative Review Committee and the Criminal Justice Commission. Yet Goss was concerned that the government should not get too far ahead of expectations. The government, Peter Coaldrake said, was 'thrifty, cautious [and] not much different from non-Labor governments'. In practice it achieved extensive reform, was re-elected comfortably in 1992, and generally undersold what it had achieved.

Within the government, there remained an inner circle of three: Goss took the lead; Swan did the politics and political management; and Rudd the policy. In the next circle were the leading ministers, Burns and De Lacey, and the other advisers, Dennis Atkins, Glyn Davis and Peter Coaldrake.

Outside the state government, Rudd's biggest impact was in federal–state relations. The Office of Cabinet gave Rudd a role in policy issues across states, a role he could not have pursued as a political staffer. Goss and Rudd had been horrified by their first experience of a Premiers' Conference where process had been reduced to theatrical routine—the federal government's offers were slipped under the hotel room door in the early hours of the morning. They wanted better process and found common ground with other state premiers, particularly Nick Greiner, the Liberal Premier of New South Wales. At the same time, Prime Minister Bob Hawke proposed the establishment of the Special Premiers Conferences, later folded into the Council of Australian Governments (COAG). The initiative created a need for whole-of-government work across departments. COAG was a meeting of premiers. All the issues had to be coordinated by the centre of government: in Queensland, it was the Office of Cabinet. Rudd became part of a key group of advisers who worked for the premiers and who oversaw the development of an agenda.

The Commonwealth officials sometimes felt uncomfortable dealing with the likes of Rudd and Sturgess, whom they termed 'political bureaucrats'. These sharp and often young state officials would, if unsuccessful working through traditional methods, be quite prepared to ring up the Prime Minister's Office to get a message across. They were certainly noticed; on one occasion an official watched in awe as Rudd and Roger Beale, associate secretary of the Department of the Prime Minister and Cabinet, argued for an hour, with references to High Court cases, the Constitution, legislation and other sources.

One subject on which Rudd took the initiative was the study of Asian languages. At his instigation, Queensland put Asian language studies on the agenda of the first COAG meeting, held in December 1992. Rudd believed that an early appreciation of Asian languages and cultures would provide a basis for trade development. COAG agreed; its communiqué explained the initiative in the context of the National Trade Strategy and as a means of promoting an export culture. It noted the importance of 'the development of a comprehensive understanding of Asian languages and cultures through the Australian education system if Australia is to maximise its economic interests in the Asia–Pacific region', and commissioned a study for the implementation of a comprehensive Asian languages and cultures program in Australian schools (and, where relevant, TAFEs) by the end of the decade.

Queensland was given the responsibility of organising the working group. By tying the proposal to trade and arguing that it was a matter of national importance, the Office of Cabinet was able to remove the issue from the exclusive preserve of the state departments of education.

Rudd chaired the working party that produced a report entitled 'Asian Languages and Australia's Economic Future'. He fought off attempts by education departments to take over the program as part of the Studies in Asia curricula. He insisted language and culture be taught together. Of course, there were interstate differences that had to be negotiated. That took time. COAG endorsement did not ensure cooperation. Nevertheless, a common approach had been developed for presentation to the COAG at its meeting in February 1994. It showed that only 4 per cent of students were studying an Asian language. It proposed that emphasis be placed on Korean, Mandarin, Japanese and Indonesian, with a target of 25 per cent of Year 12 students studying an Asian language by 2000 (later extended to 2006).

COAG endorsed Rudd's report and agreed to introduce a National Asian Languages/Studies Strategy for Australian Schools.

The question was, who would pay? The report had proposed that the Commonwealth should meet 50 per cent of the net funding for the project, but the Commonwealth agreed to fund 50 per cent of the program for the first two years only. Thereafter its support would decline, until by 2006 it would be responsible for just 6 per cent of the funding. So Goss wrote a lengthy letter asking the prime minister to resolve the question; Paul Keating agreed that the Commonwealth would be a full funding partner in the project.

Rudd retained a continuing interest in the scheme, having his department evaluate its progress and constantly emphasising the link between trade, economic performance and increased skills in the workforce. Asian Studies showed Rudd in action as a senior official. He knew what he wanted, was tactical in his approach, conscious of the need to maintain control of the process, and careful to support states prepared to push the ideas along. The combination of process and content were typical of his style. He developed the arguments, devised the strategy, maintained the momentum, drove the staff and drafted the correspondence.

Rudd's horizons had been further extended by a surprise in early 1993. He was invited to attend the first meeting of the Australian–American Leadership Dialogue (AALD). The AALD had been the dream of Australian executive Phil Scanlan. Finding himself sitting with President George Bush on a harbour cruise in Sydney in December 1991, Scanlan had suggested that the Australian–American relationship, however close it was, should not be taken for granted. He wanted to establish a link that would continue regardless of which parties were in power at either end.

The first meeting was held in Washington in July 1993. From the American side came a cohort of the significant players. They included

Richard Chaney, Bob Zoellick, Richard Armitage and Bruce Reed. Scanlan had to determine who would come from Australia. Looking to the future, he asked the secretary of DFAT, Dick Woolcott, whom he thought would be in his position of departmental secretary in fifteen years. Woolcott nominated Rudd. So Rudd was invited to the Washington meeting; he was the only official among a group of politicians, journalists and business figures. Among the political elite from Australia were David Kemp and Warwick Smith from the Liberals, and Kim Beazley and Nick Bolkus from the Labor government.

It was Rudd's first visit to mainland America. As he told his amused US colleagues, he had, by contrast, been in and out of China over twenty times. He found the United States to be stimulating, interesting and friendly. Over the next twenty years he missed only one of the twenty or so AALD meetings. He was always an active participant. Greg Sheridan recalled that: 'It is breaking no confidence to say that Rudd is frequently a brilliant contributor to the dialogue'. He became familiar with the US scene; when in the next decade he visited Washington, he could readily pick up the phone and talk to some of the people who mattered. He made good friends and developed easy and informal relationships. They were to prove useful in times ahead, and not only in mainstream politics.

Rudd may have been a powerful bureaucrat, but he still worked for the government and his was a delegated power. If Rudd was to make real changes, he had to be the leader himself. He chose to take the plunge into federal politics.

5

A POLITICAL INITIATION: FROM CANDIDATE TO BACKBENCHER

When he arrived back in Brisbane in 1988, Rudd rented a house in Figtree Pocket in the city's western suburbs. Then he and Thérèse bought a small house in Hawthorn and, a year or so later, the house in Norman Park that they still own today. Hawthorn and Norman Park are both in the Griffith electorate. That was not an accident. Griffith was then held by Ben Humphreys; he had first been elected in 1977 and was soon to turn sixty. In a state that had been reduced to one Labor MP in 1975, Griffith was seen as a Labor seat. It included meatworks and shipbuilding. Humphreys had been a member of the Old Guard. Sooner, rather than later, Griffith was going to be looking for a Labor candidate. Living there kept Rudd's options open. In 1993 he campaigned for Humphreys, even though a few weeks earlier Rudd had undergone heart surgery for the replacement of a valve and was meant to be resting.

Rudd's decision to enter politics surprised many of his colleagues. Rudd had long been seen as sympathetic to Labor causes and had worked for a Labor premier, but standing for election was another step. He told Goss and Swan about his plan a year before he publicly announced his intention to stand for Griffith. When Humphreys announced in 1996 that he was standing down, Rudd had to move. Goss and Swan, himself now a federal member of the House of Representatives, were amused that, as a consequence, Rudd had to join the Old Guard faction, dominated by the Electrical Trades Union, one of the more traditional of unions.

He organised his push for selection with the same thoroughness that he did everything else. His principal opponent for the party nomination was Norma Jones, a member of the Left, with her greatest strength in the West End branches. Rudd was the candidate of the Right, with the support of the premier. He was confident he would have won a ballot, but eventually did not need to. The redistribution commissioners changed the boundaries of the seat of Griffith and stripped out the left-wing West End strongholds from which Norma Jones would have drawn her support. She did not stand and Rudd was unopposed for Labor Party selection.

Once he had won party nomination, Rudd stood down as director-general of the Office of Cabinet. Strictly, he did not have to. He could have remained a public servant until his nomination papers were due. But he argued it was better to give up the position and undertake a number of specific tasks for the Cabinet Office as a consultant. The director-general position was advertised nationally and Glyn Davis, at that stage back working as a political scientist at Griffith University, was appointed.

Rudd campaigned, constantly, exhaustingly. He knocked on doors, talked to electors, and appeared at shopping centres throughout the electorate. He and Thérèse calculated they had canvassed 30 000 houses by the time the election was held. He developed a local machine and started to develop policies on a series of local issues, including the potential problems that might be caused by a second runway at Brisbane airport and the noise it would create for the Griffith electors. Although well established within the higher echelons of government, he was virtually unknown within the electorate. He was also a contrast to the outgoing member, a more knockabout figure than the intellectual and nerdish-looking Rudd.

For once, and for the first time, all the work was to no avail. Rudd was standing as the tide went out for Labor. Queensland electors were, to repeat Goss's memorable phrase, sitting on their verandahs with baseball bats, waiting for the chance to attack the Keating government.

Thérèse recalls the pain of that loss in 1996:

> I remember on election day as we went round the booths together, a number of people coming to him and saying, 'I really wanted to support you and I took a long time agonising about my vote'. He would say, 'What did you decide?' or 'Do you want to tell me what you decided?' And they would look at him and just shake their heads and just say, 'Sorry'.

Rudd was swept away in the landslide, with a great swing against the government. He got 47.5 per cent of the vote and was left with no seat and no job.

Kevin Rudd and Thérèse Rein felt as though they had hit a brick wall. The question now was: What next? One immediate local response was that Labor had to revert to a more traditional candidate, that the experiment with Rudd should not be repeated. When this was suggested to Rudd directly after the election, his response was visceral: 'Let them try to take it'. He had no intention of giving up so readily. But it was a shock. For all his life he had worked according to the principle that if he did everything possible, if he was disciplined and organised and persistent, then success would follow. Now he had lost, in spite of all his work, all his campaigning, all his dedication.

He explored other options. He talked to DFAT to discuss what he might be able to do there. It was a bad time as the department was required to reduce staff. Nevertheless, the response was damning. Although there was some talk about his suitability for the position of consul-general in Shanghai, that would have required ministerial endorsement; no-one expected the new Minister for Foreign Affairs, Alexander Downer, to agree to appoint a former Labor candidate. Instead, he was sent a message from the top of the department that he was too controversial, too high profile, and that it would be more appropriate if he resigned. Any possibility of a future career as a diplomat thus ended. He resigned from the department and used his superannuation to pay off his mortgage. There was also a story that he had been approached to become the head of the New South Wales Department of Community Services. Neither of these possibilities would likely have proved a satisfactory option.

These were dark times—an education in frustration. At times it showed. In September 1997 he turned forty. It was a grim night of introspection as his friends gathered on the balcony of the Rudds' Norman Park house. Labor was out of power in the state; even if it won, Wayne Goss was gone as leader and Rudd was too strongly identified with him to expect so central a position with Peter Beattie's regime. His brother Greg tried to cheer everyone up, but when later that night Wayne Goss was diagnosed with a brain tumour and rushed to hospital, the future looked bleak indeed. There were no guarantees that Rudd would keep his Labor preselection or, if he did, that he would win the seat from the Liberal member at the next election.

At this time, Thérèse was just beginning to develop her own business. On her return to Brisbane, she initially worked for a private firm that provided rehabilitation services. She enjoyed the feeling of getting people back to work, aware of the self-worth that could be created. When she parted company with the firm on a matter of principle, a friend offered to invest should she decide to establish her own business in the field. She immediately sat down to work out a mental map of what would be required, where the connections might be in a venture with a psychologist and an occupational therapist at the core: What services might be provided? Where else could the services be expanded? Could they extend to the long-term unemployed? So Thérèse established her own company, Work Directions Australia:

> I love the fact that someone can have been out of work for eighteen years and they think they're never going to work again and can be quite depressed and despondent. And three months later they can walk in and they're taking their family on holiday and their head is up and their chest's out. That is what we do.

Rudd started to plan for the future. His first reaction, to continue the fight, resurfaced. He ran again for the seat of Griffith. His faction, the Old Guard, insisted that he participate in a ballot. He won easily; his recollection was by 41 votes to 2. He was duly endorsed. One consequence was that he could continue to campaign as the Labor candidate, consistently and hard.

He also had to make a living. He founded Australia China Consultancies as a vehicle to build on his contacts and skills in China. He became a facilitator, working mainly with KPMG, flying in and out of China to deal with the range of activities that they had there. His conscientiousness continued. One observer met him in a Shanghai cafe with all the cards of people Rudd had met laid out across the table; he was writing notes to every one of them, to assist the next time he was in town. Indeed, relations with his Chinese contacts were now easier than they had been when he was a diplomat because much of the ice had thawed over the decade since he had worked there.

It was also an education. Working as a troubleshooter, he saw another side of Chinese business, the toughness of some of the business activities, the way that Australian companies could readily be out of their depth. Clients were impressed by his contacts. He 'would arrange introductions to mayors and heads of departments and all sorts of things that you have to work your way through in China'. He had a range of connections across the country, within government, business and the universities. He was engaged in project negotiation: 'Everything from what is called an upfront feasibility study of "should you get into this market", to "you are in this market and you are in trouble", through to "how do you get out of this market?"'.

The experience provided a depth to his views of China that now took him far beyond the diplomatic compounds of Beijing and illustrated the challenges and difficulties of working there. Notions that Rudd had an idealised view of the country discount many of his experiences working within the business arena for those two years.

Rudd maintained a continuous campaign even after the Griffith election: months of pounding the pavement, knocking on doors, letterboxing. His sister Loree recalls one of the team complaining to her: 'Why does Kevin expect us to work so hard?' She replied: 'I don't think it enters his head that everyone isn't geared up and going like him. He works hard; therefore if you're in the team, you just go with it'.

He had learned from the 1996 defeat. Friends like Goss noted that he would now listen rather than lecture and that he had developed a facility for grass-roots campaigning.

There were no guarantees. Governments often hold their gains the first time they run for re-election. In the 1998 election, Rudd now had to win from outside, without the benefits of incumbency. The local Liberal member, Graeme McDougall, had worked the electorate conscientiously and was standing for re-election. Campaigning against the imposition of a GST, Labor got over 50 per cent of the two-party vote, but John Howard won the majority of seats. Rudd won 52.4 per cent of the votes in Griffith, compared with 48.5 per cent in 1996. He was now an MP.

The Beginning

He was part of a new influx of MPs to Canberra. Several of the old members from the Keating era had retired from safe Labor seats. Besides Rudd, Julia Gillard, Craig Emerson and Nicola Roxon entered parliament. Wayne Swan was one of those returning after losing his seat in 1996. They joined a number of ambitious members, elected in 1993, who had watched the last years of the Keating government, including Lindsay Tanner and Mark Latham.

What were Rudd's ambitions? There was a scent of realism. No Queenslander had been prime minister since the 1940s and no Labor Queenslander had held the position substantively since Andrew Fisher in 1915. He was not a factional player:

> My own ambition was to become foreign minister. I am not simply retrospectively re-engineering stuff here. That was my principal and realistic ambition, with the fall-back that if a general bus crash occurred at some stage it would be nice to be prime minister.

That was indeed realistic, as he explains in Q&A style:

> Question: How do you stitch together a coalition to support yourself for election from the great state of Queensland?
>
> Answer: With great difficulty. Look at the history on both sides.

Still, years later, Rudd also acknowledges: 'Any honest backbencher would tell you they arrive with a [field marshal's] baton in their backpack and I was no different'.

There were four challenges. First, he had to survive. Political office goes to those with long and continuous political careers. Since Rudd had won his seat from the government, he then had to make it safe. Second, he needed to become recognised within his own party as its principal expert in one field; in his case, his obvious advantage was in foreign affairs. Third, he had to prove himself within the parliamentary caucus as a person of standing, a person who would represent the new generation post-Hawke and Keating and who needed to be taken seriously. Fourth, he needed a national public profile—recognition outside Queensland.

The first requirement was to ensure his home base. His initial electoral margin was small, a mere 2.4 per cent. So he worked his electorate hard. Rudd's mobile offices became a feature of his continuing campaigns. His 1996 defeat taught him even more about the need to listen and to understand what people are concerned about. The education of young Rudd was achieved primarily by the Griffith electors.

He developed a number of trademark schemes that brought attention and identification. He donated bicycles to schools, for them to raffle and raise funds. The idea of the 'Rudd bike' became well known in the neighbourhood. There was a running gag that he would either donate a leather-bound copy of Hansard, with all his speeches included, or a bike—no-one ever took the former. He also provided a Kevin Rudd Foreign Language Award to all high schools in Griffith for the student who topped the language class at the school. It was a striking way to make contacts across the electorate and with parents who could remember something concrete that he had done for them.

Even before he was elected, he championed opposition to the second runway at Brisbane airport. If one were developed, he argued, a large proportion of the flights would cross the electorate at low levels, causing noise and disruption. He thought the airport master plan was dodgy and inconsistent with his reading of the *Airports Act 1996*. He demanded more transparent decision-making and greater consultation. He fought a continuing battle with the Brisbane Airports Corporation, won three rounds in court and then lost on appeal in the Federal Court. He had $32 000 worth of damages awarded against him. The community rallied and raised around $30 000 to help him.

In Canberra he had to make a mark quickly. Being in the Opposition does not blunt ambition, but it channels it into a fairly narrow arc: how to get on within the party as a means to be in a strategic position if (when) the party wins office. One backbencher arriving in parliament once asked his prime minister what strategy he should adopt if he wanted to advance quickly. The advice was that he should concentrate on one or two topics and make himself a name there, so that he would stand out from the pack. For Rudd, the choice was obvious: he might belong to a number of backbench party committees but his field was to be foreign affairs and security. He was a former diplomat, even if he had by now spent more time in Queensland political life than in DFAT, and had not been directly involved in diplomatic issues for a decade. He was selected immediately to be chair of the backbench Committee for Foreign Affairs, with Julia Gillard as his deputy. In the best Labor tradition, there was only one nominee.

He was, as always, energetic. He began to write regularly for the press on a wide range of topics, always turning the articles into critiques of the Howard government and Minister for Foreign Affairs Alexander Downer. An early article was cheeky. He wrote an open letter to Peter Costello, seeking to create mischief:

> Dear Peter, You probably don't know me from a bar of soap. I'm one of the new lot elected to the Parliament last October. From the other side, I'm afraid, the Labor Party.
>
> We do however have one thing in common; we're both republicans. That's why I'm putting pen to paper.

> Like it or not the future of the Australian republic is up to you. You are the only show in town ...

He had learned from Goss the value of close links with the media, and cultivated several members of the press gallery. Some of his colleagues felt that his links were too close, that he constantly backgrounded the press on internal Labor affairs. In the first year he wrote for the *Canberra Times*, *The Australian*, the *Australian Financial Review* and the *Courier-Mail*, most often about foreign affairs, about developments in Asia. In February 2001 he reported on his visit to Jakarta, suggesting that there was a wariness there about the motives of the government. In April 2001 he attacked the federal government on its support for what he described as a great change of policy by the US Government in regard to Taiwan. He travelled extensively to Asian countries as well as maintaining his links with the AALD and building networks in Washington.

There were moments of sheer strangeness. Rudd took part in an official visit to North Korea, with Leo McLeay the leader of the Australian delegation. In general discussion with party officials, Rudd says, McLeay cracked a joke:

> The interpreter obviously mistranslated something because no-one laughs at the joke. They weren't upset, they just didn't laugh. To which Leo said: 'The interpreter stuffed it up, shoot the interpreter'. The poor old interpreter, the blood drained from his face as he had to interpret this remark, at which point I said, seeing what was going on, this is an Australian joke. This is not a serious comment, we believe that the interpreter is in fact an exceptionally professional representative of the Democratic People's Republic of Korea.

Progress within the Labor Party is seldom achieved without a cost. Parliament attracts the ambitious. Egos clash as new members size up their rivals for future office and seek to get ahead. Established figures want to defend their position against usurpers and pretenders. The first battles in the rise of any potential leader must be fought within the party, for standing and reputation. How newcomers handle these challenges determines who may be marked out for higher things. Inevitably, Rudd's push for a high profile grated, particularly with the shadow spokesman for foreign affairs, Laurie Brereton. Brereton had been a minister in the Hawke and Keating governments, with a desire to be minister for foreign affairs. He had a reputation as a tough, uncompromising opponent, a bad enemy to make for a newly arrived MP. 'Danger Man' was one nickname, not meant kindly. He wanted to change the party position in a number of areas. Rudd's greatest concern was Brereton's attitude to the American alliance; Rudd was always a strong defender of it. Although he was from the Right, Brereton was more sceptical. He 'would describe me as a CIA plant, half-facetiously and half-seriously, around the place', recalls Rudd.

Brereton's first step was on East Timor. He had advocated a referendum before the 1998 election. In January 1999 he sought, and was granted, a visa to visit East Timor. Then the Indonesian ambassador withdrew the invitation, suggesting the time was not opportune; the visit should be postponed. Brereton let fly. He suggested that previous Labor governments had been too supine on Timor; he accused them of being morally compromised, comparing Australian knowledge about what happened there with the Holocaust. Whether deliberately or not, he argued they had acquiesced in Indonesia's invasion in 1975 and had failed to push hard enough to protect civil rights. His comments unleashed a flood of anger from former Labor leaders and ministers. Gareth Evans replied bitterly in a speech to the caucus that Brereton had assaulted the moral integrity and competence of Labor prime ministers and foreign ministers.

Rudd agreed with Brereton that 'we were dealing with completely new realities'. But he saw no need to repudiate the past. Rudd joined the fray, however, giving a speech in Jakarta in April 1999 defending the Whitlam/Keating/Evans approach as necessary and appropriate. It laid the foundation for antipathy between the shadow spokesman and the caucus committee chair and indicated that Rudd was not about to be browbeaten into submission by a senior colleague with a fearsome reputation.

In May 1999 the Indonesian Government invited Rudd to visit East Timor. It was cleared with the federal government. Brereton leaned on the party leader, Kim Beazley, to order Rudd to cancel the trip. If the Indonesian Government would not invite the official spokesman, then no-one should go. It was duly cancelled.

In June 1999 Rudd was an official observer for the Indonesian elections, travelling with Labor's defence spokesman, Stephen Martin, not with Brereton. In October he wrote to the Indonesian Government asking for approval to visit the refugee camps that had sprung up in West Timor. It was agreed that he could lead a delegation, and that Brereton could come with two delegates from the government side. On 19 October Rudd announced his plans in parliament. The speaker refused to fund the trip, on the grounds that it was not an appropriate time; he cited security reasons. Everyone else dropped out. Rudd carried on, paying his own way:

> We were in Kupang which is where all the militia leaders were based ... by coincidence we teamed up with the US and British Ambassadors who were based in Jakarta and ... went to the camps up around Atambua which is the place where you might recall the World Food Program had a number of its staff chopped to death by the militia leaders. I agreed with the British and Americans that we would go around and visit all the police and military commanders of Indonesia and basically formally put

them on notice about the fact that there was now an international war crimes jurisdiction and that the safety and wellbeing of these East Timorese was in their control. If anything happened to them, the international jurisdiction would come in search of them. This was technically just before or just after the Roman Statute came into being, probably before. So we were somewhat wide of the brief in technical accuracy but my job as I saw it was to scare the living Jesus out of them.

The relationship with Brereton grew even tenser as Rudd continued to speak publicly across all issues of foreign affairs. In early 2001 the two made different comments on Indonesia. Brereton had again criticised past Labor governments for putting too much emphasis on working with the Indonesian military. Rudd, in Jakarta, talked about a return to 'Evanism, Keatingism and Hawkism all wrapped together'. Downer had made fun of Labor in parliament, accusing it of being in disarray over Indonesia. Brereton's annoyance was well known. As Michelle Grattan wrote in June 2001: 'Rudd is not a short term threat to Brereton; he could not realistically expect to jump straight from the backbench to foreign minister. He is however a negative for Brereton because no one in Labor is in any doubt about what Rudd, a one-time diplomat, thinks of the spokesman'.

Brereton decided to pull him into line. In June 2001 he wrote to Rudd and copied the letter to the thirty-five members of the Caucus Foreign Affairs Committee. It was to be a very public rebuke, since it could be guaranteed that the letter would be leaked more widely. It was—sections of the letter were reported in the media. Brereton accused Rudd of a 'complete absence of liaison' and regretted that they did not enjoy a 'productive and co-operative relationship'. He wrote:

In this election year, we must be prepared for a much greater discipline in public commentary on international affairs.

I certainly understand the urgent desire of a backbench member for personal promotion through contributions to the opinion pages of newspapers and on television. However there is a risk that gratuitous commentary can send mixed signals to the electorate, media and diplomatic community.

I don't want to cramp your style, but I think it would be helpful if you could take your time to consult with me or my office before you embark on further commentary on foreign policy issues.

In effect, he was publicly telling Rudd to shut up, in the only style he knew how. Rudd did not flinch. He wrote back, expressing his surprise

that you didn't raise any of the concerns raised in your letter personally, and instead chose to copy a letter to the 35 members of the national Security and Trade Caucus Committee. As a consequence both you and I know that there is therefore a high probability that the content of your letter will find its way into the public domain and become the subject of public controversy ...

[I have] written some 40 or 50 commentaries about the foreign policy failings of the Howard government. I'd be most grateful if you could advise me which of these commentaries presents a departure from party policy ... [I intend] to continue to contribute to the public debate, as I have done in the past, consistent with the parameters of party policy.

I can find no reference in the rules that empowers shadow ministers with an ultimate right of veto over what the chairs of their respective policy committees contribute to public debate.

He circulated the response to the same list of caucus members as had received Brereton's, with the same result. It appeared in the press.

The two argued in a meeting of the caucus committee. One account said they 'angrily clashed' in a 'blazing row' and a 'screaming match'; the official account said it was 'civilised but argumentative'. When Rudd asked whether he had breached Labor policy in his statements, Brereton replied: 'No, you're pretty good on policy'. He argued that Rudd had failed to take account of the 'nuances' of his policy statements. While it finished with an uneasy truce, neither side gave ground. Brereton acknowledged he did not have a veto and Rudd agreed to inform Brereton before publicly making any statements in sensitive policy areas. Leader Kim Beazley explained the row as evidence of 'creative tension' in caucus. In effect, it was not about policy but about their respective standing, as the old tired warhorse fought to guard his ground against the newcomer. Rudd had stood up for his rights within the party against one of its toughest operators and had come through unscathed. It was symbolically important; he was becoming well known within the party. As one observer suggested, 'No wonder the growing caucus reputation and public profile of a calm, experienced and knowledgeable former diplomat like Kevin Rudd is causing him [Brereton] some grief'.

There were other rivals, too, not of the former generation but of those competing for light and reputation with a longer-term future in mind. The most public was Mark Latham. He had been on the frontbench from 1996 to 1998 but had resigned from the shadow executive in 1998 in protest against Beazley's changes to his proposed education policy. Now he used the freedom of the backbench to write widely on a range of issues. Rudd and Latham may have been the most active of Labor's new breed, but they constantly sniped at one another in their articles.

At first, Rudd thought Latham was a

person of ideas, prepared to stand outside the Labor norm, [a] moderniser, like myself, intrinsically Blairite: in the great tradition of Labor reform, pro market on the economy and active on the social quality agenda and prepared to take the Labor party beyond the traditional paradigms. It was only after I got to know him a lot better that I began to see that it was a great exercise in policy fraudulence.

So by March 2000, Rudd could start an article, 'Mark Latham is often a thoughtful contributor to public policy debates in the country. Regrettably his latest contribution on tax policy and regional policy is not'. And finish with the comment: 'Latham has written much that is innovative in these areas. His most recent tax proposal, however, is just plain loopy'. Latham responded that Rudd might ridicule his ideas but had no suggestions of his own 'to assist the poor'.

When Rudd proposed new powers for parliamentary committees, advocating that MPs run actual or 'virtual' town hall meetings, Latham, an advocate of an email direct democracy scheme, sneered:

> The erudite Rudd is one of the brighter people in Federal Parliament. Yet, like so many of the modern political class, he has the roar of a mouse rather than the crusading zeal of a parliamentary lion. The last thing we need is another generation of political committees, poncing around the country ... Rudd wants to give the Australian people wall-to-wall political tedium and cat fighting.

Rudd in turn thought little of Latham's e-democracy: 'Mark is a bright bloke, but sometimes the brightest of blokes come up with the dumbest of ideas. We have just had the dot com disaster in the economy. Does Mark now want to deliver a tech-wreck democracy?'

On economics, Rudd wrote that Labor 'does not embrace a brand of globalisation that is no more than once around the dance floor with Adam Smith'. Latham reacted: 'Speak for yourself, comrade. I'm happy to have Adam Smith on my dance card'.

Their styles, not their backgrounds, guaranteed a clash. Michelle Grattan responded to a complaint that new Labor MPs were 'white bread' by pointing out the two feisty backbenchers:

> Rudd might be described as 'wholemeal'. He's chair of Labor's committee on national security and trade, and ambitious. He operates within the system. He also stretches it.
>
> Latham is more like German black bread. He's been in the shadow ministry, but he couldn't stand its constraints. On the backbench since the 1998 election, he's full-on critic and gadfly.

Rudd did indeed operate within the system. Not even Brereton could identify when he had worked outside party policy. When responding to Brereton, Rudd drew a distinction between his own style and that of Latham. He asked Brereton:

> Your friend and colleague, Mark Latham, is a more active participant in the policy debate than I, and is often regarded as contributing comment that is at odds with Labor policy ... Kim, a month or two ago, defended Mark's right to do so. It is curious, therefore, that you seem to regard as undisciplined my contributions to public commentary when they are not at variance with party policy, but have expressed no parallel concern about Mark's commentary.

In 2001 Rudd took on a further commitment that was to massively increase his profile: breakfast television. He had started a regular slot on ABC 612 in Queensland, sparring with the Liberal Peter Slipper. He was provided with the opportunity to expand that to breakfast television on the national program *Sunrise*. At first his counterpart was Parramatta Liberal Ross Cameron, but then Cameron was defeated in the 2001 election. A great opportunity was about to emerge with a new partner in publicity.

During the 2001 election, Rudd's seat of Griffith was not to be taken for granted. His margin in 1998 had only been 2.4 per cent. The Labor Party was threatened by the *Tampa* crisis of 2001 and the events of September 11, 2001. There were fears Labor was going backwards; its campaign issues of education, health and jobs were being swamped by concerns about international security.

Worried by the local reactions, the Rudd family held a council of war on the double bed in the family home in Norman Park to consider how they would respond. Daughter Jessica suggested a slogan: 'Keep Kevin'. Son Nick provided the variation 'Keep Kev In'. They stuck with the first. It seemed to resonate, so they swamped the local electorate with 'Keep Kevin' posters that included little reference to the Labor Party or its leader.

The Labor campaign headquarters was furious, says Rudd:

> The State Secretary went off his brain, off his trolley when he saw all these 'Keep Kevin' signs go up around the electorate rather than health, education and jobs. He rang me up and abused me and said that I would not get any campaign funding support if I didn't adhere to the central campaign. I told him I wouldn't be changing because he was wrong. I knew my own electorate and he could get stuffed.

In an election where Labor went backwards, Rudd received a 4 per cent swing towards him. The seat was looking safer.

6

STALKING DOWNER, SURVIVING LATHAM

After the 2001 election, Rudd was elected to the Shadow Cabinet. The new leader, Simon Crean, made him spokesman for foreign affairs. Laurie Brereton had decided to stand down from the frontbench. Rudd was the obvious candidate, as a former diplomat who had made a mark in the previous term. It was also to be a parliamentary term where foreign affairs was to have a much higher profile than usual. The September 11 attacks in New York and Washington had led to George W Bush's war against the Taliban in Afghanistan, which had received support from both sides of politics in Australia. However, the ensuing decision to invade Iraq as part of the Coalition of the Willing provided Rudd with opportunities to develop a profile that was rare for a foreign affairs spokesman.

In Australian politics, foreign affairs is often regarded as a sideshow in the daily battles over the future of the electorate. It seems far removed from the hip-pocket nerves that are seen to drive election outcomes. Shadow ministers in that area have a hard time getting media space or developing a public profile. Rudd was therefore lucky; he took over responsibility just as the policy area became domestically controversial. However, the manner in which he capitalised on the chances sprang from sheer hard work.

Then he had another stroke of luck. He advertised for the media adviser that Opposition frontbenchers were allowed to employ: just the one staffer to supplement the electoral office staff every MP had. He appointed a young politics graduate from the University of Queensland, Alister Jordan. Their backgrounds were similar; both had grown up on the Sunshine Coast, at least for a time with a single mother. Both had a strong sense of the need for social change. Jordan also had many of those characteristics Rudd saw in himself: a steely determination, a ferocious work ethic, a curious mind, an applied intelligence. He was phlegmatic and unruffled, and accepted with equanimity his boss's occasional bursts of temper and need to sound off. Rudd warned Jordan, 'I treat this as a vocation, not as a job'. Rudd scarcely needed to give the warning; asked if he would be there when the boss arrived and still be there when he left, Jordan's answer was: 'Of course'.

Jordan started as media adviser but quickly expanded his activities to assist across the board. Between 2002 and 2005 he was one of only two or three advisers on staff; later, some assistance came when Rudd also took on the trade responsibilities. Most of the time it seemed to be Rudd and Jordan against the rest. He was the first staffer Rudd talked to in the morning and the last one at night. He could advise, listen and sometimes take the brunt of his boss's frustrations. He said: 'We got here together, except for one week at Christmas, we worked seven days a week, 51 weeks a year and long hours each day through some pretty tough times'. As Rudd rose after 2002, Jordan was at his shoulder.

When he was appointed foreign affairs spokesman, Rudd declared that 'foreign policy is no longer marginal to the interests of the average Australian. It is mainstream'. He certainly intended it become so.

If he could leverage the role of party spokesman on foreign affairs into a high-profile position, then he could gradually build support within the party by force of performance. It was the only realistic option for a person who had no factional support and came from a small state with little representation in the federal caucus.

There was an additional element. Alexander Downer had been Minister for Foreign Affairs since the formation of the Howard government. He was all the things that Rudd was not: born to privilege and wealth, privately educated, part of the Adelaide establishment—he came from a family of conservative politicians and included a state premier and federal minister among his forebears. He also, a few years before Rudd, had been a graduate recruit to the Department of Foreign Affairs. Their paths had never crossed there, certainly not in terms of creating any direct antagonisms. It was what others thought, the conclusions they drew, that caused the later tensions. If Rudd had been regarded within the department as a diplomat with a potentially stellar future, Downer's standing was more mixed when he left in 1982. So Rudd sought to pester, to annoy, even to haunt Downer. He would chase Downer across the newspapers and airwaves, always harassing and querying, challenging his record, his motives and his competence.

In January 2002, Rudd wrote for *The Australian* in response to an article by Downer. He challenged the view that suddenly foreign affairs had become harder:

> All this sounds like the universal lament of the misunderstood foreign minister. The truth is that the region has never been a static environment. To suggest that poor old Alex has somehow been dealt a rougher hand than Evatt, Casey or Evans belies the extraordinary challenges of, for example, decolonisation, Konfrontasi and Cambodia ... No amount of 'golly gee, the region has changed

an awful lot hasn't it', can camouflage the systematic deterioration
in our regional relationships over the past decade.

Rudd argued that the government had bungled its relations with Asia, both in its failure to condemn Pauline Hanson and in its acceptance of a role as the United States' 'deputy sheriff' in the region. He suggested the Howard government was, in effect, involved in long-term disengagement and condemned its base use of immigration for electoral purposes. He concluded that the role of the foreign minister 'is to resist the political assaults of his colleagues when they seek to prosecute a domestic agenda that would otherwise undermine the long-term international interests of the nation. Downer has failed this test … Regrettably, when the nation needed him most, Downer has been missing in action'.

Rudd continued doing what he had done from 1999; writing articles in the broadsheet press became the norm. It was the persistence, frequency and sheer continuity of the commentary that made it effective.

He was also determined to indicate that, on an international stage, he knew everyone and was able to contact them. In one of his first appearances on ABC TV's *Insiders* in February 2002, he said he hoped for good outcomes from the Bali conference on people smuggling. He had not left it at nominal support but had taken action, even as part of the Opposition. He had written to the Indonesian foreign minister, Hassan Wirajuda, explaining the Labor policy and supporting the need for an outcome. In the same interview he provided evidence of his networks, talking about his discussions with the high commissioner of Pakistan, his visits with ambassadors in Europe. Always ready to attack the government, on this occasion he claimed that the Department of Foreign Affairs was dominated 'by a culture of fear; second guessing always in terms of what is the right answer'.

From mid-2002 onwards, Iraq dominated foreign affairs debates. Would the US attack, and if so, when? Would Australia be part of any coalition? Would it be under the auspices of the United Nations? Howard had been in Washington during the September 11 attacks. He was tightly linked to both President George W Bush and Prime Minister Tony Blair. The question of Australian involvement centred on the terms of the commitment. Labor wanted the UN involved. Rudd wanted the weapons inspectors, who were looking for the weapons of mass destruction (WMD) in Iraq, to be given more time and greater opportunity to find them. Everyone believed, incorrectly as it turned out, that such weapons existed.

Throughout 2002, Labor accepted that Iraq had defied UN Security Council resolutions and failed to disarm its WMDs. However, it argued that all the processes of the UN should be first exhausted before other options were considered. In August, Rudd visited Washington with Crean and received briefings from the Pentagon, the State Department and the CIA. In London, he talked to senior British politicians in the Labour government. A couple of weeks later, Blair released a dossier of evidence. When Rudd returned, he said that one of the keys for Labor to support unilateral US action 'would be evidence of a significant expansion in Iraq's weapons of mass destruction capability and threat'. On *Lateline* on 24 September, Rudd stated that he would review the new evidence provided by the Blair government. He declared: 'There is no debate or dispute as to whether Saddam Hussein possesses weapons of mass destruction. He does. There's no dispute as to whether he's in violation of UN Security Council resolutions. He is'. Labor, Rudd argued, wanted clear evidence that Iraq was a threat to regional and world peace and had weaponised its WMDs. Rudd then produced a five-point policy for UN action on Iraq.

In October 2002, the Bali bombings brought issues of terrorism closer to home. When Howard argued that he, like any Australian prime minister, would be prepared to send Australian troops onto foreign soil in a pre-emptive attack if there was the threat of a terrorist strike against Australia, Rudd attacked his presumption and the damage such a statement might do to relations with countries of the region. It brought back images of Australia as 'deputy sheriff' of the United States in the region. Labor, by contrast, would work cooperatively with countries in the region.

In February 2003, there was a debate in parliament on foreign policy and Iraq. The government argued that it would prefer to work through a UN resolution, but it left open the possibility for other options. Rudd spoke for the Opposition. Of course, he argued, 'the national security of Australia is non-negotiable. For Labor guaranteeing national security is the first responsibility of government'. Then he sought to lay down clearly what he saw as the three pillars of Labor's approach to foreign policy, the three distinctions between Labor and the government, which were to be repeated over the next five years:

1   the US alliance
2   UN membership and multilateral approaches
3   comprehensive engagement with Asia.

By contrast, he argued, the government's policy rested on a single pillar, the US alliance, while its attitude to the UN 'has ranged from ambivalence to neglect to outright derision ... The government's commitment to the UN is all politics, not policy—and certainly not principle'. Labor remained committed to the fight in Afghanistan but doubted Iraq was responsible for the September 11 attacks on New York. Rudd asked 'whether the Iraqi weapons of mass destruction represent a real, present credible danger', but said they had received no evidence they did.

When the government chose to send a small number of troops to Iraq as a member of the Coalition of the Willing, Labor had to maintain the position of supporting the troops while opposing the war. The Shadow Cabinet was badly divided. Mark Latham had declared that George W Bush was the 'most incompetent and dangerous president in living memory', and declared that Bush was at the end of a 'conga line of suckholes'. Rudd, always close to a number of US diplomats, found such language uncomfortable.

The splits put Crean in a difficult position because he was not making any impact in the polls. Crean's failure led Rudd to reconsider his position; the baton in the backpack was shifting. He wanted to be foreign minister, but unless the party won, even that ambition would never be realised:

> At some stage in this period, I can't pinpoint the time, I remember sitting in the caucus room, saying this isn't working, in terms of Simon's leadership, and therefore, we are going to have to consider an alternative. So I actually then looked right across the room, face by face, and the only person in the room that I thought was credible at that stage was Wayne Swan (I didn't think it was credible to go back to Beazley) or myself.

In April 2003, stories about the divisions within the Shadow Cabinet led to a growing frenzy about the leadership. The names of possible challengers started to be floated; Rudd was one of those mentioned. He had a meeting 'over a cup of tea and an Iced VoVo' with Crean to assure him that he was not responsible for a story in the *Daily Telegraph* mentioning his ambitions. In May, he declared that he would not be a candidate for the leadership before the next election. He then added: 'I've never given a commitment beyond that. Let me emphasise I've never said never'. He was not the only one in this position. Both Latham and Craig Emerson had stated they would put off leadership challenges until after the next election.

However, it was the first time that Rudd had been listed in the press as a potential contender in the near future. He might be regarded as pushy, but as he told the *Courier-Mail* on 26 April, 'I don't give a damn whether people like me or not. I do give a damn about whether they respect me'. He and Latham were seen as the leaders of the new generation, with Wayne Swan and Stephen Smith mentioned as other possibilities. The race was now in the open, even if the contenders had declared it was to be postponed until after the next election.

Beazley was not prepared to wait. Supported by Swan, Smith and Conroy, whom Latham decried as the 'three roosters', he launched a challenge. He fell short. Rudd kept his counsel. He did not publicly campaign for either side, even though he eventually voted for Beazley. His reticence annoyed the Beazley camp. They became suspicious of his motives. Principally, the challenge brought about a collapse in the relations between Rudd and Swan. They had inevitably seen each other as potential rivals; that created its own tension. Now their interests diverged. Swan was to remain Beazley's closest lieutenant for the next three years. Rudd was his own man. Ironically, the story about the mates falling out was written by *Courier-Mail* correspondent Dennis Atkins, who had been close to both as part of the inner circle of the Goss government.

Crean survived but was unable to build on his narrow win. As the months passed and the party remained divided, a second challenge was increasingly seen as inevitable. Tapped on the shoulder by the party elders, Crean realised he could not win. He decided to stand down. Beazley would obviously be a candidate. Latham would be the candidate of the Crean and anti-Beazley forces, representing the new generation. Rudd's dilemma was whether he should stand himself.

Others also considered his options. Matt Price, as entertaining as ever in *The Australian*, made fun of him:

The Beginning

Labor's erudite foreign affairs boffin is patently no idiot, but Rudd tends to wear his ambition like a giant Coca-Cola sign at the top of Kings Cross.

The *Courier-Mail* carried a speech he made to an Anglican breakfast calling for more prayer in politics. It contained a rare confession: 'I am a Christian ... but I'm still as failed and flawed as the rest of humanity'. This—the admission, not the imperfection—will be news to some colleagues.

He said that the interview with then journalist, later colleague Maxine McKew was 'plastered across the *Bulletin*, along with glamour photographs that look like a *Vanity Fair* spread'. But Price concluded:

> Yet the biggest problem for Rudd—tireless, intelligent and good-humoured soul—remains support. Jesus did a nice line in loaves and fishes, but even the Almighty might struggle conjuring the numbers for St Kevin.

On *Insiders*, the veteran journalist Paul Kelly assessed his chances. After describing Beazley as the safe pair of hands and Latham as the risky candidate, Kelly turned to Rudd:

> I think Kevin Rudd wants to run and he's certainly creating expectations that he will run. It is also correct to say that he doesn't want to be embarrassed. The smart thing for Kevin Rudd to do is only run if he can get a reasonable vote. But the fact that we're discussing his leadership credentials is a tribute to his ability, his drive, to his media skills. He's only been in parliament for five years.

Rudd tested the waters. He thought returning to Beazley would be a disaster. He rang around three-quarters of the caucus. Then, he says,

I got a call from Leo McLeay urging me to pull out and I said, 'You tell me this Leo, based on everything I have found out doing the ring around, Beazley is in absolute trouble and there is a risk you are going to get Latham. So why don't you tell Beazley to back out and back me. He's had his turn'. He said he couldn't do that. That would have been me v Latham. So at their request I backed out.

His friends suggested he would do better to pull out earlier rather than at the last moment. He decided not to stand this time. At that stage observers believed that he would have had fewer than ten votes. However, as Kelly also observed, he was now a clear potential candidate of the new generation.

To widespread surprise, Latham won narrowly. He became the leader of a party, many of whose leading members he already despised. Over the next year, Latham diarised that Rudd was 'whitebread', a Young Technocrat in action, an insider of the Canberra foreign-policy establishment, 'a big-noter', 'Heavy Kevvy', a non-believer, 'addicted [to the media], worse than heroin', 'king of the caveats', 'a terrible piece of work'. Latham said he would never trust him and, if he won, would make Rudd the Minister for the South Pacific, 'a junior minister at best'. This compilation of condemnations says as much about Latham as it does about the people who sat on his frontbench. Rudd had to work with a person who regarded him with disdain and dislike.

Unsurprisingly, 2004 was a difficult year, remembered with retrospective horror by members of the Labor caucus even if at the time the divisions were camouflaged by a constant public refrain that everything was fine. Almost immediately, Latham and Rudd gave a press conference to insist that relations with the US would be fine.

Behind the scenes there was tension. On the one hand, the Labor shadow ministers wanted to win, and Latham's poll figures in the first half of 2004 suggested that Labor was in the lead. On the other hand,

Latham's tendency to make policy without consulting his colleagues made public perceptions difficult to manage. In March, Rudd appeared on *Lateline* explaining that the Labor Party wanted the troops out of Iraq, but, conscious of their responsibilities under international law, would wait until an interim system of self-government was in place. He got home that evening to find a message from Latham saying that he would 'sharpen' Labor policy by announcing a timetable that would have the troops home by Christmas. Rudd left a long message on Latham's message bank, explaining why it was a bad idea. Latham backed off the next morning. A week later, Rudd returned from overseas to be told that 'Mark just sharpened the position up a bit. He mentioned Christmas'. Rudd had to explain on *Lateline*, two weeks after saying Labor would not reassess its position, why it had. Asked if Latham had consulted him in advance, Rudd responded somewhat disingenuously that Latham and he had been discussing the issue for a time.

Rudd continued to work his US connections, who were entirely out of sympathy with his predicament and made the point strongly that they disagreed with Labor's policy towards Iraq and the American alliance. In June, Rudd visited Washington to see, among others, Deputy Secretary of State Richard Armitage, whom he had known for some time through the AALD. Armitage had appealed to Latham to review his 'home by Christmas' pledge. Rudd sought to soothe the feathers ruffled by Latham's often public antipathy to US policy and explain Labor policy in private while publicly saying: 'But we are quite plain in terms of our policy and Mark has made it absolutely crystal clear that that policy is not about to change'. To an extent, the debate was distracted by the revelations about prisoners mistreated in Abu Ghraib prison, but these were times when Rudd was arguing a case that he found difficult to prosecute. To suggest, if Latham travelled to Washington as prime minister, he would be treated with 'courtesy and respect as an Australian prime minister, as his predecessors have been treated', was a careful choice of words.

The 2004 election was a disaster for Labor. Latham was blamed. However, there was no immediate challenge to his leadership. A number of people refused to serve under him in the Shadow Cabinet. Others wanted to wait to see what happened. Latham had only been the leader for a year. In the next two months, however, Latham unravelled. He decided to stand down, but did not tell anyone. When a tsunami swept across the Indian Ocean and killed over 160 000 people in Aceh alone, he declined to be interviewed or drawn back from his holiday. 'It's the middle of summer and only maniacs like Rudd are interested in interviews', he wrote in his diary. Then he called a press conference on January 2005 in the local park and announced his resignation.

Rudd met Mark Arbib, the general secretary of the New South Wales branch of the Labor Party, at the Radisson Hotel in Sydney to seek his support. The New South Wales Right had a reputation for toughness and bastardry. Its hold on power had often been used brutally, excluding those from other factions in the party. Graham Richardson's motto and autobiography title, *Whatever It Takes*, was accepted as a given. But it was becoming counterproductive, with the New South Wales branch increasingly regarded as a self-serving dinosaur.

Arbib argued that he wanted to be more consultative, working with other factions to reduce the tensions. He was realistic: 'Factions exist everywhere … They have a role to play and they assist in administration. The key is to ensure that factionalism doesn't get out of control, where people consistently put the faction's interests ahead of the party's'. At the time, Arbib even got compliments from the Left. Anthony Albanese, Minister for Infrastructure, commented in 2005 that he could 'actually sit down and have a chat with him. He cares about the Labor Party as opposed to the faction. He has made a decision to try [to] genuinely change the culture'.

Arbib wanted to win. The machine was concerned that the caucus had got it so horribly wrong with Latham that they wanted to ensure that this time the result was safe and predictable. Arbib organised a meeting with Beazley and his key supporters, including Bill Shorten and Albanese, to lock in support: 'We are still pragmatic about politics. We'll do whatever it takes to win an election—definitely—but sometimes factions have to put their own interest aside for the good of the party'. He wanted to change the focus of the party; 'the politics of envy is over', he declared. Now voters think:

> 'I'm running a business, I want to keep going up the ladder, so what's the best party for business, who's best for managing the economy and who's the best party for aspiration?' The truth is now, especially in Sydney, that envy is dead … the truth is that most of those people who are earning $50k, $60k, $70k or $80 000 all want to be earning $120 000 and think that one day they will get there. So therefore many are happy to see tax cuts at the higher end. They're not envious of it—they just want to be there themselves.

When Rudd and Arbib met, Rudd argued that, to win, Labor needed Queensland, and Beazley had never been popular there. He doubted that Beazley would be able to reignite enthusiasm. Arbib recalls his impressions:

> He was able to analyse why we lost the last election and put forward a detailed strategy where he wanted to move to, which was the mainstream. So part of me was saying, 'Gee this would be a good move for the party', but the remainder of me thought, 'This is the worst possible time to take another risk'.

Arbib told Rudd that, while he would think about his comments, he was leaning towards Beazley as a safe pair of hands. However, as Roger Price, another member of the New South Wales Right, put it, Rudd was now well positioned, one out, one back, if the leadership came up again.

Rudd was about to catch a plane to Aceh, to see the extent of the 2004 tsunami damage. He thought about cancelling the trip but decided it would be counterproductive to consider pursuing support as more important than understanding the disaster that had befallen Australia's nearest neighbour. So for three days he was out of regular or reliable contact, ringing each evening to find out what was happening. Alister Jordan rang a number of MPs on his behalf. So did Alan Griffin, a leader of the Victorian Left, who became Rudd's principal caucus contact and organiser. Their task was to gauge the level of support.

There were three potential candidates. Beazley already had a head start. Julia Gillard was the candidate of the Left and she had been in Vietnam when the vacancy occurred. By the time Rudd returned, Beazley had locked in almost half the caucus. All the weight of the party organisations and unions was brought to bear. When Rudd was finally able to hit the phones, it was too late to change the momentum. He was in Melbourne for lunch with a friend, but spent most of the time pacing up and down in the garden, listening to the reports. His desire to run was established, but too many votes were locked in and the caucus was in the mood for safety, after the rollercoaster ride that had been the Latham leadership. The more he heard the reports, the more obvious it was that he did not have the numbers. As Alan Griffin put it to him: 'Well, you are still in the ring, but you are coughing blood at the moment'. Who had how many votes was, and is, a matter for speculation. One Rudd supporter thought Beazley had almost half and the rest were split 60/40 between Rudd and Gillard.

Others put the 60/40 the other way round. A few thought Rudd's figures were far lower. Whatever the case, they were not enough.

Rudd sought advice from friends and colleagues. He decided he would not stand. In explaining his position, he took the advice of Robert Ray, who told him: 'Don't be cute about it. Your staff will give you lots of reasons to explain your decision, none of them really credible. Just say you are not standing because you do not have the numbers'. He also added that Rudd should say he would still be interested in the future. Rudd did just that. His ambition remained apparent; the time was not yet his: 'I've got a field marshal's baton in the backpack. It's just that the season is not right'. When he appeared later that week on *Sunrise*, on the day Beazley was formally anointed, he commented: 'I've been in the trenches, the political trenches. It's all been a very character-building exercise for me, let me tell you'.

Rudd rang Gillard to tell her that he was planning to withdraw. A day later Gillard too withdrew from the contest. Beazley was elected unopposed. He was a stopgap. Labor members might have argued publicly that the party could win the next election, but most did not believe it. The idea was to minimise the loss of seats and hope that the election after that might be in reach. However, Rudd was now established as one of the few likely candidates of the next generation with the public profile and image.

His reputation as a policy nerd was well established. But for a long time there were doubts about his ability to talk to a broader audience beyond the watchers of the ABC. By 2005 those doubts were being allayed.

A principal reason was *Sunrise*. Channel 7 producer Adam Boland thought it worth a try to have a political spot and gave Rudd an opportunity, stressing that it was to be relaxed and accessible. After the 2001 election, the idea took off. Almost every Friday for the next five years, Rudd appeared with Joe Hockey. They talked about politics, but in a relaxed and folksy way. They would cover both serious topics and Rudd's mother's recipes. On one occasion they talked about what Rudd should buy Thérèse for her birthday. Hockey talked about the new child his wife was expecting, and Rudd noted that he would qualify for the baby bonus. Sometimes there was a sense of immediacy: Rudd mentioned that he had been in Korea when news of the North Korean missile tests broke and explained how the South Koreans reacted. Their segment worked so well that their airtime was doubled and David Koch started to refer to them as the show's Friday All Stars. Rudd and Hockey seemed to get along; indeed, after most sessions the two would have a coffee with their staffs. The cross-party camaraderie went down well with viewers tired of constant political sniping. Rudd and Hockey were called members of the *Sunrise* 'family'.

For many people, this was the first time that they had seen politicians on national television behaving like 'normal' people. They loved it. Rudd's profile grew among a group of electors who would never have dreamt of tuning into a political program.

Others noticed too. Wayne Goss commented with a smile that Rudd 'was very astute when he managed to get himself on the Channel 7 program where you have to talk in English. This was a challenge for Kevin, but over the year he managed to increase his ability to talk in English year by year'. Rudd argues that he had learned that already in his years of building up support in his electorate. If there was a lesson, it was the 1996 defeat. After that he had become more conscious of the need to talk to different groups in ways that allowed him to get through to them. *Sunrise* allowed him to use that skill and relate to a wider national audience.

7

WINNING THE LEADERSHIP

Looking back, Rudd recalls that what he wanted to do at the end of 2006 was to 'define publicly my credo ... it was not enough to come up with some vacuous proposition that I was somehow more popular'. He did not want to be seen as a blank page but as someone 'who had a defined set of political values which were anchored in both philosophical and theological traditions'. Those values had to be defined in a way that could readily be explained.

The new year of 2006 opened in a rented villa in Sicily, with Rudd and his family seeing in the year with the Davis family. Glyn Davis and Rudd had remained close since 1989. Davis described how Rudd 'was about policy, not politics. He was not talking about how you get the leadership, but about the coming agendas'. Rudd wanted to identify 'the core issues in Australian public life, the concerns that resonated at various times in the national psyche'. Then he wanted to see if there were ways in which these concerns could bring together 'a different coalition of interests'.

The purpose was to clarify how the issues he wanted to stand for could be best presented. Davis said that Rudd knew it was 'essential to speak to people with aspirations that were properly grounded ... What are the elements of a coherent policy message? How do you package it together? What is the language?' He played around, over and over again, with sets of words, 'looking for a sentence that sums up what he offers, but a sentence grounded in his vast amount of work about who he is and what the national agenda is and what a Rudd leadership should be'.

It was an exercise in preparedness. There could be no certainty. A leadership strike needs a number of forces to line up, for opportunities to be available. Not everything is under control; *fortuna* (since these events were being discussed in Machiavelli's Italy) has a role in the rise of any leader. If it happened, if the cards fell his way, then Rudd was going to be prepared, to have the message, to know what he stood for.

Preparedness would cover a number of arenas. The public profile had to be developed, so that not only was Rudd recognised among the public, but his colleagues also appreciated the asset of public awareness. He had to be accepted within the party as a whole, not just within the parliamentary caucus, as a person who deserved support and who had a chance of leading the party to electoral success. And he had to gain the support of a majority within the caucus. That required not only enough votes to win a contest, but also the ability to persuade some people to desert Beazley. He had to be a person of ideas and substance.

He also had to be positive. He was consistent in his faith that the Labor Party could beat Howard, not in a two-stage tango, but in the 2007 election. He was upbeat that he would be leader by the end of the year, even before the vacancy was clear. Whether that was a natural ebullience or just confidence is difficult to assess because, after all, he was right.

But he could not campaign openly against Beazley, who had to be given free air to make his case. Initially, then, it depended not on

Rudd but on Beazley. Had Beazley taken off, had he seemed likely to bring victory, then no change in leadership would have happened. But, by early 2006, many in the party believed that Beazley's leadership had not taken off. On the one hand, there were Labor governments in all the states and territories, the first clean sweep since the territories were given self-government. On the other, there was the sense of an inevitable fate awaiting them at the next poll, and recriminations abounding for the debacle of 2004. Beazley performed well in the House on occasion; his supporters, led by Swan and Smith, insisted he could win. Few others believed it.

Within the caucus, Rudd had begun to work more assiduously to talk to his colleagues. The Rudd of 2006, said one grizzled Labor veteran, was very different from the Rudd of January 2005. He had already begun to reach out. In November 2004, just after the election defeat, he had invited his caucus colleagues to a meeting to discuss the interaction of politics and religion. To his surprise, around thirty people, a third of the caucus, arrived and spilled out into the corridor. They received a presentation that did not discuss philosophical issues, but tables and charts illustrating where, and why, this was an issue the party had to confront. Family First had won a Senate seat: What were the implications for Labor? The Faith, Values and Politics Group continued to meet until, later in the year, Rudd presented a detailed report to the Labor executive, analysing the size and location of the religious vote. It was an example of both thinking laterally and seeking to draw in the other members of caucus.

After the 2005 leadership election, Rudd was offered the shadow portfolio of education, a platform that might have allowed him to establish a domestic reputation. He turned it down, wanting to stay in his existing position. He asked for, and was given, responsibility for trade as well as foreign affairs. That provided him with the standing to enter the debate on economic matters. He could visit other MPs' constituencies and talk about trade prospects, issues that could have a direct impact on the local economy. So he travelled widely, appearing at functions, addressing meetings and electors. It gave him the opportunity to interact with voters; it also provided a means by which the local MPs could see for themselves his ability to relate to all types of people.

He was made a member of the Tactics Committee, the inner group of the parliamentary executive and constituting its leading members; it was chaired by Beazley. It met regularly to plan the assault on the government in Question Time. Sometimes Rudd would turn up with a long list of well-researched questions that he wanted to ask. The Opposition had ten slots and they had to be rationed. He might, on a good day, get three. It was all part of a political education. However, when the party secretary, Tim Gartrell, briefed the shadow executive on polling, Rudd said that he didn't want to know anything about Beazley's poll numbers. He feared if it leaked he would be accused of leaking it. He preferred not to be told.

If Rudd was active in caucus, he also spent time in the movement outside. He made a point of talking regularly to the more significant players within the Labor Party. Sitting in the middle of the Labor web, Gartrell kept hearing that Rudd had dropped in to see this union leader, that party operator, another party elder. He says, 'Kevin's schedule, and none of this will surprise you, was very much linked to a list that he and Alister had developed of who should be visited, who he should have breakfast with, who he should have talks with, all the rest'. There was no particular reason given for the visits. He was not immediately touting for votes or asking directly for support in a leadership challenge. He was just becoming a familiar figure for those who mattered. He identified who should be visited, who had been visited and when he might make contact again. The purpose was recognition and acceptance as a credible leader. If anyone asked these Labor personalities about him, they would at least have an opinion, formed on the basis of direct contact. His approach was systematic and continuous.

Sunrise continued to be important. The concept that in politics there are those who are interested in ideas and those who are concerned with people's everyday lives, and that the two are distinct, has always been a nonsense. Rudd illustrated that point. He could talk as readily about Sinology or the workings of local community groups. There was no need for any contradiction or pretence.

The *Sunrise* highlight was the Kokoda Trail. Rudd and Hockey agreed to walk the trail, covered by the cameras. Thérèse had already done the walk. Rudd wanted the chance to take his son Nick, then nineteen, with him. The strain of a tough walk showed in their faces. Rudd recalls: 'They never told you how hard it was before you went or you'd never go. All this notion that you have to do three months training in order to make it, it is just nonsense. You still die when you get there'.

They both made it. There were moments of pathos, as Rudd, son of a veteran of the battles for Syria and Borneo, broke into song with a rendition of *Danny Boy*. There were contrasts in instinct, as Hockey talked about the heroism and Rudd provided the information about the number of steps. There were moments of entertainment. As Rudd slipped when the two of them were washing in the stream, Hockey grabbed him to stop him falling and then looked into the camera and said: 'Sorry, Kim; I should have let him go'. It was not that Rudd was actually in any danger, but it was a great extempore gag. For both of them, what came across was their humanity, the willingness to put themselves in difficult circumstances, to struggle through tough conditions and to retain their sense of humour. They provided an unusual image of politicians in their exertions and their vulnerabilities. Kokoda was another step in the introduction of Rudd to the people of Australia.

The target of *Sunrise* was not just the people, although that was a crucial part. Labor members, too, could be influenced. One of the ministers commented:

Kevin had that rare gift of being able to discuss high level foreign policy on *Lateline* and being quite compelling, and to be mucking around in the morning on *Sunrise* and be equally engaging. Not many people could do that. *Sunrise* shows him being able to engage at a community level and also gave him the opportunity to show he could do that across a range of portfolios. One of the risks for someone who is good at an area—and it's also their portfolio—is people can easily presume that that's what they do and that's all that they do. *Sunrise* gave Kevin a very clear opportunity to say: 'I can do all this too'.

Another argued the impact broke a preconception: 'Kevin is a diplomat, an academic; he has been accused of being a bit nerdy. *Sunrise* showed he can have a conversation with the Australian people'. His backers used it as a means of persuasion. When anyone had doubts, one backer would say, 'Well, do yourself a favour, turn on *Sunrise* and watch him on a Friday morning. You'll see how good he is'.

Throughout 2005 the Labor Party struggled. By contrast, Rudd's image was on the rise. A number of Labor heavies were advocating his cause. Former New South Wales premier Bob Carr argued: 'He is making himself an inevitability. He's taken off as a political package ... He is the one with the profile'.

Rudd forced himself into the public consciousness. When Hu Jintao, the President of China, visited the parliament, he chatted to Rudd in Mandarin, causing eye-rolling among Labor members. Rudd responded:

> I seriously don't give a bugger. This business of people thinking you're up yourself if you speak another language, they've just got to get over it. The wisdom of smallness says it's incumbent on the smallest kid on the block to learn the language and culture and

history of its neighbours. Here we are in a region of three billion people, and last time I walked around there weren't a lot of people speaking English.

What is arrogance if you unpack it? If it implies an innate view that you are better than someone else, well, there's something sobering about being brought up on a Queensland dairy farm that keeps it all in check. Keir Hardie said he could not sing hymns with people on Sunday and ignore their working conditions on Monday.

The Liberal government unintentionally boosted his case as the dealings of the Australian Wheat Board (AWB) first simmered and then, with skilful prodding, developed into a long-running scandal that emerged in late 2005 and ran throughout the winter of 2006. In the US, a report from Paul Volcker, former chair of the Federal Reserve, had identified the suspicious behaviour of the AWB, accused of bribing Iraqi officials to ensure that it was able to sell wheat. Prices were inflated and the wheat transported by a dodgy Jordanian trucking company owned by an Iraqi minister. At a time when there were UN sanctions on Iraq, an Australian company was bribing its way to success. The Howard government promised to establish an inquiry to investigate whether the AWB had breached international sanctions and behaved improperly. It asked Terence Cole QC to head the inquiry, but gave him very tight terms of reference. He was to inquire into the behaviour of officers of the AWB, and them alone. Others, including ministers, would come into the scope of the inquiry only so far as they were able to throw light on the behaviour of the AWB.

The Labor Opposition described the AWB as a disgrace. An Australian company had breached sanctions, paid bribes and conspired with a rogue dictator. It was a stain on the country. But the AWB was, to Labor, almost incidental. The target was the government. The attack focused on two fronts. First, what did the ministers know about the breaches? If they did not know about them, what should they have known? The second tack was to demonstrate that the only reason that Cole could not identify what the ministers knew was because the government had tied his hands with such narrow terms of reference. Both sets of questioning were intended to lead to the same conclusion: the government was running a cover-up to protect ministers who had failed in their duty. The government was presented as devious, tricky and, by implication, guilty.

Rudd led the attack, day after day, across the airwaves. When the Cole Inquiry began its hearing, Alister Jordan sat in the court so that, at lunchtime, he could brief Rudd on the morning's events and allow a midday press briefing to get the new details across and consolidate the message: it's a cover-up.

The AWB gave Rudd a great ride as he traversed the TV and radio channels putting the Opposition's case. In January he claimed that ministers had been warned by cables from the Australian mission to the UN, and that AWB officials had talked to Downer. Rudd demanded, on a regular basis, that the terms of reference of the inquiry be expanded to ask what ministers knew and should have done. It was never likely to happen, but it provided the image that ministers were scared of having their activities investigated. In early March he talked of the six warnings that had been sent to the ministers' offices. In April he asked why ministers ignored twenty-seven sets of warnings. By 31 May he could identify even more. When ministers did appear on the witness stand, their memories were not that good. Minister of Trade Mark Vaile said forty-one times on the witness stand that he did not recollect events.

The AWB scandal also was part of the broader campaign that pitted Rudd against Downer. Rudd needled Downer, accusing him of cover-ups, ridiculing his pretensions, laughing at his claims. Downer sometimes bridled; sometimes he responded disdainfully. The direct adversarial contest, at a time when international affairs had become domestically significant, gave Rudd a prominence rare for a foreign affairs spokesman. Downer helped to make Rudd's reputation and gave him national standing; all unintentionally, of course, but he provided a target at which Rudd could fire his annoying salvos of political darts. They were never fatal to Downer or the government. But they irritated him and promoted Rudd.

Meanwhile, Beazley's standing in the caucus took a beating after he decided not to support his predecessor when Simon Crean was challenged for preselection in Victoria. The general view was that former leaders deserved better than to be thrown out of parliament in a local rebuff, particularly one organised by powerbrokers close to the leadership in caucus. Beazley argued that leaders should not interfere in the internal activities of a state branch. Crean survived the challenge, but it left an animosity that was deep-seated among Crean's friends and supporters. It was another group discontented with Beazley's leadership.

Then, in June 2005, the Labor Party decided to oppose Howard's tax cuts in the Senate, knowing that in the next month the government would have a majority there and would pass them then. To some members, it was a pointless exercise in tokenism. It reflected badly on the Beazley leadership group that made the tactical decision.

Gradually, Labor organisational leaders, concerned about the chances of winning in 2007, started to look at the alternatives. One of the first to shift was Mark Arbib. Arbib had talked to Rudd in 2005 when Latham resigned, telling him then that the New South Wales machine was backing Beazley because the party needed a safe pair of hands. One risk had failed. Why take another and, besides, why burn out a future leader?

Over the next year Arbib came to believe that Beazley could not win, and he came back to Rudd. However, before he was prepared to put his support behind Rudd, he wanted to know that Rudd was worth of the effort, that he actually stood for something. So he asked Rudd to set out his position.

Rudd wrote two papers. The first, 'What I Stand for', provided seven brief statements of core beliefs, followed by a number of supporting arguments. The seven statements were:

> I stand for *an economic vision for our country* that is bigger, much bigger, than Australia just being China's quarry and Japan's beach.

> I believe in *rewarding hard work, achievement and success* through a tax system which creates real incentives for Australian business.

> I believe it's time to *restore the balance for Australian families* because John Howard has gone too far with his extreme policies.

> I believe time is running out for Australia to develop *a long-term energy strategy that reduces our dependency on Middle East oil*, boosts alternative fuels and plays our part in protecting the planet.

> I believe in *balancing the budget.* Year in, year out. No exceptions. To keep interest rates down.

> I have a totally *hardline attitude in national security*. No ifs. No buts. No maybes. Defending our national security is the first responsibility of Government.

> I love this country of ours. My family has been privileged to live here for eight generations. And I want to *preserve the values which have made Australia great.*

Rudd spelt out under each heading a combination of policy ideas and rhetorical flourishes.

In a second paper, '28 Policy Initiatives', he laid out a strategy to deliver the ideas to the population. He noted that:

> The next task is to schedule these initiatives over a 28-day campaign across the country with appropriate visual backdrops and audiences. Week one would involve a tour of the nation with visits to each state and territory capital—a day in each against a landmark setting. This would demonstrate Labor was on the move.

It was not just a manifesto of dreams but a detailed agenda of ideas that had been formulated over the previous decade, and a strategy to promote them. There were proposals for ports, roads, research funding schemes to bring back 'the best and the brightest scientists', and the creation of an Office of National Security headed by Australia's first national security adviser.

Not all of this, of course, could be pursued, as events later made some of the promises impractical. Circumstances were to change: the financial status of the country was to deteriorate dramatically, leading to situations that could not be anticipated. But it was still a detailed manifesto, with both specific proposals and a strategy for a new leader to put them into effect. It was written by Rudd and Jordan, and many of the ideas were to surface again while he was the leader of the Opposition and later still after he became prime minister.

Arbib was persuaded. He thought: 'That's it. This guy has got it'. He became the lynchpin of the Rudd campaign, the link to the machine and the New South Wales Right. Arbib used qualitative polling to show that Beazley was unelectable because people had stopped listening. His actions were not without risk. The Right was still behind Beazley. Destabilising the leadership and then failing to topple the leader is treason. Success is good judgement.

Others joined the cause in the next few months. Party whip Roger Price had long been a supporter. Chris Bowen, a young right-wing MP from New South Wales, was chair of the caucus Committee for Economic Affairs. After the committee produced a report on trade in services, Rudd asked Bowen to discuss it with him. The report was barely mentioned, but the future of the party was. Bowen became a principal adviser. Ironically, Rudd's campaign manager in January 2005, Alan Griffin, thought that he should not challenge Beazley, on the grounds it was too near an election. So the team was different this time.

The key was Julia Gillard. Neither Gillard nor Rudd could win on their own. Nor was it likely, in a contest that pitted Gillard against Beazley, that the Rudd supporters would vote for Gillard. Combined, they provided a different picture: a team that was likely to win. During 2006 they gradually came together. Although they had been chair and deputy chair of the same caucus committee in 1999, they had not been close since. In the leadership battles, they had been on opposite sides; Gillard had been close to Latham. After the 2005 leadership challenge they had talked on and off. They met by accident in Noosa during the Easter break and shared a coffee. Victorian Left Senator Kim Carr was keen they cooperate. Although he was from a different Victorian Left faction to Gillard, he worked hard to get the two to talk. By late 2006, several observers thought they had reached an accommodation. Exactly when the two finally agreed to run as a team may be known to only a few—it did not become public until a few days before the December challenge.

Challengers need a peg on which to hang their case. Beazley provided it when he muddled television personality Rove McManus with US presidential svengali Karl Rove. McManus's young wife had died of cancer and Beazley was sympathising with his loss. Although McManus's name was all over the papers, Beazley got it wrong, a slip that by itself meant little, but which in this context was seen as another example of him losing his grip. A rambling address at the Press Club exacerbated the despair in parts of the Labor Party.

At that time Rudd was on a delegation to China with Senator Kim Carr, Simon Crean and national secretary Tim Gartrell. The purpose of the visit was to talk about climate change, and Rudd had gone over a day early to meet his contacts. Consequently there was continuing activity on mobile phones as both sides were planting stories with select journalists, about whether Rudd was undermining Beazley or whether there would be a challenge. Some did not think he would make the move, even at this stage. Others felt they were holding him back. The uncertainty outside his office was evident.

Rudd had long identified the last caucus meeting of the year in early December, the political killing season, as the best occasion for a challenge. As it was the last week in parliament, it would give a new leader time to establish himself before the parliament met again. On the other side, the Beazley camp had an Australia Day strategy: if he could survive till then, they could start preparing for an election, working on the assumption that it was too late for a new leader to establish himself in the eyes of the electorate. There was speculation that a challenge would come, but uncertainty about when the best time, if ever, might be. Alan Griffin argued publicly that Rudd should not run and said that he did not know of any plans. As he had told Rudd that he should wait, he had not been in the tent on this occasion.

There was no concerted push by the party elders to tap Beazley on the shoulder and tell him to stand down, as there had been for Crean, although some MPs did individually suggest to Beazley that it was time to go. Within the caucus there was considerable affection for him and a desire that he not be humiliated. When he was not prepared to stand down, the Rudd–Gillard alliance was made public.

Inevitably, the subterranean process of lobbying now became public. The night before laying down the challenge, Rudd was still considering his options. A string of people came in and out of his office, the last being Gillard. A meeting to discuss what he might do turned into a trial press conference, with Jordan and Bowen throwing questions at him. On the Friday morning he finally decided, made an appointment to see Beazley and told him the challenge was on. Beazley announced there would be a spill and, to raise the stakes, declared there would be a spill of all frontbench positions at the same time. It was a dramatic destabilising choice, designed to make all frontbenchers nervous and more liable to maintain the status quo.

Once the gauntlet had been thrown down, the strategy was to maintain the momentum, to try to dictate the headlines. The people in the Rudd camp thought they had a good chance, but never assumed they would win. Rudd and Gillard campaigned together, presenting themselves as a team, not a union of convenience. They immediately appeared together at a press conference, advocating the need for a new generation to take on a tired Howard government. Then they attended a previously scheduled function in a Melbourne electorate before flying to Brisbane, which was to act as the centre of the campaign for the next two days.

The campaign was run at a number of levels. The intent was that the headlines in the weekend papers, particularly the *Daily Telegraph*, were at best positive and at worst neutral. They needed to avoid any suggestions that Beazley was in front and might win easily. 'Beazley ahead' was their fear. In the event, the headlines were neutral. Second, they sought to provide the momentum, with backbenchers standing up to say that they would vote for Rudd. While it might have been nice to get one who had shifted from Beazley, the important point was to get someone in front of the cameras.

They also hit the phones: Rudd, Gillard and Jordan, all in Brisbane, held phone link-ups every two hours, checking with the principal organisers from the states, determining who was a certain 'yes' and a certain 'no', and where the others stood. While members of the support team, such as Jordan, would ring the solid supporters, ensuring their continued backing and saying that they had to leave the boss to talk to the waverers, Rudd kept working the others.

In Beazley's camp there was a degree of gloom. At the end of the weekend, his office thought the best result could be 47–41 to Rudd. Other key supporters, including Swan and Albanese, were more pessimistic. On the morning of the poll there was discussion of whether Beazley should concede without a ballot. He decided to stay in, what was called the verandah option: Did he want to spend the rest of his life sitting on the verandah wondering?

Beazley and Rudd nominated. The vote was soon announced: 49–39 to Rudd. Jenny Macklin decided she would not contest the deputy leadership; Gillard was elected unopposed.

Rudd had won the leadership without most of the props regarded as necessary for the leadership of the Labor Party. He was not a member of any large faction; indeed, he was in a faction of two and the other member, Arch Bevis, voted for Beazley. He was not directly supported by any of the faction heavies: Swan, Smith, Conroy and Albanese backed Beazley. Bob Hawke made some calls on Beazley's behalf. Crean and Carr supported Gillard, and only through her did they come to Rudd. He did not have a union block behind him; most of the right-wing union heavyweights, such as Joe De Bruyn of the Shop and Allied Workers, and Bill Ludwig from the Australian Workers' Union, supported Beazley. However, Rudd had the support of some of the old warriors, like John Faulkner and Robert Ray, who wanted a better future for the party, and some of the young members, like Chris Bowen, who wanted generational change. He had made his reputation through his remorseless drive to attack the government through the media, his public presentations of ideas, his incessant networking. It was all part of relentless self-promotion, so that he could in effect put his hand up to say, 'I am the best person here'. In December 2006, the party agreed.

After the vote, Rudd met the press. He promised fresh ideas, a new agenda and a bucketload of energy. His key phrase, much repeated, was 'the fork in the road'.

It was to be a new leader, a new generation and a contrast to an old, tired government.

8

MODELS, IDEAS AND BELIEFS

'When Christ calls a man, he bids him come and die', wrote Dietrich Bonhoeffer in 1937 in his treatise in *The Cost of Discipleship*. He was faced by a rampant Nazi party that was cracking down on dissent. They were the first words that Rudd extracted from Bonhoeffer's work when he wrote his essay 'Faith in Politics' in 2006. Bonhoeffer was involved in the resistance against the regime, was imprisoned by the Nazis and hanged at Flossenburg concentration camp on Hitler's explicit instruction, three weeks before the war ended in Europe. He was, Rudd has stated, 'the man I most admire in the history of the twentieth century'. Rudd's other model was from an earlier time. Bonhoeffer, in Rudd's eyes, 'became the Thomas More of European Protestantism because he understood the cost of discipleship, and lived it'. He speculated that 'it was the Catholic More who later inspired the Lutheran Bonhoeffer not to yield to the yoke of Hitler's Aryan race laws'. More and Bonhoeffer were Rudd's ideals by the time he left university.

Both represented what Rudd defined as 'muscular Christianity', a commitment to action. Bonhoeffer rejected the idea that the inner person belonged to God and the outer sphere to the state. Christians should be involved, and on the side of the dispossessed. Rudd cited Bonhoeffer on the need to see the great events of history 'from below, from the perspective of the outcast, the suspects, the maltreated, the powerless, the reviled—in short, from the perspective of those who suffer'.

We select our heroes with a mixture of fascination and instinct. A fascination with More and Bonhoeffer coupled Rudd's faith to a commitment to action and social involvement to bring about a better society. The lessons did not have to be paired with a martyr complex; they did suggest a sense of obligation and a preparedness to do what was necessary to achieve a more decent society. Faith and action should, in his cosmos, be inextricably linked, even where the threat to position and future may be significant.

If that combination might explain how Rudd saw the call to action, it could not of itself determine what he should do. Even the Bonhoeffer plea, that the perspective of the oppressed be paramount, did not tell anyone how those perspectives should be put into operation. If his heroes determined the approach, the priorities and programs had to be more grounded in the practical Australian world of politics.

What do leaders believe and how consistent are they? As a public servant Rudd talked about process, about the need for coordination, about policy consistency. These were technical issues, constrained by the positions he held. As a politician he was able to talk about values, aspirations and ideals and how they can be translated into policies. In the years before his election to the party leadership, he talked regularly and consistently about his beliefs. In a period where initially he had no staff, and then only one or two after becoming a shadow minister, he had to do his own research and write his own speeches. He might have had a number of contacts he could consult, but he was mostly on his own.

Rudd's maiden speech in the parliament set out three core ideas: the beneficial role of the state, the requirement for improved educational opportunities, and the necessity for Australia to be an active international citizen, particularly in multilateral organisations. He was given less than a day's notice of the occasion and spent the night with Thérèse preparing a draft. These themes were the ones that recurred over the next decade, often placed within the context of broader ideas.

In his maiden speech, he began:

> Politics is about power. It is about the power of the state. It is about the power of the state as applied to individuals, the society in which they live and the economy in which they work. Most critically, our responsibility in this parliament is how that power is used: whether it is used for the benefit of the few or the many. In this my first speech I want to speak on the fundamental principles that I believe should govern the exercise of political power and the reasons, therefore, that I am a member of the Australian Labor Party and why I have sought election to this parliament.

For Rudd, ideas were important and were the reason there were still fundamental differences between the two sides of politics on the role of the state. 'This [Howard] government's view is a minimalist view of the role of government. It is a view that holds that markets rather than governments are better determinants of not only efficiency but also equity.' By contrast, Rudd argued:

> I believe unapologetically in an active role for government. I believe that this activist role should have as its foremost guiding principle a commitment to equality of opportunity that is real rather than rhetorical. It is a principle that should permeate all that we do in education and health. I also believe that governments

must actively look after those who, through no fault of their own, cannot look after themselves.

A consequence is that governments sometimes have to regulate markets. Markets might generate wealth but they can also fail, 'requiring direct government intervention through instruments such as industry policy. There are also areas where the public good dictates that there should be no market at all'. An active state became a core theme. The state should combine a competitive economy with a just society. Talking at a time of economic crisis in Asia, he asked what regulatory structure should be put in place, 'as the market has apparently failed adequately to apply its own disciplines'.

Second, Rudd emphasised the need for better education because education 'is both a tool of social justice as well as a fundamental driver of economic reform'. He listed the problems and argued for strong Commonwealth action.

Third, he talked of Australia's role in the region: 'There is, of course, no reason for this nation to apologise for its heritage. We are proudly Australian and should remain so. But as a nation we need to understand how others perceive us, because that helps us in our behaviour towards the region'.

In particular, and consistent with a longstanding Labor tradition, he argued for Australian commitment to involvement in multilateral institutions; he feared the Howard government was retreating from 'the vigorous multilateralism of its past'. 'We have been respected as an effective international citizen. This represents the cumulative capital of successive Australian governments, ministers and officials'.

Then came a jibe that reflected tense relations with the foreign minister for the duration of the Howard government, Alexander Downer:

This capital must be husbanded and harnessed for the future. That requires leadership—leadership that the current foreign minister is demonstrably incapable of providing. Our challenge is to build across this nation a robust constituency in support of Australia's future international engagement, one that will not be hijacked by the periodic outburst of populism.

The ideas of the maiden speech of 1998 became the principles of 2003. Labor had three fundamental foreign-policy foundations: commitment to the US alliance, deep involvement in the region, and a commitment to multilateralism. These three principles emerged in Opposition and as the basis of Rudd's foreign policy when he reached office.

Rudd was concerned to contrast his ideas with those of the more strident free-marketeers. Over the years he talked about economist Friedrich Hayek as the epitome of the market and sought to identify Howard and Costello with Hayek's ideas. In 2001 Rudd asked how social democrats should respond to the challenges of globalisation, in particular to ameliorate the contemporary orthodoxy of free trade and deregulated labour markets. Rudd wanted to promote regional responses. Although he saw Asia-Pacific Economic Cooperation (APEC) as the product of regional elites, he wanted it to refashion its approach to take on new challenges. If that were to occur, then there would be opportunities: 'For social democrats, therefore, free markets should be managed markets and we should be mindful of both the effects of market failure and the fundamental and continuing importance of the social contract'. He provided a detailed list of the steps that social democrats should take to ameliorate the impact of emerging capital markets on the local social contracts, on poor countries and on currency regulation. What was required, he argued, was suitable institutional machinery, as states could not act unilaterally. The EU was a good model, but the Asia–Pacific needed its own structure, and APEC could be a useful vehicle. The challenge was for Australia to make use of its opportunities.

Rudd's ideas were eventually brought together in two papers he wrote for *The Monthly* in October and November 2006. They reflected the culmination of his personal creed, written while he was still a shadow minister. The audience was both internal and external—a manifesto to the party of what he stood for and the establishment in the public eye of a separate identity. When coupled with the manifesto that he wrote some months earlier at Mark Arbib's request, the articles set out not only what he claimed but also a framework for what he wanted to do in office.

The second paper he wrote was 'Howard's Brutopia: The Battle for Ideas in Australian Politics'. The title itself, while connecting to the conservative philosopher Michael Oakshott, is redolent of his own intellectual heritage. It can be coupled with a speech he gave to the Centre for Independent Studies (CIS), also in November 2006, to identify his broad approach to governmental involvement in society and the economy.

Rudd's argument was that if the neo-liberals considered humans to be self-regarding, then social democrats believed that they were also 'other-regarding'. If neo-liberals saw the basic principles as security, liberty and property, then social democrats added another three: equity, solidarity and sustainability. Consequently, he argued that:

> Working within a comprehensive framework of self-regarding and other-regarding values gives social democrats a rich policy terrain in which to define a role for the state. This includes the security of the people; macro-economic stability; the identification of market failure in critical areas such as infrastructure; the identification of key public goods, including education, health,

the environment and the social safety net; the fostering of new forms of social capital; and the protection of the family as the core incubator of human and social capital. These state functions do not interfere with the market; they support the market. But they have their origins in the view that the market is designed for human beings, not vice versa, and this remains the fundamental premise that separates social democrats from neo-liberals.

In the CIS lecture, Rudd sought to contrast his social democratic position with the dictates of Hayek. Social democrats reject Hayek's assertion that altruism is a primitive value. They believe that human beings have an intrinsic dignity and value beyond what the market alone determines. They argue that liberty and equity are not mutually exclusive, that education, health and the environment fall in areas where market failure is likely, and that the provision of those education services by the state provides opportunity and enhances productivity. They argue that family cannot be insulated from the market and needs to be protected, particularly in the labour market. They argue that the market should not be separated from the political domain; the task of politics is to deliver 'long-term market friendly reform—reform tempered by social responsibility'. In sum, tempering the market with social interventions does not, as Hayek asserted, push a state down a 'slippery slope' to totalitarianism.

Rudd's arguments are, of course, in a political context. They chart the Howard government's failure in terms of family values, climate change and foreign policy. The lecture gave him the opportunity to identify where he saw Labor as different. He could restate the three core 'pillars' of a Labor foreign policy: 'The US alliance, our membership of the UN and a continued policy of comprehensive engagement with Asia'. The writings also established, following the lines of his maiden speech some eight years earlier, the consistent themes Rudd saw for the role of the state and the approach to domestic and foreign policies.

If the Brutopia article provided his belief in the role of the state, the article a month earlier went to his more fundamental question of faith in politics. It stemmed from a speech he gave in November 2005 at the St Thomas More Forum in Canberra. Rudd located himself in a long Labor tradition of Christian Socialists, including the founder of the British Labour Party, Keir Hardie, and the last elected Labor prime minister from Queensland, Andrew Fisher. Rudd sought to identify what he learned from his Christian beliefs and what actions should follow.

He wanted to counter the argument that Christians should always be connected with the conservative side of politics because they talk about family values. He also rejected the notion that 'religion should keep out of politics'. He argued that the

> Gospel is both a spiritual and a social Gospel, and if it is a social Gospel, then it is in part a political Gospel because politics is the means by which society chooses to exercise its collective power ... In this respect the Gospel is an exhortation to social action ... A Christian perspective on contemporary policy debates may not prevail. It must nonetheless be argued.

To be consistent, he argued, the Church should be involved in industrial relations, in 'the fundamental ethical challenge of our age to protect the planet', in global poverty and asylum seekers. In all cases he argued for the application of Bonhoeffer's principle: 'Who speaks boldly to the state for those who cannot speak for themselves?' So he said the challenge was to build an Australia that takes the lead in dealing with poverty and climate change, in redesigning the international order to prevent genocide, and in policies not defined by 'the narrowest definitions of our national self-interest'. He returned in the end to his hero.

Bonhoeffer's vision of Christianity and politics was for a just world delivered by social action, and driven by personal faith. Bonhoeffer's tradition therefore acts still as an eloquent corrective to those who would seek to traduce Christianity by turning it into the handmaiden of the conservative political establishment. Bonhoeffer's Christianity was, and remains, a more demanding challenge than that.

Rudd obviously had a political purpose: to reclaim some of the ground that had been lost to parties like Family First and to the arguments of those like Tony Abbott, strong and open Christians who, he thought, implied that Christians should vote for conservative values. He sought to identify the other Christian traditions that had inspired social activism and commitment. On the way, he used the occasion to attack the policies of the government.

But in Rudd's articles can be found a range of aspirations that had been consistent over the previous decade. Rudd did not come to religion as a convenient vehicle to lambast the government. He had identified what he found admirable in More and Bonhoeffer twenty years before. He had explored the options at the ANU and decided there that being a Christian and an activist was a consistent position. Christians should be involved and committed. That was the attraction of Bonhoeffer and More. Furthermore, he argued, there was a Christian imperative to speak for those with no voice.

The Bonhoeffer theology of 'from below' provides a position from which policy analysis can start. Rudd rejected the uncompromising liberation theology that was all about egalitarianism of opportunity and outcome. He was not attracted to the ideas of the parable of the talents: the concept that all are given talents and have to be left alone to use them as best that they can. He agreed that those who worked hard and used those talents would be duly rewarded. But he wanted a middle path, one which allowed the use of talents through a market system but required that the state assist those, who for reasons of market failure or poor regulation, failed through no fault of their own. The Bonhoeffer dictums could go no further than that. They forced leaders to stand back and ask the question: Is this authentic in terms of the interests of the view from below, be they the homeless, Indigenous Australians, or those who will lose their livelihood as a consequence of a recession for which they had no responsibility? In international affairs, governments not only need to deal with climate change to save the planet, they must also consider those in developing countries who will be blasted by the depredations of climate change, and those who are still children, or even grandchildren not yet born, who have no voice now and who will have to live with the consequences of our actions.

That had to be a continuing concern. Rudd cited Bonhoeffer's dictum as providing a moral compass: 'Unless you stand in solidarity with the Jews at the moment of absolute despair, then who are you? How can you sing Gregorian chants on Sunday and pay no attention to the wailing of the Jews on Monday amidst the Holocaust?' His was a stripped-back Christianity, largely unencumbered by dogma, form, ritual or the prohibitions of any particular Christian creed. He was impatient with the paraphernalia of religion that surrounds much of the worship. He was comfortable in Catholic or Protestant churches. His point of reference was biblical and practical. He never pretended it was easy to translate the aspiration into daily practice:

> It is very hard to pigeonhole people like me because I have a religious faith, but I never actually bought the whole uber sexual morality regime, because on any honest reading of the New Testament it's on the margins. So when they say (a) they know I swear, I don't care, I have been trying to stop swearing for years,

I just can't, it is very therapeutic ... imagine Jesus of Nazareth growing up in a bloody carpenter's workshop. I'm sure they didn't swear in first century Galilee! [They had their own words.] That is what I mean, I regard this as so much a triumph of form over substance and most of the sex and sexuality agenda is the same.

Faith did not tell you what to do in any individual case. It did not provide solutions. It did not define what was possible or impossible. It did not give any economic analysis. It provided a moral compass that could assist when all those questions had to be answered. And therein lay the challenge. A government has to do good, but the means of ensuring benefits for the needy have to be estimated on a policy-by-policy basis. There is no easy measure against which the benefits of a policy can be determined. They have to be worked out item by item. Rudd's beliefs provided a challenge but not a pathway. The question he was to face was how to turn the ideas into practice in an adversarial, and sometimes bitter, political battle.

9

TO VICTORY

When Rudd faced Kerry O'Brien on *The 7.30 Report* on 4 December 2006, the evening of his election as party leader, he set out to introduce himself to the electorate. All the policy drivers that were to dominate the next year can be found in this first evening of his leadership. He was at pains to differentiate himself from the incumbent Howard government, and to map out what he saw as long-term challenges: climate change, workplace relations and the economy. He was about:

> making sure that we as Australia build a strong economy in the long term, a sustainable economy, one which is not just China's quarry or Japan's beach, but one with a broad economic base and one [in] which individual hard work, achievement and success are properly rewarded, and at the same time preventing or making sure that fairness and social justice aren't just thrown out the back door.

He had to be 'rock solid on national security' and 'to have economic responsibility and credibility'. Then he would be taken seriously on health, education and climate change. When challenged on whether he would take on 'the factional Daleks', he responded:

> I'll be leading this show and when it comes to the outcomes I want, I intend to get them. I don't particularly care if anyone has opposing views, that's what's going to happen. When it comes to the broader structures of the party ... I think it's time that right across the party we opened up more as a party and a movement to attract candidates of talent and ability.

To demand support was unusual in the rhetoric of the Labor Party. But Rudd had won the leadership with fewer debts than most of his predecessors. The big union bosses had mostly backed Beazley. So had many party heavies. Rudd had won because he was seen as the best—the only—chance of beating Howard. When accused of being yet another Labor Party apparatchik, he drew on his roots:

> I grew up on a farm in rural Queensland. I've run my own business. I've worked in embassies abroad and you choose, I think, probably, three years of my political career when I actually worked as a premier's chief of staff as a definition of me being an apparatchik out of twenty-one or twenty-two years of public life.

Then he lapsed into the Queensland country vernacular that had long been familiar to those who knew him in private:

> Fair shake of the sauce bottle, Kerry. Let's be frank about this. I bring a range of experience and it's that breadth that I want to see across our entire movement. The other thing I would say about my background: I elected to join the Labor Party. My family weren't Labor. I grew up in rural Queensland. I think

Mum voted DLP and Dad was in the Country Party. And the reason I elected to join the Labor movement is what it stood for, and I still believe in what it stands for, and that is, a strong economy, but not jettisoning a fair go out the back window.

From share farm to The Lodge: that was the narrative and the next challenge.

The immediate task was to secure Rudd's shadow executive; all the positions had been declared vacant by Beazley when the challenge was made. It gave his successor the chance of a fresh start, even if that had not been the intention. Rudd had promised that he would have Peter Garrett on the frontbench. Two MPs who had lost their party nomination agreed to stand down. Rudd and Gillard, with advice from the 'wise owls', senators Faulkner and Ray, settled on the twenty-nine people they wanted. They told the factions. At the caucus, only those people were nominated. It was not the time to take on a new leader and Rudd used his authority to achieve his immediate objective. He gave a conciliatory address, saying people should come and see him if they had problems.

Then Rudd sought to mend bridges damaged by the years of infighting. If caucus was to work effectively together there could be no recriminations. Wayne Swan was perhaps the key, both symbolically and personally. After a decade of close cooperation in Queensland and four years sharing a house in Canberra, relations between Rudd and Swan had broken down. Swan had remained Beazley's chief adviser while Rudd had struck out independently, thereby stymieing any ambition of Swan. Even if there had been no shouting matches, relations had become glacial. But Rudd kept Swan on as Shadow Treasurer, at the risk of disappointing his supporter Lindsay Tanner. Gradually, Rudd and Swan rebuilt some of the links that had made them so close in the days of the Goss government and beyond. He made Albanese, another Beazley supporter who had kept open communications with the Rudd camp, manager of government business in the House.

Rudd started as he had proposed in the manifesto he had sent to Arbib some months before; the thought given to presentation then was valid months later and gave him an immediate strategy. He went on a listening tour, often to the very places mentioned in the proposal given to Arbib. He visited every state and territory and announced several initiatives.

In January 2007, while most politicians headed for the beach, Rudd chose the recording studio. Labor strategists decided that a blitz at the end of January was a good way of telling people who Rudd was, and that he should do so before the government tried to define him in the public mind. The Eumundi advertisement was born: Rudd in open-neck shirt, filmed against the town and talking about education, the gateway to opportunity that had allowed him to come so far. In a second ad he stated that he was fiscally conservative: 'A number of people have described me as an economic conservative. When it comes to public finance, it's a badge I wear with pride'. Even if the government disagreed, he was intent on making it fight on his terms.

Rudd immediately received extensive boosts by his persistent high standing in the polls. Both leader and party were now doing well, with a lead that suggested Labor could win the next election. However, there had been false dawns before. Howard had trailed midway through every parliament. Latham had been popular for six months or more. Still, the honeymoon was encouraging. The government seemed tired and divided. Peter Costello was champing for the chance to be prime minister, but he never had the support in the parliamentary party to take over. Wars in Iraq and Afghanistan wore on. There appeared to be a mood for a change, even while the economy was booming. But could Rudd's honeymoon last?

Rudd had been elected because he was considered the best prospect for regaining office. Poll figures only boosted his authority. Rudd's response was typical: discipline, control and prodigious work. All the next year, the party was run out of his office. His principal staffer was initially George Thompson, an experienced hand who had been brought in to manage Latham's office after the election and who agreed to stay on. Eventually, David Epstein, a former chief of staff to Beazley, was persuaded to return to head the office. Alister Jordan was deputy and oversaw the political and media management with Walt Secord and Lachlan Harris. A tight discipline was immediately imposed on the shadow executive. Nothing was released without the approval of the leader's office. There were to be no independent shadow ministers running their own show. Desperate to win after the long period in Opposition and buoyed by the polls, the shadow ministers accepted the controls. There was little public complaint, even if there was some mumbling about the excessive power of the leader.

Gradually, policy ideas were released. Labor would abolish Work Choices. 'Working families' became the mantra; Labor would protect these families from the rising cost of living. Indeed, in mid-year it was Rudd who identified the concerns about the cost of living and who proposed a change of direction and emphasis in the advertisements. He had drawn on his conversations with voters to intuit what really worried them and he fed his thoughts back into the machinery.

Rudd had connections around the world from whom he would draw ideas. A commitment to developing a rapid broadband connection emerged, initially with a promise to connect all houses. It became more sophisticated after discussions with Larry Smarr at the AALD. Smarr, a professor at the University of San Diego and one of the initiators of the internet, talked to him about the need for glass fibre, with all its speed and capacity to go to the house, and not just the node. Rudd listened to him and others; when he was persuaded, he instructed the shadow minister to investigate what was likely to be desirable.

The 'education revolution' was intended to provide access to a computer for every secondary-school child. A climate change summit would explore the different ways in which Australia could be protected from the devastating drought that had water reservoirs down to historic low levels; climate change was to be a priority. These were the differentials from the Howard government.

So, too, came the strategies designed to reassure the voters and negate traditional Coalition advantages. In 2005, Rudd explained that he saw public policy as a set of babushka dolls:

> The outer shell of the babushka doll is national security. The public has to be able to look you in the eye and have confidence that you will maintain security. Peel that layer off. Next, people want confidence that the economy will be well managed and that you can provide them with the basics of life—a job and an income. Our experience of the last decade is that the community has had reservations about these outer two shells ... Peel that layer off. Next, people ask, 'What will happen if I get sick? Who will be there to look after me?' Next, people want to know, 'How do I provide for my kids' education?' Then, at the inner core, there is community. I think there is a deep yearning for people to be involved in community life.

Security and the economy were two areas where Labor usually lagged. If Rudd could reduce the gap so they were not vote deciders, then Labor's chances would be improved. So Rudd emphasised his closeness to the United States and his commitment to the US alliance. He was not prepared to give an inch on national security. He kept talking about himself as an economic conservative, as being fiscally responsible. He sought to set the agenda, to get everyone talking about what he thought and in the context that he chose.

There were the inevitable government attacks on his credibility and his integrity. The government trawled through his past for anything they could use against him. The attacks came, like episodes in a soap opera, one after another as ministers tried to exploit his connections, his narrative, his family and his integrity.

Episode one concerned three meetings he had had with the former Western Australian premier and convicted criminal Brian Burke. Rudd had met him in 2005 at the invitation of local MP Graham Edwards. The Labor premier, Geoff Gallop, had banned his ministers from having any contact with Burke. In the previous few months the Western Australian Crime Commission had released a series of tapes implying that Burke tried to gain benefits from Labor ministers and state public servants for the clients of his lobbying firm. Burke was now political poison. The government sought to crucify Rudd for keeping company with a convicted criminal. At Question Time, as Costello challenged Rudd's veracity and judgement, Rudd looked deeply uncomfortable, shaken and temporarily mute. Then he gathered his wits. He declared to his staff: 'If the government wanted to make this election about character, let's address this for what it is'. So he called a press conference. He denied that he met Burke to seek votes for the leadership and admitted that meeting Burke was an error of judgement. The attack rebounded as a consequence of Costello's overkill. He took out the bystander. Costello trumpeted that anyone who met Burke was morally compromised, and then discovered that a Coalition minister, Ian Campbell, had met a delegation that included Burke. Campbell, most unfairly, as he was just doing his job, was forced to resign, and the Coalition lost any moral superiority they might once have claimed.

The second target was his life history, a challenge to the story that his family had been forced off the farm after his father died. The question was not whether the family had to move; it was the speed with which it happened that was at issue. The children of the farmer-landlord thought their father was being unfairly labelled as unfeeling and inconsiderate. In a rather heavy-handed way, Rudd and his office rang the newspaper editors and ineffectively tried to kill the story. The reaction, rather than the precision of the account, became the news. However, the attack misfired because it was seen as slightly distasteful to use the memories of a distraught eleven-year-old to accuse him of misrepresentation forty years later.

Episode three was the accusations that Rudd had sought to bring forward the timing of an ANZAC service in Vietnam to suit the convenience of *Sunrise*. Rudd denied he had tried to do anything of the sort. It transpired there were some emails to his office, but he argued he was not told about them. Hockey initially defended him on air, but then under pressure argued that there were questions for him to answer. The incident ended their weekly appearance on *Sunrise*. The government wanted a more senior minister to take on Rudd.

Fourth, stories emerged that Thérèse Rein had taken over a company and paid workers a mere 45 cents an hour in exchange for their holidays and other rights. Rudd was defensive at first, as Thérèse was overseas. He pointed out that, once the anomaly had been discovered, the workers had their conditions adjusted and all entitlements paid retrospectively. He turned the attack into a more general point; he defended the right of the modern woman to have a career independent of her partner. When Thérèse decided to sell her Australian business, in order to minimise any future chance of clashes of interest, Rudd regretted the need to do so.

As a series finale, there was Scores. Rudd had been taunted across the chamber by Downer with the comment: 'We know all about you and Col Allan in New York'. In 2003, Rudd had accepted an after-dinner invitation from a former News Limited executive, Col Allan. He was taken to the strip club Scores. There was never any evidence that anything improper occurred; indeed, it seems the party left after thirty minutes because Rudd was 'freaking out to find himself in such a place'. The next morning he rang Thérèse to confess to being silly.

When, four years later, Glen Milne from *The Australian* rang for comment before running the story, Rudd was really worried about the damage it might do. He pulled Gillard out of a meeting to tell her what was about to happen. He seemed so perturbed that he thought it necessary to develop a strategy for dealing with it. Gillard thought it was funny and was not concerned. Rudd had an uncomfortable twenty-four hours. He appeared on *The 7.30 Report*, where he suggested both that he had been too drunk to remember what had happened and that he was certain that nothing untoward had occurred. He copped the flak, accepting he had been unwise to be there at all. It was another error of judgement.

Gillard was right: the story did Rudd no harm. Rudd's popularity increased: some people thought it made him more human; others were amused. A Labor frontbencher was startled when a constituent rushed up to announce, 'I'm going to vote for Rudd now'. Besides, most people thought the Liberals were behind the smear and, to an extent, it rebounded. When Downer was asked if he had ever been to a strip club, he denied he had ever gone to one in his official capacity. His office responded that he had never been to Scores with Col Allan.

The election year was full of potential hurdles within the Labor Party too. At the ALP conference in late April 2007, Rudd opened his speech with the self-deprecating quip, 'My name is Kevin and I'm from Queensland'. The conference itself was highly disciplined. With the leader's standing in the polls so high and victory a possibility, the party was tight behind him. When a union leader tried to advocate more radical action and condemned Rudd's conservatism, Rudd had him expelled. If the party was going to win, it would do it his way. There was an edge to his determination to remain in tight control.

The government tried to 'wedge' Labor on policy. It suggested a citizenship test. Rudd accepted that it sounded like a good idea and said he would wait for the details. The government intervened directly in the Northern Territory to attack problems of Aboriginal deprivation. It was announced fifteen minutes before Question Time and without notice. Rudd and shadow minister Jenny Macklin agreed that the stories in the report 'Little Children Are Sacred' were so terrible that the Labor Party would give bipartisan support to the actions.

When Howard agreed to take over the funding of a northern Tasmanian hospital, Rudd did not reject the federal takeover; three weeks later he unveiled the proposal that 'a Rudd Labor government will seek to take financial control of Australia's 750 public hospitals if State and Territory Governments have failed to agree to a national health and hospital reform plan by mid-2009'. It was a dramatic but conditional response. Howard, having established the precedent, found it hard to oppose on principle.

The most dramatic event was the arrest of an Indian doctor, Dr Mohamed Haneef, who was working on the Gold Coast and was planning to fly home to be with his pregnant wife. He was a cousin of a doctor involved in failed bombings in London and was accused of providing the cousin with a SIM card. After it was agreed he had no case to answer, the Minister for Immigration ordered he be detained on the grounds he was not a person of good character. Dr Haneef was guilty of nothing except his relationship with a cousin in the United Kingdom, but ominous hints of more information were designed to catch Labor in a bind. Rudd refused to bite. Remembering the 2001 campaign, Rudd simply stated that he had to rely on the information provided by the security services and federal police. He promised an inquiry. It frustrated Howard, who was reduced to complaining that Rudd was just copying him.

Arbib attributed Rudd's success to his work rate and discipline, but also to his political instincts: 'He was so in touch with the electorate ... While he would get regular briefs from people on polling, he didn't need them. He'd know what was going on in the electorate anyway and his innate response to questions would almost always be the right response, without polling'.

Arbib thought it was easy to have a disciplined campaign when the leader was going well. He cited Bob Carr's comment that 'to win from Opposition you've really got to hate every day. If you feel comfortable in Opposition you're not going to win. Kevin would get up and probably hate every minute of it, I suspect—and that was a good thing'.

In turn, Rudd could have his fun. On Howard's sixty-seventh birthday, Rudd gave him a goat, or rather nominated a goat for the World Vision gift-in-kind program in Darfur, Sudan. A milking goat could provide a family with milk and an asset. In doing so, Rudd encouraged the prime minister to increase Australia's Donate to the World Food Program, which was running out of funds.

By September, the pressure had shifted from Rudd to Howard. The Sydney meeting of APEC leaders was designed to bolster Howard's standing, but for the prime minister it was a disaster. While the comedy troupe The Chaser made a mockery of the much vaunted security arrangements, Downer convened a meeting of ministers at Howard's request to consider his position. They decided that he should go. But having loaded the gun, they weren't prepared to pull the trigger. Meanwhile, Rudd met US President George W Bush and spoke with him on relaxed terms, and welcomed the Chinese leader in fluent Mandarin. As Howard's fortunes seemed to wane, APEC gave international credibility to Rudd's aspirations to be a national leader.

When the election was called, Rudd was prepared and still ahead in the polls. The expected decline in his popularity had not occurred. The government's wedges had failed. The attacks on his integrity had been deflected. The two issues that were normally Coalition assets, national security and economic management, had largely been neutralised.

Rudd remained in tight control during the course of the campaign. The team that travelled with Rudd included his press adviser, Lachlan Harris; his chief of staff, David Epstein; and his deputy chief of staff, Alister Jordan. It also included John Faulkner, who had travelled with Labor leaders for the last three elections as a voice of wisdom and experience. Later in the campaign, Rudd's daughter, Jessica, joined the caravan. She had been working in his office on and off for the year; now she was able to bring a more-relaxed air of amused tolerance. She was able to say when he needed a break, when it was time to call an end to the day; she could also, with greater difficulty, give advice on wardrobe—'Not that tie!'—and let him relax and laugh.

The election became a combination of responding to the government and setting Labor's own agenda. When the government announced tax cuts on the first day after the election was called, in an attempt to seize the initiative, Rudd agreed to do the same with the difference that they would not be handed to the highest income earners. For every bid by the government to undermine the credibility of the Opposition, Rudd responded coolly and effectively. While the government began to implode, the standing of the Opposition leader improved.

The most striking image was the 'Kevin07' picture plastered across the Web. The secretariat developed an ad that had jogging crowds wearing Kevin07 T-shirts. Rudd came into a meeting and asked: 'Whose idea was that and why wasn't I told?' It was explained as an oversight, that everyone thought someone else had told him. In practice, as Rudd admitted, he might well have felt uncomfortable with the idea and not have agreed. It turned out to be a striking success and became the symbol of the campaign. Rudd became Kevin to everyone he met; they all felt they knew him.

That was about the only part of the campaign in which he was not heavily involved. He has never been a person who is comfortable merely reading someone else's words. He would play with the text of any advertisement, until the secretariat decided that it would not schedule a shoot until the final words were agreed. Even then, he would still fiddle and edit.

Everyone thought the televised debate between Rudd and Howard could be crucial and large slots of his time were set aside for trials. He prepared assiduously for the three sessions in which Robert Ray played Howard and Faulkner was the anchor. The office developed nine pages of potential questions. They were sometimes policy driven, sometimes purely political and sometimes downright personal. Sometimes they tried to discover what he knew himself, about the cost of child care, or when he last did the grocery shopping for the household. Others covered international issues, such as whether Osama bin Laden, if captured, should be executed. Others looked at the record of economic management of former Labor governments: 'Should Keating apologise for 17 per cent interest rates?', for instance. Ray taunted him throughout: 'Do you have a glass jaw?' Rudd kept focused.

He was cool in the one debate, carefully presenting a statement suggesting the government was out-of-date and a new generation was needed. He reacted with a degree of polish. When the Liberal ministers in the front row started to catcall and the moderator asked them to be quiet, Rudd asked: 'Were you reprimanding the Treasurer then?'—just in case the viewers did not get the message.

As the public learned more about him, they warmed to him. His poll figures, far from falling, stayed firm and sometimes rose. They reflected the warmth and ease with which he was now responding to the electors he met in all forums. One Labor member, Anthony Byrne, recalls one such visit to a local shopping centre. It was a spur-of-the-moment decision when a gap in the schedule developed, so there were no cameras. As he and Rudd went down the escalators, the reaction was unbelievable. They'd be looking but there's no TV camera, so what is he doing? He was just talking to people … People were literally running out of the shops. A lot of mums were there, and they're getting out their cameras, getting photos with him. Young shop assistants that are charging out getting their shots taken. Talk about a powerful reaction when he appeared.

It had been Rudd's decision to take the walk. He dealt well with people in crowds who did not agree with his point of view. He had learned the skills of relating, of treating those he met personally. His campaigning was effective when he mixed with the public. He had developed the capacity to be both policy nerd and grass-roots campaigner, whether arguing on *Lateline* or walking through shopping centres. Both were essential for success, so he did both.

His most striking line was during the Labor launch, days after Howard had laid out promises of $9 billion: 'This sort of reckless spending must stop … I have no intention today of repeating Mr Howard's irresponsible spending spree … That's why the commitments I announce today will cost less than one-quarter of those Mr Howard announced on Monday'.

A Labor candidate seeking to underspend a conservative government was a novelty. It bolstered the argument that Rudd was indeed a fiscal conservative. That line dominated the coverage; it was the five-second grab that everyone could remember.

He and his staff remained cautious. Even when the polls held firm, there was nervousness about what could go wrong. The office prepared two responses for election night. One was in case of a cliff-hanger. It started: 'Well, I said to Labor's colleagues and candidates that they should be knocking on doors until their knuckles were bleeding. I didn't mention they'd be chewing their fingers in such a nail-biting finish as we've seen tonight. I've always believed this would be a close election. So it is—closer than we'd like'.

Observers could afford to be more confident. Leading into the election, journalists started to ask what sort of prime minister Rudd would be. The conclusion: 'He will demand the best-quality advice from public servants and fact-based submissions from ministers. He will listen carefully to all arguments but he is determined to carry the day. "I do have a belief that leaders are elected to lead", he says'.

He had already announced that as prime minister he would choose his ministers, rather than allowing caucus or factional fragments of caucus to select them. The announcement overturned 100 years of Labor tradition: the practice of caucus election had been established by the Labor conference of 1904. Rudd thought:

> If the Australian people put their trust in me to be their next prime minister, I think they'd have a parallel expectation of me because in my heart of hearts I'm a meritocrat. I don't care where people come from geographically or by way of party background or non-party background—I'm interested in what works, and who has the talent to make it work.

On election night the numbers rolled in. The result had been so widely forecast it seemed inevitable. Nerves remained taut until the right number of seats, plus a couple for a margin of safety, were won. Then Faulkner turned to Rudd and said, 'Kevin, I think I can inform you that we have enough seats to form the next government'. Less than two minutes later, Howard rang to concede. Rudd never had to give the 'too close to call' speech. The other draft, the victory speech, could now be pulled out of his pocket.

Eighteen years earlier, Rudd had heard Goss advise his victorious party to take a cold shower. Now, Rudd suggested they have a strong cup of tea. He gave a concession: 'You can even have an Iced VoVo on the way through'. Thereafter, the work would start.

PART II
GOVERNING

10

TAKING OVER

There is no extended period of transition in the Australian parliamentary system, nothing like the leisurely three months in the United States when incoming presidents can choose their new team and move from campaign to governing mode. For new Australian prime ministers and their advisers, the transition is immediate, with no time even to recover from the celebrations of election night. Winning the election is the beginning. The very next day they have to start exercising the levers of power. The new leader may not formally be prime minister; the resignation of the incumbent and the swearing in of the fresh government can only take place when the full election results are known and the new ministry selected. In the meantime, the prime minister-elect effectively has all the authority and will exercise it. Therefore for Rudd, the discipline of office applied immediately. A number of important decisions had to be made.

On the Sunday morning, Peter Shergold, the secretary of the Department of the Prime Minister and Cabinet (PM&C), flew to Brisbane to meet the incoming Prime Minister. The department had developed a series of papers designed to assist the transition to government. One set dealt with issues of administrative routine: when the prime minister would resign, when The Lodge would be vacated, when the new ministry would be sworn in. A second paper looked at the possible administrative arrangements. It is the prime minister's prerogative to decide how the government will be organised and what portfolios will be allocated to which ministers. The department's brief picked up on whatever statements had been made and proposed ways of implementing them. It had to be done quickly, before any ministers were sworn in. The third package raised broader issues of policy. It took the policy statements of the new Prime Minister and suggested ways in which they might be implemented. Of course, the vaguer the ideas, the harder it was to be precise. All departments prepare this brief so that incoming ministers can be presented with ways of doing whatever they have declared they want to do. The department had already had some discussions with Rudd's chief of staff, David Epstein, during the campaign, but inevitably, in a number of areas they were not certain what decisions the new Prime Minister would make.

Rudd had not been heavily involved in preparations for the transition before the election. He had left it to the Opposition Spokesperson for the Public Service, Penny Wong, to the experienced John Faulkner and Robert Ray, and to David Epstein. In part it was superstition; he did not want to appear to presume to take the people's vote for granted by spending time blatantly preparing for office. He would concentrate on the responsibilities of office only when they were won. In part, it was simply the need to ensure that everything that could be done was done in the fight to win the election. However positive the polls, however confident the observers, Rudd and his close colleagues would not allow themselves to relax until it was too late to do anything. Only then did they really acknowledge to themselves that they would win.

On the Sunday, the officials from PM&C worked through the arrangements of government with the Prime Minister. In particular they talked about routines of transition. Rudd wanted the government sworn in that week, but he was in no hurry to insist that his predecessor vacate The Lodge or his parliamentary offices.

They also talked about administrative arrangements, the distribution of responsibilities between departments. This has always been a prime ministerial prerogative. One of the promises made by Labor under Beazley's leadership was that Labor would establish a Department of Homeland Security. A shadow minister had been appointed. PM&C had done a considerable amount of work on what might be involved, which departments and agencies would be brought under the new entity's umbrella and how it would work. Rudd decided to commission a study, to be undertaken by a former head of the Defence Department, Ric Smith, on the advisability of such an innovation. Several months later, Smith recommended against the idea. It was shelved. Rudd realised from experience that the amount of time taken to settle new structures and procedures could be extraordinarily long. So he preferred, as far as possible, to work with the existing arrangements and people, and make changes only when and if it became apparent that the elements were no longer working.

There were three specific innovations, creative ways to tackle challenges. Each concerned a different issue. Julia Gillard, as Deputy Prime Minister, had the traditional right to identify her own portfolio. However, Rudd had already said that she would be Minister for Industrial Relations, with the responsibility for rolling back Work Choices. The two leaders decided she would also be responsible for the education revolution. So they asked for a mega-department to be constructed that merged several departments under the one minister.

Rudd was keen to bring John Faulkner into the ministry. Under Howard, the Cabinet Secretary had been made a political appointee, responsible for Cabinet management and for some long-term planning. However, the three people who held the position were not elected parliamentarians. Rudd made Faulkner the Cabinet Secretary, but his principal concerns were areas of governance: freedom of information, codes of conduct for ministerial staff, government ethics. This was the agenda about which he cared. He thought that processes of governing, transparency and accountability were issues to be pursued in government as well as in Opposition. The creation of the Cabinet Secretary within the Prime Minister's portfolio was an innovative way of driving that agenda.

It also kept Faulkner at the Prime Minister's shoulder for when he needed sage political advice, particularly when trouble was brewing; he was the 'wise owl', the consigliore. When political problems occurred, Faulkner appeared in the Prime Minister's Office. Rudd trusted his judgement, his political sense and his ability to cut through issues.

Third, there was a need to prioritise climate change as a government initiative. During the campaign, Rudd had not been precise about the administrative arrangements that he might want to develop. So PM&C arrived with a number of alternative ways in which units with climate responsibility, currently spread across departments, might be consolidated into a single office. After listening to the suggestions, the Prime Minister asked if they could be incorporated into a department. Creating a new department from scratch is always a challenge that invariably takes longer than anticipated. A Department of Climate Change would not be totally new, as an office already existed within PM&C. So the head of the climate office was asked to come up with a structure for a new department within three days. As a symbol of its importance, it too was to be placed within the Prime Minister's portfolio. The new administrative arrangements had to be settled before the ministry was announced.

On Monday it was Treasury's turn to meet with the Prime Minister and the Treasurer, Wayne Swan. The officials went through the current economic circumstances, identifying the state of the economy and potential threats. For many of the officials, it was the first time they had met the new Prime Minister. They soon understood his way of working: asking questions, raising issues, arguing the points. He did not pretend that he knew everything but was concerned that he understood the issues they were analysing. Some of them noted they were pleasantly surprised by his preparedness to assume that officials would be required to make a positive contribution to policy-making.

At the same time, Rudd was talking to Gillard about the make-up of the Cabinet and the ministry. For a century, the Labor caucus had elected the ministers. That principle—and it was seen to be an important principle for the ethos of the party—had been agreed at a Labor conference in 1904 and had become one of the guiding organisational characteristics that made Labor different. Prime ministers did not choose their ministers and could not dismiss them without the agreement of caucus. After 1984, ministers could be dismissed by the parliamentary leadership group, but not by the prime minister alone. The comparative lack of prime ministerial authority had, in the past, led to momentous struggles between Cabinet and caucus in all the governments before 1984. Thereafter, some factional concessions had limited the brawls but still restricted prime ministerial choices. During the 2007 election campaign, Rudd announced that he would choose the ministry, both to prevent it being seen as a stitch-up between all-powerful unions, working through the factions, and as part of moves to modernise the party. He also stated that Gillard, Swan and Tanner would hold in government the portfolios they had shadowed in Opposition, thus anticipating the choices of the caucus. No-one challenged his statement at the time; the middle of an election that Labor might win was no time to be undermining a leader. Once Rudd won, he had the authority to do what he had promised. Indeed, he selected the ministry before caucus met and then had the process endorsed, ex post facto. That was one way to overcome Labor tradition.

The caucus motion looked anodyne:

The executive shall consist of the Leader and Deputy Leader, who shall be members of the House of Representatives, and the Leader and Deputy Leader in the Senate, who shall be elected in accordance with Rule 38. All other Members of the Executive will be appointed by the Leader of the Federal Parliamentary Labor Party.

And of course the leader could thereby dismiss them too. The secretary of caucus, Daryl Melham, formally spoke against it, arguing that the power could go to the leader's head. Rudd said that if the caucus thought he had not made selections on anything but merit they could get a new leader. The motion passed.

Apart from the endorsement of Gillard, Swan and Tanner, Rudd declined to make any commitments about who would hold which portfolio. He argued that he would take no notice of factions but would select the best ministers in the caucus. Initially, he talked to Gillard. They drew up a provisional list. Then they brought in the experienced senators John Faulkner from the Left and Robert Ray from the Right. By one account (not universally remembered), Ray looked at the listings and congratulated Gillard on promoting more Left-faction members than their numbers justified. He also said that it was 'a brave decision to simultaneously declare war on the AWU (Australian Workers Union) and the SDA (Shop, Distributive and Allied Employees Association)', which were two of the biggest right-wing unions. Ray compared it to fighting a 'war on the Eastern and Western front at the same time'. The Cabinet had been eighteen ministers; it was extended to twenty with the inclusion of Tony Burke and Joe Ludwig, with connections to the SDA and AWU respectively. The ministry inevitably still had to take some account of state, Senate and factions. Ironically, Rudd himself came from a faction of two; the second member failed to make the transition from Shadow Cabinet to the ministry. One of his close supporters noted: 'When we were in the shadow ministry he rang me and said basically what job do you want. This time he rang me and said this is the job I'd like you to do, which I was perfectly happy with, but it was a subtle change there'.

There were thirty ministers—twenty in Cabinet and ten in the outer ministry. Then there were ten parliamentary secretaries. Rudd used these positions to reward the high-profile candidates who had entered parliament: Greg Combet, Bill Shorten, Gary Gray, Mike Kelly and Maxine McKew. He also eased the regrets of some whose careers were in their later phases and rewarded a few supporters. It was a mixture of experience and promise.

There were a number of people chosen by Rudd with whom he had had his differences and who had sniped from the sidelines, not publicly but noticeably, during the previous year. However, they also had sufficient weight and talent that the Prime Minister wanted them in positions in the new government. He was, however, not prepared to see a continuance of backstairs whining. He called five of his selections to meetings, usually in Canberra, with his staff and the two 'wise owl' senators attending as witnesses. The five were told that any continuance of disloyalty would see them out of the ministry. It was their last chance. They received, in one euphemistic phrase, a frank character assessment delivered assertively and at length. In effect, they were told: Step out of line and you're gone. Rudd was showing who had won and who was boss in a display of his power. There was an element of triumphalism.

Early in the week after the election, Rudd and Gillard flew to Perth for the funeral of the much-loved journalist Matt Price. He had written entertainingly about politics and that forlorn football hope, the Fremantle Dockers. He died of a brain tumour the day after the election. He had texted Rudd on election night with congratulations. Rudd and Gillard used the time on the plane to discuss the allocation of departmental secretaries with Peter Shergold. Rudd had promised that all departmental secretaries would be retained and given an opportunity to show their ability to serve the new government; it was, he argued, time to restore the Westminster system. He did not want a 'night of the long knives', like the one that Howard had adopted when he fired six departmental secretaries in 1996; it had scarred relations with much of the public service from the beginning. Rudd was, after all, a former bureaucrat and wanted the public service to assist in the plans for reform that the new government had; he had learned from his Queensland experience. Faulkner too had strongly argued the case during the previous two elections. Rudd gave two reasons:

> If you wanted to restore a Westminster public service, then you had to play by those rules and make a specific and decisive point about independence and continuity. The second was that, with our big agenda of policy implementation, we might have sent the place into either structured chaos or personnel-related chaos. I didn't want that.

So he gave the incumbent departmental secretaries the opportunity to prove their professionalism through their performance.

The Prime Minister had to decide where they could be put to the best use. Some were self-evident: the secretaries of Treasury and Finance, both of high repute, kept their positions. Others were harder. By the time the plane reached Perth, the decisions were largely made. Shergold had argued his case and the ministers were told who their secretaries were when their positions were confirmed later in the week. All, that is, except the Prime Minister himself. Shergold had announced earlier that he thought he had served long enough in the position as secretary to PM&C. He now told the government that he was going on leave at the end of December and would not be coming back. PM&C was left without a head at a time most difficult for a new and inexperienced government.

Over the next six weeks, a number of names were considered. The press speculated on whether Glyn Davis would take the job. But he had made it clear that his first commitment was to the University of Melbourne, where he had just made major changes to the degree structure. Ken Henry was mentioned, but his services were needed in Treasury. The best-known state official was Terry Moran, head of the Premier's Department in Victoria, where he had played a significant national role in driving the COAG agenda. Before moving to Victoria he had lived and worked in Brisbane, first as head of the federal Australian National Training Authority and then as head of the Queensland Department of Education. In late January, Moran was invited to The Lodge to discuss the position. He agreed to start in March. However, the space between Shergold's departure and Moran's arrival meant that the Prime Minister was supported in his own department only by deputy secretaries, of whom just one, the Deputy Secretary International, Duncan Lewis, was going to stay. It made for a more difficult transition.

The first international challenge came within a week of Rudd taking office. The Bali Conference on Climate Change was held in December 2007. Rudd had promised to ratify the Kyoto Protocol on climate change immediately; he would therefore go to Bali with the benefit of being the leader who had committed Australia to the international agreements, doing so as soon as he had taken office. He still had to be briefed on the details. So did the new Minister for Climate Change, Penny Wong, who had not expected the portfolio and needed to be across the areas of contention. The briefing in part took place on the VIP plane as they flew to Bali and continued during the conference. Wong was appointed joint chair of a committee responsible for drafting the communiqué, a task that went on into the early hours of the morning. The new government had shown it was different to its predecessor.

On Rudd's first international visit as Prime Minister, he took the opportunity to meet with the Indonesian President, Susilo Bambang Yudhoyono, the Prime Minister of Singapore and the leaders of Papua New Guinea and East Timor, Michael Somare and Xanana Gusmao. If Rudd intended to be an activist prime minister with plans to influence the regional architecture, some level of empathy was useful. In addition, he talked to the heads of two international organisations: the Secretary-General of the United Nations, Ban Ki-moon, and the President of the World Bank, Bob Zoellick, an old friend from the AALD. He was immediately either building new networks or consolidating old ones.

There were two activities where the symbolism was as important as the content. Before the end of December, he met the state premiers and territory chief ministers, all of whom at the time were Labor, at a session of COAG. A new approach to federalism had been at the core of Rudd's election campaign. He promised to end the blame game, to reintroduce notions of cooperation. Many of his commitments, whether to put computers in schools or ensure better health services, would have to be delivered through state governments. One of the premiers noted the precision with which Rudd moved from item to item through the agenda. The problems lay ahead, when state ministers started demanding more money or special treatment.

The second symbolic gesture was an unannounced visit to Iraq and Afghanistan. He flew into Iraq on 21 December to address the troops at Tallil, and then on to Baghdad to meet the Iraqi prime minister, the US ambassador and General Petraeus. He returned via Afghanistan. He met the Australian troops at Tarin Kowt to deliver

Christmas goodwill and stopped briefly in Kabul to meet President Karzai. He was thus able to reassure the troops that a new government appreciated their efforts and had not forgotten their contribution, while seeing for himself the conditions under which they were working, and meeting the leaders the government was supporting.

Prime ministers set the tone and the direction for their governments. One British account from the 1960s described all ministers as the prime minister's agents. Over the years in Australia, a quite formal process developed by which prime ministers could make clear what they expected of the ministers. Under John Howard they were called Charter Letters. They spelled out the responsibilities for portfolio ministers and junior ministers, identified the priorities within the portfolio and established the targets that the ministers were expected to meet. Initially, the Charter Letters were developed after each election, but gradually there was a move to make them annual. They became both a vehicle for the prime minister's priorities to be transmitted to his ministers and a means of accountability and evaluation.

In February, Rudd began a series of portfolio meetings with his ministers. It gave the Prime Minister the opportunity to canvass the main issues, to identify what he saw as priorities and problems, and to make clear what he wanted the ministers to do. He essentially asked three questions: What are the pre-election commitments? What are your other reform proposals for the portfolio? What are the incoming threats that you can anticipate in terms of external events? Here were twenty-one meetings over a two-week period with nineteen ministers. There were two each with Wong and Macklin. On three days, Rudd held four separate meetings with different ministers, a hefty commitment of time and concentration on the future strategy of the government. Faulkner described it later:

> I sat down with the Prime Minister … as I believe most if not all my ministerial colleagues did, and discussed these issues at great length. There are records of those meetings, as I think 'conversation' would not be putting it at a formal enough level. I have a very clear record of those meetings and I am treating that, of course, as a charter in relation to my own conduct of my own ministerial responsibility.

Initially, Rudd announced that he would be issuing Charter Letters, but he changed his mind. He had a 'minute' of the meeting that contained the agreed benchmarks. After all the meetings were held, Rudd decided that the ministers had an adequate set of instructions and there was no need to issue Charter Letters.

Rudd at times showed his disappointment with the advice that the public service provided. He still believed in it as a profession and a calling. He felt that the culture of policy innovation had been

> throttled out of it, to be blunt. I had a halcyon view of the Commonwealth bureaucracy, a policy arcadia, in the Hawke and Keating days of which I was a part, albeit as a relatively junior officer. This was an exciting and innovative time. … (a) that's been drummed out of them and (b) a lot of people who were capable of it were either drummed out or chose to go of their own accord … the bureaucracy after a decade has become a bureaucracy whose job it was to issue-manage, rather than a bureaucracy which is capable of policy innovation.

He felt he had met not malice or political bias, but policy inertia.

He talked to the secretaries at a regular meeting in early February. He explained how he saw the public service as part of the Westminster system, the need to gather ideas from the community and the importance of good delivery of services on the ground. The phrases he used—'the mandarinate', public service 'as a vocation'—reflected his attitude to, and instinctive support for, the public service as a vehicle for change. When on 30 April Rudd more formally addressed a meeting of departmental secretaries, he emphasised his belief in continuity. He proclaimed appreciation of the work that had been done thus far and of the qualities of the public service. He then declared, 'Westminster, by and large, has served our system of government well—and the time has come to rebuild the Westminster tradition in Australia'.

He stressed the need for professionalism and evidence-based policy advice. He declared that 'Public servants will not give frank and fearless advice if they think their career prospects or the continuity of their employment rest on them simply echoing the government's own prejudices'. He used Nugget Coombs as the model to which public servants should aspire. He set a high bar.

When, a couple of months later, there were complaints that he worked the public servants too hard for little return, he was unsympathetic: 'I've news, there's more'. Many senior officials agree. Their role is to serve, and if that brings long hours and high expectations, they will live with it; it is the compact for being partners in the running of the country. But they want to feel their work is at least considered and appreciated too.

11

REACHING OUT

In Opposition, leaders can talk constantly to get their message across and present ideas. But those messages can be no more than promises, aspirations concerning what might be done if they manage to win office. Help is usually welcomed. When government is won, suddenly the relationship is transformed. Governments can deliver. Ideas are needed to determine what the problems are and how they should be tackled. Every new acquaintance has a barrow to push, an idea to promote, an interest to protect. Everyone wants an audience. Ministers have to be careful and selective, without cutting themselves off in a way that isolates them from the opinions of those who elected them.

All prime ministers have to take positive steps to reach out to meet those who might otherwise not get access, both as a source of ideas and as a means to get their message across. Strategies will depend on choice and personality. Rudd used several vehicles, each aimed at a different group and with quite deliberate objectives. He developed new systems, presented symbolic visions, unveiled dramatic initiatives and capitalised on new technology. The first was the Community Cabinets, the second the apology to the stolen generations, the third the 2020 Summit and the last his use of blogging and Twitter to talk to a new, sometimes apolitical, audience.

Community Cabinets became a regular feature of the Labor government; they had been initiated by the Beattie government in Queensland and Rudd decided to develop them in the Commonwealth arena. The Prime Minister and his ministers would meet the public on a regular basis, answering citizen queries. The first Community Cabinet was held in Canning Vale, Western Australia in January 2008, less than two months after the election; it set the form that most others followed. After a Cabinet meeting in the vicinity, Rudd and his ministers trooped in to sit behind a long table. Rudd introduced himself and talked for a short time about the issues of the moment. Then he asked for questions from the floor. As Rudd put it at one Community Cabinet:

> Now it is a very simple system this evening. I am going to move from right to left and as people whack up their hand I'm just going to take a question in sequence from each block and then move back and the rules are very simple. I make them up as I go along and if I can't answer the question directly I will refer it to a minister or you may wish to refer it directly to a minister yourselves and then when the allotted time is up we will then break this part of proceedings and then head off to the individual discussions.

These meetings were genuinely unscripted. Rudd just picked out people with their hands up. It was not possible to anticipate what the questions would be. Rudd answered some himself and referred others to ministers. The Q&A often lasted up to ninety minutes. Then, in the second half of the function, the ministers sat with their departmental secretaries and responded to specific questions about their own portfolios. Citizens had put in requests in advance, saying who they wanted to see and what issue they wanted to discuss. That allowed some research to be done, so that genuine answers could be provided for particular problems. Many departmental secretaries were initially sceptical about a Community Cabinet for a federal government; ministers thought it would take them out of their immediate comfort zone and force them to see the citizens they worked for in their own environment.

By 1 October 2009, seventeen Community Cabinets had been held across all states. The numbers attending varied from 300 to 600, a total of around 8100 people. Over 200 questions were asked from the floor. Ministers held 980 individual meetings. Over 250 inquiries were followed up after the event. The Prime Minister himself had eighty individual appointments in those seventeen Community Cabinets.

Community Cabinets had their political benefits. One of Rudd's entourage recalled a particular meeting at Geelong. A large, gruff man sat down with Rudd and somewhat aggressively asked a question. He seemed dissatisfied with the answer when he wandered off. So an assistant minister approached him to ask if his concern had been satisfied. The response was: 'Mate, the fact that the bloody Prime Minister of the country is prepared to come down here and bloody do this, he's got my bloody vote'.

If the Community Cabinets were to be a running dialogue, the apology on 13 February 2009 was an occasion of drama and symbolism. Whether the government should apologise to the stolen generations of Aboriginal children had been an issue since the publication of a 1997 Human Rights Commission (HRC) report entitled *Bringing Them Home*. Howard had regretted the past but had not been prepared to go further; the apology had become a sticking point that enmeshed Indigenous policy and relations. Rudd had announced that, if elected, he would give an apology on behalf of the nation. It was one of those issues, like the signing of the Kyoto Protocol, where there was a distinction between the two sides of Australian politics.

Rudd worked with Jenny Macklin, the Minister for Indigenous Affairs, to organise the occasion, the first item of business for the newly elected parliament. The new backbencher Mark Dreyfus had been a barrister in one of the related cases, so Rudd sought his advice. He visited Nanna Nungala Fejo, a member of the stolen generations, and talked with her for two hours. She had been taken screaming from her mother outside Tennant Creek in 1932 at the age of four. She never saw her mother again. When the state decided to send the children to missions, they were put into three lines: one declared to be Catholic, a second Methodist and the third Church of England. So as a new Methodist she then was separated from her now Catholic brother.

Rudd related her tragic story to parliament, and told how she emphasised the importance of family and did not want to blame the Aboriginal stockman who had handed her over to the state authorities. He collected opinions through Macklin and William Dean, former High Court judge, governor-general and principal author of the HRC report. Planning was required to bring members of the stolen generations to parliament, and to organise the broadcasting of the event on screens outside. There were also legal issues; Rudd wanted to discover whether the issue of an apology in itself created legal liabilities for the government.

The speech was Rudd's own; he wrote out the initial draft by hand and it remained the core of the delivery. There were several iterations as he talked to people, changed the text, talked to more people and made more changes, even on the morning it was delivered. It was not a speech that could be delegated. The voice to be heard in parliament had to be authentic Kevin Rudd. He moved that today we honour the Indigenous peoples of this land, the oldest continuing cultures in human history.

We reflect on their past mistreatment.

We reflect in particular on the mistreatment of those who were stolen generations—this blemished chapter in our nation's history.

The time has now come for the nation to turn a new page in Australia's history by righting the wrongs of the past and so moving forward with confidence to the future.

We apologise for the laws and policies of successive parliaments and governments that have inflicted profound grief, suffering and loss on these our fellow Australians.

We apologise especially for the removal of Aboriginal and Torres Strait Islander children from their families, their communities and their country.

For the pain, suffering and hurt of these stolen generations, their descendants and for their families left behind, we say sorry.

To the mothers and the fathers, the brothers and the sisters, for the breaking up of families and communities, we say sorry.

And for the indignity and degradation thus inflicted on a proud people and a proud culture, we say sorry.

We the Parliament of Australia respectfully request that this apology be received in the spirit in which it is offered as part of the healing of the nation.

For the future we take heart, resolving that this new page in the history of our great continent can now be written.

He then explained his position: 'There comes a time in the history of nations when their peoples must become fully reconciled to their past if they are to go forward with confidence to embrace their future'. He had promised to say sorry to the stolen generations as a step towards reconciliation, and to do so early in the next parliament. His statement was open and explicit:

> To the stolen generations, I say the following: as Prime Minister of Australia, I am sorry. On behalf of the government of Australia, I am sorry. On behalf of the Parliament of Australia, I am sorry. I offer you this apology without qualification. We apologise for the hurt, the pain and suffering that we, the Parliament, have caused you by the laws that previous Parliaments have enacted. We apologise for the indignity, the degradation and the humiliation these laws embodied. We offer this apology to the mothers, the fathers, the brothers, the sisters, the families and the communities whose lives were ripped apart by the actions of successive governments under successive parliaments.

He reached out to those who had come to Canberra and to those listening across the nation, 'from Yuendumu, in the central west of the Northern Territory, to Yabara, in north Queensland, and to Pitjantjatjara in South Australia'.

> I know that, in offering this apology on behalf of the government and the Parliament, there is nothing I can say today that can take away the pain you have suffered personally. Whatever words I speak today, I cannot undo that. Words alone are not that powerful; grief is a very personal thing.

It was parliamentary drama at the highest level, as the speech was televised across the nation. Many of those watching from the forecourt of Parliament House were in tears. They declared that it would make a difference, that reconciliation would follow. Others, such as Noel Pearson, were more sceptical. Writing the day before, he had asked whether an apology without compensation was adequate.

Rudd also had an eye to the political impact. He sought to incorporate the Opposition into the initiative, announcing that its leader, Brendon Nelson, would be part of a committee to oversee progress. The bipartisanship did not last long. A number of people ostentatiously turned their backs when Nelson spoke, including Rudd's press secretary. Soon afterwards, the adversarial process and debate about what else was required made further bipartisan cooperation difficult and Nelson withdrew from the committee.

Just as dramatic was the announcement of the 2020 Summit. After the election, Rudd had sought to extend his connections beyond his established networks; he wanted to find new sources of ideas. He had asked Glyn Davis to host a number of dinners in Melbourne and had done so himself at Kirribilli House, the Prime Minister's harbourside Sydney residence. He also thought that the public service was not yet providing him with the range of innovative ideas that he wanted. He wanted access to more people more quickly, and to encourage debate. He invited Davis up to Canberra and they worked through the options in classic Rudd style.

Davis recalls that, as they walked around the gardens of The Lodge,

> The Prime Minister had already developed a firm sense of how a summit might run. He said it was time to encourage a national conversation and this is something a new government can only do once and must do early. The choice of ten topics reflected the key issues he felt should dominate national policy discussion, with bullet points under each to ensure as comprehensive coverage as possible. This was a familiar expression of how Kevin Rudd thinks—broadly but systematically.

Once the shape was worked out, Rudd asked Davis to act as co-chair. A week later, Davis flew back to Canberra for a media conference in the courtyard outside the Prime Minister's Office. He used the opportunity to invite Australians to be part of a new policy conversation.

The way the summit was organised gave an insight into Rudd's approach to the problems that his government would face and the priorities he wanted to tackle. There were ten strands:

1. productivity agenda (education, skills, training, sciences and innovation)
2. Australian economy
3. sustainability and climate change (population, sustainability, water)
4. rural Australia
5. health (long-term strategy, preventative health, ageing)
6. communities and family (strengthening communities, supporting families, social inclusion) / Indigenous Australia
7. creative Australia (the future of arts, film and design)
8. the future of Indigenous Australia
9. Australian governance (democracy, open government structure of the federation, rights and responsibilities of citizens)
10. Australia's future in the world.

Each strand had four sections. Here then were the forty areas on which Rudd wanted some thinking done and some ideas proposed. Ten ministers were coupled with ten prominent citizens to drive the debate in each of the strands.

So in April 2008, just after Rudd had returned from his first big overseas tour, 1000 delegates arrived in Canberra for a two-day summit. The government had invited applications and received thousands. It wanted the final groupings to be, in part, representative of all areas, ages and interests. So it tried to appoint a balance.

Rudd and Davis addressed the first plenary session, followed by a keynote speech from Michael Wesley, formerly of Nambour High and then a professor at Griffith University. Then the delegates broke into their ten groups and forty subgroups, working through a more detailed agenda.

Rudd presided, enjoying the debate and the occasion. He moved around the sections, listening to reports and talking to delegates. He promised that the government would respond to the proposals, but the reaction after the event was initial excitement and then a degree of cynicism. All these ideas, many feared, would come to nothing. Rudd and Davis disagreed. Davis commented in 2009:

> A surprising number of the 2020 Summit proposals made it into policy within eighteen months of the event. A number of further important initiatives, such as fully funded care through a no-fault insurance for disability, are still being finalised but seem likely to be adopted. In other areas, the Summit alerted government to concerns about a policy area without necessarily throwing up acceptable or affordable proposals.

What we will never know is how much the subsequent global financial crisis (GFC) cut short action on some recommendations. By the end of the 2020 Summit year, however, all attention had swung over to fiscal policy. Timing is everything in politics, and in public policy.

Rudd was able to use modern media and the internet with a degree of skill that left the Opposition flat-footed. He set up a blog that allowed anyone who registered to receive news alerts. He provided the capacity for citizens to email him and developed a series of live web chats that operated rather like the Community Cabinets. The first topics of these web chats were young Australians and climate change.

He also used Twitter and amassed a large following. His messages went out to reinforce his position. For example, on 28 November 2009, he tweeted:

4.26 Been working on new Commonwealth Declaration on Climate change at CHOGM.

4.26 UN secretary-general, the Danish PM (Chair of Copenhagen Conference) and other countries all working on declaration.

4.26 Queen gave strong speech on need for action.

4.27 Only 21 days to Copenhagen. Further delay and further inaction not an option for Oz or the planet.

Then on 30 November:

5.53 Good meeting today with President Obama in Washington. Long discussion on climate change. Only 18 days to go to Copenhagen.

5.54 All countries now need to push as hard as possible for the strongest global action possible.

5.54 We need it for the environment, the economy, for jobs and our kids.

And on 2 December:

4.15 Back in Oz early this am. Out to a local primary school at Fadden.

4.16 The kids introduced me to the wonders of worm farming, what to do with worm poo—all part of the work for their sustainability ctee.

4.17 Action on climate change now critical for these kids' future.

Rudd used the new technology in part because he was fascinated by it, and in part because it allowed him to reach out to people who might never attend a party meeting or public event and never meet the prime minister. The office gave a degree of gravitas, of awe. Electors do not forget when they have talked to or received messages from the prime minister.

12

PUNCHING ABOVE OUR WEIGHT

Kevin Rudd wanted to change the tenor of Australia's engagement with the world. While he accepted the US alliance as a cornerstone of foreign policy, he believed the country had the opportunity to do more than reflect the interests of the United States. Labor had opposed Australia's participation in the Coalition of the Willing in the war in Iraq, was embarrassed by the Australian Wheat Board scandals and felt that the notion of Australia as a 'deputy sheriff' was an indication of a lack of independence. All those stances were regularly expressed in Opposition.

Rudd wanted to provide a contrast; he thought that Australia should play a constructive and active role as a middle power. To be effective as a middle power, he considered there were two criteria:

> First, sufficient global, regional or local standing to be taken seriously by the other global, regional or local players in bringing about either systemic change to a problem or dealing with, or devising, a different solution to a particular problem. The second thing you need is the intellectual and policy software to develop

the ideas and solutions necessary and negotiate them through the international system.

Australia needed credibility and ideas.

Rudd did not argue that Australia could fix things, but hoped to build a consensus behind the scenes. Furthermore, if much of the drafting of papers was to be done by Australia, he could help to set the terms for that consensus. That required a creative and informed bureaucracy, a network of personal contacts and a consistent drive for impact. Rudd already had a clear vision of what he wanted to achieve, plans that he had developed in Opposition. He also had carefully built networks across the region. He was never going to be an internationally reactive leader or one who was satisfied with one or two main themes.

Australian leaders suffer from the tyranny of distance and time zones. While European and South American leaders have in-built networks through which they see each other on a regular basis, Australia is out of those loops. Rudd argued that, therefore, an Australian leader

> has to work harder and smarter than the rest of the world to be regarded and accepted as a normal player in regional and global deliberations because of the time zones and geographical separations and lack of knowledge of the Australian government position. Smarter: you have to be able to constantly deliver ideas which are not just rants and raves but practical solutions to immediate problems … It is the way to frame agendas. Here is the problem. We have commonly a sense of the problem. How do we define it further? Here is a paper. Here are a range of solutions. Here is what we think we should do. It is an extrapolation of domestic briefing methodology.

Rudd came to office with three distinct and often-repeated pillars of policy. They had been pronounced in 2003 and had remained unchanged. Labor was committed to the American alliance, it sought a deeper involvement in Asia, and it was intent on working with and through multilateral institutions and processes. The question was how the balance between them would be maintained and how each could be advanced. It was also a case of where the ideas would come from.

Rudd had, in some respects, idealised the DFAT that he had left in 1989, an ideal that epitomised a creative, responsive and intellectual public service. Although he had become disillusioned with the lack of impact the department had, others thought that DFAT had been an implicit gold standard for service against which he had judged the Queensland public service, to the detriment of the latter. He believed that was how the public service should work. It may have been nostalgic, but he talked consistently about the Westminster values in public service. A DFAT officer commented that:

> He was soon disappointed. He did not find the Australian Public Service in general, and DFAT in particular, as creative as he had wanted. DFAT had become less effective in the previous years. It was partly driven by the minister. Downer had been foreign minister for a decade and did not see the need for a creative department with policy ideas. Internally, its critics argued, the former secretary, Ashton Calvert, had maintained a tight grip on the department and its proposals; arguments that countered the orthodoxy were said to be discouraged.

Many of the departmental staff wanted to continue to maintain existing relationships within the region and not to disturb the ways things were done.

Rudd was extensively briefed for every overseas visit. An adviser recognised that, while many of the ideas came from Rudd, he sought assistance to develop and consolidate those directions. He needed facts and figures, sometimes a clever form of words. If he was preparing for Question Time, he might want three or four topic sentences, supported by data. According the adviser: 'He much prefers data to argument. I've never known someone so fascinated with data'.

Rudd had a distinctive style of working. One adviser said:

> He thinks about what's the outcome that he wants and works backwards ... how to get there, rather than sort of trying to edge there without really knowing what it is that you want. I think of his method of working as being essentially Socratic. He talks and wants feedback, and he's never happier than when he's in an environment of people whom he trusts and whose views he appreciates, coming back, not negatively, but in a sort of constructive way, and they work together to build ideas. He doesn't just want to know for knowledge's sake. Or, maybe he does want to know for knowledge's sake, but he also wants to know in order to use that information, and ... how it works with global leaders.

The last point was crucial. Rudd, as many leaders do, saw value in personal contacts. There is often camaraderie between national leaders. They see the world from a unique perspective within their countries, a perspective that only their counterparts as national leaders can really understand. They, and they alone, can speak for their countries. The personal chemistry between the Australian prime minister and other national leaders is crucial, as an adviser noted:

> If the chemistry is right, you can pick up the phone with far fewer constraints and barriers than if the chemistry is not right

View across the paddocks to the Rudd family Eumundi share farm. (Courtesy of Loree Rudd)

Father, Bert Rudd, in the caravan during the 1967–68 family trip to Kevin's brother Malcolm's graduation in Melbourne. (Courtesy of Loree Rudd)

Kevin, aged nine, in the 'far paddock' of the farm, during a typical Queensland summer flood. (Courtesy of Loree Rudd)

Kevin, aged 16, with sister Loree. (Courtesy of Loree Rudd)

The Rudd family (from left to right): Malcolm, Greg, mother Margaret, Kevin, Loree. (Courtesy of Loree Rudd)

Kevin and Thérèse at his graduation from ANU, 1981. (Courtesy of Loree Rudd)

Left: Browsing in a tiny bookshop in Gothenburg, Sweden. (Courtesy of Loree Rudd)

Below: After a year as a graduate trainee, Kevin was appointed as a diplomat in Sweden, 1982. (Courtesy of Loree Rudd)

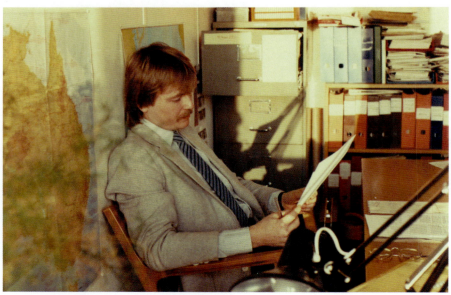

Left: Maiden Speech, House of Representatives, November 1998. (AUSPIC)

Below: Rudd had worked with former Queensland premier, Wayne Goss, as his Principal Private Secretary. Goss showed his support on election night, 2007. (AUSPIC)

The inner circle of the 2007 campaign team, Lachlan Harris, John Faulkner and Alister Jordan on the phone. (AUSPIC)

The Rudd family on election night, 2007 (from left to right): Albert Tse (Jessica's husband), Jessica, Nicholas, Rudd, Thérèse and Marcus. (AUSPIC)

The Apology, 13 February 2008. Rudd with Jenny Macklin and Lowitja O'Donoghue. (AUSPIC)

Five Prime Ministers at The Apology (from left to right): Bob Hawke, Gough Whitlam, Malcolm Fraser, Paul Keating, Kevin Rudd. (AUSPIC)

Rudd and Glyn Davis at the 2020 Summit, April 2008. (AUSPIC)

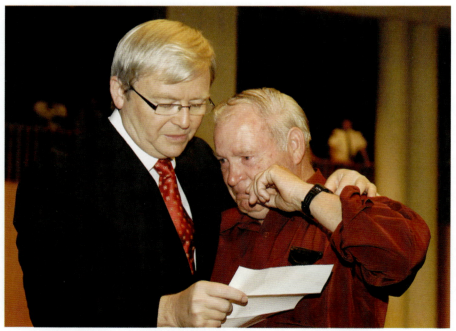

Rudd comforting a member of the 'Forgotten Australians'. (AUSPIC)

A contemplative Prime Minister at the 2020 Summit held in Canberra, April 2009. (AUSPIC)

For better … (AUSPIC)

Or worse. (AUSPIC)

A new system introduced by the Rudd government was the Community Cabinet. This Cabinet was held in Emerald, June 2009. (AUSPIC)

Four key points—with Penny Wong at the Copenhagen Climate Change Conference, December 2009. (AUSPIC)

Greeted by former President of the United States, George W. Bush, at The Oval Office, March 2008. (AUSPIC)

Discussions with former British Prime Minister, Gordon Brown, July 2009. (AUSPIC)

Rudd greeting Indonesian president, Susilo Bambang Yudhoyono, in Bali, December 2007. (AUSPIC)

President of the World Bank, Bob Zoellick, Rudd and UN Secretary Ban Ki-Moon at the Pittsburg Summit, September 2009. (AUSPIC)

President Hu and the Prime Minister at the APEC Summit, 2007. (AUSPIC)

Breakfast with United States President, Barack Obama, November 2009. (AUSPIC)

Before the Pittsburgh Summit Rudd met with former President of the United States, Bill Clinton, September 2009. (AUSPIC)

Rudd, after losing the prime ministership, June 2010. (Cameron Richardson/ Newspix)

Still here: on the backbench, June 2010. (AFP/Newspix)

Re-elected: the twice prime minister. (AAP Image/Lukas Coch)

> ... It is not much use trying to open a sensitive discussion or negotiation with somebody you've either never met or you don't get on with.

That, of course, meant that Rudd had to be well prepared. One adviser was reported as saying, just after a successful meeting with Bill Clinton: 'Whether he sits down with a tea lady or the president, he prepares equally. He doesn't wing it'.

Rudd spoke to some leaders regularly from the beginning. He would ring Gordon Brown in the UK to 'shoot the breeze', to discuss their common problems; the two had quickly found common ground. In Washington he had built on the links he had made through the AALD. He could arrive in town and ring people from both sides of the political divide there. He had known Dick Cheney before he became vice-president. Among the Republicans, he regarded Richard Armitage and Bob Zoellick, now president of the World Bank, as friends. On the Democrat side were Bruce Reed and Kurt Campbell; the latter became the undersecretary for the Asia-Pacific region under President Obama. In China and Indonesia, he had gradually built extensive sets of contacts, some going back a decade.

The first 'grand tour' was scheduled for March and April 2008. He was to visit the United States and the UN, then go on to Europe for a meeting of the European Community, then China. The first stop was Washington and a meeting with President George W Bush. It was sensitive, since Bush and Howard had been close mates, with Howard an enthusiastic member of the Coalition of the Willing in Iraq. For Rudd, the US alliance was also a priority, the keystone of Australian foreign policy. But he wanted it to be reflective, rather than reactive.

The first visit to Washington was important because the links with the US president were always important. Looking back, an adviser noted that the meeting in the White House that we had was a lengthy one-on-one, then followed by a group discussion ... It is important that they have that time together and they are able to sort of identify whether they're kind of travelling soulmates on something or not.

Since the US presidential campaign was underway, Rudd either met or talked to the three candidates still in the race: Democrats Hillary Clinton and Barack Obama, and Republican John McCain.

He used his connections too. Bob Zoellick said:

When the Prime Minister came to Washington, he asked if I could organise a dinner so that he could hear more views from the US about the crisis. So I invited Larry Summers and the chairman of CEA [Council of Economic Advisers], but also some economic journalists and one or two policy professors, and a thoughtful former colleague from Wall Street. We had a very engaging dinner conversation; it gave him a chance to pick people's brains but also gave them a chance to see that he's [a] very sharp leader on the cutting edge of thinking how to solve problems.

Thereafter Rudd flew to Brussels for a meeting with the European Community, then attended a session in Romania before heading back to Britain to talk to Prime Minister Gordon Brown for the first time and to attend a meeting of the Progressive Governance Summit, where he sat on a panel with Chile's Michelle Bachelet.

China was the next stop, one that was watched with particular interest. Rudd had chatted in Mandarin with President Hu both in the Australian Parliament and at APEC. Would he be too soft on China? What would he say about human rights, particularly in Tibet, where there were growing demonstrations against the Olympic torch relay?

His first public appearance was at Beijing University, where he gave a speech in Mandarin and answered questions from the students with a relaxed fluency. He explained what he thought Australia's position should be. It was to be not an unquestioning ally but a critical friend, speaking the truth even when it was unwelcome:

> A true friend is one who can be a '*zhengyou*', that is, a partner who sees beyond immediate benefit to the broader and firm basis for continuing, profound and sincere friendship. In other words, a true friendship which offers unflinching advice and counsels restraint to engage in principled dialogue about matters of contention. It is this kind of friendship that I know is treasured in China's political tradition. It is the kind of friendship I offer China today.

For Rudd, China always presented a challenge. Because he spoke Mandarin, some critics thought he would get too close to China, even while problems between the two countries and economies emerged. Rudd, experienced in the mores of the country, had fewer illusions: he thought it necessary to be clear-cut about the areas where he disagreed and then navigate those waters; there was the danger of self-censorship.

As soon as he returned to Australia, Rudd was accused of snubbing Japan by visiting China first. When he continued to travel to meet leaders, it led to the inevitable quip that Kevin07 had morphed into Kevin747.

Rudd decided that Australia would seek a position on the UN Security Council, a position it had not held since 1986. He worked out a strategy for calculating support and identifying who could best talk to the relevant leaders. He shrugged off criticism from the media and within government that it was a forlorn hope and likely to be expensive, as Australia would have to canvass for votes. It was precisely the type of negative response that he found unsatisfactory.

Regional engagement has always been a Labor priority, as Australia has struggled to be accepted as a full member of the regional groupings. APEC had been one of the arenas where Australia was able to sit at the table with the big powers. Rudd had identified, in his maiden speech in 1998, the need for improved regional cooperation, although he hoped then that APEC might develop into a more useful vehicle. However, APEC had remained primarily concerned with economics. He thought there was no forum that had as comprehensive a membership as APEC and covered security. He wanted to explore whether a new forum could be developed for that purpose. There was nothing new about his belief in this initiative. Within government, a series of discussions were held to see how it might be managed.

In June, Rudd asked Dick Woolcott, the former head of DFAT, to lead the initiative. Woolcott had been the head of the department when Rudd had gone on leave in 1989 and had recommended Rudd to Phil Scanlan, who was then establishing the AALD, as a person who might be departmental head in fifteen years' time. In the ensuing years, the two had got to know each other much better, with Rudd often having dinner in the Woolcott household while he was Canberra.

Rudd's logic was that none of the existing organisations had the broad membership or the mandate to deal with all the economic, political and security issues that he wanted to discuss. India was not in APEC. Russia and the United States were not members of the East Asian Summit. Any effective security organisation had to include them all. There had to be discussions at the head-of-government level. So Rudd commissioned Woolcott to consult the other countries in the region, to discover whether they thought a new body should be developed and what sort of arrangements such a body might require.

Woolcott visited twenty-one countries and talked to over 300 people: sometimes heads of state, sometimes prime ministers, many of them officials. He presented a final report to the government in March 2008. His remit emphasised that Australia wanted to play a constructive role in the region.

Rudd addressed the issues in the report in a speech at the Shangri-La Dialogue in Singapore on 29 May 2009:

> I look forward to a free-flowing and open discussion about our region, its future and the institutions we might need to maximise our future peace and prosperity.
>
> There will inevitably be disagreement along the way. This is natural and normal ... That is why I have deliberately set a target of an Asia-Pacific community by 2020: comfortably removed from the present but still sufficiently close to focus our collective mind.

His thinking was intended to be long term. While he acknowledged that there was no desire for another organisation, he did see the need for a continuing discussion about appropriate forums for debate. He followed up the ideas with letters to heads of state. The Asia-Pacific community did not appear, at that moment, to be a high priority, but the need for some such body was clearly put on the table. In December 2009, Australia hosted a conference in Sydney; the delegates included officials and academics from across the region. Some of those who had at first condemned the initiative as hubris now thought it might eventually come to something. Others, particularly those from Singapore, were still hostile. There were clear divisions among delegates about where the next steps might lead, and how much support the plan had.

Rudd also asked Gareth Evans, former Labor foreign minister and for the previous ten years the chief executive of the International

Crisis Group in Brussels, to head a commission to explore the global prospects for nuclear non-proliferation and disarmament. He argued the region simply could not afford to not evolve: 'In fact I believe this is potentially dangerous. We do not bring to the table a misty-eyed idealism about some pan-regional utopia'. He thought there needed to be 'a high degree of structured regional and global engagement'. Evans delivered his report late in 2009. Rudd launched it with the new Prime Minister of Japan, Yukio Hatoyama. Rudd praised the report and sent a copy to Obama.

Some observers close to DFAT suggested that both initiatives created a certain amount of anxiety. An active prime minister with a belief in shifting the status quo made the routine management of the regional relations a little harder. In late 2009, Rudd appointed Dennis Richardson, former ASIO head and ambassador to the United States, as head of department in the expectation that he would act as a change agent.

Rudd was also Chair of the Pacific Islands Forum (PIF), a meeting of Pacific Islands among whom Australia itself is the superpower. He secured agreement that all governments would submit a national plan to the forum secretariat. There would be peer review of those national plans. When the donors came to the region (and some of these were the big players: the EU, Japan and China), they would be required to explain to the forum secretariat how their donations fitted with the regional plan and the national plan. These initiatives evoked a degree of enthusiasm. Instead of the traditionally long silences that used to dominate the leaders' retreat, the activity was described as helter-skelter. Rudd was serious about finding out what others wanted and harnessing that for something everyone would be happy with.

He was able to use his connections with the World Bank to develop aid to the Pacific Islands, to help resettle refugees, and to organise trust funds so that small, fragile states would not have to deal with twenty or thirty donor countries but could work through one neutral multilateral organisation. Australia contributed to a World Bank Trust Fund for this purpose.

Each of these initiatives was, in Rudd's view, an exercise of middle-power diplomacy where Australia could use its position and talent to influence the debates, and structure the way that problems were conceptualised and shaped.

He also had to deal with the great powers. This took place against a backdrop of looming financial disaster and economic uncertainty, as the prospects within the United States had become grim since the collapse of global investment bank Bear Stearns in March 2008. When Rudd spoke at the UN in September 2008, just after financial services company Lehman Brothers had gone broke, he appealed to the memories of Bretton Woods in proposing that the GFC provided a new opportunity for collective action. What was required was 'political will exercised through ministerial forums working in cooperation with the IMF, the Financial Stability Forum and the G-20. The G-20 is well placed to provide political authority to have these actions implemented urgently and comprehensively'. He promised that Australia would work with the incoming chairs of the G-20, and that the G-20 Finance Ministers' meeting in November was an important opportunity to review progress. He also referred to climate change, terrorism and Afghanistan, nuclear weapons, Doha and the Millennium Development Goals, and Australia's candidacy for a seat on the Security Council.

Later in the year there was further strain. Bush rang Rudd during a dinner party at Kirribilli, attended among others by Chris Mitchell, editor of *The Australian*. The next day *The Australian* ran a story that reported Bush had not known what the G-20 was. The Prime Minister's Office denied that any such comment was made; so did the White House. But the story ran and ran, with widespread speculation about who actually said what. It did not help good relations. When Rudd visited Washington in November for a G-20 meeting, the press commented on the somewhat abrupt way in which Bush appeared to welcome Rudd to the White House.

If overseas visits were one illustration of Rudd's international interests, they were reflected internally in late 2008 by two white papers, one on defence, the other on security. The former was officially the responsibility of the Minister for Defence. Security was the Prime Minister's. Both were considered in detail by the National Security Committee (NSC), which had sent them back for further work on a number of occasions.

The Defence White Paper emphasised the potential power of China in the region and also proposed the building of an extensive naval fleet, including twelve submarines. As Rudd later explained:

> Australia is also a strong believer in the importance of military cooperation and military transparency as contributing to long-term security. That is why Australia is building on our already strong defence and security relationships around the region. And it is why we have recently released Australia's first Defence White Paper in nearly a decade.
>
> If sovereign states are clear about their strategic perceptions and their military forces, the risk of miscalculation is reduced. The White Paper is a frank document that describes how we see the world and how we are shaping our military forces to respond to possible challenges ahead.

The white paper reaffirmed that the alliance with the United States was the bedrock on which Australia's national security was built, and that Australia wanted the United States to maintain its presence in the Asia-Pacific region. It emphasised Australia's maritime interests, with the need to conduct independent military operations in the defence of the country by controlling both air and sea approaches, and denying any potential adversary the ability to operate in our immediate neighbourhood. Australia also needed effective regional institutions.

The National Security Statement was, in part, a response to the decision not to create a Department of Homeland Security. In mid-2008, Rudd presented to parliament what he described as the first coherent statement of the security challenges facing Australia and the coordinated response the government proposed to develop. He identified the most obvious issues of importance, of which the US–China relationship was at the top. He listed the varied organisations, from defence forces to police to intelligence services, that assisted in keeping Australia safe. Rudd accepted the recommendation of the Ric Smith report to establish an Office of National Security within PM&C. Most significantly, a national security adviser was created who would be the Prime Minister's go-to person for advice. A deputy secretary of PM&C, Duncan Lewis, was appointed. Lewis had been a former SAS commander and was well respected in Defence by both the civilian and military wings. He was to serve as the de-facto Chair of the Senior Committee on National Security (SCNS), which pre-digested all items that went to the NSC and provided support for its meetings. Lewis was to be responsible for coordinating intelligence and responses to crises.

Rudd's advisers argued that, as a leader, he was difficult to categorise because he saw the world as complex. That was not because he did not stand for anything. An adviser commented:

> He knows what he stands for, but it's not always necessarily well understood across the board ... Because he is a very complex individual, there's no doubt about it, and he's extraordinarily

knowledgeable. He knows a lot about a lot, and that's a good thing. You'd hope that your national leader did know a lot about a lot, but he is a particularly studious and scholarly sort of individual.

Australian prime ministers are often seen to be trying to inflate their own influence. They can translate diplomatic welcomes into signs that their views matter to great powers. International visits to the White House or Number 10 as a head of state allow Australian prime ministers to talk to the world's leaders, but influence cannot be taken for granted. Access has to be translated into impact. Every prime minister gets access; not all become part of the world's inner circles.

Rudd wanted to run an active international agenda because he thought Australia could contribute and because he felt comfortable in the role. By the end of September 2008, most of the initial proposals were underway, but they were then overtaken by new economic challenges. Rudd did not give up on those initiatives, but he found himself playing on a more pressing field.

13

FACING THE GLOBAL CRISES

There is a traditional view concerning Australian politics that Labor governments are profligate with taxpayers' money. It was born of the Whitlam government and takes no account of the way in which Hawke and Keating reoriented and opened up the Australian economy. In 2007 the economy was booming and the Howard ministers argued that it was no time to entrust the economy to an inexperienced Labor team. Rudd responded by insisting that he was a fiscal conservative. Initially, he argued that Australia should stay in surplus. He wanted to do things differently from his predecessor, but within the limits that could be interpreted as fiscally and economically conservative. His platform plea—'This madness has to stop'—was designed to finally dispel the idea that Labor governments are irresponsible and cannot be trusted to manage the Australian economy.

His economic briefing started immediately. Although not as conversant with economics as with other subjects, he began immediately to learn. As one adviser noted, while some leaders want to play to their strengths and leave other complex or technical areas to their ministers, Rudd was not prepared to do that. He believed that, unless he understood the economics, he was not going to be able to command in the crises. So he read widely, not only policy briefs but also clippings from financial journals and articles; he wanted to draw information out of all those around him. His learning process was always organised. The adviser said:

> He has a mind like a mobile phone menu. So he thinks of things, he says, right, there are five issues and you scroll the menu and click on one. Then underneath that you get five more, and you click on one and underneath that are five more and you choose one of those.

Rudd broke ideas into categories and subcategories and thought in those terms. Sometimes he read a book and then wanted to know what implications the author's insights might have. While on holiday, he would ask for a reading list and then commission a paper on, using Donald Rumsfeld's description, the 'known unknowns', what might occur and what impact might ensue.

Some advisers quickly got the message that the process of briefing was, in effect, an economics seminar. One said:

> I have heard him many times say, 'Why do people keep coming to me with problems? I want then to come to me with solutions' … he's not going to be at all interested in the solution till he understands the problem inside out … he has a greater need for that than any other [prime minister] I've encountered.

Others did not realise it and continued to treat briefings as a policy development exercise rather than an economics tutorial dressed up as a policy development process; they could find it frustrating that every meeting did not lead to instructions.

Rudd wanted to tackle areas like economics or climate change head-on. He needed to know the connections, the logic, not just for his own satisfaction but so that he could present the cases. He would say to his advisers: 'I have to understand the links and the connections because I am going to go out there and explain this. I have to announce it and so I have to understand it'. He would run through the logic and then ask if he had it right. As an adviser said, 'It's a testing of ideas, a testing of understanding. That comes at the end. In the lead-up he is actually dissecting the issue and understanding its causes'.

Some advisers question whether a prime minister needs to know the economic logic. Many leaders will skate over those details and take the formulations they are presented on trust. However, Rudd was not comfortable until he understood. 'Sometimes I felt like saying "Because it just is"', said an adviser. But, as an economist, the adviser accepted that he had a model in his head that could link the data in a particular way, and Rudd did not. Indeed, the absence of such a model meant that Rudd sometimes asked questions that a trained economist might not, leading to some interesting discussions. He had to make the connections for himself: 'I don't like givens; it also allows me to strip away much of the superfluous language from the core logic of what was going on'.

It was Rudd in typical mode: start with a broad approach and then drill down into whichever policy areas are likely to be significant. Since economic crisis seemed likely, he needed to master the topic at a level of detail that ensured he could speak with confidence. He explained his thinking:

> If you are in the business of national or international political leadership, you ... have to deal in specifics, talk about financial market reform as it affects capital adequacy ratios; you've got to know what they are talking about ... It doesn't mean you would have done a Masters in it, but it means you've got to know what

the problems are, what are the possible solutions and why you are using this solution and not others, what are the range of costs and how you measure them.

Even if, as Prime Minister, he could not afford to let other topics slide, he drove his advisers relentlessly, asking for more information, more explanations and more papers.

Economics was so central to government reputation that Rudd was always involved and kept informed. Even as Wayne Swan grew in confidence, it was a joint endeavour. In Britain, when close friends Tony Blair and Gordon Brown split over the party leadership, with the more senior Brown feeling he had been unfairly bypassed, the animosity infected the Blair government. As Chancellor, Brown ran a parallel court, insisting on his economic predominance and constantly undermining Blair. They were the core of government: fighting, cooperating, ever competing. It was a rivalry of legend. In Australia at different times, the Hawke–Keating and Howard–Costello duets were sometimes cooperative and constructive, often discordant and dysfunctional, albeit not so much in the first term of their governments.

Rudd and Swan were determined there would be no repeat of this. What to do with Swan had been a key decision for Rudd when he won the leadership. Swan had been Shadow Treasurer, a dogged and effective parliamentary performer who could niggle Treasurer Peter Costello. Rudd appointed him Treasurer, both as a sign that the commitment to 'no recriminations' would be honoured and because Swan was a hard worker, desperate to be a member of a Labor government. Gradually over the next twelve months, more cordial relations developed. Indeed, by this time, with the emergence of Rudd and Gillard as Labor stars, Swan's ambitions may have been tempered. Before the election, Swan was confirmed in his position—if Labor won, he would be Treasurer.

Initially, Swan was hesitant in parliament and struggled in press conferences. But by the time of the GFC, his confidence had grown. He was well supported. He became more confident in Question Time. In government, Rudd and Swan—and significantly also their principal staff and departments—began to work together closely.

Preparations for the 2008 Budget began immediately. There were clouds on the economic horizon. The sub-prime crisis in the United States was unfolding, but there remained the hope that it would be restricted to that one country. In February 2008, the British Government had to take over the failed Northern Rock Bank. However, the Australian economy was still growing, with interest rates rising, and a fear that it was reaching full capacity. The government's initial objectives were to dampen inflation and increase productivity. It established Infrastructure Australia and Skills Australia to advise on means of easing bottlenecks and increasing skills. The early discussions, particularly with the Cabinet's Expenditure Review Committee (ERC), were about the level of the cuts that might be required. The emphasis was on getting interest rates down.

Only gradually did doubts emerge. Every night Rudd was given a collation of economic data from the world's financial media. It raised questions for him. In February 2008, on a flight from Gladstone, Rudd asked Ken Henry to look at some of the eventualities that might occur over the next year: to survey the known unknowns. He asked big questions: What were the possible consequences of the problem in the US economy? If everything went bad, what would happen in Australia? What were the contingency plans? Rudd liked to be prepared. The advice then was that the deterioration in the US economy would not be a fundamental problem for Australia.

The collapse of Bear Stearns in March 2008 raised more warning signs. Rudd and Swan travelled to the United States in April, where they were briefed on the potential dangers of the oncoming crisis and its likely broad impact across the globe. Talks at the World Bank and the International Monetary Fund (IMF) uncovered a degree of pessimism. There were conflicting currents. When Rudd and Swan came back to Australia, both required that the depth of budget cuts be lessened, even though they were in no position to explain to the public what the fears might be, lest they become self-fulfilling. They did not want to discover that deep cuts would then stall the economy if the global crisis hit. They did not want to talk the economy down. Rather, they provided for a large surplus and sought to use it for nation-building schemes.

During the Australian winter, the American economy floundered. The two big mortgage companies, Freddie Mac (Federal Home Loan Mortgage Corporation) and Fanny Mae (Federal National Mortgage Association), needed to be rescued by the US Government. The big insurer AIG (American International Group) was also in trouble. On the other hand, Chinese demand for iron ore remained high, so for a while Australia was insulated.

Then, in September 2008, Lehman Brothers became insolvent. The US Government decided not to develop a rescue package, as it had done in other cases, and all hell broke loose. A week later, Rudd was in New York to give a speech at the United Nations. He used the opportunity to talk about the looming economic crisis. It was, he argued, a consequence of the rapid globalisation of the economy without the development of an adequate global regulatory framework. There had also been a globalisation of security and of the environment. So, he argued, the community of nations had to respond. He proposed that all important financial institutions be regulated (including investment banks and hedge funds), that a capital buffer be built up and that the IMF be given a strengthened mandate. He advocated the need to revamp the global rules and regulations. He wanted to be part of the process of responding to the crisis. While in New York, he talked widely with bankers and economists.

When the world economy hit a wall in early October, the government had to react. On 7 October, the Reserve Bank of Australia (RBA) cut interest rates, and the Strategic Priorities and Budget Committee (SPBC) of Cabinet held its first crisis meeting. A number of small banks were in trouble. Over the weekend, the SPBC was in almost continuous session, whether formally in the Cabinet Room or swirling across the corridor in informal meetings in and around the PMO. One insider said: 'That was the time we went into hyperdrive, and the PM in particular'. SPBC was the de-facto inner Cabinet. It consisted of the Prime Minister, Deputy Prime Minister, Treasurer and Minister for Finance. They were supported by the heads of PM&C, the Treasury and Finance, and by a number of key advisers: Epstein, Jordan, Phillip and Charlton from the PMO, Chris Barrett and Jim Chalmers from the Treasurer's office, and Anthony Baker from the Minister for Finance's office. The SPBC had a core membership and a floating support group. Everyone contributed to the debates, but the ministers made the decisions. The committee met as required and at short notice. Because of its personnel, what SPBC decided in a time of crisis could be taken to be the policy of the government. Other ministers were brought into the meetings if there were potential impacts on their portfolio. So Albanese was involved when an infrastructure stimulus was under consideration.

The crisis hit while Swan was in Washington at a meeting of the IMF, so the SPBC met in the Cabinet room, with Swan a disembodied voice over a phone loudspeaker. He and Chalmers were working from the bedroom of the Minister-Counsellor's son in the Washington embassy, because that was where they could access a secure phone line. He was able to provide real-time reports on what was happening in other developed economies. The message was 'This is a catastrophe'. It was clear that developing nations, too, would be affected and it was uncertain how much China would suffer, or what the consequential impact on the Australian economy might be.

Essentially, in crises of this sort, the number of participants solving the problem will be few. While the principals meet in constant session, there is little time to brief others, to commission research, to draft detailed briefs. Timeliness requires immediate discussion, so the same few people become responsible all the time.

On the day of the crisis, no-one quite knew what was happening. It was, according to one witness, 'one of those fundamentally buttock-clenching moments', when everything was uncertain. What would the next weeks, days, even hours, bring? What to do? Would it work? The Reserve Bank had cut interest rates. The dollar was falling spectacularly. The committee had to make decisions on the basis of limited and ever-changing information. The circumstances were seen as new; there were no precedents that could comfortably be used as examples of good policy. The ministers were, as they saw it, looking into the abyss. The problem was that the international credit system had ground to a halt. There was a freeze on international lending. Australia had a large current account deficit. The Australian banks relied on overseas borrowing to keep the wheels turning. Car dealers needed to borrow money to cover the stock on the sales floor; these credit schemes were taken for granted, until they were threatened. Overseas banks were collapsing and there were fears that a run on the banks would undermine their buoyancy. Iceland's economy was in freefall. Australian banks were getting calls from customers asking if their money was safe. The Irish Government had guaranteed deposits in their banks, leading to a transfer of funds there by those worried about losing all their savings. Other nations were following this precedent. The fear was that the Australian economy would hit a wall, too, leading to a sudden cessation of activity, to unemployment and to recession.

It appeared to be the greatest economic crisis since the Great Depression of 1929, when cuts in government spending deepened the problem. No-one's personal experience went that far back. At one stage Rudd asked what the advisers had learned from the 1991 recession and, if anyone could remember, the one in the early 1980s. Several officials in the room could remember 1991. The Treasury had, on a couple of occasions in previous years while the economy was flourishing, 'gamed' the next economic crisis. Without knowing in what form the crisis might appear, they had tried to identify the best strategies and estimate the impact of the alternative responses. That preparation was now useful. They understood the lags that occurred when fiscal or monetary solutions were adopted. Currency variations, falling interest rates and infrastructure spending would all be levers to be used to stimulate the economy, but they would take time to have an impact. By the time they had an effect in 1993, some six months after they were introduced, the worst of the recession was over. On this occasion, six months seemed too far away. The period between October and the time that traditional methods might work was seen as a Valley of Death. The challenge was to determine what could be done to get through that period.

Precision in forecasts was impossible. Events were moving fast. No-one knew what would happen even in the next twenty-four hours. Treasury developed a series of forecasts, trying to estimate the impact of the crisis on the Australian economy. Advisers were in contact with colleagues in overseas governments to discover what they were planning to do. Responses ranged from the optimistic to the dire. Should the government wait to see what happened or should it seek to pre-empt? If the government chose to act, it had to decide what was going to happen and respond accordingly. The Treasury believed the downside risks of doing nothing were enormous.

The advice from Treasury Secretary Ken Henry was 'go early, go hard, go households'. Rudd determined to assume the worst and to pre-empt. His thinking was: 'If you are going to have an effect, then do what is necessary to have an effect'. Even if, at the time, the Treasury figures did not yet support the direst of the forecasts, Rudd decided that that was the eventuality that policy should be designed to guard against. It was an intuitive judgement, a sense that the meltdown could be worse than people expected. There was so much uncertainty that it was better to go hard. It was a bold decision; there were plenty of people around the table who were uncomfortable because they were not used to such dramatic action. In the event, the direst forecasts proved to be the most accurate. Rudd's instinct was justified.

The SPBC made a series of decisions in those first few days. It agreed to guarantee all bank deposits, a total of $800 billion. It also guaranteed the funds raised by Australian banks from offshore markets so that foreign lenders would continue to provide credit to the Australian banks. It knew that it would be criticised because it supported bank deposits and not those in other financial institutions, but did not see any option when other countries were acting in the same way. It decided to provide a $10.4 billion stimulus package to ensure that the economy kept moving. The best way to keep the economy on the move was to send cheques to the people who needed them the most and were the most likely to spend them. They included pensioners, carers and families with children.

These were not simple solutions and much of the detail was contested: the nature and urgency of the challenges, the size and composition of the stimulus, its likely effect. Rudd was always the person who wanted to prepare for the worst-case scenario. As one economic adviser remembers: 'The worst cases were constantly being proven to be the right ones. The IMF kept re-forecasting and then every forecast was too optimistic, they kept making it worse. He [Rudd] was pushing Treasury to go harder'.

Rudd acted before most other countries did, and went further than they did. One observer argued that in responding to crisis, many people worry about what might happen if they are a little wrong in their responses. Rudd, he suggested, thought about all those potential problems but still acted: 'This is a man who thinks that the danger of getting it wrong by being too conservative is greater [than by being too bold] and acts on that basis'.

He wanted to know the full range of possibilities, no matter how unlikely. He wanted to prepare for the 'full spectrum of missiles that could hit us from every possible direction'. He was prepared for the worst. An adviser noted:

> The strong view of the Prime Minister was that, regardless of what Treasury's forecast might be saying about the state of the economy, there was not a high degree of certainty because nobody really knew, we were in uncharted waters and pre-empting was better than waiting.

That October weekend demonstrated one basic truth. The number of people who were likely to be involved in managing economic crises was small: the ministers, their senior staff and the top officials. As one official said: 'You can have all these vast bureaucracies but at the end of the day, particularly in a crisis situation, it's only a few that actually are doing the work and it becomes done at the high level of the organisation. It couldn't be done any other way'.

The combination of a policy seminar technique and the need for speed meant that the officials around the table had to have the technical skills to estimate the consequences of the different options under consideration. This was never the Prime Minister alone. He worked with his key ministers: Swan, Gillard and Tanner. He listened, argued, considered. After a long period in which there were divisions between prime ministers and their treasurers, in this government, at least at this time, they were working closely together. There is a traditional budget occasion when the prime minister and treasurer stand on a little table in the Cabinet anteroom and thank the Treasury staff for their labours. Rudd did it again after the pressure of the October package. This time he bought a copy of John Maynard Keynes's *General Theory of Employment, Interest and Money*, inscribed it to Ken Henry with the comment that he might be needing it, and presented it to him.

In the meantime, the SPBC needed to know what was going on in the world. The world's economy worked during the Australian night. By the time ministers came to work, the previous day's global disasters could be identified. So Rudd instituted a daily meeting to brief senior economic ministers on the events of the previous day. He equated it to a rolling security crisis. A Treasury officer, starting work very early, coordinated the data into a coherent account. Another Treasury officer, based in Washington, would send back details daily about financial markets, and about retail figures in Europe and the United States. They monitored finance companies and car finance, hence the push to establish the OzCar scheme, to provide support for dealers, so that they could continue to present stock on the floor. The discussions were often detailed; one small finance company under threat was discussed four times. One official said: 'The PM likes to go into frenzied detail on all these sorts of things'. The intent was to develop a daily 'dashboard' of everything economic. Rudd said he wanted 'to be sure that we had identified everything that could possibly have implications for Australian financial markets, and that we had the full toolkit that might be required to respond to developments'. The officials then had to work out what might happen down the track. Decisions had to be made on whether to act, what sort of action might be taken and with what weight.

So at 8 a.m. every morning from 20 October, Rudd, Swan and their principal advisers met the heads of Treasury and PM&C for a briefing on the events around the world and the likely implications. Sometimes junior Treasury ministers were also invited to attend. Sometimes it was, in part, linked by video. The meeting lasted as long as was necessary, generally thirty minutes or so, sometimes longer, as

Rudd and Swan asked questions about the data and its implications. The process was structured. Treasury would do a brief on overnight events. Rudd would systematically follow up ongoing issues or developing problems, asking what progress had been made. There was concern about the consequences of the bank guarantee, concern about Ford and GM dealerships. Mortgage brokers were going out of business. Some managed investment funds were freezing redemptions.

Occasionally the meeting would be held in Sydney, or wherever the Prime Minister was for the day. The meetings continued until the end of the year, when the more immediate pressures seemed to be off, and by the end of January they had stopped. Three months of daily briefings was an indication of the concerns that the government held as it entered that Valley of Death. In addition, on a daily basis when parliament was sitting, Rudd had to be briefed for Question Time, using the latest economic data and overseas reports to best effect.

The first economic stimulus package in October 2008 was designed to put money where it was most likely to be immediately spent. Thus much of the $10.4 billion was directed to tax payers in the form of cash bonuses and to boosting the First Home Owners Grant. As an adviser explained:

> The fastest thing you can do is just push this money out the door. Now, of course, the advice was: if you're going to stimulate the economy, spend it on good-quality things—spend it on infrastructure, roads and bridges. Now that's all very fine, but then you get the problem we had in the early 1990s. The stimulus spending focused on grand infrastructure was too late; the money didn't start to flow for two years after the recession had finished. So, very early action. There was a sense we had to do something fast, this was the way to do it. We announced it on the Tuesday after doing the bank guarantee on Sunday night. Extraordinarily,

breathtakingly bold action. There were a lot of very nervous bureaucrats.

Over the medium term, infrastructure was an obvious possibility, and Rudd instructed that proposals be brought forward. 'Shovel ready' projects were hard to find. Others might take some months to get approval. Immediacy was the most important criterion. A second round of stimulus expenditure, $4.7 billion, came in December and mostly focused on transport infrastructure projects.

In January, Rudd took a holiday, spent mostly at Kirribilli House in Sydney, where he did a huge amount of reading. He also wrote an essay for *The Monthly*, 'The Global Financial Crisis'. He sought to make the case that the old neo-liberal orthodoxy that had underpinned economic policy had been discredited, that the move to deregulate had failed: 'It is a crisis which is at once institutional, intellectual and ideological'. Social democratic governments were now called on to 'save capitalism from itself'. However, he argued, the challenge for social democrats was

> to advance the case that the social-democratic state offers the best guarantee of preserving the productive capacity of properly regulated competitive markets, while ensuring that *government* is the regulator, that *government* is the funder or provider of public goods, that *government* offsets the inevitable inequalities of the market with a commitment of fairness to all. Social democracy's continuing philosophical claim to political legitimacy is its capacity to balance the private and the public, profit and wages, the market and the state.

He also argued the need for 'global co-operation if governments are to prevail in their task'.

In part, the essay sought to demolish the neo-liberal intellectual structure, particularly its insistence that labour was no different from any other commodity. His conclusion was that

> [t]he time has come, off the back of the current crisis, to proclaim that the great neo-liberal experiment of the past 30 years has failed, that the emperor has no clothes. Neo-liberalism, and the free market fundamentalism it has produced, has been revealed as little more than personal greed dressed up as an economic philosophy. And, ironically, it now falls to social democracy to prevent liberal capitalism from cannibalising itself.

Social democracy could now be presented as a white knight coming to the rescue, with its belief that 'the pursuit of social justice is founded on the argument that all human beings have an intrinsic right to human dignity, equality of opportunity and an ability to lead a fulfilling life'.

Rudd used the opportunity to argue for an international solution based on three principles: that national financial markets need effective national regulation; that global financial markets need effective global regulation; and that the means for achieving effective regulation can only be achieved by national governments working together, hence the need for action through the multilateral channels of the G-20.

He quoted with approval American historian Arthur Schlesinger Jr's definition of a political economy cycle as 'a continuing shift in national involvement between public purpose and private interest'. Now social democrats had to harness the creative energy of government: 'Government is not the intrinsic evil that neo-liberals have argued it is. Government, properly constituted and properly directed, is for the common good, embracing both individual freedom and fairness, a project designed for the many, not the few'.

Rudd used the opportunity to restate, in terms reminiscent of his maiden speech, his belief in the proper role of the state. His opening words then were: 'Politics is about power. It is about the power of the state. It is about the power of the state as applied to individuals, the society in which they live and the economy in which they work'. Now he was seeking to explain how he was exercising that state power.

In late January he set off on a tour of Australia, talking about the economy, while keeping in contact with other world leaders, encouraging them to take action through the G-20.

In February, what had been done was seen not to be enough. The earlier packages might have kept the economy above water, but the news from overseas continued to be dire. The collapse seemed to be longer and deeper than people had feared. So Rudd determined that the government could not wait for the 2009 Budget to provide a further impetus and that more had to be done. A third package was developed on the run as the Prime Minister, in normal mode, zigzagged across the country.

The SPBC and their advisers effectively followed him around, grabbing time where they could, often on planes, to discuss the options. There were meetings in all the capital cities. They had to be short and rapidly effective. The third package targeted schools, services housing, home insulation, universities and personal cheques to taxpayers. Schools were the simplest. The government, even if it was a state government, owned them and could move quickly to start building halls or classrooms. They would be spread around the nation, providing opportunities in the regions and the cities. Cheques for $900 to taxpayers below a certain income provided another way of keeping spending up. Rudd says:

> Cash payments were the short fuse, to support the economy this month, and next month and the month after. Local infrastructure

projects, grants to first-home buyers, an investment tax break for small business, service housing and school maintenance projects to support the economy in three to six months. School building to support the economy in six to twelve months. Then long-term infrastructure to support the economy beyond that. There was this trade-off between timeliness and worthiness.

No-one really knew if it would work, but it was the best solution they could see for the rapid action required.

The test was to be whether Australia withstood the expected recession and came out in a good position. In developing the package, the government knew the risks. They anticipated many of the criticisms of their opponents. If speed was essential, then inaccuracies that might not be found in a more measured scheme had to be borne. Some needy non-taxpayers missed out; some people who got the cheques had moved overseas; others had died. But the best way the government could think of to determine recipients was to use the previous year's tax returns. They knew there would be some problems. The proposal that the government should develop a type of Australia Card and then pay out on the basis of cardholders had merits, but it would take two years to put in place. Where the choice was between speed or accuracy, fast or worthy, speed was to be the determining factor. Not all school buildings would be needed or always appropriate. Even the advisers could not have anticipated all the inefficiencies that emerged from the insulation package, but again, the purpose was to keep people in employment and the economy moving.

At the same time, the question of retaining confidence had to be calculated. Over the years, the rhetoric of economic management had proposed that every government should run a surplus, and that to go into deficit would be an indication of economic mismanagement. In terms of economics, that was nonsense; in terms of perceptions, it was significant. Rudd was conscious of the spendthrift reputation of Labor governments: he did not want to push the budget into deficit. The government did not want to talk about a recession or even a deficit lest they became a self-fulfilling prophecy. So all sorts of euphemisms were used instead; ministers sought to keep the emphasis on the problems that were appearing, the challenges that had to be met. When, in the opinion of the senior ministers, the time was appropriate, the language changed. When he returned from Lima in late 2008, Rudd started to talk about the need for a deficit to stimulate the economy. Other ministers took their cues from the Prime Minister and also talked about a deficit. The exercise was to ensure the message was consistent, the essence of spin; inconsistent messages are pilloried by the media.

The good news came in May 2009, when Australia, alone among major advanced economies, did not go into recession. The Budget then was meant to be about the long term.

The ministers expected the debt argument, but saw it as just good economics. Educating the public would be yet another, different challenge. If the first instinct, inside and outside the government, had been to protect the surplus, that would have been bad policy. If the government had waited until unemployment started rising and growth declined, it would have been too late. There was, however, a political price to pay.

The political battleground covered the expected terrain. The Opposition complained about the level of debt; it acknowledged that a deficit was necessary, but stated that it would have been smaller and better targeted under a Coalition government. They pointed to problems in the delivery of the school building programs, selecting particular cases where the money seemed to be applied less effectively. Rudd's strategy was to accuse the Opposition of talking down the economy and to point out, on a regular basis, that Australia was the only major advanced economy that had not gone into recession. He cited the opinion of the IMF, the World Bank and other gurus that it would be a mistake to wind back the stimulus too early.

The challenge was how to reduce expenditure once the immediate crisis was over, to balance the budget in the foreseeable future. When the worst of the crisis was over, Rudd had to determine the next steps and how to respond to the specific criticisms of schemes designed with speed, but not always precision, to meet immediate demands.

Rudd explained what the government had done and why in a long article published in the Fairfax press—*The Sydney Morning Herald* and *The Age*—on 25 July 2009. Its title, 'Pain on the Road to Recovery', delivered the message. Here was the justification of his approach. He described how the crisis had occurred, with the boom in debt. He lambasted the Liberals for hypocrisy, for attacking the government when they would have reacted almost identically. He provided details of what the government had done and how the first signs of recovery were beginning to show. He justified the need to go into debt, while pointing out that both the deficit and the debt, as a percentage of GDP, were 'the lowest by an order of magnitude of all major advanced economies'. He repeated the challenges for governments: the need to maintain strong finances and improve economic efficiency. He acknowledged that there might be pain in the next months: rising unemployment, rising interest rates, price rises for commodities as global demands grew, and some painful decisions if the government was to return to surplus. It was, in effect, a report to the nation, with a partisan political swipe on the way. While there was a long march ahead, the immediate economic crisis seemed to have been weathered.

14

A WEEK IN THE OFFICE

Prime ministers regularly appear in the headlines, but most of what they do is never noted. They must fulfil several roles: politician, salesman, security chief, diplomat, policy analyst. But for prime ministers, these roles are not distinct. Prime Ministers must adapt to the environment, understand the expectations and satisfy the audience, whenever and whomever they are. The pressure and demands are constant. As an example, here is a sketch of one week in November 2008, when the GFC remained a threat but Rudd was still loved—when the clouds on the horizon were no bigger than a man's hand.

Monday
The Prime Minister's arrival at Parliament House always has a mark of authority. The barriers holding back other vehicles are pulled aside. The gates to the courtyard within the complex are opened, and the Prime Minister's car, accompanied by the inevitable police escort, pulls up right outside his office, where staff await his arrival. Some of the press staff have been there since 4.30 a.m., checking the newspapers, and monitoring the media coverage and the talkback shows.

A Week in the Office

The senior staff have already met in the office of the chief of staff, Alister Jordan, to begin planning the week. The Prime Minister arrives and sweeps straight across the corridor into a meeting of the economic taskforce. Some of his staff run to ensure they are not late.

Every morning since the GFC began, the Prime Minister, the Treasurer and their staff have had a briefing on what has happened overnight, and it's the same this morning. The European and US markets slump while Australians sleep. Treasury officers have to work from the early hours to collate the details and prepare a brief. For the first thirty minutes, the economic news from around the globe is reported and its impact on the Australian economy assessed.

Mid-morning there is the formal launch of the National Australia Bank's Reconciliation Action Plan. A crowd of around 100 awaits the Prime Minister, mingling and drinking tea in the Mural Hall. When he arrives, the occasion starts. There is a moving welcome from the land's traditional owners, speeches from the NAB leaders. The Prime Minister talks for eight minutes. He compliments the NAB on the plan which, he admits, he has browsed through only while listening to the speeches. He uses the opportunity to muse on the ways that the country must build on the apology to the stolen generations. At the end, he adds the aside that a copy of his comments may have been circulated in advance, but they bear no relationship to what he has actually said. His comments were ad-libbed.

Then it's back to his office. Since it is the first Question Time for a couple of weeks, it is preceded by prime ministerial statements. The Prime Minister records his horror at the terrorist attack on Mumbai. He puts on record his tributes concerning the death of former Labor deputy prime minister Frank Crean, the father of his Minister for Trade, and that of Jørn Utzon, the Danish architect of the Sydney Opera House, whose soaring sails he can admire from his Sydney residence across the harbour.

At 2 p.m. Question Time begins, the daily contest between government and the Opposition. Half the questions come from government, half from the Opposition; a balance of defence and offence, of justification and glorification, of turning the Opposition's questions back on their own record and performance. The more detailed business of governing inevitably remains out of sight.

A meeting with the Attorney-General occurs on the hoof, on the way back from Question Time; even walking is an opportunity for a discussion. The Prime Minister returns to his office, and then there's a lengthy session of the Cabinet committee on climate change. The government's statement on carbon trading is due to be released in two weeks. The subject is brutally difficult; the science is contested, the cost uncertain, the impact distant, the politics divisive. Ministers know that, whatever they determine, they will be criticised by environmentalists and industry, but from diametrically opposed perspectives. Besides, the global crisis has changed all the calculations; what seemed so possible a year ago during the election has become that much more difficult. Jobs and carbon compete for significance.

When Cabinet is over, around 9 p.m., there are Christmas drinks with Queensland members and senators to attend.

This first day has been bookended by the two great global challenges the Prime Minister must understand and tackle: the economic crisis and climate change. In both, Australia can never be anything but a bit player; its decisions will be marginal relative to the world's progress. In both, the Prime Minister will be judged by the Australian people. That is the lot of a prime minister: to take office when the world goes crazy and yet to have to understand the complexities of these crises, know how to explain them and react. Public policy can be hard. Prime ministers are not given the luxury of specialisation; they must be on top of every big issue the government has to tackle.

Tuesday

At 8 a.m. there is a meeting in the Cabinet anteroom to plan the government's tactics for its half of Question Time: Who will ask questions, and on what topics? The committee is chaired by Anthony Albanese, the leader of the government in the House of Representatives; he is a left-wing warrior, hardened in battles with the right-wing Labor machine in New South Wales and by eleven years in Opposition. The Prime Minister is formally a member of the tactics committee. If he does not attend, his chief of staff acts on his behalf. Also present are the Deputy Prime Minister, Julia Gillard; the Treasurer, Wayne Swan; and the government whip in the House, Roger Price. Their staff fill the table and debate the options readily.

When parliament is sitting, Question Time dominates the atmosphere. Not for an Australian prime minister is there the comfort of Question Time in the British House of Commons, where twice a week, for twenty to thirty minutes, the prime minister answers questions as though it were high drama. Australian prime ministers answer questions on any topic, on every day that parliament sits. The tactics committee meets twice on most sitting days, to take a first cut at the batting order and then to confirm its decisions. It decides which ministers will answer questions from their backbench, questions that are scarcely challenging and entirely lacking in literary merit or forensic capacity. The backbenchers ask ministers to tell the House what great achievements have been completed in the past few days. The ministers thank the questioners, commend them for their interest and deliver the good news. Some are Mogadon questions, designed to put the House to sleep, serious if uncontroversial. Others are meant to be provocative, providing opportunities for the Prime Minister or his ministers to go on the attack. While the public is often sceptical about the significance of parliament, ministers see it differently. When parliament meets, it dominates the day, at least until Question Time is over.

This week, the intention is to celebrate the successes of COAG the previous weekend.

This Tuesday, the Prime Minister attends the daily economic taskforce meeting and then the weekly Labor caucus meeting. This is the last caucus meeting of the year, so it includes a group photograph. Caucus elected Rudd as party leader; he has to retain their support and keep their confidence. There is no problem at this stage. He boosts their morale after a year in office.

Then there is a staff meeting to consider the arrangements for an upcoming visit to Bali to co-chair a democracy forum with Indonesian President Susilo Bambang Yudhoyono. Foreign visits have to be justifiable to the Australian community, as a worthwhile expenditure of the Prime Minister's time and national funds. How will the electors view the trip? Will they understand the value of the links with Indonesia?

On this occasion, time gets away and there is a need to keep rescheduling the afternoon. A recording of a message for the Clinton Global Initiative meeting in Hong Kong has to be delayed because the Prime Minister is scheduled to make a statement in the House to celebrate the sixtieth anniversary of the UN Declaration of Human Rights. The government gives multilateralism, human rights and international organisations a higher standing in its hierarchy of values than its predecessor.

Then it is back for the SPBC. Finally, back at the Lodge, the Prime Minister hosts the Christmas reception of the federal parliamentary press gallery. At 8.30 p.m. the function ends.

The day emphasises the politics of the Prime Minister's job as a politician: maintaining political support, boosting the confidence of backbenchers, determining strategy. Prime ministers have to be conscious of the internal and external politics that underpin their position. 'Being political' is essential for survival.

Wednesday

The routine of the morning follows the pattern of the previous days. The economic taskforce meets as usual. There are two meetings of the tactics committee, but the Prime Minister does not attend. Question Time remains intensive, but there is little sign that the Opposition rattles the government. There is a diversion when a member of the public jumps from the gallery into the chamber and is hustled away by the police and attendants. In the middle of the questions, the Prime Minister is told that the Opposition intends to move a Matter of Public Importance, deploring the 'dismal performance' of the Rudd government. The Prime Minister stays at the end of the questions and listens to the Leader of the Opposition enumerating the government's failures. He has the opportunity to make a few notes while his opponent talks. Then he responds in aggressive style, damning the Opposition for its divisions and weakness, and extolling the achievements of the government. It's been a year since the government was sworn in and a catalogue of its record is released. Any prime minister has to be able to dominate the House. Even if Rudd does not exercise the excoriating wit and sarcasm of his deputy, Julia Gillard, he has no problem speaking strongly off the cuff.

In the meantime, his schedule has had to be redone once again. A meeting with the head of the Department of Prime Minister and Cabinet is put on hold and eventually cancelled. The Prime Minister goes from the House to a Cabinet committee on climate change. There is no time afterwards for the head of department meeting because he has two public functions to address.

First there is the opening of the National Portrait Gallery. The Prime Minister is joined by his wife, Thérèse Rein, and with a police escort, sweeps down the hill to the new gallery on the lake. The guests are already there, including representatives from portrait galleries overseas, and much of the art world's glitterati. Once the Prime Minister arrives, the official part of the ceremony begins. His speech recognises the contribution to the gallery of the former government, particularly the former prime minister, John Howard, who is in the audience. The Prime Minister reflects on some of the great portraits of history: Vermeer's *Girl with a Pearl Earring*, Rembrandt's *Self Portrait as an Old Man* and 'most hauntingly, disturbingly, Goya's great image of *The Third of May, 1808* depicting the execution of young Spanish citizens who defended Madrid against the French. An image of fear and death, yet defiant pride, heroism and fervent nationalism'. He declares the gallery open and is taken on a tour of the exhibits. He clearly enjoys the occasion, a symbol of the victory a year before, with the vanquished present and obliged to applaud.

Then it's off to another audience, another constituency. It is the annual dinner of the Australian Chamber of Commerce and Industry. Here, the Prime Minister's speech is longer, denser and more serious. In a sense, for a Labor prime minister, this is hostile territory, the natural home of Coalition ministers and therefore all the more important. The Prime Minister explains the nature of the international crisis and the government's policies in reaction to these events. He exhorts, explains, justifies and defends everything from COAG to the Fair Work legislation.

Prime ministers must always be the government's chief spokesman. They must spruik in a wide variety of forms. What prime ministers choose to do, where they choose to go, will always attract attention because they give weight to an occasion by their very presence. What they say is significant because of their standing. Every public statement can be deconstructed for inner meaning and stored for future use against them.

Thursday

Choice and misfortune make security the theme of the day. Though not, of course, to the exclusion of other issues. There is a visit from the Speaker of the Indonesian House of Representatives, who is welcomed by the Australian Speaker in public and the Prime Minister in private. The principal event in the parliament is the presentation of the National Security Statement and the announcement of the national security coordinator. The Prime Minister's speech spells out the 'enduring principles': self-reliance, the US alliance, regional engagement, commitment to multilateral institutions, creative middle-power diplomacy, a risk-based approach, and partnership with state governments. It covers both detailed engagements and broader issues, such as energy security. It is followed by a speech on the second reading of the Fair Work Bill, the Bill that was to bury Work Choices. The Prime Minister wants to put his contribution on the record.

Then he flies to Sydney with the Leader of the Opposition to attend the memorial service at Holsworthy barracks for Lieutenant Michael Fussell, who was killed in Afghanistan. Fussell is the first Australian officer to die in either Iraq or Afghanistan. The mood is sombre, for a young man has died in the service of his country in a war determined by its leaders. If the Security Statement relates to security on a larger scale, the memorial service is that ever-present reminder that decisions made by Cabinets and prime ministers are translated into the risks that service personnel must take, and into the tensions and fears that parents and families must face. Sometimes the results are fatal. Prime ministers must be the lead mourners and personify a sense of national loss.

The Prime Minister decides to stay in Sydney at Kirribilli House rather than fly back to Canberra; he has a meeting there the next morning. This means he misses the meeting of the SPBC. However, his staff ensure that the preferences of the Prime Minister are known to his colleagues when they meet that evening.

Friday
A day of formal meetings, initially in Sydney with the big end of town, on global crises and climate change. The economic taskforce meets there, too; it moves with the Prime Minister. Then a book launch at Fairfax and a plane to Melbourne for the 2008 Australian Export Awards.

Weekend
In Melbourne still. Today, Saturday, will be a combination of work and social activity; on Sunday there will be a Community Cabinet meeting in Geelong.

First, the Prime Minister attends a private breakfast, then a formal occasion to turn the first sod for the Western Ring Road in company with the Minister for Transport and Infrastructure.

After the formal functions there is time to relax and meet some old friends for lunch. The arrangement is that they will meet at the bookshop Readings in Lygon Street, Carlton. Even here, there is a security team to watch over the Prime Minister. Initially, there is almost a circle of space around him. Then celebrity takes over. 'Hello, Kevin', says a young teenager who is leaving the bookstore with his father. The weekend manager introduces herself; a book buyer wants an autograph. It is all unscheduled. As the Prime Minister walks up the street to a restaurant, the enthusiasm grows: 'Have a coffee with us, Kevin.' 'Good to see you, Kevin.' As he crosses the road, a young woman going the other way sticks out a hand to say hello; the child with her gives him a smile. It is the same after lunch as, by this time, the local press wants a picture at Readings. It takes time to return there. Some passers-by want a photograph with the Prime Minister; others have a quick chat or offer a word of congratulation. Back at the bookstore, shoppers nudge their companions: look who is there, they say. Some stare, others pretend not to notice.

A Week in the Office

It is always Kevin. Not Mr Rudd, not Prime Minister. Even the kids call him Kevin. Kevin07 caught on. And that, the Prime Minister thinks, is how it should be. In part because it is quintessentially Australian; it is difficult to imagine a US or French president or British prime minister being treated with such informality, or indeed being allowed to walk up the street in so unscheduled or relaxed a manner. In part it is the right of those who elect prime ministers to have access to them; they should be permitted to talk and be photographed with them. In part it is just good politics; the people will not forget that brief conversation and picture, and they will tell their friends and relatives. The prime minister belongs to the people.

That evening, at a party to celebrate a friend's son's twenty-first birthday, the Prime Minister is in relaxed mode, breaking into song with another guest with whom he had been in the same school musical thirty-five years before; he remembers the words for her songs as well as his own. It now seems appropriate that Rudd was cast as the Minister of Pleasure and Pastimes in *Salad Days*. Serendipity?

Melbourne teases out another side of the Prime Minister: off-duty and relaxed, but mixing comfortably with the passing electors. There is still a need for caution. Wherever he goes, security checks it out, finding the best way in and out. They will never take him unnecessarily through a forum where people are drinking. Australians are informal; caution still prevails, as it should.

★ ★ ★

Every week is different, but the variety and challenges are constant. Prime ministers must at once be policy experts, political warriors, public spruikers, security overlords and national celebrities. They must move from one to another seamlessly, understanding the complexities, determining where the priorities are. The roles cannot be separated.

Policy solutions cannot be devised without considering political implications. Foreign visits have to be domestically defensible. Security has to be ensured, but at what cost? Decisions have to be explained, again and again, in different forums. The public demands access.

15

A TIME FOR QUESTIONS

Every sitting day, around fifty-five days per year, the prime minister sits at the dispatch box in parliament, just across from the Leader of the Opposition, like the royal champions at a joust. It is direct, personal and inescapable. In Australia, every question may be directed at the prime minister, designed, if the Opposition is organised enough, to put mounting pressure on the government's leader. The prime minister is at the core of the battle. When Rudd became Opposition leader, he said he wanted to 'play with Mr Howard's mind'. His cricket may have been with Yandina thirds; his tactics resonate with Steve Waugh's desire for the opponent's mental disintegration. That approach is not limited to political opposition. The intent of prime ministers is to maintain their superiority by dominating and splintering the Opposition, by destroying the confidence of its leader and by destroying its credibility as an alternative government. Prime ministers can never be above the party politics; it is what they must do to survive. In turn, Opposition leaders seek to undermine the confidence and credibility of prime ministers.

Question Time is at 2 p.m. when parliament is sitting. Each side is usually allowed ten questions without notice. On the government side, they were carefully scripted. They are called 'Dorothy Dixers' (in the style of letters to a magazine agony aunt), planted by ministers to give them the opportunity to provide information and attack the Opposition. The first went to the Prime Minister. Thereafter it depended on what issues were running, and what needed to be announced. If there was a need to drive home an economic message, then the Treasurer would follow. If there was a need to launch an attack on some idiosyncrasy of the Opposition, then a question would be shaped for one of the more aggressive ministers. Every morning the government tactics committee met at 8 a.m. and 11 a.m. It was chaired by the leader of the government in the House, Anthony Albanese, and nominally included the Prime Minister, Deputy Prime Minister, the Treasurer, the government whip and members of staff. In practice, the prime minister left the task to his staff and got a report at the morning briefing when he could make further suggestions about tactics. The 'Dorothies' were written primarily by the PMO and then distributed to backbenchers for them to ask; it was the only opportunity in Question Time for them to make an appearance. There would be no surprises from the government side.

'Incoming' traffic had to be anticipated. The Prime Minister had a constantly updated briefing folder that included all the data that might be useful to deploy. Each morning before Question Time, the staff tried to leave a couple of hours free for the 'PM's paperwork', preparation for the ensuing challenge. It was primarily a test for the Prime Minister.

In 2008 there were 1290 question asked, 641 from the government and 649 from the Opposition. Of the government questions, 91 were directed to Rudd (14 per cent). Gillard got 89 (13.8 per cent), and Swan, 77 (12 per cent). The tactics committee ensured that every minister got some questions from backbenchers during the year, although not so many that it was onerous. By contrast, the Opposition 'incomings' were more focused. Rudd received 362 (55.7 per cent); Swan, 111 (17.1 per cent); Gillard, 56 (8.6 per cent)—between them over 80 per cent of all questions. In 2009, Rudd got a few less, and Swan and Gillard a few more, but they remained the principal players. No-one else was asked more than fifteen, while four ministers got no Opposition questions at all in 2008; Simon Crean, Minister for Trade, got not a single Opposition question in two years. Another eight got five or less in 2008; they included the Ministers for Defence and Foreign Affairs, although Joel Fitzgibbon got enough (twelve) in the first half of 2009 to undermine his position. The Opposition was concerned only with the big players.

Rudd would prepare in detail, particularly in the early days. One observer said:

> He'll get all the inputs, all the raw data and he'll spread it across the floor and across his desk and he'll shuffle the bits and pieces of paper. I've counted up to thirty piles of paper and you couldn't possibly comprehend them all but he's pulled bits and pieces out and he's shuffling them and reiterating, deconstructing and then reassembling.

In the House, Rudd would lay out on the table in front of him a series of organised piles of notes to which he could refer. As he became more practised, so his style developed. He would lean with one elbow on the dispatch box, look across at the backbench and talk without reference to his papers. He knew the points he wanted to make. The Dorothy Dixers gave him the opportunity to lambaste the Opposition, to point to their weaknesses or divisions. He would answer at length, annoying them, riling them. His parliamentary performances lacked the withering contempt of Keating or the eviscerating ridicule of Costello. They depended on evidence, data, repetition and a consistent message, delivered day after day; they celebrated the government's successes and the Opposition's shortcomings. After years in Opposition, Rudd understood the frustration of that position and appreciated the pleasure of winning the divisions in the House.

In the first year there were few problems. One was a leak that identified the contrary advice that had been provided by departments over the introduction of Fuel Watch, a monitoring program for fuel prices; it was of disputed value and was defeated in the Senate. The leak identified divisions between departments. Why ministers should be concerned if departments had different views was not clear; it was just advice. Nor were there more than the normal hiccups in the media coverage. Rudd's views on the Henson photograph of a nude girl were the source of argument. They were an instinctive reaction from which he would not resile.

Opposition leader Brendan Nelson struggled and lost his position, the second Liberal leader that Rudd had faced. Turnbull became the third challenge, even as the GFC developed. The Opposition focused on the level of debt while admitting that a fiscal stimulus and temporary deficit were appropriate responses. It was a predictable strategy, with the government asking how much less the Opposition stimulus would be. 'Less than Labor's' was effectively the only response.

In May and June 2009, the government came under serious parliamentary pressure for the first time. As a government it had been well disciplined. Ministers had stayed on message. There had only been an occasional leak of intentions. There were no obvious ministerial errors. Most notably, there had been no forced resignations, unlike the first year of the Howard government, when there were several. To an extent, this discipline came from the centre. Tight controls ensure a common message and less egregious behaviour.

Nevertheless, in late May 2009, the first chinks in the discipline appeared. Minister for Defence Joel Fitzgibbon had, for a time, been seen as struggling. He had been unable to answer satisfactorily in parliament when administrative blunders had left serving SAS soldiers with no money in their pay packets. They may have been paid in advance. He might have demanded it be fixed, but it continued to happen and he was unable to explain why. He blamed it on the department, never a sign of a minister in control. Then stories emerged about a connection to a Chinese businesswoman, a family friend with apparent links to the People's Liberation Army, who had paid for trips to China which had not been entered into the pecuniary interest register. As the stories broke, the PMO went into crisis-management mode. John Faulkner, the political strategist, settled into the chief of staff's office. Other senior ministers and advisers dropped in. The Prime Minister came through the connecting door from his office. It was decided that there was carelessness in record keeping but no hanging offence.

The next day the gloom lifted. The quarterly figures came in and Australia had a positive result. Alone among developed economies, Australia was not in recession. Question Time saw a rampant Prime Minister, driving home the message that the stimulus had worked, that Australia was growing and that all the Opposition could do was to talk down the economy. The mood went from crisis to exultation. But then it went back to crisis when more stories emerged about Fitzgibbon's brother using his office and his connections to try to advance his business. The party leaders reconvened in the PMO. They decided that was one accident too many in a growing litany of accidents. On the Thursday morning, Fitzgibbon resigned before he could be subjected to an Opposition grilling in Question Time. Instead, he quietly retired to the back row. He was replaced by Faulkner. That proved to be a cost to the government. Burdened by the massive ministerial load in Defence, Faulkner was not able to spend much time at Rudd's shoulder, as his consigliore, his adviser. Only as things went badly was it realised how much that mattered.

The government expected an attack on Fitzgibbon. Ministerial resignations are grist to Oppositions. Instead, the first question from Turnbull came as a complete surprise. He noted that on the Prime Minister's register of interests he listed a car provided by a John Grant. He asked if the Prime Minister, or anyone on his behalf, had made representations to the Treasury in support of Grant for OzCar, the scheme to assist car dealers over the global credit crisis. Rudd answered he was unaware of any and that he would check. The Opposition followed with a series of questions to the Treasurer, asking if he had made special representations on behalf of Grant. Swan acknowledged one conversation, but no special treatment. Then the Opposition returned to attack the Prime Minister again. Later in Question Time, after quick checks had been made in his office, Rudd stated that he was advised that neither he nor his office had ever made representations on Grant's behalf.

The attack had been a surprise, drawing from the Senate estimates hearings where there were hints that something had been brewing. The PMO took the precaution of going through the email traffic to see if anything came up, but was not unduly concerned as nothing was found. It was seen as a fishing expedition. It simmered. There was a request that the Treasury officer responsible for OzCar, Godwin Grech, be recalled to give evidence to the Senate committee. The government did not object. However, it raised concerns and triggered a second round of checks within the PMO.

In the next week, there were more questions in parliament, with the Opposition hinting to the gallery that Rudd and Swan were in trouble. There were some allegations being thrown around, but nothing precise. When asking the questions in parliament, Turnbull had pointed at Rudd's adviser Andrew Charlton in the adviser's box and smiled at him. Then, at the Press Gallery Ball, Turnbull approached Charlton and told him he shouldn't lie for his boss. The two had a public argument. PMO staff across the room noticed the confrontation and, for fun rather than any other purpose, took a picture of the two on the nearest mobile phone, which happened to be the Prime Minister's. Turnbull's outburst warned the office that something was going to happen and that Charlton was going to be the focus.

On the Thursday, with more accusations flying around about Swan, there was yet another search through Charlton's email traffic. Swan's emails were all released and, as a countermeasure, pictures of Turnbull's confrontation with Charlton were circulated. It could provide a distraction and remind people of his reputation for impulsively crashing through.

On the Friday morning, the newspapers were claiming that there was an email that implicated the government. That caused concern because, even though the emails had been checked several times, there was a fear that something might have been missed. The PMO staff waited for the Senate estimates hearing on the Friday to see what would emerge; several watched the feed from the Senate hearing room in Jordan's office. There was silence as they waited to see whether Grech would say there was an email, or whatever else might emerge. Then they heard Grech say that Andrew Charlton had sent him an email from the PMO making representations for John Grant. There was a gasp of surprise, but it also immediately narrowed the focus: Could any email be found from Charlton to Grech that made that request? As the hearings went on, Grech started to talk about contacts with journalists. No-one asked if he had had contacts with Turnbull or other Liberals. That came out later.

The decision was made to send all the papers to the Auditor-General to provide a third, independent opinion. At the same time, the News Limited reporter Steve Lewis rang the press office to ask for comment on the email. He provided a typed copy of it. By this stage the search was totally focused. For the first time there was a specific allegation. The PMO knew the precise timing and wording of the email. It was couched in the style that Charlton used. Other staff went through Charlton's files again and found nothing. Both PM&C and Treasury were asked to examine the files since it is not possible to delete email from the official files. A deputy secretary of PM&C went through the emails, ticking them off. So did Treasury. By 7.15 p.m. both departments had stated that they could find no such email.

While the PMO was planning a response, with Faulkner still acting as consigliore, Turnbull had gone public. He declared that the email proved that Rudd and Swan had misused their position, that they had lied to parliament and that therefore they should resign. It was a gung-ho, take-no-prisoners press conference. The Prime Minister was a liar, unworthy of his position, and Turnbull had the evidence to prove it.

Then Rudd re-entered the fray. He had been away for the day for a minor medical procedure on his back. He had been kept informed and now came to parliament to answer the charges. He asked Charlton if he sent the message. Despite the inevitable fear that he might have forgotten about sending it, since the PMO had no copy of it, Charlton was sure he had not. Rudd accepted his word. There was no question of distancing himself from a staffer, standing the staffer down while inquiries were made, or leaving the staffer to face the music on the grounds that staffers were dispensable when the credibility, even the position, of the Prime Minister was under challenge. Rudd decided immediately to stand by him. He and his staff began to plan the press conference, although, with a certain ghoulish humour, a stack of cardboard boxes was dumped outside Charlton's office. Advice from Treasury, PM&C and the email itself were run off for the convenience of journalists.

Rudd agreed the allegations were serious and announced that all the documents would be given to the Auditor-General to allow the accusation to be tested. He had received written advice from Treasury and PM&C that no such email existed. Then he turned to Lewis for the first question. As the interaction continued, Rudd thought Lewis was increasingly uncomfortable and his own position became firmer:

> So, just to go back to the other part of what Steve has raised, or what he has raised separately with my office. What Steve has said in his communication to my office, and I will just quote it:
> 'News Limited plans to publish the following email, sent by Andrew Charlton from the Prime Minister's Office to Treasury official Godwin Grech. The email was sent on the 19th of February. "Hi Godwin, the PM has asked if the car dealer financing vehicle is available to assist a Queensland dealership, John Grant Motors, who seems to be having trouble getting finance. If you can follow up on this asap that would be very useful. Happy to discuss. A"'
> All I am saying to you Steve is, we cannot find, anywhere in the system, any such email. We have searched in our own office, and we have had other officers apart from Andrew Charlton go through his own system. Secondly, he has assured me personally, along the lines I referred to in my remarks before, but thirdly, out of a complete abundance of caution, [we] then ask[ed] Prime Minister and Cabinet, who control the PMO's communications system, to go specifically to the date where you claim you have an email which says that. They cannot find anything or anything that has been deleted there, and that is from our end. And finally, on the question of Treasury, that is a communication from one person to another, the recipient is alleged to be Treasury, that is, the public servant concerned. Treasury's IT unit have advised us this evening, they can't find anything either.
> And I go back to my earlier remark, that were this sort of communication in existence, did I have information to that effect

or the office had information to that effect, I would have informed you all at the earliest opportunity and informed the parliament ... Based on the evidence we have ... all I can conclude is that the email ... is false.

Rudd became more and more convinced that there was no evidence for the accusation. He was angry that his integrity had been impugned on that basis. Once the press conference was over, he took Charlton back to The Lodge for dinner. After three torrid days for Charlton, it was a vote of confidence and encouragement from the boss, a personal touch that was deeply appreciated.

The next day, Saturday, some of the media were still pushing the line that the government was in trouble. Turnbull was talking only about Swan, ignoring the fact that he had demanded the Prime Minister resign just the day before. Rudd determined to move onto the attack. After all, he and Swan were under fire even though they were not only falsely accused but had done nothing wrong. He used all the weapons of government, the benefits of incumbency. First, the Australian Federal Police was called in to discover who had forged the email. Then he gave a press conference. He was focused and determined; indeed angry at the charges. He stressed the fact that the email was fake.

By the Sunday, the newspapers had backed off the accusations against Rudd, but continued to attack Swan. Rudd, Gillard and Swan all ran the same line: 'Give us the evidence. Turnbull should produce the document on which he demanded my resignation or resign himself'.

The Prime Minister pursued Turnbull in parliament the next week as the Opposition position unravelled. The email was fake. Turnbull tried to attack in parliament, moving a vote of censure and thereby providing the government with the excuse to trawl though his own past. Hockey and Turnbull acknowledged they knew Grech.

Then they admitted the collusion between Grech and Turnbull in determining when Grech should be called, what questions he should be asked and what answers he would give; the Opposition case was further undermined. The challenge to Turnbull was relentless, even with an edge of venom, an element of nastiness, as though Rudd relished the demolition. This was politics, raw in tooth and claw.

One observer, often critical, commented:

It's clear that Rudd has what Civil War historian Shelby Foote called, in relating to U.S. Grant, 'four-o-clock-in-the-morning courage', a capacity to deal with the worst news at the worst time with coolness and detachment, not merely working out how to respond to it but how to turn it to his advantage. [On the Friday] he calmly and assuredly disputed the email, repeated his central claims, produced documentation to support it and ended with a joke about having gone to the 'quack' and had a cyst removed from his back. For someone who had been accused of corruption and lying, it was a nerveless performance.

This week he has progressively ratcheted up the pressure on Turnbull, first with cold fury on Monday, then with a calculated assault on the man's reputation on Tuesday, switching the focus to Turnbull's leadership and incapacity to lead his party on Wednesday, before using yesterday to show he was focussed on real issues rather than sleaze. It was a carefully prepared strategy and it redoubled the damage Turnbull had inflicted on himself.

Rudd came out of what came to be called Utegate with an enhanced standing and a damaged opponent. Over the next months, the Liberal leadership became the story, with rumours of coups and spills, but for a long time it seemed no-one else in the party actually wanted to become leader in the face of what they thought was a likely electoral disaster. Then the internal battle over climate change saw Turnbull replaced by Tony Abbott.

Utegate also illustrated that, for a time, Labor was comfortable with both the reins of government and the powers that came with it, and the potential lethality of sudden crises. Political crises disrupt the regular process of governing; they demand attention. The press becomes excited; the Opposition smells blood; and the tension rises, whether or not the crisis is real or constructed. Crises can destroy a political career in a blink. They matter to the participants because if they cannot win in the political bear pit, they will never have the chance to govern, to make a difference.

16

PLAYING ON THE INTERNATIONAL STAGE

Rudd wanted Australia to be at the top table in international meetings. If big decisions on the international economy were to be made, he thought Australia, as the world's fourteenth-largest economy and a substantial regional power in the Pacific, should be there. The G-7 and G-10 had been transatlantic in outlook; these forums represented a European past, not the Asia-Pacific future. The G-7 contained the United States, Canada, Britain, France, Italy, Germany and Japan, but not developing nations such as China and India; it was seen as unrepresentative. The 2008 economic crisis assisted Rudd's case. The problems that were emerging could not be solved by the old international architecture because it excluded the emerging powers.

In Washington in September 2008, Rudd picked up vibes through the Australian ambassador, Dennis Richardson, that a new scheme of international collaboration was under consideration within the US Government and related circles because the old system of the G-7 was too restricted. A number of alternatives were suggested. It was usually the G-7 plus some number. For instance, G-7 plus 5, to include the new developing powers, was one proposal. The World Bank was suggesting a G-7 plus a few. Rudd rang his old friend, World Bank president Bob Zoellick, to push Australia's case. Zoellick reflects that:

> Kevin properly ascertained that there are informal networks within the formal group, so in addition to trying to advance the G-20 as a forum, he drew on a combination of personal, historical and geographic ties to maximise Australian's influence. So, for example, he would take Australia's role as an Asia-Pacific economy and work some of the Asia-Pacific players; and as you saw he successfully joined hands with the Koreans and others and that has a connection to the [World] Bank in that Korea and Australia are part of one 'chair', that represents multiple stakeholders.
>
> Secondly, he built a relationship with President Obama and drew on his strong ties with the US.
>
> Then there was what I'll call the English-speaking democracies group. So he would reach out to Harper of Canada, Gordon Brown. He also was working some of the other European capitals, leaders such as Chancellor Merkel who is an intelligent, thoughtful person with whom Kevin could establish a rapport.
>
> So part of his diplomacy—and I don't know to what degree this has been recognised in Australia—is not just to make the G-20 effective but to use informal channels to extend Australia's influence.

The G-20 was Rudd's arena of choice. It already existed, but as a forum for finance ministers. It had been created by the G-7 in 1999, as a response to the 1997 Asian financial crisis, to bring together ministers from a range of developed and developing countries. The G-20 included nineteen countries and the EC. In addition to the G-7 countries, representatives came not only from the big players, China and India, but also a spread from around the world, including Mexico,

Turkey, South Korea, South Africa and Australia. Indonesia was added later. The first meeting was in Berlin in 1999, with Canada in the chair. Its intent was to develop regulations that might prevent a repetition of the contagion that had spread from one country to another. Australia had acted as the host to the finance ministers in Melbourne in November 2006, although in the midst of violent demonstrations.

In an article submitted to the journal *Foreign Affairs* in March 2009, Rudd summarised his case for the G-20:

> The G-20 is the best on offer ... It straddles all continents and all major regions: five from Europe, five from Asia, five from the Americas, and five from other regions including Africa. It is not an almost exclusive Western enclave as is the case with the G-7. It contains the emerging powers of China, India, Brazil and Mexico. It includes the largest Muslim nation in the world, Indonesia. Its combined membership makes up 80 per cent of global GDP and 85 per cent of global trade and two thirds of the world's population. It is small enough to take decisions and large enough to be representative.

He argued that it was the diversity of these countries, together with their economic and strategic reach, that made the G-20 a good 'driving centre'. If they could agree, then they had the capacity to deliver on an agreement.

Rudd argued the G-20 should be 'a lightning rod for global leadership: articulating principles, defining broad objectives and crafting the political consensus which can then be given expression in the individual institutions which are best equipped to deal in detail with the relevant policy and/or technical deliberation'. And, of course, it had the advantage that it gave Australia a seat at the top table, whereas all the other suggested formulations left Australia out. So it was logical that, in a time of economic crisis, a body that was created to deal with international financial stress should become a vehicle for the leaders of the same countries to discuss the GFC.

The theme of Rudd's address at the United Nations in September 2008 was the need to develop a coordinated international response. Globalisation had led to integrated economies, to the extent that no-one could be isolated from the effects of the crisis. If, initially, the hope had existed that the worst effects of the sub-prime debacle would be restricted to the United States and Europe, by September it was clear that all the developing countries, and particularly China, were going to be badly hit. Australia would be at the mercy of international meltdown and had limited capacity to solve problems unilaterally.

By himself, Rudd could do little. He needed the support of other national leaders. He could push, prod and cajole. Whether Rudd's activities made a difference may be debated, but the effort he put in cannot be. The drive came mostly from the Prime Minister, his office and his department. Whenever the leaders at an international meeting were determining who should draft the papers for the next meeting, Rudd was always willing to volunteer Australia's resources. As one observer quipped, he would have taken responsibility for all the background papers if he could.

Rudd began an extended campaign to ensure that the G-20 become the forum of choice. When Lehman Brothers collapsed on 15 September and the crisis hit on 10–11 October 2008, he immediately began to talk with national leaders to argue the need for a more representative body than the G-7. He wanted to piggyback a meeting of the G-20 on the G-7 meeting in Washington in November. His arguments were consistent. The meeting needed to be representative; it needed to cover all continents; it needed to include the great developing countries of India, China and Brazil. He recognised that there was a trade-off between numbers of countries and the ease of getting agreement. He circulated a paper to all G-20 leaders explaining why he thought that it should be the forum of choice.

A number still doubted the logic. The French were not keen to dilute their influence and were consistently to propose that the G-7 be expanded by as few as possible. Many of the countries from outside the G-7 were annoyed that Brussels gave the impression that it knew all the answers and yet the problems had emerged from the developed, not the developing, economies. Rudd canvassed support in a series of ten or more calls in October, including the ill-fated conversation with Bush regarding the G-20 that became the subject of stories in *The Australian*. The first set of calls was designed to persuade and even educate. The later ones, after the G-20 leadership meeting had been convened, were aimed at turning a potentially one-off occasion into a regular event, designed to deal with problems of international political economy. An official commented:

> They take the calls because he's not just calling to ask them what the weather's like. It's assisted by the fact that he's not calling them to ask them to do things but rather he's calling them to float an idea with them or to volunteer that we will do something.

Rudd circulated to the leaders a Memorandum on the International Financial System. It proposed five action points: important financial institutions should be licensed only if they make full disclosure of balance and off-balance sheets; supervisory frameworks should be developed that are counter-cyclical; financial institutions should have internal incentives to promote internal stability; a better medium-term perspective for risk management should be created; and the IMF's mandate for prudential analysis should be supported and strengthened. He argued that the G-20 was well placed to provide political authority to the IMF and the Financial Stability Forum. He wanted the IMF to provide robust and regular reports on the world's financial systems and the threats to them. The principal purpose was to argue for a continuing and coordinated approach to the financial crisis that had just enveloped all the countries.

Former World Bank President Robert Zoellick thinks he had some advantages:

> Frankly, influence at the summit level reflects a combination of factors: one's country, the individual, credibility of national policies, relationships ... Kevin would recognise those assets and how to leverage them ... Having the good fortune to having inherited what was a relatively solid economy; secondly, having performed well in the crisis, with a good stimulus program, well-respected, good growths; and, three, using one's personal relationships, one's country's reputation and any other assets to maximise your impact. All these factors can help add weight to the ideas one brings to the table. In Kevin's case he's a workhorse, he uses assets to the fullest to advance ideas to solve problems.

In the international jargon, a leadership summit requires a 'sherpa', an official who 'prepares the way for the leader to the summit'. It is a term that has been used for over thirty years. The sherpa will always be a person trusted by the leader and has the responsibility to liaise with the sherpas of the other leaders. So each country has a single person who can speak with authority on behalf of their boss; they settle what they can before the meeting, and work out the communiqué in advance where it is possible. They smooth the way, make the connections. Consequently, much of the preparatory traffic goes primarily through the one person (hence the need sometimes for a sherpa to be assisted by a yak!). Initially, Rudd's sherpa was David Tune, who was the associate secretary of PM&C (and later appointed secretary of the

Department of Finance). In early 2009, the task was handed on to Andrew Charlton in the PMO.

The sherpas will have two or three meetings in advance of the leaders' summit. The host country is always in the chair. At the first meeting they will consider the items that could be on or off the agenda. In the second they become more specific, talk about possible proposals, and gauge the feelings and national interests of the countries. The host country then usually closely guards the draft of the communiqué as it does not want too many objections. So there is always a scramble the day before the leaders meet. The sherpas may work throughout the night because they have a really hard deadline. As one experienced negotiator noted: 'People may be willing to compromise at four in the morning on issues they might normally not compromise on if they had more time. That is a normal part of the tactic'. The areas that cannot be settled are left in square brackets for the leaders to discuss. All the way through, the leaders are directly represented by an individual they can trust.

The first G-20 meeting of leaders was held in Washington on 15 November 2008. It was to be the first of three in the next year. Rudd prepared assiduously for them. An adviser explained the challenges. A strategy needed to work out what everybody's position was and then determine at what level the caucusing should take place: national leader to national leader; in communications between finance ministers, at the myriad officials meetings; and then with or without the involvement of the IMF and the World Bank.

The G-20 was convened by Bush, by then a lame-duck President awaiting his departure from office, even if the push came from Brown and Sarkozy. Rudd declared as he left Australia that the purposes of the G-20 were to work with the president in three areas: stability for the financial system, growth in the economy and rules for the financial system for the future.

Rudd arrived in Washington on 14 November with time for a day of meetings with national leaders. They included the presidents of Brazil and Argentina, the heads of the World Bank and the IMF, the secretaries of the US Treasury and Defence, and a meeting and press conference with the UK's Gordon Brown. The next morning were the plenary sessions and a working lunch. After the G-20 ended, Rudd met the presidents of Indonesia and the Republic of Korea, and spent an hour the next morning with President Hu of China.

After his return, he wrote to all the leaders arguing that it had been a good meeting and there was a need to maintain the momentum. In January 2009, he wrote an opinion piece drawn from his *Monthly* article on the GFC. It was translated and appeared in the press in twenty-eight countries, including *Le Monde* and the *China Daily*. A second article, 'Leaders Must Act Together to Solve the Crisis', appeared in the *Financial Times* on 7 January. It was either published in, or sent to the national leaders of, another fifteen countries. In the next months, he wrote a lengthy article that was submitted to the leading US journal *Foreign Affairs*. One of the themes was the need to create a new international architecture. It was not accepted, but became available to some journalists who then wrote about its ambitions.

In the weeks before the London G-20 summit in April, Rudd talked on the phone with twenty-six leading participants, including sixteen national G-20 leaders, the EC president, four leading US officials and the heads of three international financial institutions (IFIs). The messages were the same. There were three big issues that the meeting had to pursue: a common approach to toxic assets; coordination of the global stimulus packages; and reform of the IMF, both in terms of an increase in its resources and its voting rights, whether determined by the size of the national economies or, as a secondary criterion, by a readiness to contribute. A number of additional issues, such as the need to pressure the United States to provide adequate financial regulation and the necessity to make progress on the Doha Trade Round to lower barriers and assist development, were part of some of the discussions.

The other common theme was the future of the G-20 itself. Everyone was aware that not all leaders were keen to see the G-20 replace the G-7 as the principal gathering of world leaders. France and Italy did not want to see their influence reduced, as it would be if they became part of a much larger forum. The key was of course the United States. So many of the calls between those who supported the G-20 as the primary international forum, often at the expense of historical European hegemony, discussed the best way ahead: who would talk to whom to put the case for the G-20; who would lobby President Obama before they met in London; who else needed to be persuaded. Particular issues included who would host the next meeting and whether the membership should be fixed. As one leader put it, the membership should not be made a point of breakdown; even if there were more than twenty members, it could still be called the G-20. There was no need to get in a bind about numbers. As Zoellick says:

> the G-20, I sometimes joke, is an organisation for our age because the numbers don't add up. In fact there's more than twenty members. The Europeans have managed to invite the Dutch and the Spanish and so you have a large number of Europeans around the table. Some of the G-20 meetings sought to advance multilateral diplomacy by inviting representatives of groups; for example, ASEAN representative at the Summits and Singapore's and APEC representatives with the finance ministers. So there's more than twenty national attendees. Then the heads of the international organisations.

Rudd often followed up the calls with letters. He was co-chairing a working party, established at the Washington meeting, so in some cases he included copies of the two principal papers that he had had drafted and which were both described as the Australian Prime Minister's Working Papers. The first was 'Global Economic Recovery—An International Framework for Toxic Asset Management (IFTAM)'. The second was 'Renewing the IMF: A Practical Resourcing and Reform Plan to Deal with the Crisis'.

The paper on the IMF defined the problems of the organisation: inadequate resources; an inappropriate toolkit that lacked the flexibility in lending instruments; a deficit of trust after its response to earlier crises; and a lack of legitimacy because its structure was not representative of current global economic conditions, with Europe having eight times the quota of China but only 1.7 times the GDP. So Rudd proposed that the London meeting should triple the IMF's resources, support the establishment of new IMF policy and lending instruments, and provide better surveillance monitoring and reporting roles. He also suggested it set a path to reform the IMF ownership structure and its governance. Attached to the paper was a detailed implementation plan for each of the proposals that had been suggested in the short paper itself. The paper on toxic assets included a series of detailed steps, including what Rudd described as the seven critical elements for acting in a coordinated way to deal with the issue. In typical fashion, Rudd went to London in April 2009 with lengthy preparations, detailed proposals and a persistent effort to get the other leaders working together. The Australian priorities were a strong macroeconomic focus, with an emphasis on toxic assets, further stimulus, trade and protection, major reform to the IMF, effective financial sector reform, and an ongoing role for the G-20 Leaders' Process.

Rudd went to London via Washington. It was his first chance to meet the members of the new Obama administration and the President himself. He also talked to a number of significant people: Jim Wolfensohn, former president of the World Bank; Henry Kissinger;

two leading economists, Jeffrey Sachs and Joe Stiglitz; former vice-president Al Gore; diplomat Richard Holbrooke; and the editorial board of the *New York Times*. Rudd wanted to find out not only what officials were thinking but what other possibilities could be suggested. When he arrived in London, the hectic pace continued. Formal meetings with the Queen, the Archbishop of Canterbury and the Leader of the Conservative Opposition were intermingled with preparatory talks with Gordon Brown, Foreign Secretary David Miliband, and the presidents of Indonesia, Korea and Russia. After the formal G-20 proceedings, there was once again time for a meeting with President Hu of China.

The G-20 communiqué covered a range of issues. It committed the countries to a continued stimulus; required greater regulation of financial institutions, including hedge funds; raised possibilities of taking action on executive pay; reaffirmed a commitment to the Millennium Development Goals for a fairer world economy; and agreed to resist protectionism. The IMF was given more funds, with an agreement of a continued process of review and reform. Finally, the official document stated that: 'We have committed ourselves to work together with urgency and determination to translate these words into action. We agreed to meet again before the end of the year to review progress of our commitments'.

There was to be at least one more meeting. To that extent, the G-20 as a leaders' forum was a going concern. In June, President Obama announced that the next G-20 summit would be held in Pittsburgh in September 2009.

However, there was still no commitment to a continuing role for the G-20. In July, Rudd attended the Advanced Economies Economic Forum held at the margins of the G-8 meeting in L'Aquila in Italy. One phenomenon of these summits is that the formal figure (G-7 or G-20) seldom reflects precisely the number of heads of state or other leading participants. So several other leaders attended this G-8 meeting. On the way, Rudd visited Berlin to talk to German Chancellor Angela Merkel. As the world's economies began to show signs of recovery, an exit strategy from the stimulus packages became the next point of discussion. Rudd was interested in the German Charter for Sustainable Economic Activity, which sought to combine open markets and sustainable growth. The Europeans were still uncertain about the G-20; they still hankered for the influence they could wield in a G-7, or even a G-8+5. But they recognised that the big developing countries needed to be involved. Merkel came out in support of the G-20. Rudd also talked to the head of the Financial Stability Board (FSB), established in 1999 to assist the finance ministers of the G-20, and now assisting the G-20 leaders in their efforts to manage the GFC and in the push for global accounting standards and reporting.

In L'Aquila, Rudd saw Berlusconi and argued once again for a 'global clearing house, a place where leaders could broker a deal'. He put a similar case to the Japanese Prime Minister and the Korean President, and to the heads of the UN, the IMF and the World Bank, all of whom were in attendance. A coordinated strategy, he argued, was vital. Climate change too became an issue as the Copenhagen conference was only six months in the future. The message he received was that the G-20 was firming up as a preferred option, in part because President Obama wanted 'fewer summits and more consequences'.

Between July and the Pittsburgh summit in September, the pace of preparation was frenetic. Rudd asked for four papers to be prepared: he then worked through them in detail with his working party. The papers covered the transition of the global economy to stable growth, exit strategies from the stimulus, the reform of global governance and climate finance. In the last of these, he argued that the leaders should use the G-20 to build consensus towards a comprehensive agreement, and use the expertise of their finance ministries to estimate the quantum of finance required, the mechanisms for raising finance, the role of carbon markets and the areas where public funding were needed. He sent copies of the papers to all the national leaders. There were additional letters on IFIs, sent jointly with South Africa, the co-chair of the G-20 working party. He also worked with the Italian Prime Minister to produce suggestions on dealing with financial speculation. Rudd had already talked to fourteen leaders on the phone in the three weeks before Pittsburgh.

Rudd went to the United States a few days before the Pittsburgh Summit. On the first day, 20 September, he had breakfast with former president Bill Clinton, and received a laudatory testimonial. He pursued his regular round of meetings with people whom he thought could assist in one way or another. He had dinner with Rupert Murdoch, gave an interview with CNN and had another discussion with economics guru Jeffrey Sachs. In the next three days he met fifteen heads of state and several dignitaries, including George Soros and Henry Kissinger; attended two climate change working dinners hosted by the UN Secretary-General; participated in a UN climate change session, which included facilitating a round-table discussion; and attended a Security Council Summit on non-proliferation and disarmament. Every day, the program started at 7.30 a.m. and ran through to 10 p.m. in the evening.

On 24 September, Rudd flew to Pittsburgh. There was a leaders' dinner that evening and two plenary sessions the next morning. Rudd's interventions were carefully planned and scripted. In the first morning session, he proposed that there was a short-term problem: the danger of a double-dip recession and a jobless recovery; and a long-term one: the IMF prediction of a shrinking of the world economy by 2012. He proposed that the short-term response should be a continuation of the stimulus; a medium-term issue was how governments would elaborate an exit strategy; and the long term could be based on the US Framework for Strong, Sustainable and Balanced Recovery, because it sought to rewrite the economic orthodoxy with the aim of preventing the 'boom and bust' cycle. It had, he argued, to be led by the nations, not the IMF. He added other items he saw as drivers for recovery: the completion of the Doha round, the digital revolution, the need to link climate change and development with green technology, the need for education skills and the importance of development. In the second session he argued for better regulation, whether macro-supervision or individual institutions, and for greater transparency. So he agreed with President Sarkozy that, if there were not globally consistent rules, countries would face regulatory shopping, as firms decided where best to nominally operate, and a race to the top for executive remuneration. In a contribution to the debate on climate change, he suggested that if the finance ministers could not come up with a climate change financing scheme, then perhaps the G-20 leaders should commit to meeting 'virtually or physically' before Copenhagen. When the meeting discussed the future of the G-20, President Obama, in the chair, asked Rudd to open the discussion in recognition of his contribution to the debate.

The communiqué had been drafted, although one head of state had noted to Rudd how welcome, and unusual, it had been to see the leaders themselves actually redrafting clauses in order to reach some agreement. The leaders pledged to sustain the strong response 'until a durable recovery is secured', but at the same time 'we will prepare our exit strategies, and when the time is right, withdraw our extraordinary policy support in a cooperative and coordinated way, maintaining our commitment to fiscal responsibility'. They accepted the Strong Sustainable and Balanced Growth compact; committed to improve their regulatory systems for financial institutions; decided to take steps to improve access to food, fuel and finance for the world's poorest; and to move towards greener, more sustainable growth. They also agreed to 'reform the global architecture to meet the needs of the 21st century'. The leaders 'designated the G-20 to be the premier forum for our economic cooperation'. They also welcomed the efforts of the FSB in monitoring and improving financial regulation, delivered on the promise to contribute over $500 billion for the IMF to utilise, and agreed to change the governance arrangements of the IMF and the World Bank. Finally, they agreed to meet twice in 2010, in Canada in June and Korea in November, and thereafter annually, with the 2011 meeting in France.

Rudd's objectives were achieved: the continuation of, and support for, a stimulus package; the agreement to develop a coordinated exit strategy; the acceptance of a need for consistent financial regulation; and the push to develop some climate change financial package to take to Copenhagen. In terms of policy responses, the cases that he had advocated were largely adopted. So too, crucially, were the decisions on architecture, including not only the reforms of the IFIs but the acceptance of the G-20 as the 'premier forum' for economic cooperation. Acceptance of that had been far from certain: at L'Aquila, some European countries had still been in favour of G-7+5, or G-7 plus as few extra as they could get. The lobbying had been organised and intense. The supporters of the G-20 had consistently agreed who would talk to the key players. Those who would have been left out of the G-8+5, Argentina, Korea, Indonesia, Turkey, Mexico, Saudi Arabia and Australia, interacted to push their case, particularly to the United States, China and Japan.

It worked. A senior US official, who had known Rudd through the AALD, asserted he was one of the key figures in making the G-20 central to the response to the global crisis. Kurt Campbell, the US Assistant Secretary of State for East Asia and the Pacific, and an old colleague of Rudd from the AALD, saw the development of the G-20 as 'the biggest innovation in global politics in decades', and as a recalibration of global power towards Asia. He described the development of the G-20 as an eight-month period of institution-building. He commented:

> The process behind the scenes was much more fraught and complex than was generally recognised in the public discussion ... I think Australia's role was a decisive role. Prime Minister Rudd was relentless in making the case with world leaders. He was intimately involved in persuading key players, he especially made his case with a number of players who might have been reluctant.

Or put another way, a year before, very few people were talking about the G-20 or thought it would emerge as the dominant institution. The idea that no-one listened to Rudd was disproved by his success. Very few people had made a major effort to make the G-20 happen. Rudd did. The United States was still the key, but Rudd and his international colleagues assisted to maintain the push.

Zoellick suggests why Rudd's style of working assisted his influence:

> the G-20 is a formal group which culminates in meetings. But one needs to use informal networks to prod people's thinking and build cooperative solutions. Whether it's Kevin's diplomatic background or whether it's his intellectual background, or whether it's his ability to be party coalition leader, he was a natural for working those networks. In addition to having personal relationships with other heads of government, he does his homework first. Yet I also think he's evolving his own thinking as he talks to other people. Perhaps simultaneously, he's trying to kind

of understand the politics of his colleagues' positions so as to try to integrate policy directions with politics at the highest level.

Why so effective? An adviser comments:

The G-20 was an institution born in crisis. It was first established at finance-ministers' level in the wake of the Asian crisis. It was established at leaders' level in the wake of the great crash of 2008. It has always been an institution born in crisis and as a result has been an institution of action.

It suited Rudd and his ambitions.

17

RESETTING PRIORITIES: CLIMATE CHANGE

The babushka-doll imagery Rudd proposed in Opposition in 2005 argued that policies are layered: get the security right, get the economy right, and then a government can develop domestic policies in education and health. In government they all arrive at once and they are often interconnected. Prime ministers must live with the complexity. They work where the difficult and the troublesome policies are, where issues cut across portfolios, where there are international connotations. They must also ration their time to determine where they will be deeply involved, and what they will leave primarily to their ministers, always with the proviso that they will re-enter any policy arena that becomes contested and thus attracts media scrutiny. Every prime minister has a hierarchy of policy arenas. Working with his office and department, Rudd developed a strategic document that sought to relate the principal policy initiatives to one another and to classify them by their importance and by reference to the ministers who should have primary carriage of them within government and in the public arena.

At the top, as Rudd identified, were issues of economy and security, the sine qua nons of political life. A government that gets these issues wrong does not survive. Prime ministers will be involved in depth and continuously with the development, management and presentation of both, and will be constantly explaining them.

Second were areas Rudd described as signature policies: initiatives for which the government will wish to be known if it can succeed. Some signature policies for Rudd were choices: broadband, the education revolution, the reworking of the federation, and the abolition of Work Choices. Others would be thrust upon the government by circumstances: health reform and climate change are the most obvious. Rudd would be heavily enmeshed in these policy areas. They were his priorities, the policies on which he chose to campaign, the ones to which he had given attention. Rudd would drive them, work closely with ministers, assist in their development and presentation, and monitor their implementation. Ideally, the number of signature policies would be few, to concentrate the Prime Minister's attention. It did not, perhaps could not, quite work out that way; his interest would often be drawn to the issues before him. But the intent was that signature issues were the ones that needed pressure from the top and on which any re-election battle could be fought.

Third were the major policies of change and reform. Some might take place within the broader COAG agenda; some would be necessary amendments to existing regulatory systems. Superannuation and industry policy were two important examples. When significant developments emerged, Rudd would be briefed and he would oversee developments with watchful attention.

Fourth, there was ministerial policy, often within a portfolio, where initiatives are driven forward by ministerial direction and interest. Rudd would approve the initiatives; they would have been part of those planning meetings he held with individual ministers in the months after the election. They would attract active involvement primarily if something went wrong. All the time, the ministers kept Rudd's staff informed of what was happening. Ministers concentrated on their portfolios, on the particular challenges. Many ministers quietly got on with their job, steered clear of controversy, and delivered what they promised. The press never wrote about them; the Opposition asked them no questions; and the Prime Minister was delighted that he did not have to get deeply involved. Some ministers quickly learned the value of getting approval and working below the horizon.

The Prime Minister potentially had to deal with them all. Crises, whatever their provenance, would end up on Rudd's desk, in part because the Prime Minister's role was to fix problems, but in part because the media would always ask him about them, indeed about anything that was in the news; he needed to know the state of play within any policy field. Thus, immigration policy might be quietly developing under the immigration minister, but when boat people, or an intractable issue such as the refugees on the *Oceanic Viking*, become front-page stories, Rudd had to respond.

As the worst threats of the GFC began to recede in mid-2009, other priorities took centrestage. Some of these issues were primarily domestic, but still huge in their implications. Health reform and COAG were there because they were among the government's signature polices. The health commission had reported and the government had to present and explain its ideas. COAG needed to deliver on its reforms. Broadband and telecommunications policies had to be developed. Throughout, the Senate was rejecting government proposals with a degree of unpredictability.

In these areas, solutions were seldom simple or obvious. Rudd was cautious about imposing unconsidered policy onto society. When he won office, he established a series of reviews, to the extent that it became a standing critique of the government that its policy was to establish another review. His logic was simple: the government might know in general terms what it wanted to do, but in Opposition with limited resources it could not often determine in detail how to get there or whether there might be better options. Rudd argued: 'In anything that is substantial in terms of public finance or really substantial in terms of wider public policy, you want to be deliberative because I have been around long enough to know what I don't know'.

So he established the reviews to provide the details that the government could follow through in the second half of its term: 'There is no way in the world I will touch the health and hospital system unless I have been systematically through the lot. Most of these things are quite sensitive and highly finessed which means you can't just blunder in'.

Once the commission report was submitted, Rudd and the Minister of Health, Nicola Roxon, held a series of meetings, often in hospitals, to explain the findings to an auditorium full of medical professionals. Between late July and November 2009, Rudd addressed over fifteen of these health forums, from Cairns, to Perth, to Hobart. In each case, Rudd began by describing the characteristics of the problems and presenting the overall directions of the report. He then answered questions from the floor, occasionally diverting questions to the minister or the Chair of the Commission.

The first year of a term might be spent assessing the evidence. The second year, when the report is available and the contours of the problem are evident, is about consultation. The third year can bring forth policy proposals. In a highly sensitive area, and with the restrictions caused by three-year terms, it is a cautious but necessary progress.

The Council of Australian Governments was another forum where, of necessity, there had to be a long process. Rudd would chair the COAG meetings and set the agenda. He was, a state premier reported with pleasure, highly organised, working through the agenda and pushing for clear decisions and plans for action. He could set the tone and create the expectations. Much of the detail then had to be channelled though the ministerial councils chaired by his senior ministers.

The national government has to work cooperatively with the states and rely, to a degree, on their goodwill. Each signature policy area can provide its own story of debate and development, of consultation and sometimes confrontation, of hope and disappointment. The challenge of health reform was a saga of its own.

Many of these issues combined domestic and international politics. Refugee arrivals needed negotiations with the President of Indonesia at the East Asian summit. China wanted to invest in energy supplies, while it held a Chinese mining executive with Australian citizenship without charges being detailed. Climate change and the GFC were on the agenda of the G-20 meeting in Pittsburgh. Copenhagen was to be the test for the world: Could any deal be struck to reduce carbon levels? It is used here as one illustration of the way that Rudd worked, with ministers, across a complex field of policies.

★ ★ ★

Climate change has been described by Rudd as one of the great moral issues of our time. It was obviously one case where Rudd had to be deeply involved from the beginning. Establishing a separate Department of Climate Change, entrusting it to Senator Penny Wong and placing it within the Prime Minister's portfolio were all indications of the priority that Rudd gave to the topic. Signing the Kyoto Protocol at Bali was the first and easy part. Rudd had indicated to the international community that the change of government meant a new outlook: his government believed that climate change was real, that the scientific evidence was persuasive, that some action was needed and that Australia would be at the fore in responding.

There was a local history within which Rudd had to operate. The Howard government had, recently and somewhat reluctantly, created a joint government–business Task Group on Emissions Trading. The group included six current or former departmental secretaries and a number of business leaders. It was headed by the secretary of PM&C, Peter Shergold. It published a discussion paper in August 2006 and a final report in May 2007. The committee accepted the existence of climate change and agreed that the only practical response was to use market forces and put a price on carbon. It proposed an emissions trading scheme. One important issue was the level of compensation that should be paid to the bigger polluters; the proposal was generous to them.

A second review was also underway, headed by Professor Ross Garnaut, an economist of international standing, a former economic adviser to Prime Minister Bob Hawke and ambassador to China. He was commissioned in April 2007 by Rudd, then Leader of the Opposition, and by the state premiers, then all Labor, to develop ways in which they should respond to climate change. Garnaut insisted on terms of reference that gave him independent status; he worked with administrative support from the Premier's Department of Victoria, and some of the review's modelling was done by Treasury in Queensland.

By the time of Rudd's election victory, Garnaut's review was well advanced. An interim report was issued in February 2008 and his final report in September 2008. The report provided ideas, guidelines, possible solutions and a point of reference; Garnaut did not underestimate the difficulty of the project; he described climate change as a diabolical policy problem.

However, even while anticipating the Garnaut reports, the government, once elected, had to start discussing the structure of an emissions trading scheme (ETS). Rudd faced a political challenge of exquisite delicacy. Whatever he might want to do, he would have to get the legislation through the Senate. The Coalition victory in 2004 had given it a Senate majority until July 2008. Given the senators elected would then serve until 2011, the consequence of that defeat lived long for the government. After July 2008, Rudd had to depend at a minimum either on the support of the Greens and the two, often conservative, independents, or on the Liberal Opposition. The Greens wanted radical action, but the Family First senator, Steve Fielding, was in the thrall of climate change sceptics. The Liberals had a hard core, led by the Liberal Senate leader Nick Minchin and Nationals leader Barnaby Joyce, which did not believe any warming was a consequence of human actions. At first sight, neither option seemed to be viable. What satisfied the Greens would repel the Liberals. If both rejected any legislation, it would be for different reasons: the one because it did not go far enough, the other because it went too far. However, since any action with the Greens also needed Family First, that route was off the table. The ETS could only be passed with some Liberal support. Any strategy would require a combination of skill and good fortune.

The government chose not to wait. Rudd believed quick action was important for two reasons: to demonstrate Australia's serious commitment to tackling the issue, and for domestic political reasons because it had been a clear electoral commitment. The possible divisions of the Opposition on the topic were a bonus.

In his Cabinet arrangements, Rudd established a committee on climate change. He chaired it himself. Over the next year there was an inner troika of the Prime Minister, Treasurer and Minister for Climate Change who worked through the details. Climate change was always going to be brutally difficult. The climate impacts were gradual, affecting the planet over the next century, with forecasts of extreme weather events and rising sea waters in 2050 or 2100. The great preponderance of scientific evidence supported the case, with the International Climate Change Committee and the Stern Report (named after the economist Nicholas Stern, who headed the committee) providing an overview of the evidence, the likely consequences and the need for action. However, their opponents, whether for political advantage or genuine scepticism, challenged the need for action, the timing of any unilateral Australian policies and the desirability of any particular strategy the government chose to adopt.

Any government decision had to take account of the science, the cost of not acting now, and the actions (or inaction) of other countries, particularly the big polluters, the United States and China. It also had to explain to its electors why action was needed and what it might cost them.

The government's policy was one of gradual development. With an issue of such complexity, which would have an impact on much of the Australian population, it wanted to move fast, but with due consultation. In Opposition, the capacity to develop policy is limited by time and personnel. In government, the ministers have much greater capacity to access information and use all the resources of their departments to consider the alternative options and to model their consequences. Establishing inquiries to explore what the situation really was, rather than rushing ahead on the basis of what was known in Opposition, might have been cautious, but it was also good risk management. Often the ministers knew they wanted to tackle a problem, and in general terms they knew how they would act, but they needed those ideas to be developed and tested, and for the operational implications to be calculated.

The government decided to explain its intentions through the publication of a Green Paper that would lay out the arguments and the government's preferences. Rudd recalls: 'We sat in the Cabinet Subcommittee on Climate Change for literally weeks on end, for hours on end, in each meeting to go through that agenda for the carbon pollution reduction scheme, line by line, until everyone was on the page and on the bus'.

The committee met every day from 23 to 27 June, for a total of over eleven hours. While meeting time was formally 8.30 p.m. until 10 p.m., it could in practice go on into the early hours. The next week the committee met a further three times. In addition, the climate troika of Rudd, Swan and Wong met another six times in the same two-week period for at least another twelve hours or more. The final committee meeting was on 7 July, and the Green Paper was signed off. The ministerial commitment was intense.

The committee went through the sections of the draft with great care and at excruciating length. It had already been both a learning and a decision-making process. In the first meetings, the ministers had to get their heads around the problems and the likely impacts of any decisions. Then they began to make choices, on the extent of the scheme and on levels of compensation. Many of the tough decisions were taken in the process of developing the Green Paper in the first six months of the government. If it was accepted that there should be a 'cap and trade' system, by which the government decided the acceptable level of carbon emissions; that level could be gradually reduced. It would then sell permits, each of which gave the holder a right to emit a determined level of pollutants. The permits could be traded. A company could decide whether it was preferable to buy permits at the then market price, or to alter its practices to reduce the volume of carbon that it produced. The government would have to decide what the overall targets would be (a 5 per cent reduction, or more, on 2010 levels, and what target by 2050), what permits would be given rather than sold to the big polluters, and what compensation should be paid to citizens at what levels of income to counter the price increases in electricity and other goods.

The Green Paper was published on 16 July 2008. Rudd appeared that evening on *The 7.30 Report* to explain the initiative. The reaction was predictable. The Greens declared it was a sell-out, failing to take the perils of climate change seriously. The Leader of the Opposition began to back away from the policy that Howard had taken to the 2007 election, a cap and trade system based on the Shergold report of

Resetting Priorities: Climate Change

2006–2007. The logic was that, whereas electors might be prepared to accept in principle the idea of action on climate change, when they saw what it might cost they would change their view. It was one of the reasons for which Brendan Nelson was overthrown as leader of the Liberal Party by Malcolm Turnbull, who believed in the existence of climate change and was an advocate for stronger action.

Late in the year, issues of climate change became swamped in the deluge of economic crises. Rudd insisted that the process keep to schedule. The departments continued to hold consultations around the country at every stage of the process. A White Paper was produced on schedule in November 2008. The legislation proposed a cap and trade scheme covering some 1100 firms; it determined the rate of compensation that would be provided to consumers, particularly those at lower-income levels, faced with rising prices because of the cost of traded permits.

That was to be the basis of the government's legislation that was introduced in mid-2009. It was passed by the House of Representatives but rejected by the Senate. The government announced that the Bill would be reintroduced later in the year. If it was rejected a second time, the government would have the trigger for a double dissolution of the parliament, forcing both houses to an election. Rudd insisted that he did not want an early poll and that governments should go full term; he wanted the Bill and wanted it before he went to Copenhagen. However, the prospect of a double dissolution certainly spooked the Opposition, which feared electoral disaster. Furthermore, the Coalition leader, Malcolm Turnbull, had pushed for a similar system as environment minister in the Howard government and insisted he did not want to lead a party that did not want to take it seriously.

For six months, Rudd watched while the Coalition split and split again on the issue. The National Party's de facto leader, Barnaby Joyce, who was in the Senate, said he would not support the Bill under any circumstances. When Turnbull declared that the Liberals would agree if its amendments were adopted, Rudd sent Wong to negotiate with Liberal spokesman Ian Macfarlane. The two managed to engineer a compromise that both found acceptable; it excluded agriculture permanently (rather than until 2015) and increased the compensation to some big polluters. Rudd and Wong took it to the Labor Cabinet and the party room; Rudd told the Liberals that the deal stood for that week. The Coalition parliamentary parties met all day on 25 November, and debate raged. Without going to a vote, Turnbull declared the majority of the room were in favour and the Coalition would vote for the Bill. He told the government it had a deal. It appeared that the government's measure would pass on the basis of the compromise and with Liberal support.

But then the Liberals disintegrated. Those opposed to the measure, and not coincidentally to Turnbull's leadership, first attempted to call for a spill of the leadership. It was easily lost. Then a substantial group, led by Senate leader Nick Minchin, resigned from the Shadow Cabinet; they were also determined to prevent the Bill reaching a vote in the Senate by talking and talking on every clause. There was no way the government could force votes. Its deal with the Liberal leader was not honoured. A second challenge was organised, with Tony Abbott arguing it was about policy, not personality. Ideas of promoting Joe Hockey as a compromise disappeared when Hockey said he would give Liberals a conscience vote on the issue. While the government watched, Abbott defeated Turnbull by one vote, 41 to 40, and the party voted to oppose the climate change Bill. In the Senate, two Liberals voted with the government, but that was not enough. The coalition of Liberals, Nationals, Greens and independents easily voted the Bill down.

In Abbott, Rudd faced a different type of opponent: religious, intelligent and educated, but a political street fighter who argued that the role of the Opposition is to oppose, not provide detailed alternatives.

Rudd had wanted to go to Copenhagen with his legislation in place, in part as an indication that Australia was serious in its determination to tackle climate change (even if not serious enough in the minds of many critics who wanted more drastic action). He also wanted the legislation passed because he believed that action was not just a political tactic, but a necessary response to the problems. The numbers in the Senate made that impossible.

While climate change was a divisive domestic issue, it was an equally divisive international one. The UN Climate Change conference at Copenhagen was to be held in December 2009. Many leaders hoped a successor to Kyoto would be negotiated. But little progress was being made. Rudd's opponents accused him of being hasty in seeking to rush through a scheme that would cost Australian producers and citizens, even though it would have no real impact on the world's climate unless the big polluters—China, India and the United States—signed on. They argued, primarily as a tactic, that they wanted to delay action until they saw what the rest of the world decided to do. Rudd insisted that Australia should do its part, and that delay would be costly.

However, the prospects for Copenhagen looked grim. Rudd still kept pushing the agenda at a range of international forums. As chair of the Pacific Island forum, he was well aware of the fears of the inhabitants of the small and low-lying Pacific Islands, places like Kiribati and Tuvalu, which rose only a metre or two above the ocean and could disappear if the sea levels rose as much as anticipated. Since Rudd had a voice in forums such as the G-20, he could speak for them there and emphasise the urgency that they felt. The issue was raised at the G-20 meeting in London and at the Major Economies Forum at the margin of the G-8 meeting at L'Aquila. It was a significant item on the agenda at Pittsburgh, where Rudd pushed for some coordinated action on research to mitigate the rise of carbon levels. He wanted countries to specialise, with Australia taking the lead on clean-coal technology.

In October 2009 the pace increased, as it appeared possible that no agreement would be reached. Rudd was asked to be one of the friends of the Chair in Copenhagen; that is, part of an inner group who would be able to assist in pushing the leaders to some solution. He became one of the video-linked Copenhagen Commitment Circle (CCC), a group of national leaders and the chiefs of international organisations, such as the United Nations and the European Community, who talked of ways that the agenda might be advanced. The link was chaired by the Danish Prime Minister, who would be the host and chair of the Copenhagen conference. The members included heads of state from Britain, Norway, Bangladesh, Ethiopia, Mexico and Australia, as well as the Secretary-General of the UN and the President of the EU. They represented diverse countries, in terms of both geography and economic standing. They all knew that the perils of climate change were real and that some action was required. They accepted the overwhelming scientific evidence; at the very least, prudence and risk management required some cooperation and progress. They were all also conscious of the problems of getting commitments from the great powers: Would the US be spooked by targets? Would China be prepared to accept reductions in carbon when its people blamed developed nations for creating the problem in the first place? How should compensation for adaptation or mitigation be paid?

They could discuss what options could be pursued, and what tactics might work. Most important was the issue of how both China and the United States could be engaged. The very fact that all these leaders were prepared to put aside an hour in their busy diaries, working across time zones and interests, indicated the importance they gave to the events. One such meeting was held on 25 November 2009. After dinner, at midnight, Rudd returned to Parliament House to attend a meeting of the CCC. Time zones make such arrangements difficult. On this occasion, the leaders came from four continents; often the meeting covered five. So midnight in Canberra was midday in Europe and early morning in the Americas. Rudd joked that he was having his late-night Scotch when the President of Mexico had his morning coffee.

The Danish Prime Minister as Chair called first to Gordon Brown, the British leader, who put a suggestion on the table. The leaders were discussing a 'non-paper', the diplomatic jargon for a draft proposal that was circulated for discussion but did not commit the author or anyone else. Sometimes it was called a 'non-existent non-paper', for emphasis. The Danish Chair crossed to the Norwegian Prime Minister, to Rudd and to the leaders of Mexico and Ethiopia. Each contributed his own ideas on ways that some thorny problem could be tackled. New ideas were appreciated and accepted. They were all heads of government. When they talked in these forums, they spoke for their nations. The Secretary-General of the United Nations entered the debate, although technical failures meant that his contribution was interrupted until communications were restored. The President of the European Union explained the position of his members. They all sought to make constructive suggestions on the best strategies to advance the international negotiation. They all wanted Copenhagen to succeed in moving international responses along.

There was an agreement that it would be useful for an Op-Ed piece, under all their names, to be published. Rudd had already provided his colleagues with a draft. After an hour, with leaders coming in and out of the discussion, the conference ended. Some of the participants planned to meet the next week at the Commonwealth

Heads of Government Meeting (CHOGM) in Trinidad. The leaders of Denmark and the UN had been invited to talk to Commonwealth leaders about the proceedings at Copenhagen; any international forum, particularly one that brought together over fifty countries, was too good an opportunity to miss. The meeting finished at 1 a.m., and for the Prime Minister it was then back to The Lodge.

Rudd took every opportunity to push the case. He co-chaired a working breakfast with APEC leaders at the meeting in Singapore on 15 November. When the Commonwealth Heads of Government met in Trinidad, the Prime Minister of Denmark, Lars Lokke Rasmussen, the French President, Nicholas Sarkozy, and the Secretary-General of the UN, Ban Ki-moon, talked to the fifty-three heads of state about climate change. Rudd chaired a small group that drew up the three-page statement in which the fifty-three countries represented at Trinidad threw their support behind a climate change declaration. Rudd joined the UN Secretary-General and the Danish Prime Minister in a press conference. The statement gave support to Gordon Brown's proposal for a $10 billion 'fast start' fund to assist poor countries to deal with the consequences of climate change. Rudd claimed: 'That single voice is saying to the world that we, as the Commonwealth representing one-third of the world's population, believe the time for action on climate change has come'.

Rudd then flew on to Washington for a hastily scheduled meeting with President Obama to brief him on the discussions that had taken place at CHOGM.

The preparations continued apace. The last CCC video conference had been held on 10 December, just before the Copenhagen conference began. Rudd had also talked to several leaders, including Ethiopia's Meles Zenawi, who acted as a spokesman for many African countries; Chancellor Merkel; and Danish Prime Minister Rasmussen, the conference Chair. He talked to Gordon Brown on the phone twice in that week.

RESETTING PRIORITIES: CLIMATE CHANGE

Rudd flew to Copenhagen in hope rather than anticipation. The conference had been in session for a few days and was going nowhere. The hope was that when all the national leaders arrived they would be able to break the deadlocks. The key players were Chinese Premier Wen Jiabao and President Obama, as leaders both of the biggest polluters and greatest powers.

Rudd arrived late on Tuesday, 15 December. He met Rasmussen and Brown almost immediately. Since the conference was clearly not making progress, some alternative strategy was needed. Rudd suggested that Rasmussen prepare a Chair's draft and try to introduce it to the conference. Then, at 11.15 p.m., he met Ethiopian Prime Minister Meles to see if he could broker a compromise on his financing proposal that would make it acceptable to the United States. Africa needed funds for mitigation. The poor countries there would be the first affected and could least afford to respond.

The next morning Rudd met with the leaders of a number of small states, such as the Maldives and Guyana, and with a number of less-developed countries such as Nepal. These were the countries that might suffer dramatically from the physical consequences of climate change and needed assistance. The conference still had no workable text that could form a basis for agreement. When Rasmussen took the chair, the conference neither supported the introduction of a Danish draft, nor gave him permission to convene a small group of leaders and ministers to develop a draft.

With the conference due to end on the Friday, no outcome seemed possible. At 7.30 a.m. on the Thursday, the group who had worked for the previous six weeks as 'friends of the Chair' agreed to prepare a leaders' draft as a last-ditch effort. The group included the leaders of Britain, Norway, Vietnam, Bangladesh, Mexico and Australia. They set their officials to work. At noon, they reviewed the draft text and suggestions on how they might sell it. Over the afternoon, Rudd talked to more than twenty leaders to try to build support.

It was in these environments that Rudd's insistence on knowing all the connections and details paid off. His powers of persuasion were based on that detail. An adviser commented:

> He is much more across the detail than most of his counterparts. He was able to explain things, leader to leader, and obviously, when something is being explained from one leader to another leader, they take it that much more seriously … Most of the leaders operated, necessarily, at the higher level of principle, but when it came to doing what they needed to do at Copenhagen, which is to personally negotiate the text of an accord where there are some enormous complexities and technicalities, then, as one of the people who were across the detail, he had an important role that enabled those in the room to move forward.

There was one positive step that afternoon when Secretary of State Hillary Clinton announced the United States would be prepared to join other countries to commit US$100 billion by 2020 to assist poor countries adjust to the effects of climate change. The friends of the Chair met for the third time that day at 6.30 p.m. to determine the next step.

That same Thursday, Rudd addressed the conference. He identified the four major points of disagreement: on the need for mitigation, on climate change finance to deal with the needs of the poorest countries, on verification, and on the future of the Kyoto Protocol and its intersection with any new Copenhagen accord. He noted those who would lose: 'the washing away of villages in Tuvalu, Kiribati or the Maldives … the melting of the glaciers of the Tibetan plateau … the thirty million of the most vulnerable people in the low-lying areas of Bangladesh … the Chinese peasants dealing with unprecedented drought on the North China plain'. And he appealed on behalf of the children of the future: 'History will be the judge of each of us today'.

At 11 p.m., Rasmussen convened a meeting of twenty-five leaders who agreed to work on a final statement. It would ultimately be based in part on the draft of the 'friends of the Chair', rather than the drafts of the different working groups. The twenty-five countries came together for a midnight meeting. Again, ministers and officials were tasked with the responsibility to work through the night to seek agreement. However, when the twenty-five leaders convened the next morning, little progress had been made; the Chinese Premier did not attend but sent a more junior official. Then Obama arrived and began to work the room, while Rudd sat down with others to negotiate a text. At 3 p.m. the leaders reconvened, with a number of issues outstanding, particularly questions of verification. The Chinese withdrew their support and by 4 p.m. some of the leaders had given up and left the venue. A few, including Rudd, urged leaders to keep going, even if only with officials there and with no Chinese representative.

In the meantime, Obama and Wen agreed to meet and try to settle on an outcome, while Rudd and Meles worked up a compromise on financing that could be acceptable to the United States. Obama returned to the conference centre with agreement on some issues with Wen and sold the compromise to India, South Africa and Brazil. Rudd continued until midnight at the centre, negotiating compromises on a number of issues of concern for small island states, particularly from the Pacific. By 11 a.m. on Saturday, a text was agreed by the small group of twenty-five leaders and finally noted by the conference.

Copenhagen had an outcome—of sorts—but no guaranteed action, no legally binding targets, only aspirations at best. It was far less than any hoped for. That is not atypical of international conferences. Some of them work. Others are too divided to reach a conclusion. The caravan moved on to Mexico in 2010. In the meantime, questions would arise as to whether there would be forward action in other forums, such as the G-20.

So, for reasons entirely outside of Rudd's control, the results on climate change were disappointing. In the second half of 2009, the government had taken a low public profile while the Opposition fought its internal battles. While the Opposition was the issue, Rudd could concentrate on the external management and the lead-up to Copenhagen. Had one vote in the Liberal leadership been different and Turnbull been returned, the emissions trading scheme might have passed in the amended negotiated form. Had Copenhagen developed real clout internationally, then external pressure would have put moral pressure on Australia to keep in step as part of international commitments. However, the Copenhagen conference failed to reach binding agreements, and Tony Abbott was elected.

With the Opposition committed to oppose any legislation that put a price on carbon—a great big new tax, as Abbott described it— and with the Opposition and Greens combining to reject his ETS proposals, Rudd had to reconsider his options for 2010. Should he call a double dissolution on climate change and an ETS that was less than optimal because it had had to be negotiated with the Coalition? Any joint sitting rising from that poll could only consider the Bills on which the election was called; he could not reintroduce his preferred scheme. Should he reintroduce his proposals, knowing that they would be defeated again and again, but as an indication that he was serious? Or should he take the issue off the table temporarily, on the grounds that little progress had been made internationally?

Of course, climate change was just one of the stories running at the time. It has to be understood within the broader context of the standing of the government within the community. There, Rudd's reputation remained high.

By the end of 2009, Rudd had continued to maintain consistent support in the electorate for two years. According to Newspoll, when respondents were asked who would make the better prime minister (against whichever Opposition leader was in the position at the time), Rudd had always rated 54 per cent or more—for long periods, well into the mid-60s. On the question 'Are you satisfied with the performance of the Prime Minister?', he had not rated below 50 per cent, and had not gone under 55 per cent between October 2008, when the government tackled the GFC, and December 2009. The Labor party too had been ahead, on the two-party preferred vote, with support between 52 and 60 per cent, all the way to the end of 2009; it was always in a winning position. It was a long, sustained record of support, far longer than any anticipated honeymoon. There was nothing to suggest in the polls that the government was soon to be in electoral or political trouble.

These were the circumstances in which Rudd found himself at the beginning of 2010. Many of his initiatives had been be rejected in the Senate. Yet governments had some advantages. They could set the agenda by what they did, while the Opposition could only promise and criticise. And yet it is the impressions, not the details, that determine elections. Managing those impressions, presenting the picture of a government in control of its agenda and knowing where it is going, what it believes and what it wants to achieve, would be for Rudd the key to continuing success in 2010. That proved harder.

PART III
STRUGGLING

18

CHALLENGES

From its green room, the Copenhagen conference looked different from the disaster that it was seen to be in Australia. Certainly there was no great deal to which the world was committed, but some groundwork had been laid and many heads of state had been involved. In Australia, however, the picture was one of chaos and deadlock, playing to the Opposition's claims that Australia should not act until the rest of the world had moved too. Most affected were the numbers men of the New South Wales Labor branch who feared that climate change would be a millstone around the government's neck; they thought it should be dropped. If that was too drastic, it was not clear what the best alternative strategy might be, either to prepare the electorate for changing the approach or redefine the issue.

Rudd had an immediate choice to make. When the Opposition, with the support of the Greens, rejected the ETS in December 2009, it created the conditions for a double dissolution. Rudd could take both Houses to the people and then, if he was returned without a majority in the Senate, could use a joint sitting to pass the legislation. A double dissolution would cause problems in the future. The Senate terms would be backdated to 1 July 2009; the next Senate election would have to be held by June 2012, thus effectively ensuring that a House of Representatives vote would have to be held then too, so its term would be just over two years. But a successful result might have allowed the Bills through.

There is, and will continue to be, dispute about whether there should have been a double dissolution and who favoured and opposed it. In hindsight, more and more people wish that the government had gone to the polls then; perhaps consequently more and more people remember how much they favoured it at the time. There is never likely to be consensus amid the swirling array of revelations now emerging. Labor's New South Wales branch opposed the idea on the grounds that the election could be lost—a pessimistic evaluation that illustrated how much Abbott, with his 'one great big tax on everything', had already spooked the party apparatchiks. Rudd recalls that Gillard agreed with this perception, and told the Prime Minister in a meeting between the two at Kirribilli that she would not support an early election on climate change (an interpretation that Gillard disputes). Nor was there much support when cabinet ministers were consulted in another meeting at Kirribilli. Faulkner alone pressed for action, as he had done for months. There was little backing for him in the Cabinet room; others demurred or opposed. Rudd had long argued that governments should run their terms and that the Australian people did not like early elections. Besides, at the time it looked likely that the government would win whenever they went. So Rudd, after listening to the prophets of woe, the pessimists, decided not to go. Of course, the option remained open until August; according to the Constitution, a double dissolution can be called any time until the last three months of a parliamentary term. Still, in retrospect, this proved to be a pivotal decision: had the Prime Minister called a double dissolution, even against the advice of senior ministers and party officers, then he might have been returned with greater standing and carried the legislation; even had he lost, he would have done so fighting for the greatest moral challenge of our time. Hindsight is easy.

Problems now emerged on two fronts: the home insulation scheme and the Building the Education Revolution (BER). Both had been part of the response to the GFC. Both were intended to assist in filling the gap before other monetary measures had an impact. The idea was that, by introducing funding for schemes that could be implemented quickly, employment would be maintained, particularly in unskilled areas. Australia stayed out of a recession; in that respect, the policy worked. But the rush with which the schemes were introduced meant that there were problems of oversight and implementation. That these problems were in part anticipated did not reduce the difficulties in dealing with them.

The BER was delivered by state governments; it consisted of providing funds to build new halls, classrooms and other facilities. Since the states already owned the land, there was no need to gain government approval for new buildings. Consequently, the process could be expedited. It was done in a rush. There were a number of issues: sometimes the cost was higher than it might have been if more careful assessments had been undertaken. In a few cases, buildings were allocated to schools where decisions had already been made to close them in the future. In some cases, locals complained that the most appropriate building was not selected. Some such problems were perhaps inevitable in a scheme intended to provide employment as much as buildings. A later review found that, given the size of the scheme, the dissatisfied schools were really very few. But they were given attention and the picture of constant complaint began to grate. The BER was in the Deputy Prime Minister's portfolio; Rudd left the running to Gillard, but often had to defend the details of the program in Question Time.

The home insulation scheme was much smaller, but became more controversial. By supporting an extensive expansion of home insulation, the government had allowed newcomers to rapidly enter the industry to take advantage of the new funding. Not all were qualified, experienced or scrupulous. Sometimes, occupational health and safety guidelines were ignored. That said, the regulation of the industry's standards was the responsibility of state governments; the federal department did not have the personnel, the expertise or the systems to regulate the installation of insulation at the many sites.

In broad terms, the scheme led to a large number of houses being insulated. In the year before the scheme, 67 000 houses had insulation installed; in the year of the scheme, the number was 1 100 000, and about 10 000 jobs were created. From that initial 67 000, there had been 80 reported fires from poor insulation; from the 1 100 000, there were 120 reported fires: a massive *reduction* in the incidents per installation. There were about 10 000 complaints: that is, 1 per cent of the installations. One calculation suggested that the reduction in carbon from the insulation of half the uninsulated residences in the country was the equivalent of taking a million cars off the road (or in another guess, 300 000). Whatever the real number, there were benefits in carbon reduction too.

The administration of the scheme, however, fell far short of acceptable standards. Stories about failings in the rollout began to emerge; stories of fires circulated. In late 2009, four young people died in Queensland and New South Wales when they were installing batts in roofs. One man in New South Wales died from heat exhaustion. Of the three deaths in Queensland, one man died from faulty wiring in the roof before the pink batts were installed, and two other young men died when using steel staple guns that hit live electrical cables. In all three Queensland tragedies, the companies that employed the young men were fined by state authorities because they failed to follow health and safety regulations; the companies were negligent. It mattered not that reviews of the scheme suggested that the great majority of installations were effective and welcomed. Pink batts became bywords for government incompetence.

The government administration had failed too. The massive expansion of the scheme brought into the industry a number of dodgy operators, because there was no way the existing firms could expand to meet the increased demand in time. The introduction was rushed; an important factor in the scheme had been speed: to get the projects moving fast to protect the unskilled labour force from many of the consequences of the GFC. Initially, there was a need for a co-payment and the householders could claim their costs. Later, it was amended so that contractors could claim directly through Medicare. There were a small number of false claims. But in the preparation, some corners had to be cut if the fundamental intention, employment, was to be achieved. The costs were high.

The 1 per cent complaint level raises questions about risk management in the public sector. What is acceptable in the private sector can never be taken as given in the public sector. One of Thatcher's businessmen in government told a House of Commons Committee that

> if you are running a business in the private sector, to be successful you have to be right more often than you are wrong. If you are right 51 per cent of the time, you are just on the right side of that line. If you are right 60 per cent of the time, you are doing better. If you are right 70 per cent of the time, you are doing well. If you are right 80 per cent of the time, you are doing brilliantly. However in the public sector, if you are right 98 per cent of the time, people are not interested in the 98 per cent; they are interested in the 2 per cent that you are wrong because the 2 per cent will be the ones that people are concerned about, where things

are not being done properly, where things are not being done the way people would like to see them done. Therefore the difference you mentioned is that you cannot say, 'I will not worry about the few per cent that I got wrong'.

What had been scattered and occasional problems with insulation now became part of a set of interconnected phenomena. Fires from insulation were reported, whereas earlier they had not been. The 1 per cent of complaints became regarded as an avalanche and were now on the front pages of the newspapers. The successes of the scheme—insulating half the houses that had no insulation, introducing training schemes where none existed, maintaining employment for 10 000 unskilled workers—were lost in the emphasis on the mistakes, albeit mistakes that were perhaps inevitable in the rush.

In making the decision to launch the scheme, the government had had to make choices. It had been looking for a scheme that would have an immediate impact on employment and could start at once. There may have been some advice raising questions about the capacity of the government to introduce and oversee a scheme that would be so decentralised, delivered by a multiplicity of micro firms on the ground. If the intent had been insulation, rather than employment, the scheme might have been introduced more gradually; there were plenty of people who raised such issues while the initiative was being planned. Not all the caveats were passed on. The public servants stressed that they had deadlines, imposed by government, that they had to meet. Anyway, the Cabinet had to decide between introducing it slowly after extensive discussion and thus losing the benefit of the employment bonus that was a principal purpose, or moving fast and accepting there would be some costs. These are the hard decisions governments must make and there can be no single correct answer at the time (which is different from retrospective wisdom).

After a number of problems emerged in the first eight months of the home insulation project, the Minister for the Environment, Peter Garrett, who had responsibility for the scheme, wrote to the Prime Minister reporting on progress and asking for some variations in the program. One of the letters was taken to a Cabinet committee, which approved the recommendation of the minister. Rudd remained supportive of a scheme that seemed to be delivering both insulation and employment benefits. But early in 2010, the tragedies and the general complaints began to have an effect. Rudd asked a task force of departmental secretaries to report. They argued that the administrative arrangements were flawed and could not be rectified. They recommended that the scheme as it stood should be ended.

The issue for Rudd was how to respond: he decided that, as the scheme was introduced by, even if not overseen or delivered by, the federal government, he had to formally take responsibility. In such cases it is not enough to point out that state governments should fulfil their supervisory obligations and all firms should follow the rules and the law.

On 25 February 2010, Rudd went on *The 7.30 Report* to respond to the critics. He took the blame:

> Let's not try to sugar-coat this, Kerry, and I don't for one minute. This program has created real problems on the ground; it has resulted in a lot of difficulty for a lot of people. As Prime Minister of the country I accept responsibility for that. My job now is to fix it up.

The charge was that the government had tried to introduce the program too quickly. As Rudd admitted, those who were rorting the system or ignoring the guidelines were not picked up by the compliance mechanisms. As he later testified to a royal commission, ministers were not told the program was in trouble until that February. It had received a satisfactory progress rating in the system of program reports.

Perhaps for the first time since he had won the election, Rudd looked rattled. Taking personal responsibility may have been an instinctive reaction: where problems occurred, he wanted to fix them. But it also connected him with the furore about the scheme's record.

Rudd removed responsibility for the program from the Minister for the Environment and gave it to his fix-it man, Greg Combet. A few days later, on the advice of the task force Rudd had convened, the scheme was cancelled. But the poor image never went away. The industry complained that a perfectly sound small sector had been swamped and then deserted, leaving them with a bad reputation and oversupply of goods. Those who had had insulation installed, particularly the foil that had had to be stapled in, were concerned their houses might catch fire. The Opposition blamed the government for every misdeed of every small firm across the country. The image of the 'pink batts debacle' lived with the government: If you cannot install pink batts, how can you govern the country?

The Prime Minister did another mea culpa on *Insiders* (compere Barrie Cassidy was not a fan of Rudd; over five years he rarely missed an opportunity to snipe and denigrate Rudd, whether as the prime minister present or past). He admitted that the decline in the government's fortunes had occurred because 'we haven't been up to the mark so far'.

> We are taking a whacking in the polls now. I'm sure we'll take an even bigger whacking in the period ahead. And the bottom line is, I think we deserve it, both not just in terms of recent events, but more broadly. Where we have to improve and lift our game, where I need to lift my game, is in delivering in the key outstanding areas of reform in health and hospitals, in education and getting on with the business of action on climate change as well.

He argued that he would have to work harder, a proposal that those who watched him knew to be impossible. First the Copenhagen failure and then insulation; the until-now continuous levels of support from the Australian people were beginning to falter. The party numbers men were nervous.

For Rudd, the next two months were all about health. Health was one of the government's signature programs, those programs where, from the beginning, the Prime Minister was going to take a leading role. But health, for federal governments, can be a frustrating slow-burn area. Whatever is decided takes time before it can be implemented and the results are even slower to see in terms of service. Furthermore, hospitals, the area of health most obvious and stressful for patients, were delivered by state governments, which wanted to protect their prerogatives. Rudd had promised that, if there was no progress in the negotiations with the states, he would put a referendum to the Australia people proposing that the federal government take over responsibility for health. As he saw it, health policy was confounded by the constant shifting of blame. Every level of government accused the other of failing to provide the appropriate level of resources.

The plan that Rudd announced on 5 March had been a long time in the planning. The Prime Minister had established the National Health and Hospitals Reform Commission to review the arrangements. Over the previous year he had visited a number of hospitals, in company with Nicola Roxon, the Minister for Health, and Dr Christine Bennett, the chair of the commission. A number of interim reports had been released, and a final report came in late 2009. The main components of the government's proposals were that the federal government would take over acute and preventative care, aged care and primary community care (to be seen in the establishment of community clinics); hospitals would be run by local committees; and the new initiatives would be funded from an agreement by the states to return 30 per cent of the GST that they received from the federal government. These needed to be negotiated.

In March, Rudd faced Abbott in a debate on health at the National Press Club. He knew his material and was confident in his presentation. To one journalist, 'Rudd was all smiles and softly spoken solutions; Abbott was all aggro accusations'.

The next four weeks were dedicated to visiting hospitals, taking the reforms to the front line where they would be felt most directly. In March, the Prime Minister visited sixteen hospitals or clinics, talking to the staff, the nurses and the patients. In April, even while the details of the health package were being negotiated with the state governments, he went to a further twenty-one sites, sometimes taking in two hospitals in a day: Mackay and Rockhampton; Lismore and Port Macquarie; once even three: Canterbury, Campbelltown and Illawarra. This type of forum was one in which Rudd was comfortable: talking to practitioners about policy details, about the ways that health funding and delivery could best be improved, about evidence, statistics and data. Health was for him a key area, a vital priority.

Negotiating with the state premiers was altogether different. Before the speech to the Press Club, Rudd had rung each of the premiers to inform them about what was proposed. He had several meetings, sometimes over meals, with the premiers of New South Wales and Victoria. Some states were agreeable from the start. Others had very different agendas. Western Australia's Liberal Premier was happy to take the funding but was never going to agree to concede a third of the GST income back to the federal government. It was not a matter of money but of state rights. New South Wales wanted, and eventually got, more funding. Victorian Premier Brumby did not want to concede control over his hospitals. The Victorian Government believed that they had the best hospital system in the country and were not about to hand over the reins. Of course, New South Wales and Victoria did the bulk of the spending, so without their involvement the grand plan would be worth little.

COAG met in April to endorse the agreements that had been negotiated state by state. Western Australia did not sign up to the altered GST conditions; the rest of the country did.

Health was not the only policy area with which the Prime Minister was concerned at this time. In the same seven weeks between the announcement of the health plan and the COAG decision, he maintained activities in other areas. He hosted visits from the President of Indonesia, the President of Botswana, the Prime Minister of Thailand and former US secretary of state Madeleine Albright; he talked on the phone to the leaders of Chile, Pakistan, Spain and South Korea, to the President of the USA and his Treasury Secretary, and to the Director General of the IMF. There were continuing meetings of SPBC, Cabinet and its committees, and regular meetings with the Deputy PM and the Treasurer.

But health was the key; it could be the big reform and the cornerstone of Rudd's re-election campaign. His determination to know all the details that were needed, his obsession with being as well informed as, if not better informed than, anyone in the room, so that he would not be caught out and would be seen to be authoritative, meant that his concentration on this limited his continuing interest in the other issues that were on the boil.

That was illustrated by a meeting of the SPBC just as the Prime Minister came out of the final COAG meeting with the premiers. The Treasurer was trying to finalise the Budget, due the next month. He needed to know what he should put in the forward estimates: in terms of revenue or in terms of potential compensation for the introduction of the EFTS. Because the compensation would be paid before the income was raised, the differential would be a hit on the size of the deficit that Swan preferred to avoid. A meeting earlier in the year—after the Senate combination of the Coalition and Greens had again rejected the proposal—had not decided what to do next, waiting until a new Senate was elected; no other actions had been taken. Alternative ways had been considered, but not adopted.

At the SPBC meeting, a range of opinions was voiced. Gillard thought that any plan to price carbon should be put on hold until there was a consensus for change in the country, as it would otherwise be electoral poison; as long as Abbott was leader of the Opposition, that effectively meant permanent postponement. Swan wanted to fix his budget and thought it better to put the proposal on hold, even if some expenditure on alternative energy options was left. Tanner understood the fiscal problems but believed that climate change was such a high-profile commitment that it would be politically damaging to be seen to reject it; he believed that to dump the policy would have a devastating impact on the Prime Minister's credibility. Wong, attending the committee as the responsible minister, wanted to keep pushing. They all knew that the party operatives, particularly in New South Wales, by then wanted any carbon tax dumped. Rudd, frazzled and exhausted from the long hard grind over health, felt he was being railroaded into making a decision, and the committee agreed put it off until the next morning. When the meeting was reconvened and there'd been further discussion, Rudd agreed that a recommendation that expenditure on climate change should be deferred and thus not be included in the forward estimates should be sent on to Cabinet for consideration and endorsement at its next meeting. To some of the committee, this was seen as a routine, technical discussion: what should go into the budget papers. It was not an endorsement of a proposal to dump the commitment. How the deferral would be presented in public was to be determined later. That might have been the subject of Cabinet discussion.

But the belief it was just routine was belied by the violent reaction when the proposal was leaked to Lenore Taylor and published in

The Sydney Morning Herald. The story was released about four days after the meeting; the leak must have been immediate. Taylor said later: 'I did not write the story for four days because I just couldn't believe that it could be right. I kept going around and asking more people and, yep, it was right'. She could not have asked Rudd, as he was shaken and flabbergasted when the story appeared in the paper.

The immediate interpretation was that the Labor government was dropping its commitment to 'the greatest moral challenge of our time'. That had not been the intent. Unable to get its proposal through the Senate, the logic was that there was no point in pushing it up again and again. The government already had the trigger for a double dissolution on climate change and could use it any time up until August. Deferral seemed a sensible strategy and then it could try again with a new Senate after it was re-elected.

But if that was the intent, the account never surfaced. Instead, the government had to explain why it was running away from its promise. Rudd was on a visit to the Nepean Hospital when he was asked why he was dumping a commitment to carbon pricing. Since the report was accurate, in that Lenore Taylor had all the key evidence, Rudd did not think he could defer comment until the recommendation had been considered by Cabinet. So, flustered, he tried to explain what the choices were and what had been done. The responses seemed lame and poorly considered. He did not get the message across. The reports reiterated that Labor had dropped its commitment to climate change. Taylor suggested that putting climate change on hold smacked of political cowardice. The polls collapsed.

The leak was the most devastating of the year. It destabilised the government and undermined the standing of the Prime Minister with the public. Yet that public standing was one of the government's most potent assets. The leak's timing, almost straight after the SPBC meeting, suggested it was deliberate, and the detail in the report implied it was based on more than just a casual conversation. If senior officials were right and it had all the characteristics of a ministerial leak, then who had the most to gain? Whose position was bolstered by the information becoming public? It was possible that the New South Wales party officials, the most strident opponents of a continuing commitment to climate change, had been briefed on the decision and chose to lock the Cabinet in by making the recommendation public. That was one suggestion, but would they have been given the degree of detail that Taylor's report included, rather than just a general account of the committee's decision? The one member of the SPBC that everyone excluded was Rudd. Among the ministers, the leak locked the government most into the position that Gillard by then seemed to hold. But who actually gave the story to Taylor will have to wait until one of the two (or more) people concerned reveals the answer.

The consequences were dramatic, the collapse in support sudden. Prior to the leak, Newspoll recorded that Rudd had been preferred prime minister for well above 55 per cent of respondents. That now dropped to 49–50 per cent, but this still put him way ahead of Abbott. The Labor two-party preferred vote had been above 52 per cent, but now slipped to 49 per cent. The worst damage was elsewhere: in the standing of the Labor Party, whose primary vote declined from 43 to 35 per cent; and for Rudd himself—whereas previously his satisfaction rating had only fallen below 50 per cent in one poll over two years, now it collapsed, from 50 to 39 per cent, and did not recover.

The dangers were then exacerbated by what seemed to be a mishandling of the proposed mining tax by the Treasurer. Rudd set off the next storm with the announcement, on 2 May, of the new Resource Super Profits Tax (RSPT). The Henry Review of the tax system had been delivered late in 2009. The government needed to determine what would be done with the recommendations. The initiative was left with the Treasurer, who wanted some plans to indicate his reformist credentials. In the ensuing months, he and his department had been developing the RSPT. Rudd and Gillard trusted him to cover all the angles; they assumed that he would move only when he had the support of the big mining companies and the state governments. There was, however, evidence to the contrary. As one COAG meeting wound down, Rudd commented to the premiers that he would be talking to them all soon about the RSPT, which, he said, he understood all of them had agreed to. Not me, responded WA Premier Colin Barnett. Barnett recalled that Rudd's jaw dropped when he said that. Rudd thought that Swan had gained agreement. Swan's office later argued that it had never said that Barnett was on side.

Nevertheless, the RSPT launch went ahead. It was presented as a step that would provide equity for the Australian people. At a time when mining companies were reaping record profits, it seemed reasonable that Australian taxpayers should benefit from the high prices, not just from the quantities that were the subject of royalties. Through the tax, Australians would benefit from a range of measures, including higher superannuation contributions.

This was not a surprise to the mining companies, who had been talking about profit-based (rather than quantity-based) taxes with Henry over the past year. They did, however, claim to be surprised when the Budget came down. They claimed that they had talked about the principle of a profits tax, but not the detail or the settings. Yet the Budget not only included the parameters but also spent the money that the tax raised. The mining companies began a campaign, funded from their deep pockets, to undermine the proposal. In the next four weeks, as the temperature rose, more and more of the pressure of selling the proposal fell on Rudd, assisted by Mines Minister Martin Ferguson, who had barely been kept informed about the plans. Swan was overseas.

When the government began an advertising campaign to counter the claims of the mining industry, Rudd was accused of hypocrisy. He had been highly critical of the Howard government using public funds to support their initiatives. Now he was doing the same thing. Even if the amounts were less, the picture was the same.

The RSPT was complex and hard to explain. Rudd struggled, defending the government's initiative on grounds of equity. Behind the scenes, too, negotiations were difficult. The big mining companies, particularly BHP Billiton and Rio Tinto, effectively refused to participate in discussions; they sent junior staff to Treasury to talk about details, not principles. They could see a government on the run. As the weeks ran on into June, Rudd began to talk to Andrew Forrest, CEO of Fortescue Metals Group to try to get the support of the smaller mining companies. Those negotiations made progress, but were never completed.

The introduction of a new profit-based tax on mining companies, six months out from an election, was a courageous decision. There was little time to develop any public discussion to prepare the population for the change, or to ready them for the inevitable highly funded fightback from the mining companies. If the principles sounded reasonable, the details were complicated in the explanations and the refutations of the negative claims. The process seemed replete with misunderstandings, about who had agreed in advance to the tax, about what would go into the Budget, about who should negotiate. Those initial steps had been the responsibility of Swan; the tax was his and the misunderstandings were his. But by June, the Prime Minister was fully identified with the tax as, day after day, he sought to negotiate a compromise with the most powerful and intransigent international corporations working in Australia. At the same time, he had to explain his problems and the decline in his standing. Kerry O'Brien asked him on *The 7.30 Report*: 'You've spent the best part of two years building up your political capital. How have you managed to damage brand Rudd so comprehensively in such a short time this year?'

The continuing negotiations did not help his case. Later, when a new prime minister managed to have the mining company campaign called off within a day or so, in exchange for a revised tax that collected virtually nothing, it would merely add to suspicions about why Rudd had been left to carry the can.

In the meantime, the pressures of government continued. While Rudd's capacity to concentrate on the one issue, almost to the exclusion of much else, was a cause of frustration, the administration of government did not cease. Cabinet continued to meet regularly: weekly throughout February, March and May. So too did the SPBC. Sometimes it would meet several times in a rush when there were significant issues, at times for lengthy periods: for six hours on 11 April and for another three the next day when the last parts of the health package were under consideration. The Prime Minister attended other Cabinet committees in these six months: on climate change, on health. There were meetings of the National Security Committee when it was required.

In the first six months of 2010, only one minister suggested to the Prime Minister that the SPBC was dealing with too much material that should be sent to the Cabinet; that was Simon Crean. The others were prepared to accept the way the government was running without complaining to Rudd. They may have grumbled among themselves. They may have felt on the outer. They may have seen the number of issues being dealt with by the SPBC as a reduction of Cabinet government because they felt they should have been involved. But not all did; some commented they were quite happy to leave much of the grunt work to that committee and the senior ministers, because they had plenty of their own work to do.

Senior colleagues had many opportunities to talk to the Prime Minister. In late January, the PMO started to try to schedule what were described as 'daily' meetings with the Deputy Prime Minister and the Treasurer. They did not actually occur every day. It depended on where they were. Sometimes they were cancelled because the two ministers had been with the Prime Minister in the SPBC for several hours. Sometimes only one of them was there. Occasionally, another minister came in. But the intent was for regular contact, and three or four meetings were held most weeks, including fifteen in the first three weeks of June. There was opportunity aplenty to raise with the Prime Minister issues about his style, his approach or his directions. The leading ministers took the access, worked in the committees, talked strategy and government direction, but gave no indication that they were intent on changing the leadership.

19

THE COUP

The first half of 2010 was, in policy terms, a mixed bag: problems of implementation, an agreement on health that fell short of universal, a mining tax that was still shaking the foundations. It was coupled with declining popularity for the Prime Minister. That is principally the story of government. There is a parallel universe: the story of the party. That was an even less pretty picture.

Rudd's standing in the party had always depended on his capacity to win elections. He was chosen in 2006 because the party thought he could win when Beazley could not. He did. For two years Rudd rode high in the polls, a continuing record as one of the most popular prime ministers in Australian history. As long as he held that position, as long as the party felt that it would win again, he was untouchable. But he had run and won the leadership as an individual, not as a member of any faction. Indeed, he had openly challenged the very presence of factions in the party, both rhetorically and practically, by taking over from the caucus the selection of ministers. In the event, of course, he had consulted widely and paid attention to the advice of the canny veterans John Faulkner and Robert Ray when he chose the

Cabinet. Their warnings about the potential difficulties that might be created by leaving significant faction players outside Cabinet were heeded. The factions had lined up support for him when he took the leadership: constantly talking to Arbib and the powerbrokers of Sussex Street had underpinned his election. But he was not seen, and did not see himself, as a creature of factions or as being beholden to them.

Indeed, he gave short shrift to members of the caucus when they came as faction leaders to push their narrow interests. On one occasion in particular, soon after the GFC had thrown the country's economy into danger, he had reacted strongly. Senator David Feeny had led a delegation of backbench heavies to ask for an improvement in the pay and other entitlements of members of parliament. They were said to speak for their members on the backbench. Rudd thought the delegation inappropriate and insensitive. When the national economy was struggling, when electors were losing their jobs, how could a group of parliamentarians ask for a pay rise when they were already well paid? The symbolism of a group of people who only cared for themselves would not be missed. The Prime Minister got angry and told them in clear, expletive-laden terms what he thought of their requests. They did not forget. When months later his popularity began to slide, he could not rely on their support; rather, he could assume their hostility.

Rudd was not well positioned to respond to the growing discontent behind him in the parliament. The chief whip, Roger Price, regularly arranged for cohorts of backbenchers to have dinner with the Prime Minister at The Lodge, but these occasions were not seen as venues for too frank discussion. Rudd never had a praetorian guard to protect his back, a group of supporters who would have constantly monitored the sentiment and grumblings. It was not that there was no-one prepared to work that way: no-one was asked. Doug McClelland later told Maxine McKew:

> If Kevin had been able to buy himself some time and two weeks earlier had said, 'Look, these self-serving bastards are moving against me and I need some decent people to sandbag around me', I, along with others, would have done it and I reckon the coup would not have happened.

Others agreed that they would have been prepared to serve in that role too.

Rudd rather assumed, as it turned out naively, that he had been elected leader, that he had taken the party to government, and that the government had kept the country out of recession. Governing was hard and time-consuming; he was seeking to provide solutions. In those circumstances, he assumed that he should be allowed to concentrate on the issues at hand and take as given the loyalty of the backbenchers without having to constantly play to their feelings. And, as one of his supporters commented, he had a right to expect that support. The Labor Party had, throughout the twentieth century, proved to be reluctant to remove its leaders, even those without a history of success. In the last twenty years, the sense of loyalty had declined, but Bob Hawke had won four elections before he was ejected. In Opposition, the removal of Crean and Beazley shortened the tenure, but neither had led the party into government, let alone winning from a position where many had thought electoral success unlikely.

However, some on the backbench strongly resented the lack of attention, the fact that Rudd had relied on them to collect the numbers but now seemed to have no time to hear their views or their concerns; the Prime Minister simply thought he had enough on his plate and really did not sense the need. They became disgruntled and, when the polls suggested that Rudd's hold on the public's support was shaky, the disaffection became coupled with self-interest and festered.

Rudd's key links in government became more tenuous. In retrospect, he had the sense that Gillard was beginning to distance herself from him: there was the remembered opposition to any suggestion of a double dissolution on climate change and the determination that the government should put the issue of the ETS on hold until there was some sort of consensus on the topic. Then she had begun to raise questions about the organisation of the marginal electorates planning: Were the arrangements for ministers to visit these seats adequate and did they need greater attention? Visiting marginal electorates to assist threatened members was a well-established means of making connections. Rudd had been a master at it before elections in the past, not least when he wanted support. When Gillard's interest in the management of the visits was raised, Rudd responded that she was being sensitive to national needs and concerned about the government's standing. He did not see it as a process of positioning. Others were less easily persuaded of this. One account has the leader of the House, Anthony Albanese, telling Gillard that she did not have to position herself for the leadership, that she was the only possible successor to Rudd and that, when the time came, she would have the support of the party.

The discontent was boosted by a coruscating *Quarterly Essay* on Rudd by David Marr. The cut was in the final pages. After a walk on the beach in Mackay, Rudd had asked what the argument of the essay was. When Marr said he would pursue the contradictions of the Prime Minister, Rudd got annoyed. Marr wrote:

> I realise Rudd is furious. I have hurt him and he is angry. What follows is a dressing down which registers about a 3.8 on his Richter scale. He doesn't scream and bang the table as he does behind closed doors. We're in the open. The voice is low. He is perfectly composed ... What he says in these angry twenty

minutes informs every corner of this essay. But more revealing is the transformation of the man. In his anger he becomes astonishingly eloquent. This is the most vivid version of himself I've encountered. At last he is speaking from the heart, an angry heart.

Then Marr lapses into pop psychology:

Face to face, it's so clear. Rudd is driven by anger. It's the juice in the machine. He is a hard man to read because the anger is hidden by a public face, a diplomat's face. Who is the real Kevin Rudd? He is the man you see when the anger vents. He's a politician with rage at his core, impatient rage.

Rudd felt he had the right to be angry, because the conclusion of the essay had nothing to do with what they had discussed during the walk on the beach. There, Marr had been principally interested in whether Rudd had been sexually assaulted at Marist Brothers Ashgrove, because he never talked about his time at the school. Rudd insisted there was brutality but not assault. After such a narrow if repetitive conversation, when so many other issues could have been canvassed, he was indeed annoyed when Marr raised themes he had never talked about when he had the opportunity. He told Marr that he did not get what drove him: the desire to improve education and health were priorities. He did not think he should apologise for not pushing gay marriage because the party had told the electorate it would not. His priorities and Marr's were very different. That was the core of the conversation. To translate that into a conclusion that anger was the driving force of Rudd's persona was a big jump.

But Marr's attack had resonance because Marr writes well and succinctly, with good phrases for headlines. He promoted himself and his essay with panache; he had people talking. Here was an articulate and entertaining darling of the left hammering a Labor prime minister with a deeply cutting portrait, albeit one that was highly contentious. To some it was seen as a licence to hate: if that is what a leftie like Marr thinks, then their dislike of the Prime Minister was justified.

By then there were stirrings as the faction leaders sought to gain support. It was a revolt of the NCOs, not of Cabinet ministers. Arbib and Bill Shorten, the most prominent of the plotters, were not yet Cabinet ministers; the others were figures virtually unknown to the public. Most of them had only been in parliament since 2007; none had been through the demoralising struggles in Opposition. They were practised in the dark arts of politics and had no experience of the difficulties of actually governing. Politics continued to be party politics, not the politics of office. If, as one observer put it, to a hammer everything looks like a nail, then to faction leaders, any drop in polls means a change in leaders. It had become the pattern in New South Wales, although with no sign that the prospects of the party there had been improved. Faction leaders were accustomed to plotting and counting. Their lord was the focus group, their target winning elections at any cost: 'Whatever it takes', as their godfather put it. Rumours swirled.

It was reported that Arbib rang Feeny and said: 'You know we are going to lose. So do I. We can win this with Gillard. If we both know it, don't we have an obligation to the party to fix it?' The decision to toss a leader became a first choice, not a last resort. There was no discussion about how to get things back on track.

A poll was taken in New South Wales on the same weekend that a state by-election in Penrith was being held that everyone knew would be a disaster for the state government and a portent of things to come. Whether it was possible to get an accurate reading of federal standing might be questioned, but a fair view was not what was wanted. The results, it seems, were selectively circulated to backbenchers as a warning of what might happen.

But it all depended on one person. If Julia Gillard was not a runner, there was no race, as no-one else could fill the spot. It was her choice, her responsibility. Publicly she continued to pledge her support for Rudd, suggesting it was more likely that she would be full-forward for Footscray than prime minister. What happened in private remains unclear. It was later revealed that a member of her staff had drafted a possible victory speech for the time she took over. Freelancing, it was argued, just anticipating what might eventuate, being prepared; that seems ingenuous in an office where time was short and where any leak of such a draft would have been little short of volcanic. If the chief of staff did not know, he should have.

In late May, while travelling with Swan during the selling of the mining tax, Rudd asked his Treasurer if he was still with him, and was given assurances that he was. Swan said so publicly, too. On 14 June, he stated to the *Financial Review* that Rudd would lead the party to the next election. The party was 100 per cent behind Rudd. Gillard was perfectly happy being Deputy Prime Minister.

> There's absolutely no way in the world this party's going to be making a call on the leadership prior to this election, I can assure you of that. We have a very committed leader in Kevin Rudd, he's hardworking, he's passionate about Australia and he's got a very good record.

That was clear and unequivocal. And untrue.

On 20 June, Xi Jinping visited Australia on a state visit. At that stage he was seen—accurately—as the likely next leader of China. The Prime Minister regarded it as essential that he make connections with the potential new leader of the superpower. Two days were spent on his program: meeting the Cabinet and the parliament, talking in private, all the work that is essential to build up sufficient empathy to allow future discussions to start on the right foot. For those two days, Rudd was effectively tied up.

But others were active. Martin Ferguson says he was approached by Gillard on a VIP flight from Melbourne on 20 June to test his support: 'She said, "If you could see the polling you would see how much trouble we are in"'. McClelland was shown polling data by one of Gillard's supporters.

On 21 June, Gillard sent an email to Rudd and Jordan. She argued:

> To state the obvious—our primary is in the mid 30s, we can't win an election with a primary like that and the issue of asylum seekers is an enormous reason why our primary is at that low level ... it is an issue working at every level—loss of control of the borders feeding into a narrative of a government that is incompetent and out of control.

She noted the decision of the Political Strategy Group to develop a paper about the areas that were hurting the government but said nothing had been done. She complained she had spent time chasing process issues. She admitted 'I do not normally email you directly Kevin and I don't intend to make it a habit', but she wanted to know how they were going to learn from the past problems. The key negative areas, in her view, included asylum seekers and climate change. The message was critical but said nothing about a challenge. The polls suggested that, on a two-party preferred count, Labor led 52–48.

The next day Gillard had a meeting with Kim Carr, who had been her lieutenant when the Rudd–Gillard alliance was conceived and who was then (but not later) firmly in her camp. Carr recalls she wanted to test his feelings about leadership change and showed him polling that indicated a change of leader would be beneficial to the government. Carr, on the Left, had been unaware of the preparations that the Right had taken for a change; he swung in behind her but, in retrospect, believes he was manipulated to legitimise the Right's coup. He thinks he should have immediately warned Rudd, but he didn't.

By then the preparations were well advanced, but the Rudd team was not fully aware of just how advanced. Crean was shown some of the survey results. 'You are not seriously suggesting we challenge, are you?' he asked. He was assured not. When the challenge was on, he saw Gillard and argued that a debate was required before an ambush of this sort was launched. He, after all, had been the one person to raise with Rudd the excessive use of the SPBC. But he soon realised he had no chance of changing her mind.

There was some fear that the rebels might move at the caucus meeting on 22 June, the last meeting before the recess, and potentially, the last meeting before the election, depending on when it was held. However, casualties in Afghanistan were reported in the meeting and it did not seem appropriate to move then. That evening, Rudd addressed a Business Council dinner. Before they sat down, the president of the council offered to persuade the mining industry to call off their campaign against the Prime Minister if he publicly agreed to consult more readily. Rudd was not prepared to concede to such a half-considered offer. He used the dinner to remind the business community of what he and the government had done for them. It was aggressive.

In *The Sydney Morning Herald* the next morning, Peter Hartcher wrote an article revealing that Rudd's chief of staff, Alister Jordan, had been contacting backbenchers to confirm their loyalty to Rudd. The impression was misleading. Jordan was always in contact with backbenchers; he saw it as part of his job. There had been nothing extraordinarily active about the past three days. Indeed, in 2012, Dennis Shanahan wrote that the calls never took place, and the story was planted to generate a challenge. Certainly no MP has stood up to say they were asked by Jordan if they still supported the Prime Minister. Nevertheless, Gillard took objection, summoned Jordan and tore a strip off him. It was not as though they were strangers. For months they had walked together on Sundays, talking about the issues of the day and the problems that the government was facing. Their two offices had sought to cooperate over the period of the government, even if not as closely as the PMO had cooperated with the Treasurer's staff.

But the truth or otherwise of the story was not the point; it acted as a lightening rod for discontent, proof that the Prime Minister did not trust his senior ministers and was using staff, rather than MPs, to talk to other MPs. Rudd sought to have a proper discussion with Gillard and agreed to meet after Question Time, but apart from a quick word on refugees, he could not seem to contact her. Meanwhile, reports reached the PMO about a lot of people going in and out of Feeny's Senate office. Rudd asked Senator Faulkner to find Gillard, but in the meantime, the Prime Minister's program had to continue. The East Timor President, Jose Ramos Horta, was on an official visit and meetings with him went ahead. Then Rudd had promised to talk at the farewell of Senator Sherry, whose term was about to expire, so he addressed that meeting. Many of the ministers were unaware that anything was happening; one Rudd colleague points out he would not have gone out to dinner with his wife if he had appreciated a coup was underway.

Around 7.30 p.m., Faulkner and Gillard finally came to the Prime Minister's office. There were only the three of them there, although in the break between meetings a number of staff and colleagues were briefed on the tenor of the discussions. The discussion covered the general performance of the government and of the Prime Minister in particular. Perhaps it was the conversation that should have taken place months before, but no-one had been prepared to have it. In essence,

Rudd agreed that, if the discontent continued over the next few months, and if Faulkner, as a respected mediator, concluded that nothing had improved, then Rudd would stand down. At one stage Albanese came in to tell them they had better settle their differences as the government was in danger of collapsing around them. As Rudd put it, he had not spent all the time and effort in getting Labor into power only to see it fall if there was something that he could do to prevent it. He wanted time. He and Gillard shook on the deal. By one account, she also said she was not going to challenge. Faulkner and Gillard left. Rudd briefed staff and colleagues. Gillard rang Conroy, who was sitting among the conspirators, and he told her that the impending challenge was all over the news, that she could not back out at this stage and that she had the numbers to win easily. Minutes later, Gillard was back in the Prime Minister's office. She said she wanted a ballot. Rudd asked if she was reneging on the agreement on which they had just shaken. She was. It was a brief conversation, quickly terminated. Whether the whole discussion had been prolonged as a tactic to keep Rudd and Faulkner out of circulation, depriving Rudd of the capacity to shore up his defences, and Faulkner of the capacity to provide advice on the way forward, or whether it was a genuine discussion remains in question.

Whether or not Gillard only finally decided to challenge at the last minute, she was certainly aware of the activities of the conspirators and had talked to others about the progress of the government. As one person observed: 'When she rang, it was not as if she was asking for support, but Gillard would just ring out of the blue and ask for an assessment as to how the government was travelling'. If she did not lead, she did not discourage her supporters or insist in private that she was standing by what she said in public, that there was no chance she wanted to become leader.

As the evening progressed, the coup leaders sought to drive home their advantage. After years of complaining that Rudd had surrounded himself with, and relied upon, 'inexperienced kids in short pants', they put their own kid forward. The 28-year-old National Secretary of the AWU, Paul Howes, went on *Lateline* to gloat about the way the faceless men had toppled a prime minister without many of the Cabinet knowing what was going on. His graceless triumphalism emphasised the use of raw, unrepentant union brutality. It was their party, their leader, and the Australian people should be grateful for what they were allowed to have, the message seemed to suggest. Howes's performance showed the Labor Party at its ugliest, and factional power at its most ruthless. Howes became the face of the faceless men, the personification of unaccountable power.

Rudd convened a press conference in which he announced that he was calling a caucus meeting the next day to hold a ballot for the leadership, and that he was going to be a candidate. He did not have to call a ballot immediately. He could have delayed it until the following week, after the receipt of a petition asking him to convene a caucus. That would have taken a few days. The delay would have allowed him to call into play his public standing and support as a means of counterbalancing his lack of it within the party. It is possible to imagine the public outcry (it came, but by then was too late). But he was about to leave the country to attend a G-20 meeting; he could not represent his country overseas while at home stories were circulating that he was about to be removed as prime minister. So by calling an immediate meeting, he surrendered the opportunity for a more public fight and went meekly to the guillotine.

Looking back, Rudd sees the coup as a case study on the importance of momentum. As long as the impression remains that the numbers are all shifting, it gets harder to stop the process. So there were drip-feeds to Sky News that there had been a meeting of the Right that had decided to remove Rudd, that others were throwing their weight behind the cause, even if the accounts were not always true and never mentioned the people who had remained loyal; momentum was thus retained. When Swan shifted also is unclear. Hartcher claims Swan had been appalled, arguing that even if they had problems with the Prime Minister, 'We have to roll with it—he's the PM'. But he did not warn Rudd. Some claim that it was only on the Wednesday afternoon that Swan threw his weight behind Gillard; others are much more sceptical. By the time Rudd rang Swan, he said he was voting for change (and the deputy prime ministership) on the grounds that, if change was to happen, then it was better that is was decisive and conclusive, and did not become a running sore for the government. It was indeed to be decisive; it was not conclusive.

The next morning, it was clear that Rudd did not have the support to win; indeed, his numbers haemorrhaged as MPs wanted to be seen to be on the winning side. Had he contested the ballot, his numbers would have been low: in the 20s, perhaps 30, a long way short of what he needed. So he told the caucus he would not stand. At the same time, he put on the record the divisions that had split the inner group over climate change. He said that Gillard and Swan had been in favour of ending the commitment, but that Tanner and Wong had preferred to stand firm and that the latter two should not be blamed for the consequences of a decision that he now said had been wrong. He argued that the government should not shift to the right on refugees: 'There is no mileage in trying to out-right the right on asylum seekers'. He also expressed concern that the federal party was catching the New South Wales disease:

> I'm concerned about a principle whereby if someone says a leader of a party is to be challenged, that the conclusion we automatically reach as a caucus and a party is that the fear of the leader being terminally damaged by the fact of the challenge itself, that the challenger should therefore automatically prevail.

Rudd allowed Gillard to be elected unopposed. There was recognition that he did not have the numbers to survive. But it had an additional advantage. She would never have the benefit of being able to point to the degree of support she had in caucus. He could later claim that he had been ambushed by the faceless men, that they had leant on the caucus members and threatened their party selection, but that there was really support for him. If untested, it was a sustainable position.

That meeting was the last time Rudd really accepted his loss. Flanked by his family, he spoke in the prime minister's courtyard of his best memories in the job. The apology to the stolen generations loomed large. It was one of the things of which he was proud. He wanted to continue to serve. He attended Question Time, sitting in the back row, reminding people that he was still there.

He offered to remain in Cabinet as Foreign Minister, after Gillard's chief of staff had asked him what he wanted. A day later the message came back that, after consultation, the new Prime Minister had decided that he would not be a member of the Cabinet. That was another blow. Rudd moved into limbo.

And yet, that condition was a sign of how rushed the whole affair had been. Gillard and her colleagues could argue that theirs was a good government that had lost its way, but the new leaders could not disassociate themselves from the key decisions. They could not trash everything the government had done because they were at the core of those actions: far more so than many appreciated at the time. But more important was what they would do about Rudd. Asked what the coup leaders had planned for Rudd after he was toppled, one answered that they had not thought about it. They assumed that he would just go away, perhaps even that he would not contest the ensuing election.

There is a long history of lasting antagonism between prime ministers and their assassins. Malcolm Fraser backed John Gorton for the top job and years later brought him down. Gorton never forgave him and in 1975 ran as a Senate candidate in the ACT in the hope that he could thwart him. Paul Keating was Bob Hawke's treasurer for eight years before he unseated him at the second attempt. Hawke's memoirs are evidence of the continuing rancour; that bitter fury was entirely predictable. In both these cases the prime minister had been in office for a number of years before being toppled, yet even so they never accepted what they saw as a betrayal.

In the case of Rudd, the coup leaders knew him; they knew his drive, his determination, his commitment and his self-belief. They surely anticipated too that he could be vindictive, not very likely to forget or forgive what they had done to him. They said, so often enough, that he was self-interested and aggrandising. None of those character assessments suggested that he would quietly fade into the background to nurse his wounds, or that he would be easily reconciled to his new lot. If the management of the coup received some plaudits for its rapid success, the seeds of its disaster were there in its inability to think about the medium-term, let alone the long-term, consequences.

20

HOW RUDD GOVERNED

Crises encourage a lack of perspective. Every issue, every complaint, is magnified to suggest that never before has a government been in such chaos, never before has a leader been so disorganised. It is seldom true. The reasons given for moving against Rudd were presented in cataclysmic terms. He was Captain Chaos. It was a dysfunctional government. The government tried to do too much too fast. Cabinet was ignored. They painted a picture of ineffective management that had blotted the practices of good governance in a way that had never been seen before. The verdict, that a 'good government had lost its way', was repeated constantly as though the government was personified by one person and his dysfunctional decision-making. There was no point of reference, no comparison to provide a standard against which Rudd could be judged. It just was. The victors write the story. It is worth, therefore, seeking to put the performance in some comparative perspective, to look at the practices of the Rudd government in the context of other prime ministers' activities.

It is not possible, nor desirable, to write a job description for prime ministers. There is no one way to tackle the role, no approach to the job that will guarantee success. The activities of prime ministers must be contingent: on time, place and circumstance. Prime ministers may make their own history, but never entirely as they choose. Their choices will depend on personality, economic and international circumstance, and political necessity. To understand Kevin Rudd as Prime Minister, we need to appreciate the characteristics he brought to the job, the way that they were translated into his approach and working style, and the impact of that working style on the prime ministership and governing of the country.

The prime ministerial characteristics of Kevin Rudd reflect those working habits he developed long before, habits that took him to the position. From his school days at Nambour High through to his dedication to learning Chinese, to the thoroughness of his work as a diplomat, Rudd was a ferocious worker who did all that was required. When he returned to Queensland as a new staffer, he established a program of meetings to familiarise himself with the players in the town and in the party. As a candidate, he door-knocked extensively. As a Member of Parliament, he mastered his subjects and learned to play the media game. He would go where it was necessary to talk to people.

These working practices were yoked to a strong self-belief. At a time when few people in the Labor Party thought Howard was beatable, Rudd consistently argued the case, with himself as the person who could do it. He possessed a confidence that masked a toughness and resilience that was initially unrecognised. The ingenuous Tintin visage of the cartoons from his early leadership, the round smiling face under a thatch of blond hair, may have looked soft, but the character behind never was. He had known poverty and 'bleak charity'; he had known family loss. He had taken risks in his career. The period from 1996 to 1998 gave him insights into failure—the possibility that careers in diplomacy and politics might be closed to him. He learned, and fought back to win at the next poll.

Rudd had a solid Christian faith—that has not changed in over thirty years. Rudd was a Christian and was prepared to say so in a secular political system that rarely spoke openly of belief. He could express his admiration for a German theologian and his challenge: 'Who speaks for the poor and the dispossessed?' He never pretended that it was easy to translate the aspiration into daily practice. When castigated for his language, for the occasional burst of temper or for being seen in a strip club, he shrugged and acknowledged that he was far from perfect.

Rudd's style as Prime Minister reflected those characteristics. He worked whatever hours proved necessary. Leaders' capacity for work in part depends on their need for sleep, and Rudd could get by on only a few hours each night (a useful metabolism, even if the lack of sleep sometimes showed!). His attendance at leaders' forums demanded international travel, by necessity and inclination. His constant meetings elsewhere were his choice. He was always on the move when parliament was not sitting. Prime ministers try to work to their own timetables. However, the idea that he was the first '24/7' prime minister short-changes many of his predecessors, who worked similarly long hours because that was how they, in turn, saw the role.

Being Prepared
For Rudd to feel well prepared required a continuing, sophisticated service from his office and the public service. Rudd needed to understand not only the issues but their underpinning logic too. Some meetings took the form of a de-facto seminar because they pursued a particular objective: to ensure the Prime Minister was comfortable with the material. His analysis of topics followed the same trajectory: break a subject down to its basic elements, explore the connections, understand the foundations, then build it up in terms and phrases that he was comfortable with. 'Is this right? Does this make sense?' he

would ask. Then he would rebuild the edifice into a coherent pattern and image. He not only wanted to know what the issues were but also why they were the way they were. He would not let go and move on until he was satisfied. Rudd's adviser Bruce Hawker identified the characteristic trait:

> I have worked out that you have to pick your time when dealing with difficult issues. He has a 'silo' brain; he deals with one issue at a time—in depth—and then moves on to the next. If you jump in before he has finished with an issue, he is bound to stop you and finish what he is dealing with.

So there was a persistence, a determination to sort and shape until Rudd achieved a model he understood. Another adviser commented:

> Whether it's climate change, whether it's the GFC, whether it's the education policies, whether it's the health and hospitals policy, he would go end-to-end on the policy. There would not be a single detail which he would not know about, or if he did not know about it, ask about it and then know about it, in very quick succession. If it was a keynote policy of the government, you could bet your bottom dollar that he had had a fingerprint on every single detail of it.
>
> Did that cause other things to go by the wayside through the periods? Of course it did, because you can't spend all of that time. Is that the right way to govern? Well the question is, is there a right way to govern? That was his way. That was him.

In Rudd's view, prime ministers may not need every technical detail, but they must know how they connect. Prime ministers must be able to explain policy directions in public and then answer questions. If they don't understand the links, they can very readily be tripped up. He liked data and information that he could use persuasively in argument. When he did not get it, he could react badly. One adviser recalls:

> To be perfectly honest, I stuffed up a bit and he got a bit irate. He didn't actually yell at me, but he was cranky and I apologised and he sort of said, 'Okay'. He stormed out of the room and he didn't come back for fifteen minutes … he went out to blow off steam. I think he might have gone into Alister's office. I don't know … Then he came back in and it was fine. He said, 'Look, you know the reason I was cranky was tomorrow I have to go into a COAG meeting. I have got to have this right'. We spent the next two hours as good as gold and focused on the job … if I had got the material in the right order it probably would have been fine. We had the material there; it just wasn't in the right order. He couldn't understand something and he got frustrated.

His impatience could sometimes be confronting, even scary, for public servants, as he dissected their errors and challenged their competence in fairly direct ways. It is difficult to argue back to prime ministers. Being informed allowed him to stay on top at meetings, to appreciate where he was going, and what the likely outcomes would be. Sometimes he wanted to show off that knowledge; he had a disconcerting habit of talking at length to experts about their own field.

For Rudd, advice had to be linear and logical: if A, then B and so C. Yet his advisers said that he could think laterally in a way that often surprised them, pulling in information or ideas from other fields and applying them to the topic under discussion. He was always full of ideas about ways to tackle problems, sometimes too much so for those who were required to service the sudden notions and provide supporting detail for them. Once his mind was made up, once he had come to a conclusion about the best approach, he could be hard to shift; it seemed as though it became the only way forward. In the economic crisis, Rudd was the one who pushed for the strongest action, working on political instinct that was later justified by the figures when they came in. Many officials were nervous. One adviser says: 'He is a totally different personality to bureaucrats. He's very forward thinking, always trying to do things early, in advance, stay ahead of everything, act quickly, respond quickly, turn on a dime, get it done sooner rather than later'.

Rudd's personality and style would never allow him to be a Reagan, who presided while others laboured, or even a Hawke, who left many of the initiatives to his more competent ministers. They both adopted legitimate and sometimes effective styles of delegated leadership. Rudd's personality did not allow him that relaxed sense of distance. Their ways could not be his.

He liked to be out and about meeting people. Talking to people about their concerns was for him better than any focus group for understanding the fears of the community. How, the critics thought, could an academic (a term used pejoratively of course) policy nerd understand ordinary folk? But Rudd was not simply an academic nerd. He had long and assiduously worked his electorate and built up his ties there. He connected with the family viewers at *Sunrise* for years. That was a skill. One (admittedly admiring) observer says:

> People don't get the authenticity when … on a Saturday night he just decides he wants to go to a homeless shelter. He doesn't want any media, he doesn't even want coppers or staff. That's the Kevin Rudd who is in politics because he wants to make a difference. There's this thing about him that really wants to reach out and connect with people. He will sit and talk with people.

The smoothness with which he could shift from policy analysis to greeting people led to charges that he was insincere, that the smile was confected and the interest feigned. Rudd saw no inconsistency if he was both a policy nerd and a populist who understood the struggles of working families, the one person dealing with different parts of the prime minister's job.

Finding Answers

His style of work precluded easy answers and that sometimes affected his ability to communicate. He was not a person for soaring visions. Where some saw images, he saw complexity. However, he did want to tackle big issues: regional architecture, the quality of schools, the viability of the G-20, hospitals and health, climate change. He wanted to alter them in substantive, not incremental, ways. He did not have an immediately identifiable vision to which everything was connected, a single overarching narrative that observers wanted to isolate. Rather, he had an ambitious agenda, a list of complex and difficult issues, all to be tackled at once, even if they could only be solved in a way that had an impact over the next decade, not the next weeks. That was harder to sell than a simple message. The challenge, when seeking to do so much so fast, was one of prioritising and management: how to keep all the strands running while explaining why they were to the advantage of the electors. There was often an internal strategy and timetabling; indeed, given Rudd's history, it would have been surprising if there were not. However, the public presentation did not always reflect the depth of knowledge he almost certainly had about the intricacies of policy.

That had a downside. An appreciation of the complexity of, for instance, health reform or climate change made it harder to reduce those intractable issues into a glib solution or an immediate panacea for presentation. Explanations could be complex, not eased by Rudd's tendency to use technical language. How to explain that it took time to solve these problems? He sometimes struggled in seeking to put them in simple terms because they were not simple issues. The easy one-liner, the ten-second grab, was smothered in the search for a more accurate and technical response.

As one big policy announcement quickly followed another, he created a sense of haste, even with policies that had been developed over many months. His rhetoric overstated the challenges and the possible achievements. There were too many 'wars', too many unprecedented promises and national achievements. He cared about policy and its impact, with a dedication to detail that was perhaps much greater than many of his predecessors'. But he felt the need to get everything right, to keep everything in line, to keep searching for the big solution. This exhaustive, rational, data-based approach, a determination to get the right answer, had its problems. If the answer was not clear, then it needed more analysis, more study, more data. That search for an answer could lead to paralysis: wanting everything precluded interim, incremental steps on the way to that target. It all took longer than he hoped, goals getting pushed back into a rush of proposals in the last year of the brief three-year term granted to Australian governments. Rudd believed in analysis, not intuition—the feeling that some leaders have that this solution is just right, so they will go for it. Although he sometimes acted on instinct, that was not fundamentally Rudd's way.

Rudd wanted to ensure he controlled what was happening. If it could be controlled, it would be. If it could not, then it should be anticipated. Most of the hard work flew under the radar. Some decisions might have been made on the run, but most policy announcements usually followed an interactive process as items went through a series of committee meetings and staff briefings. A major policy might have gone to SPBC three or four times before it was announced.

It did not always appear that way, with some decisions apparently announced suddenly. Some saw this as a response to the 24-hour media cycle, but it also perhaps reflected a need for achievement, for showing that the government was producing meaningful reform. In political practice, there is a long agenda for action, which is identified and prepared for well in advance. It is hard to sell a plan for several related actions as a coherent whole.

The Geography of Power
In government, Rudd as Prime Minister sat at the centre of several circles. They were each designed to provide advice and assistance in the running of the country. Some worked through him and in his name. Others had statutory responsibility to act, but would do so only with his explicit agreement or general approval. Understanding how a prime minister uses those resources is one key to unlocking Rudd's approach and philosophy of governing. Rudd operated differently from both Hawke and Keating.

His principal colleagues were his top two ministers, Gillard and Swan, and his senior staff. The two key advisory agencies were the Department of Prime Minister and Cabinet (PM&C) and the Prime Minister's Office (PMO). PM&C is part of the careerist Australian Public Service; its staff are required to be non-partisan, serving any elected government. They must be politically sensitive and operationally active. By contrast, the PMO is meant to be operationally sensitive and politically active; its members under Rudd only had positions as long as he survived. While PM&C serves the office, PMO serves the person.

In the calculus of influence, geography counts. The PMO stretches all around the prime minister's suite. An entry hall opens onto the prime minister's courtyard, into which the official car is driven. On the left, when entering from the courtyard, is a wide foyer, just outside the Prime Minister's own office. To the right are a sitting room and a dining room. Opposite the Prime Minister's door are the staff who run his diary and routine. Then the corridor narrows. Around the corner sit the advisory staff, with the internal windows to their offices partly covered by venetian blinds that can be closed to provide any necessary privacy for a meeting inside. Further away, through a door that requires a swipe card for entry, past the switchboard and with a separate entry from the corridors, are the press staff. For the power centre of the country, the offices are cramped, often internal and far from luxurious. The power is in the presence and the proximity.

When the new Parliament House was built in 1988, it provided twice the space for the prime minister as for any other minister. Prime ministers have since taken the opportunity to increase their staff as there is room for them. More staff can increase prime ministerial capacity. There was one further change after 1988. As prime minister, Keating wanted to be able to slip away from his office without going through the foyer, sometimes to avoid someone waiting there. So he added a door from the changing room behind his desk that led to the office of his chief of staff. It has the advantage that the prime minister and chief of staff can consult without anyone else being disturbed. On occasion, Rudd slipped through that door to ask a question or join a meeting in the chief of staff's office.

By contrast, PM&C is down the hill. The secretary has an office in the Cabinet Suite, across the corridor from PMO, but does not have the ease of access of the chief of staff, the ability to walk unseen into the prime minister's office. Appointments have to be made, and are sometimes cancelled, victims of the backlog of meetings that can bunch throughout a day. The prime minister's relationship with PM&C is, properly and necessarily, more distant and formal than that with PMO, whose staff are there for the prime minister alone—theirs are normally the last voices the prime minister hears.

Decision-making

All prime ministers face issues with which they must be personally involved: economic management, national security and international diplomacy are the principal examples. Rudd ran the first two through his key Cabinet committees, the SPBC and the NSC. At any given time, there are also a number of signature policies that are emblematic of the government. In Rudd's case, climate change and health were the obvious examples. He had been deeply involved in their development and in their presentation, working with the Treasurer and relevant ministers.

While nothing significant was settled without Rudd's direct knowledge or his implicit consent through his office, those ministers in areas where there was no crisis and where Rudd had a general, rather than a detailed, interest could run their own departments: as long as nothing went wrong. Issues thrust themselves on Rudd's attention when there was a crisis. Prime ministers become involved of necessity, not least because their opinion is asked for and they must be seen to be on top of breaking news. They need to publicly defend specific policy and the government.

Control is usually welcomed as a sign of coherence and discipline while it is working effectively. But when it is not, this degree of central direction can lead to grumbling about delay and interference and questions about whether the prime minister trusts their ministers. Invariably, the discontent is expressed in terms of the shortcomings of the PMO. Where none dare criticise the king, they blame the court. Similar concerns have been expressed at some time about all prime ministers, and for familiar reasons: central control is accepted only when the results justify the frustrations. If things start to go wrong, administrative style is blamed.

What is seen as oversight, control and domination from one perspective is coherent policy and effective political management from another; the terms can be used positively or pejoratively. In Rudd's case, ministers often both sought and wanted his consent; it made life easier and was seen as appropriate risk management. For Rudd, and for many of his ministers, the principal test was: How well is the government going?

Within the Rudd government, there was a strategic planning mechanism that related all proposals to three themes: building a stronger Australia, building a fairer Australia and building an Australia for the future. Policies were categorised as signature reforms (for which the government wanted to be known over time), major reforms (the responsibility of ministers) and other reforms; they were then broken down in terms of time lines and measures of success. Each had milestones by which to judge progress and the officials responsible. It was a structured, detailed and practical way of knowing if the government was on track. Rudd took such accounts seriously and checked on performance; he said: 'I can think in thematics. But once you move into practice mode, you've got to think in boxes, otherwise boxes get lost and therefore things don't get done'. Signature reforms were his concern; the question was whether there were too many of them.

Prime ministers have never been modest in their ambitions to control, from Alfred Deakin (prime minister 1903–04, 1905–08, 1909–10) onwards. None has been as determined to direct every facet of government as Billy Hughes (prime minister 1915–23), who tried to run the country from overseas for fifteen months. Ambitions and styles differ. Robert Menzies presided with the unquestioned authority of a master; what he said went. Malcolm Fraser's interests were broader; he wanted to have an impact across the spectrum, and he did. Nothing was decided by Cabinet with which he did not agree. If he felt uncomfortable, he put it off for anther day. Bob Hawke was more inclined to delegate, but history will surely show that when there was an important issue or a policy where he cared about the outcome, his influence over the decision was evident. Paul Keating dictated where he cared, which was not about everything.

It is choice, not a lack of power, which has determined how involved prime ministers are in particular policy initiatives over the decades.

Schedules

To be suitably involved in initiatives requires a suitable allocation of the prime minister's time. That time is the scarcest resource at the centre of government. There are many things that others want prime ministers to do, but very little that they have to do. So scheduling and time management are vital for effective government. In every case, the scheduling is arranged around the prime ministers' convenience: their priorities shape the day. There are obviously regular formal occasions such as parliamentary Question Time, when the commitments are well known in advance. There are state and international conferences to attend. But within that framework the choices of the leader take precedence. For every meeting there are briefs that need to be prepared. For every paper that is required, there is some official responsible for ensuring that the research, the writing and the recommendations are available on time.

Prime ministers decide the schedule. Some will convene meetings at their convenience, will ring colleagues and officials at all hours, and will assume that when they are ready to discuss an item, that is the right time. Malcolm Fraser would sometimes hold meetings of ministers and officials in the early hours of the morning at The Lodge. He would phone officials in the early hours to ask advice (once even on Christmas morning). Keating, too, ran on his own sense of time and would not worry about keeping others waiting, even while he went back to The Lodge for dinner. By contrast, Howard was far more regular in keeping to time and, it is said, would himself leave a meeting to go out to speak to those waiting and apologise for the delay, pointing out there were issues that had to be settled before the meeting ended. It was a matter of choice.

Rudd fell into the first category. He was often late to appointments as meetings piled up and were sometimes cancelled. Early in Rudd's first term, he was criticised for keeping the Chief of the Defence Force waiting for a scheduled meeting. On other occasions, a group of public servants might have waited for up to ninety minutes before the Prime Minister arrived to conduct a meeting. This was not simply a characteristic of being Prime Minister and keeping people waiting to show who was boss. Rudd often needed to settle an issue in his mind and would stay in a meeting until he was satisfied with its progress. He held meetings when he was ready. He had always had a somewhat relaxed sense of time; it was merely exacerbated by the demands on him as Prime Minister. There were always more people wanting to see him, and when they got in they wanted to settle things to their satisfaction. The secretaries had to play catch-up all day.

There was usually a recognition that officials served at the convenience of the prime minister, and there were at first few complaints, just grumbling when work for a meeting was done on time but then the meeting was delayed, the brief left untouched. But the more often these things happened, the more officials resented it. Willing to do whatever was needed if they felt their efforts made a contribution to the final policy, they were unimpressed if their work was not even read.

If the essence of the prime minister's working day is that decisions need to be made and only the prime minister can make them, then the schedule is designed to create that effect. It is organised around the prime minister's needs. As Rudd said, 'If we make a judgement that ministers need to meet or I need to become better briefed prior to a meeting of officials, then we'll do that'. So Rudd's schedule ran to his own demands and priorities. This is a defensible proposition, but it can be frustrating for those sitting and waiting. Did people complain? Not to the Prime Minister, but they did to his staff. It left battered egos and dissatisfied advisers in its wake. Over time, that mattered.

Even when there was no crisis, the pressure on Rudd's time was constant. The extent of his interests had to be balanced with his insistence that he interact regularly with the public. Being cloistered in meeting rooms was not his recipe for re-election. Rare was the day in his diary, even when parliament was sitting, that he did not meet some group or speak at some function. The challenge for the PMO was to determine what was important, what were the priorities, and to protect Rudd from the unnecessary or the trivial. If someone wanted to see Rudd, it was preferable that he knew why and was given a brief. That included ministers.

Rudd liked to be briefed on paper (double spaced, 12 point, Arial). He wanted the briefs provided in a systematic way. One adviser said: 'He is not after a distillation … What he wants is a certain way of looking at it … What is the issue at hand? What is the context for it? What's our position? What's the other side's position? What's your recommendation?'

The Prime Minister's Office
The PMO is headed by a chief of staff. For his first eleven months in office, Rudd's chief of staff was David Epstein, an experienced campaigner who had worked for Labor governments for a decade. When Epstein left in October 2008, having stayed longer than he initially intended, Alister Jordan was promoted from the position of deputy; Jordan had been with Rudd since he had become a shadow minister in 2001. Lachlan Harris headed the Press Office. Because Jordan and Harris, and economic adviser Andrew Charlton, were all young, around thirty (about the age Rudd was when he became Goss's chief

of staff in Brisbane), the PMO was criticised for being full of 'kids in short pants', inexperienced in government. That was unfair on the many experienced practitioners, like deputy chief of staff David Fredericks and foreign affairs adviser Garry Quinlan. It also undervalued Jordan and Harris, who were crucial advisers on a daily basis and provided the continuing support that the Prime Minister needed: they had a number of appreciative supporters around the Cabinet room.

The PMO provided a 'yellow' when it put political advice on top of policy papers and briefs. The notes tended to follow a template and were kept relatively short, as far as possible to two or three pages. One adviser described Rudd as 'a logical and linear thinker, so papers are prepared to satisfy the thought process. That is a wonderful organising principle. He is also a lateral thinker, so he can actually pull an idea out from over there that none of us had thought of. It's quite interesting'. Another said: 'The key for him is a good brief. He is not a Power-Point person'.

Rudd had a great appetite for empirical data to support an argument. He liked figures, statistics and appropriate corroborative detail. Upon receiving a paper, he would ask for more information, and then more again, for comparative figures, for any Opposition statements that could be used against them to drive home his case.

At the beginning of most days in Canberra when parliament was sitting, there was an initial briefing, undertaken by Jordan, Harris and sometimes another policy adviser or press officer. The briefing canvassed what was in the news, what other information had emerged from overseas, what issues were brewing and what events would take place. If parliament was sitting, the briefing considered the ways that issues could be presented and what the likely directions of attack from the Opposition might be.

Rudd and the senior ministers worked to ensure their message was coordinated. They sought to both present the government case as effectively as possible and to identify the failings and inconsistency of the Opposition. Both were decried as 'spin', as simply ensuring the message was always the same. But ministers made no apology for staying on message because, as they pointed out, they would quickly be pilloried if they were not consistent; furthermore, they needed to get the message out to the broader public. They wanted to run the media on their own terms, hence the symbolic locked door between the offices of the policy advisers and the media staff. The press could walk in on the latter, but not the former. Within the PMO, an observer could see ministers, chiefs of staff, senior public servants, escorted members of delegations, and the occasional retired Test cricketer, but almost never journalists.

Relations with the media were, perhaps inevitably, more taut. At an intellectual level, Rudd did not care about columnists; their output was only one person's opinion and they were often either fighting old battles or uninformed about what was really happening. He did not see why he should dance to the tune of the media. He decided when and where he would talk to the Australian people and did not need to work through the press as an intermediary. Nor did he need them to set his agenda. He believed that he should stay true to the instincts that got him elected and which were renewed by the constant contact with the Australian people.

On the other hand, like all politicians, he was deeply sensitive to media criticism. For any leader, the 'gotcha' stories and often poorly informed personality analysis, coupled with the tendency to provide constant gratuitous and sometimes ill-informed political advice, can be frustrating. Rudd could get riled by the media, so much so that he was accused of being thin-skinned. At times he would go over the heads of journalists to their editors when he wanted to deliver a message.

In Opposition, Rudd's advisers had to be 'very nimble' because much of the time they had to respond to the government's agenda.

They sometimes had to provide a policy paper within forty-eight hours. They relied on their own resources. They inevitably expected that in government they would still be the policy powerhouse. But while they may have remained one source of policy, they could no longer be the sole one. They had to adjust, and that took time. In Opposition, as one adviser said, it was 90 per cent politics and 10 per cent policy. In government, the ratios were reversed. The PMO had to understand that the transition required a new approach to managing the daily issues, that it alone could not make the running in all the policy arenas.

Initially, the PMO continued to work in Opposition mode. The government's media drive was inexorable, day after day. Why, its critics complained, couldn't the government relax, rather than insist on winning every 24-hour media cycle? Rudd's office explained:

> We are focussed on winning the 24-hour cycle. We are focussed on winning the week cycle. We are focussed on winning the month cycle. We are focussed on winning the year cycle. We can't win a week without winning the day; you can't win a day without winning the week.

If the government lost, they argued, the Opposition won. Media management was not seen as an optional extra. Rudd had won the party leadership and then the election by talking to the Australian people on his own terms.

In addition to serving Rudd as an individual, the PMO acted as a link between all the ministers and their offices. It acted as a conduit to Rudd, a hub-and-spokes system. If a person wanted to see the Prime Minister, it was useful first to talk to Jordan. Often, items could be fixed there. Ministers had to take Epstein, Jordan and Fredericks on trust and accept that they could speak for the Prime Minister, could accurately assess when he needed to be consulted and could gauge what he wanted to know and when. On any day, half-a-dozen ministers came into the PMO and talked to one of its staff. Sit there for long enough and you could see almost the whole Cabinet pass through. When there was a crisis, the chief of staff's office became the command centre, planning the response; Rudd would join the strategy-making from his office. As a minister said in 2008:

> there is a large number of things where I'll have to make a decision. I'll say, the leader's office view here is important, so I'll get my office to have a chat with [a PMO staffer], or I'll have a chat with him myself ... A lot of the stuff is just office to office.

The staff of the two will keep each other informed to save Rudd's time:

> [The minister] says we've got this issue coming down the track, he thinks this, what do you think? Or, [the minister] thinks Kevin needs to know, he doesn't want to bother Kevin with it, add it to the list of things that you will raise with Kevin, just get the green light. And often it will come back: yep, that's fine, or very occasionally, Kevin wants to have a conversation or the office might just say, we can deal with that one ourselves.

The ministers accepted as a fact of life that the Prime Minister wanted to know what is happening. One minister argued:

> Any sensible minister would work up their submission and take it to the Prime Minister's Office and say 'What do you think of this?' and try to deal with their concerns. So that when the Prime Minister comes to Cabinet he's got a piece of paper in front of him which says 'This is a great idea'. You're going to get a

smoother passage. Any sensible minister in any reasonable government would do that.

That has been true for the past thirty years, to a greater or lesser degree, depending on the choices of each prime minister. In such an exchange, PMO staff could provide guidance on where the Prime Minister might be going with an item. An adviser said:

> You have to be careful to say, 'I've spoken to the Prime Minister and this is what he thinks', or, 'I haven't spoken to the Prime Minister, but I can tell you I reckon he's going to be here'. At the end of the day people do look to us for that advice, and providing that advice can sometimes resolve a difference.

Rudd expected his staff to work with ministers on issues that came to Cabinet and ensure that differences were resolved. As an adviser noted, 'We will be pushing issues that are the electoral commitments or priorities of the Prime Minister. The Prime Minister will often ask what ministers think'. He needed to know where any proposals were coming from. He could be annoyed if the ministers were not fully informed. There was always a caveat; as a senior adviser explained: 'The thing about the argument of power of these officers … it's derivative. I don't have any power in my own right. Zero. And then it's highly qualified because your power is only as much as you credibly represent the Prime Minister'. That is true, but it sounds a little ingenuous. What was crucial was that the advisers were there all the time and they had the ear of the Prime Minister. That was why a request from the PMO preceded by 'The Prime Minister wants …' was so pressing.

When a prime minister has an insatiable appetite for policy ideas, the PMO will always be talking to him about data, ideas and options, whether as a sounding board, source of new ideas, critic of public service proposals or integrator of other ministers' proposals. A policy-active prime minister could never survive with a policy-quiescent office. The PMO remains crucial and active; everyone expects its staff to offer alternative policy advice, or at least a comment on what is provided. But as confidence in PM&C grows, so PMO shares those functions more and more.

Rudd expected his office to stand at the intersection of three worlds: policy, politics and the media. When a policy proposal emerged, they had to advise him: Would it fly in a policy sense, so that there was no body of criticism in the public saying that it was bad policy? Would it fly politically: was it saleable to their own side? Would it sell in the media so it could be presented to the public? That, in Rudd's view, was the value the PMO could add in terms of policy. Everything worked best when bureaucrats, the private office and media advisers worked well together.

Rudd was a hard person to work for, although he generated considerable loyalty from some of his staff. He never understood, observers say, that not everyone had the same drive, the same determination, the same resilience, the same stamina, the same total commitment, that he had. He often burnt out advisers. It was all work, focused, driven and unforgiving. He could be snarky if dissatisfied. He could focus on one issue, and when it was done, abruptly turn to another person and move on to the next item. It was about the results more than the people, a means to the end of a policy or a decision. He joked that working in his office was a dog's life: one year there was the equivalent of seven years in a normal job. But then, the staff were working for the Prime Minister; it was not a normal job, and some of Rudd's people stayed and stayed.

In 2010, the PMO became a particular butt of criticism. As some issues seemed to get out of control, the common argument was that the staffers were inexperienced in the ways of government, that they saw the world through the lens of media manipulation and daily deadlines. As a consequence, the argument went, the Prime Minister had become more isolated. But all such comments were heavily determined by the perspective of the observer.

The Department of the Prime Minister and Cabinet
In January 2008, Rudd appointed a new secretary of PM&C: Terry Moran. Moran was a career public servant who had worked primarily for Labor governments, part of a network that had developed across the country in previous decades. Since 2000, Moran had been the head of the Victorian Premier's Department and had built up a public service machine that was the envy of other states. Victoria was seen as the driver of many of the better ideas that emerged from the workings of COAG.

Moran himself was seen to have been influential in the Victorian Government. By one account, he was called 'Bracks' brains'. However, he admitted to preferring a low profile: 'It's inappropriate to have a profile of any sort—our democracy works best when ministers are the source of public comment and the public service gets on with the job'. Moran was called The Cardinal by some, a reference to both his religion and his approach. Public service to him was a vocation, a service that could assist the Australian people. He argued that to be a public servant was 'not about boring administration, but about improving things—the Benthamite concept that the role of government is to achieve the greatest good for the greatest number'.

When Moran was appointed as secretary of PM&C, he had clear visions both in terms of what the federal public service should do and how it should be developed and organised. He revamped the department, bringing in a number of senior officials who could provide the type of advice that the Prime Minister needed. He re-engineered the advisory system for Cabinet so that it became easier for ministers to identify what the points at issue were and what they had to determine. He wanted a public service that was creative, cross-departmental and conscious of its responsibility to provide services for the Australian people.

Moran felt PM&C had become too passive, primarily because of a lack of demands from the previous government. The attitude was encapsulated in the comment attributed to Howard's long-term PM&C secretary, Max Moore Wilton: 'When I am asked for advice, I give it; when I am not, I think about it'. Moran wanted the department to respond creatively to the Prime Minister's wishes.

The consequence was complaints that PM&C wanted to centralise decisions. In part, that was inevitable. Three factors had brought about a centralisation of policy-making in government, with influence shifting to the prime minister and the central government agencies. First, more issues had become cross-portfolio, so there was a need for more integrated policy-making and coordinated responses. Whether climate change, COAG, health delivery or the GFC, these were not issues that could be determined by a single minister. Whole-of-government responses were needed and therefore the centre of government, particularly PM&C and Treasury, would be involved in developing advice for government. Second, the demands of the media and the continuing cycle meant that the prime minister could be asked at any time, in any place, about the issue of the moment, whether it be the ethics of photographing naked girls, an international incident or the mis-statement of one of his ministers. Prime ministers had to be protected from being found wanting; they needed to be kept abreast of everything that was happening. Third, technology had begun to allow the prime ministerial desire to maintain control to be more fully met. It was not that modern prime ministers had suddenly become control freaks. That had always been true to some extent—never more so than in the case of Billy Hughes, prime minister from

1915 to 1923—but now, instant and cheap communication ensured that, wherever they were, in the air, on the move or on the ground, in Pittsburgh, Lima or New Delhi, prime ministers could, if they wished, receive instant information and convey immediate instructions. They controlled because they could and because they needed to.

Rudd stated publicly that he was disappointed because the public service was not creative enough; initially, he was frustrated with the incoming briefs. He wanted more from his department than reaction. He wanted a rolling policy dialogue with the bureaucracy.

He had a standard matrix he wanted covered:

1   What problem are we trying to solve?
2   How is this problem measured?
3   What is the range of possible solutions to this problem?
4   What is the recommended solution to this problem and why?
5   What will that mean in terms of from and to?
6   How much will it cost?
7   How will it be measured in terms of whether you have moved it from and to?

Rudd said:

> My constant refrain after asking those seven questions is 'What works?' It is a very confronting question but I am not faintly interested in appearing to be active on something. I would rather say, 'This is a big problem, I have no idea what the answer is', rather than pretending we have the answer when we don't. Once we've hit upon the answer, then go for it.

So PM&C was gradually revamped. In a number of areas, Moran brought in impressive advisers: David Tune from Treasury, Mike Mrdak from Transport. They were made associate secretaries and given responsibility to develop the capacity of the department across areas of policy. They acted as principal advisers to the Prime Minister where appropriate. And soon they were promoted to departmental secretaries.

PM&C provided support in four modes. First, it provided answers to urgent requests from the PMO to help in daily political battles, such as data or analysis of economic trends. Second, it undertook conventional policy work, providing advice and sometimes developing policy proposals. Moran established a strategy unit as a response to the desire of Rudd to look further ahead. Third, it serviced Cabinet and its committees, providing briefs and ensuring that administrative arrangements were effective. The staff checked that due process was followed and that Cabinet documents met formal requirements and provided the proper information. Fourth, it acted as a coordinator across the public service, particularly when there were complex issues that needed to be worked through for Cabinet consideration. As a senior officer put it: 'We are doing our job if, on the basis of advice or how we do things, we enable ministers to make good quality decisions'.

Rudd was demanding; his interests were wide, his curiosity extensive. Like many prime ministers, when he wanted information, he wanted it quickly. Sometimes his capacity to absorb information did not match his ability to initiate. He asked for briefs that were generated through long hours to meet tight deadlines, but then they did not receive immediate attention. On other occasions he wanted a brief in a hurry, allowing little time for its preparation. Officials felt aggrieved when he then complained it was not of a high standard. They argued, legitimately, that they did not mind the rush, but that the papers would be better if there was time for them to be done properly. Neither of those, however, were unusual prime ministerial phenomena.

PM&C was the one department that sought to look at issues through the eyes of the head of government. It wanted to see how items fitted together. At times, it may have been given the responsibility to develop alternative strategies in areas where there was doubt about the capacity of the department to deliver. Then it might have arranged a meeting where its officers, staff from the PMO, and possibly ministers could lay out the issues before the Prime Minister to allow him to appreciate the alternative possibilities of a topic. Rudd also had regular meetings with Moran where they would run through a list of items: appointment of departmental secretaries, policy advice sessions or other issues of interest.

The PMO and the PM&C acted as the Prime Minister's surrogates. They exercised the power that Rudd had chosen to delegate to them. They could speak in the name of the Prime Minister; they had impact because others knew that he trusted them. As chief of staff, Jordan acted as an effective conduit only as long as others believed their cases would be presented fairly. Otherwise, they would insist on their own audience.

Cabinet

Rudd was accused, primarily in retrospect, of running a shambolic Cabinet process. But it is difficult to be precise about what a working Cabinet system would look like; the idea that in an ideal Cabinet, every minister should be present for the discussion of every item, would be a recipe for paralysis. What matters is how best each government can manage its affairs while fulfilling the two keys roles of Cabinet: ensuring sensible, coherent decisions and maintaining political support for them.

Under Rudd, ministers worked individually, through Cabinet committees and through Cabinet itself. Cabinet was nominally the heart of government. It met weekly, usually on a Thursday, after the heat of the parliamentary battle was past and the ministers could concentrate on their policy business. Rudd often started the conversation with 'secret politicians' business', a discussion of the political circumstances and future eventualities, which took place without officials in the room. Cabinet usually endorsed the proposals from some of the Cabinet committees, then had an agenda of submissions to consider. Rudd would allow the sponsoring ministers to introduce the topic before asking for comments and then seeking a consensus. Once in a while he might lead off with his views, setting the scene in the way that all prime ministers do. If in doubt, he could ask for further papers. There was nothing unusual about any of those practices.

Ministers described Rudd's Cabinet style in 2008 and 2009 as civilised, ordered and restrained:

> Rudd is a good Chair. He listens. He canvasses opinion. He never gets angry, although he can be a bit testy in a civilised kind of way …
>
> The Cabinet does not vote …
>
> No-one is ever humiliated. He never lets that happen. But in the end he listens and makes the judgement call about what people can live with.

The discussions were not dominated by Rudd; he allowed extensive debate. Bob Carr, writing only about the second Rudd term, observed that meetings were tightly organised and provided very serious analysis of problems.

Once Cabinet met over dinner at Kirribilli House. Sometimes it would meet at The Lodge. There, the conversations were reputedly more strategic; in one meeting in mid-2008, each minister gave a presentation about the plans and problems regarding their portfolio.

Cabinet Committees

While Cabinet did high-level work, it was in Cabinet committees that much of the hard grind took place. Four were especially important. The Expenditure Review Committee (ERC) was responsible for shaping the details of the Budget; it was chaired by the Treasurer. Rudd chaired the other three groups: the Climate Change Committee (CCC), the National Security Committee (NSC) and the Strategic Priorities and Budget Committee (SPBC).

The CCC considered in detail the green and white papers for the Carbon Pollution Reduction Scheme (CPRS); the ministers spent hours going through the papers, often line by line, until they all understood the principles they were adopting and the implications of the scheme. Between the formal meetings, Rudd, Swan and Wong acted as a trio of ministers, an inner core of the Cabinet committee itself.

The SPBC was the driving force of the government. Every prime minister has had some inner group. At times it has been an informal gathering in the prime minister's office; at others, it has become part of the formal Cabinet terrain. The SPBC was created for the GFC; it became a convenient vehicle for pre-digesting many of the difficult items that the government faced. The committee included the government's four most senior ministers—Rudd, Gillard, Swan and Tanner—and usually the portfolio minister. There was often a swathe of advisers and officials in the room too. The committee in part was useful because the full government too often leaked; this membership made it harder (although as the debate on the ETS illustrated, there were still leaks). It also ensured that conversations between senior ministers were part of the Cabinet process and protected from any Freedom of Information requests.

The SPBC had the same powers as the NSC. It could make final decisions. It was not required that they be forwarded to Cabinet for approval, though they were often sent there for final agreement. The fact that the SPBC was seldom challenged in Cabinet was not a surprise. When the government's four senior ministers and a portfolio minister have come to a conclusion, it would be rare for other ministers to question their judgement. After all, the committee included those with an interest in the broad government strategy (the Prime Minister and the Deputy Prime Minister), the financial implications (the Treasurer and the Finance Minister), and the minister who had to implement it—all supported by official opinion from the relevant departments. Who else had the expertise to question the decision, or to challenge the political hierarchy?

Ministers are busy people. Their time is precious. Their portfolios are demanding. In Cabinet, they are asked to consider whether to accept proposals from their colleagues; ministers speak as members of the government. Some are well prepared to contribute. Others will assume that their colleagues are best placed to decide what is appropriate and will spend less time preparing to contribute on others' issues, hoping too, perhaps, that when they bring a proposals, others will give them the benefit of support. Cabinet is not a court of law, laying out the advantages and problems of every proposal before it. Much of that work should have been done beforehand. Rather, it is a forum that combines administrative and political perspectives, ensuring that there is a degree of coherence between programs and that the proposals have the political support, or at least the acquiescence, of the main players. They are forums for political decisions. If there is something prime ministers want badly, ministers have traditionally let them have it: as long as they do not push too often and have retained a strong political position. Pressure is always on the senior members of Cabinet. Governments are pyramids, not flat structures. Cabinet is not, cannot be, and never will be a meeting of equals. The attention and time of the top few is crucial for anything to be settled.

The SPBC did not just involve the Prime Minister working with a range of ministers in their areas of interest. His senior colleagues were also involved; their judgement was trusted too, and they certainly did not complain about the process. Indeed, some ministers commented they did not mind the fact that they did not have to spend long hours in the SPBC, agonising over policy areas that were far away from their interests, and where they might make only an occasional contribution. They were content to spend that time on the work of their own portfolios. The retrospective discontent with the SPBC was rarely voiced at the time.

Rudd's general approach was not new. Fraser had a Coordination Committee to pre-digest tricky issues. Hawke used a sophisticated system of committees, designed in Opposition, to make the initial decisions: their proposals went to Cabinet, but as part of a folder of decisions for endorsement. A minister who wanted to challenge them had to request consent from the prime minister before doing so. Howard often used the National Security Committee for the discussion of sensitive items. Rudd's use of the SPBC was no more exclusive than the systems used by his predecessors. Only one minister, Simon Crean, complained that more should come to Cabinet. The other ministers were, they said at the time, satisfied with the way that Rudd ran his Cabinet.

The SPBC often tackled the big issues over a series of meetings. In the first discussion, the committee would get their heads around some complex issue, both in terms of policy concerns and political implications, and perhaps commission some work from officials and establish a series of options. The next meetings would then concentrate on particular choices. Almost nothing was done without careful consideration. However, there was little public knowledge of the way that the Cabinet process worked; it was more intricate and detailed than observers thought. Policies often went to the SPBC two or three times before going to Cabinet.

The rhythm of meetings can also tell a story. The SPBC might meet all afternoon until 7 p.m., reconvene the following morning at

9 a.m. and then work until 1 p.m. At 2.30 p.m., Rudd and his senior ministers might move on to an NSC meeting that ran to 7 p.m. Two days later, the SPBC might hold another five-hour meeting. On one occasion, the SPBC met from 8.30 a.m. to 11 a.m.; the NSC, from 3 p.m. to 6 p.m., and then there was a strategic Cabinet discussion from 7 p.m. onwards. Some Cabinet meetings were dedicated to specific topics, such as industrial relations. If Cabinet government is taken to include meetings of both Cabinet and its committees, then Rudd invested considerable time and effort in meetings with his ministerial colleagues.

The stress grew as the SPBC became a rolling meeting wherever the Prime Minister was, and as sessions were convened and then cancelled. When ministers and their secretaries had to fly interstate to attend and were then kept waiting, dissatisfaction about the use of that time grew. There might have been fewer complaints if the meetings had remained in the Cabinet Suite in Parliament House.

The reliance on the SPBC, in particular, led to some retrospective rumblings about whether other ministers should be consulted more as part of Cabinet. The tension between the efficiency of decision-making by small groups and the need to consult more widely with all members of Cabinet is common to all prime ministers. When Andrew Peacock resigned from Cabinet in 1981, he complained that Fraser used the Coordination Committee to pre-empt decisions without consulting Cabinet; the Expenditure Review Committee of Hawke and the National Security Committee of Howard were similarly criticised. For the last decade, the British Cabinet has also worked as a forum for information exchange and political tactics, but not for making decisions. Policy decisions have been made by Cabinet committees or in bilateral discussions with the prime minister, as part of the phenomenon described as 'sofa' government. Cabinet always fulfils two very different functions: to make policy decisions and to maintain political support for those decisions and the government's strategy.

So the grumbles that Cabinet should have been consulted more widely were not new. Rudd was historically correct when he argued that many decisions had traditionally, and most efficiently, been made by committees. Indeed, in the past, Cabinet was often explicitly *not* given that formal opportunity to endorse decisions; committees have often been authorised to make final decisions on behalf of Cabinet, and in some cases other Cabinet members did not even receive copies of the decisions. It is moot whether, in the case of the insulation program, for instance, a Cabinet minister would have raised issues that were not mentioned in the SPBC; it cannot be assumed.

In retrospect, some of the ministers and advisers of that time think that more items should have gone to Cabinet, and that the effectiveness of the SPBC during the GFC led to too much belief in its capacity. It is not that anything might have been done differently, and ministers would have been far busier in meetings, but the sense of involvement may have been greater. On the other hand, the SPBC dealt with many issues that in other circumstances would have been settled in the PMO. Because it existed and met so often, the senior ministers and their advisers became part of the core of government in an unprecedented way. Collegiality in the SPBC should have led to joint responsibility.

The issue at stake was not procedural; rather, it was political. How does a prime minister maintain the support of the ministers who are not involved in the inner circles and want to be? How do they retain political cohesion and policy direction? Balancing these two imperatives—effective decision-making and political support—is a constant challenge for prime ministers that will never be finally settled.

A Dominant Prime Minister?

Did Rudd dominate and centralise? All prime ministers do so in the areas they choose. They may sometimes announce decisions without informing all ministers, or take a decision to Cabinet as a fait accompli and effectively tell ministers to back it as a matter of confidence. For instance very few ministers were told of the Hawke government's decision to float the dollar. Howard gave a commitment to back President Bush in Iraq and only then consulted his Cabinet: they had no choice about whether to agree—they would have anyway, but the decision was pre-empted.

However, during the first two years of the Rudd government, there were frequent comments that the Cabinet looked talented compared with its predecessors, that individuals were allowed to shine. Gillard was a powerful deputy—by some accounts the most powerful in history. She could be so because the Prime Minister gave her the space to shine as Minister for Education and in parliament; she was an energetic Acting Prime Minister when Rudd was abroad. There is no evidence that Rudd sought to clip her wings; he enjoyed her success. Wong, Tanner, Albanese and Macklin all similarly developed individual profiles as competent ministers who argued their cases; they too were encouraged by Rudd. Certainly the government was going well at the time, but that was in part because ministers had individual standing. It was not seen as a one-man government.

Rudd worked closely with his ministers on the signature policies of the government, taking the lead in many cases, such as health, and allowing senior ministers their head in key areas, such as Gillard on education and Swan on tax reform. While he left other areas largely to his ministers, his innate curiosity and his desire to control meant that he would sometimes become involved by asking questions in policy areas where he knew only bits and pieces. But that has always been the responsibility of the prime minister: to ensure that all decisions are politically and administratively feasible. Others have, over the years, used different methods to inform themselves on possible alternative conclusions. Rudd had a deep policy interest in many areas and wanted to have an impact.

So the critique that Rudd undermined the Cabinet system with his insistence on knowing everything in an unprecedented manner is not sustainable in a comparison with the activities of earlier prime ministers. The issue was not one of administrative precedent, but of political management.

Three other key questions have been raised concerning Rudd's leadership:

1   Did Rudd become too focused on one issue to the detriment of others?
2   Did he try to do too much too fast?
3   Did he fail to maintain the political support needed for his position?

Regarding the first question, from his days in Queensland, and doubtless earlier too, Rudd demonstrated the ability, and the desire, to immerse himself in topics, to become as expert as he could. This approach had its advantages. In relation to climate change, he was on the committee that met daily to go through the green paper line by line. In Copenhagen he had been a friend of the chair, working with other heads of state before the conference to try to develop a consensus on what could be achieved. He knew enough of the detail that in Copenhagen he could chair the negotiations when the heads of state became a drafting committee to try to save the conference. That would not have been possible without his understanding the detail as well as anyone in the room. If Copenhagen failed to reach its grander goals, that was not due to a lack of effort by Rudd. In terms of health policy, he could talk to clinicians about their problems because he had absorbed the detail. When he was interested, when it involved one of signature policies about which he cared, Rudd would indeed manage in detail.

Sometimes, his commitment to the one area had to be at the expense of others. He lived health in March and April 2010. He wanted hospital reform to be one of the initiatives on which the government could seek re-election. There is no question that the proposals put to COAG had his stamp on them. It is right and proper that a prime minister should dedicate his time to bedding down a reform that was so central to the national welfare. But, critics ask, did he need to spend so much time on it, to visit so many hospitals, talk to so many clinicians, once the principal details were established? His focus might have put upward pressure on state governments. It also put other initiatives in which he had interest on hold until he could give them the time they needed.

Perhaps there was a lack of balance. Perhaps Rudd lacked the ability to keep several balls in the air at once, an ability that British prime minister Harold Wilson declared to be the essence of the prime minister's job. The decisions on the ETS and tax reform, taken on the advice of his colleagues, were the worst decisions of that year and fundamental to his defeat. As Prime Minister, he had to take the responsibility for them, but they were not decisions taken independently without consultation with senior colleagues, or taken outside the Cabinet process. Both cases may have benefited from more discussion, and perhaps more time for thought, but again, in both cases his colleagues were pressing for a quick decision. Rudd was at fault for agreeing, which is not the usual charge.

The second question concerns the pace of change. It points to a broader disease: the Opposition syndrome that new governments can suffer from. In Opposition, leaders want attention. They need to get their messages across even though all they can do is promise. As they move from one group to another, they make commitments that suit the occasion. One Opposition leader argued that to get an issue in the headlines for one day was possible; the real challenge was to keep it there for two or three days. Attention in Opposition is primarily on the news cycle, on the daily drive. The transition to government is often hard to make, in light of the fact that reporters are constantly looking for stories. So there are two challenges on coming to government: the need to balance the possible with the promised, and the need to be less responsive to the daily media grind. All new governments take time to learn how to deal with these demands.

For the Rudd government, the GFC interrupted any learning process. Suddenly, everything *had* to be done at an accelerated rate. The meetings were constant as information came in from round the world; the SPBC proved its worth. The fact that Australia survived so well meant that the processes devised for crisis became more deeply rooted.

As for the third question, Rudd's leadership style involved persistence, resilience, faith, self-belief, a tough core and a political ruthlessness: the qualities that brought him to office gave him the wherewithal to continue there. He wanted to change things, quickly. And the prime ministership gave him the levers of power to do so, and the opportunity. But that power was held leasehold, not freehold. Rudd had access to it only so long as he retained the support of his party. Without a praetorian guard, without constant duchessing of the backbench, he had little resilience when the coup leaders came from behind. Rudd was interested in policy and public presentation; he was a wholesale politician: selling himself and ideas to the public. Although he could charm and persuade in small groups, this did not come easily to a person obsessed with policy results; nor did he see the need to constantly massage the people who had chosen him as leader and whom he had led into government. His primary task was to rule; he was most comfortable on the stump or in a policy-driven committee.

By contrast, Gillard was an instinctive retail politician, working in small groups, persuading, encouraging; she was a parliamentary, not a public, performer. She was less comfortable in the public arena and was to prove to have a less firm grasp on the elements of good policy. As a pair they worked well for two years, but when they split, the lack of complementary skills left both of them exposed. Rudd was appreciated for his poll standing and public support; now he had to work in small groups to recapture the support of those who felt distrustful. Gillard had to add to her interactive skills the ability to develop strategic policy and public support; ultimately she never connected with the public and her reign was to be littered by policy blips. Rudd and Gillard needed each other's strengths. After 2010, both had to fight on ground that only drew attention to their weaknesses.

21

LIMBO

The leaders of the coup had got rid of Rudd, but they had no idea what to do with him afterwards. No-one in the camp seemed to have anticipated that he would not surrender, would not leave politics, but would stay on, remaining popular, with a high profile—and very angry. The belief was that, in a week or so, it would seem that Gillard had been prime minister forever and that life would be back to normal. That did not happen. If Gillard's first press conference seemed controlled, that was the high point. The polls rose temporarily and then declined, never to recover.

The government seemed to quickly haemorrhage. On the day of Gillard's promotion, Lindsay Tanner, the Minister of Finance, announced that he would not be contesting the next election. The two events were not connected; Tanner had decided to leave politics weeks before and the PMO had known this. Indeed, he had had a meeting scheduled to talk to the Prime Minister about it on what would turn out to be the morning after the coup. Then Senator Faulkner confirmed that he would fulfil the understanding that he would serve as minister for one term only and would not remain in

Cabinet: the period as Minister for Defence had been tough. Even if not as a consequence of the coup, two of the best-respected ministers under Rudd were departing from the ministry.

Gillard almost immediately called an election, to benefit from the honeymoon factor that often envelops new prime ministers. While Gillard campaigned, Rudd sought to look after his own backyard. He had to keep his seat. Everything he did was under the media's glare. He was also ill; he needed a gall bladder operation, which he underwent after the campaign began. Even then, his state of health was a news item.

In the first week of the campaign, Labor looked strong. In the second week, there was a story in the press that Gillard had opposed in Cabinet the introduction of a parental leave scheme and an increase in the age pension, on the grounds that the recipients would never vote for Labor anyway. She did not deny she had raised the questions, arguing that Cabinet debates were the proper occasion to identify any potential problems, and that raising issues was not the same as opposing a proposition. She was right. Someone has to raise in Cabinet the unpopular or controversial alternative possibilities; by doing so, they should not simply be labelled as holding those views. That is why Cabinet discussions are private; it is a forum that allows tough debates. There is no record of what ministers say in Cabinet, not even the summary of debate that can be found in British Cabinet minutes, where the views but not the speakers are recorded. The note takers in Australian cabinets keep a record only to the extent that they need to be sure what was said, so they can properly construct a Cabinet decision. It is likely that there is no written record of what Gillard said or in what context her opinions were voiced, just the recollections of her ministerial colleagues. But by the time the stories reached the public arena, whether these were Gillard's own views or merely a necessary part of the Cabinet process became irrelevant. She may as well have had them imprinted on her forehead.

Who knew about the comments? Budget discussions had taken place over weeks. Even if in the SPBC there were only four ministers consistently in the room, the issues may also have been considered in the ERC. In all committees, there was likely to be a myriad of advisers and public servants who could have heard the comments. Nevertheless, when Laurie Oakes reported them, the immediate reaction was that Rudd had leaked them as a means of undermining his conqueror. Rudd denied it then, and he denies it to this day. The orthodoxy is that these leaks killed the Labor campaign by damaging Gillard's reputation. Whether the connection is that precise is open to question. According to a Fairfax Nielsen pollster, approval was already heading downwards. The leak came at the same time as the fiasco that was the Citizen's Assembly. Gillard announced that, after the election, she would convene such an assembly to consider all the information on climate change and recommend what action should follow. Critics observed that the country was electing a government and did not need to delegate authority to some committee of citizens. Another furore erupted when a plan was announced to settle refugees in East Timor; Gillard had only rung that country's president but not its prime minister before announcing the scheme.

The leak was therefore not the only story in the media. If it was crucial, its impact was strangely regional, as Labor did badly in three states (New South Wales, Queensland and Western Australia) but maintained its vote in the other three. No-one has been able to explain why a vote that was supposed to devastate the Prime Minister's credentials had such a differential impact. It was, however, to be a convenient scapegoat. Again, what is true becomes less important than what people believe. It scarred relationships and damaged the government, just as the leak of the climate change decision had done in April.

Rudd continued to actively campaign, under constant media attention. He gave radio interviews; he would not take a low profile. It would have been difficult, even had he wanted to. Wherever he went, the media reported his activities as though he was an alternative party leader. What was in question was what role he might play in a future government. Gillard had promised he would have a senior role. Rudd wanted foreign affairs. The incumbent, Stephen Smith, declared he was prepared to make way for Rudd; his consolation prize was to be an uncomfortable and unpopular period as Minister for Defence. Faulkner acted as go-between.

When the Queensland vote for Labor looked like collapsing, the party arranged a joint meeting between Rudd and Gillard. It was strained beyond imagination; the two sat there carefully not looking at each other, staging a stilted conversation for the cameras. If it was meant to indicate reconciliation, it fooled no-one. However, it was essential that Rudd and Gillard be seen together and in those terms the meeting was a success. Rudd endorsed Gillard. Rudd would become foreign minister if Labor were re-elected.

The government was still doing badly in Queensland. The dismissal of Rudd, Queensland's only elected prime minister in almost a century, was a principal reason for the antipathy to the federal government. But there were a number of mistakes, such as the decision to launch 'the real Julia', raising questions about who had been campaigning before. These errors had nothing to do with Rudd. The government seemed to stumble from one problem to another.

In retrospect, there was always a defensive counterfactual. It has been argued that had Rudd not been in the contest, fighting for his own seat and thus attracting attention from the media, Gillard would have been given a clear run and would not have been under so much pressure. But for Rudd to give up so readily would have been to accept the justice of his removal. And that he would never do. Nor would anyone who knew him well have been surprised by his reaction: to hunker down and keep fighting. That had been the hallmark of his career, to succeed by hard work where others did not think he could succeed. He was not about to give up; that would have conceded that his political career was over. He would not agree with that proposition either.

Indeed, his support for Gillard may have saved a number of seats in Queensland. If so, it also saved Labor. Gillard was eventually able to cobble together a minority government, relying on the votes of one Green MP and two conservative independents.

Rudd became Foreign Minister, sitting at the Cabinet table with those who had engineered his removal. He was probably as independent as any foreign minister has ever been, for two reasons. First, Gillard was essentially uninterested in foreign affairs. On one of her first overseas trips to Europe, she declared that she would much rather be back in Australia dealing with issues such as education that she saw as vital to the country's future. Not until later in her term, essentially after Rudd's departure, did she start to build any overseas contacts that made international negotiation more enjoyable. Second, Rudd was quite happy to keep it that way. He had extensive connections. He could talk to the president of the Word Bank or former US presidents; he knew the problems and the ways forward, he had been a player in the creation of the G-20. His active international role as prime minister had meant that he could take the initiative. This did not lead to clashes between the Foreign Minister and the Prime Minister; they did not see the world differently.

So Rudd was able to travel, and to push Australia's case for election to the Security Council, a campaign he had initiated as prime minister. Of course, given the narrowness of the parliamentary numbers, he had to be in Canberra when parliament was sitting. He duly attended meetings of Cabinet and meetings of the NSC. When Cabinet considered the revised mining tax, it must have been hard. And when a revised health deal with the states was presented for discussion, he could question what had been dropped from the original agreement. But the difficulties were indeed manageable.

On two occasions, he made comments that raised eyebrows. First, he argued that the Japanese Government should be transparent about the problems at the Fukushima nuclear power stations. Was this, his critics asked, appropriate? (In retrospect, the answer is surely yes, as the government allowed the utility company to hide the level of damage.) Then he played an active role in seeking to generate an international response to the Libyan crisis. The last-minute commitment by NATO of air cover to protect the citizens of Benghazi from an imminent attack by Gadhafi's tanks probably prevented a horrific massacre. Whether Rudd's participation made a difference can always be disputed. His critics carped that he had no right to become involved in a crisis that had no direct impact on Australia's interests. His retort was that if his involvement helped to save lives, then it was worth the effort.

Rudd's competence as Foreign Minister was never in doubt. He worked with Gillard as required to represent the country. He travelled extensively, a choice that all foreign ministers have; it is perhaps not a coincidence that those who were thwarted leaders or whose ambitions were greatest became foreign minister: Richard Casey was seen as a threat to Robert Menzies; Paul Hasluck was a defeated candidate for prime minister; William McMahon was an aspirant; Andrew Peacock was a leader in waiting; Bill Hayden and Alexander Downer were past party leaders who had to be accommodated. The foreign minister is part of the government, but so often being overseas, they are never part of the inner economic core. There were no great disputes within the Cabinet about foreign policy.

But that, of course, was only half the story. Rudd's determination to right a wrong was still strong. His street-fighting characteristics came to the fore when he reminded people of the failings of the government and its new leader, though he rarely if ever did this in a forum where it could be reported. The press talked about his anger, his ambitions, while he insisted he was content with his role as Foreign Minister.

A comeback was only feasible on one condition: a poor performance from the government. Had the government performed well, had the polling figures remained solid, had the mistakes been minimised, there would have been no speculation about Rudd's return. Only if Gillard was going badly could Rudd's ambitions remain alive. Even if he was using every opportunity to undermine Gillard, as his critics argue—and he does not concede this—the ploy would not have worked on a dominant prime minister.

Gradually, as the polls got stuck in the low 30s, questions were raised about the survival of the government. The contrast was constantly drawn between Rudd's popularity and Gillard's low figures. Towards the end of 2011, Labor members began to talk seriously about the party's position. If political parties are organisations dedicated to the winning and maintenance of political power—and that is a core definition in most analyses—then there was always going to be something unreal about one that was resigned to annihilation when there were alternative options available that promised better results. The potential of the party to lose votes on a large scale had already been shown by Labor's devastating defeat in New South Wales in 2011; the Queensland state election, which would reduce the governing Labor party to just seven seats in a House of eighty-eight, was looming.

The press coverage was constant. Rudd's opinions were not unknown. In September 2011, the polls suggested that if Rudd were leader, the government would get a 15 per cent boost in support; he was preferred to Gillard by a margin of 57 per cent to 24 per cent, although what that might mean if he became leader again was open to question. In October, Lenore Taylor reported that Rudd was trailing his coat; the issue was said to be on what terms a challenge might be launched, whether there was a requirement that Rudd be assured of a clear majority before he moved. Whether or not there was a challenge in the offing, whatever Rudd did was news, so in a sense he could not win: if he did nothing, he was asked why; if he did something, then he was raising his profile.

There were also a number of provocations. Gillard used Labor's National Conference to praise her party leader predecessors, but ostentatiously left Rudd off the list, even though he was one of only five Labor leaders in Commonwealth history to lead the party from Opposition to government, and she had worked closely with him in government. It was churlish and pointless. The media, of course, allowed the omission to dominate their reporting (as they probably would have done, in other ways, had she included him). There was also talk of leaking the sealed section of the report on the Labor campaign that had been written by Faulkner, Carr and Bracks, and which, it was suggested, criticised the Rudd government's excessive concern with media presentation.

The leadership rumours rattled around throughout January and early February 2012. Press reports that a challenge was 'on', that numbers were shifting to Rudd, and that he was waiting for the next Gillard mistake, were common. It remained speculation—the best story in town. The door was then reopened by a Gillard mistake. She agreed to appear on a *Four Corners* program to discuss her government's performance, but in the small print was a reference to the government's leadership. She was asked two questions about events in the lead-up to the coup. First, had she or her supporters shown MPs secret polling data that had not been available to the then prime minister? And, second, had a member of her staff drafted comments for a possible victory speech in the weeks before the coup? Gillard did not deny either story outright. She stalled. She did not know if any polling data had been shown. On the draft speech:

> Look, I am not surprised that ... whether it's people in my office or people more broadly in the government or the Labor party were casting in their mind where circumstances might get to, of course. Political people look at political circumstances and they think about where they might go to.

When asked again what she knew, she provided a careful formulation of words: 'I did not ask for a speech to be prepared'. She would not answer the question of whether she was aware that one was being prepared. When she would not reject the proposition, the media reaction was that the claims were true. And if they were true, then she had been at least aware of the plotting and preparations underway, even if she had not endorsed them. Indeed, she admitted that people had raised the leadership with her, but said that she had not participated in any discussions. However, she had not ordered that they cease. The media response was that she had looked uncomfortable, even shifty during the interview. The reluctant draftee of 2010 had morphed into an active conspirator.

Then, on 18 February, the Member for Corio, Darren Cheeseman, holder of the most marginal seat in the country, demanded that Gillard stand down as Prime Minister as she could not win the next election, and that the Party return to Rudd. It was not a planned opening shot in a Rudd run for the leadership, but rather took him and his colleagues by surprise. They had been determined to wait until the Queensland election before they decided on their next steps; if it turned out to be as bad as they anticipated (it was worse), then the demands for action might increase.

The PMO reacted rapidly to take attention away from Cheeseman and the Prime Minister. A YouTube video, titled 'Not a Happy Vegemite', suddenly hit the airwaves, made up of outtakes from Rudd trying to record a message in Mandarin for the local Chinese community. He kept messing it up, getting frustrated and upset at the complexity of the language, blaming the authors of the message, swearing at his failure and generally looking cranky and out of sorts. It certainly attracted the attention hoped for by those who had suddenly put it on the internet. But soon it was no longer the content—a frustrated former prime minister who often swore—that was the story. It became a debate about who was seeking to damage his reputation by releasing a tape that had probably been lying around the PMO for a while.

Rudd was about to go Mexico for a meeting of G-20 foreign ministers and then to New York. He and his colleagues discussed whether he should remain in Australia, but thought that to cancel such a significant trip would itself be a provocation. They determined to try to neutralise the story. Rudd arranged a late-night interview with Sky News to respond to the stories arising from the release of the video. He said it was a bit odd that it had been released, and admitted that when he was frustrated he tended to swear. He also argued that he had learned from the past:

> I've reflected a lot on that, and some of the criticisms made of me were a fair cop and a lot of them were exaggerated and sort of produced after the event ... but the bottom line is I think you do learn and what I've tried to learn from all of this is to do less in a given working day rather than trying to do everything.

He invited people to speak to his colleagues, including at DFAT, to check this was true. (Unattributed comments from DFAT suggested he had not changed!) He reiterated that he was happy as Minister for Foreign Affairs.

Rudd might have hoped that such statements would end the imbroglio, but the PMO determined that this time they wanted to kill him for good, to remove him from office and from any future consideration as a possible rival. They developed a strategy to create a crisis. First, Simon Crean went on air to suggest that Rudd needed to decide what he wanted to do: namely, to either be a member of the team or get out. Then Tony Burke circulated around the press gallery, telling journalists that the Prime Minister intended to sack Rudd as soon as he arrived back from overseas. It was reported as a story but not attributed; it was designed to raise expectations. Gillard was then asked whether she had confidence in her Foreign Minister. She prevaricated in terms that clearly indicated she did not, even if that was not exactly what she was saying.

The reopening of the leadership debate allowed others to revisit the 2010 events. In *The Australian*, Dennis Shanahan wrote that the story about Alister Jordan polling backbenchers, which had been seen as a catalyst for the challenge, was a con; there was no-one who was prepared to acknowledge they had been approached by Jordan. It had been a story fed to the press to create an excuse for the challenge.

In Washington, Rudd was faced with precisely the dilemma his opponents intended: he was a long way away from Canberra, where his Prime Minister was not prepared to commit to his position as Foreign Minister. Whether Gillard would really have sacked him remains open to question. But he regarded his position as untenable and believed he could not speak on behalf of Australia in those circumstances. So he convened a late-night press conference in Washington and announced his resignation as Foreign Minister. With a degree of chutzpah, he claimed that the Prime Minister was displaying a lack of loyalty in not supporting her foreign minister. What might have occurred if he had ignored the provocation, returned home and effectively left Gillard to sack him, thereafter presenting himself as the wronged soul, can only be a matter of speculation.

Rudd flew back to Australia believing that he would have to challenge, and that he would lose. A loss in itself was not fatal to his future. It had taken two ballots to remove prime ministers Gorton and

Hawke. Keating won just a third of the vote in his first attempt. He was back six months later to win narrowly, when the party thought it could not survive the next election. Challengers need to appear credible in the first tussle, then they become the point of alternative reference. And everyone waits.

The government, meanwhile, orchestrated an array of violent condemnations from ministers. There seemed to be two objectives. The first was to win the immediate battle, though that never seemed to be in doubt. At no stage over the weekend of campaigning did anyone suggest that Rudd was close to winning. The second objective of the strategy was to so damage Rudd's reputation that he could never again be a contender, not least because his colleagues had provided so many vitriolic comments that they had effectively written the Liberal campaign advertisements for them. After all, they could argue, 'If this is what his colleagues, those who are on his side, think, what would others say?' (Indeed, in this, they proved correct.)

Gillard stated:

> It's very well known inside Labor the extraordinary lengths I went to, as deputy prime minister holding the equivalent of two cabinet portfolios, and then knocking myself out each and every day in things well beyond my own portfolio responsibilities and going to organisational matters in Mr Rudd's office to try and get the government functioning. Increasingly, senior bureaucrats and senior advisers came to me in the course of all that chaos, as did my senior colleagues, because I became the touchstone, the person who had some prospect of going and getting things done during those days of dysfunction.

Conroy argued: 'Kevin Rudd had contempt for the Cabinet, contempt for the caucus, contempt for the parliament'. Roxon claimed that he would never listen, though she then provided an example of a case where he had been talked out of a proposal.

But the most virulent was Swan, which was significant because he and Rudd had worked together so closely in Queensland in the 1990s and then again during the GFC. When he became leader, Rudd had made the big concession of keeping Swan as shadow treasurer to maintain party harmony, rather than giving the role to his supporter, Lindsay Tanner. Nevertheless, Swan unleashed a broadside:

> For too long Kevin Rudd has been putting his own self-interest ahead of the interest of the broader labour movement and the country as a whole and that needs to stop.
>
> The Party has given Kevin Rudd all the opportunities in the world and he wasted them with his dysfunctional decision making and his deeply demeaning attitude towards other people including our caucus colleagues. He sought to tear down the 2010 campaign, deliberately risking an Abbott Prime Ministership, and now he undermines the Government at every turn.
>
> He was the party's biggest beneficiary then its biggest critic, but never a loyal or selfless example of its values and objectives …
>
> The Labour Party is not about a person, it's about a purpose. That's something Prime Minister Gillard has always known in her heart but something Kevin Rudd has never understood.

Swan was asked if Rudd still held Labor values. He responded that he was not sure he ever had. This was from a person who had been part of a leadership triumvirate in Queensland under Goss and who had shared a house with Rudd in Canberra for years. It was of course a complete contrast to what he had said in June 2010 when supporting Rudd, who he had then described as a person 'with a passion'. Which to believe? In both cases, he was supporting the incumbent prime minister. His chief of staff writes that he had thought carefully about the statement, that he might have tolerated either the leak in the election campaign or Rudd's refusal to concede he had been campaigning for months, but he was not prepared to do both.

The virulence of the attacks then had to be balanced by a number of ministers who supported Rudd, who did not agree with the view that he had been dysfunctional. They did not return fire in kind, although there were examples they could have used. They included long-time supporters like Chris Bowen and others like Kim Carr who had initially been one of Gillard's key numbers men in both 2006 and 2010; he had since changed his view. Most notably, Anthony Albanese in an emotional press conference, declared that he would vote for Rudd because a wrong had been done in 2010 and this was the first opportunity to right it. Not everyone agreed with the condemnations.

The question was who would define the cut-off point for a 'good' loss; that is, one that enabled Rudd to survive despite the mauling. The figure seemed to sit around thirty, about a third of the caucus, the same proportion Keating had got in his first tilt at Hawke. Rudd got thirty-one. The ballot was followed by the usual protestations of loyalty to the newly re-elected leader and commitment that there not be another attempt.

Rudd stayed out of Cabinet. His supporters were retained as ministers, although in later reshuffles they were to receive reductions in seniority.

And that, many thought, really was that. Rudd's supporters had been rushed into a contest they were really not prepared for; they would have preferred to wait for a more propitious occasion, possibly after the anticipated debacle in the Queensland state election a month later. They had been thoroughly beaten. All Gillard and Swan had to do was to govern well, to recover in the polls, to look like election winners, and they were invulnerable to any further attacks from within the party. For months there was no counting of heads within the parliamentary party: grumbling maybe, concern, but not counting.

But the situation did not get any better. Rudd remained on the backbench and gave no indication that he was about to leave the parliament. The media kept talking about him. If he liked the attention, he certainly continued to get it. When he assisted his constituents in the Brisbane floods, the media was there to report on his efforts as he waded through floodwaters to help evacuate the waterlogged streets. Even if no-one was counting, equally, no-one really believed he had given up on the belief that another chance would come. His ambitions still shone. And meanwhile, the government failed to make its mark, failed to generate support. As it struggled, as the Labor party faced annihilation at the polls, so concern rose.

In early 2013, the government seemed to move from one crisis to another. Gillard announced the election date nine months in advance, thereby not only removing the one advantage she had over the Opposition, but ensuring that everything was seen through the prism of an election. Her suggestion that certainty about the date would allow her to concentrate on governing was at best naive. Then she went on a week's tour of the electorates of western Sydney. This was Labor's heartland, but polling had its support as under 40 per cent in places. Gillard didn't seem to connect with the constituents, and that left many of the local members in despair for their seats, and the New South Wales branch now disillusioned about her capacity to lead.

For two weeks, Cabinet contemplated changes to the taxation arrangements for superannuation. The lengthy debate worried those who were on, or about to go on, their superannuation. The final proposal was sensible and minimalist, but unease about it could translate into concern about what Labor might do if re-elected.

Senator Conroy introduced plans to regulate the press, plans that he had dropped without notice on the Cabinet table. He announced that if they were not passed within a week, he would withdraw them.

The suddenness of the proposals, presented without notice but with an ultimatum, drove more to the Rudd camp; Bob Carr thought the proposals insane and the process infuriating. Given the 'take it or leave it' demands, one crucial independent noted that, in those circumstances, he might leave it. The proposals also infuriated the press. They were then withdrawn, leaving only more enemies.

The Prime Minister announced that she would accept the proposals of the Gonski Report for additional funding to schools, but these were coupled with announcements of massive cuts to university funding, so education as a sector was doing no better and a good news story became submerged in complaints about the needs of the tertiary sector. Every story was a disaster, every scheme became a tale of woe, every poll suggested the Labor Party would lose as badly as it had done in New South Wales and Queensland. Annihilation beckoned, and many backbenchers became even more nervous.

Within the caucus, Rudd remained the only alternative. Crean had been at the forefront of demands that Rudd go the previous year. Now, in March 2013, he was concerned by the continuing errors of the government. There was a series of discussions between Crean and Rudd. Rudd argued that he would only stand if there were an overwhelming demand for him to do so. He was not prepared to run a ticket with Crean as deputy leader, although he was happy for the caucus to determine the position by ballot. But before there was any concerted action, Crean announced that he was going to tell Gillard to stand down and that Rudd should run for the prime ministership again. Rudd sent a message asking him to delay doing this, but to no effect.

Gillard immediately decided to call a ballot. Rudd's backers wanted to know how many votes Crean would bring across. The answer turned out to be only his own. Even if Rudd's numbers had increased from 2012, he was still short of a majority. He declined to stand. He had consistently argued that he would only run if there was a clear majority, and there was not one. Crean insisted that Rudd had to challenge. There was a meeting to endorse the one candidate. The situation appeared a farce—a coup attempted without the support of the key player. But why would Rudd have run in those circumstances?

The consequences seemed terminal for his political aspirations. Pushed by Crean's actions, Rudd said he would not run again. Gillard sacked Crean, removing some suspicions that he had actually been an agent provocateur seeking to lure Rudd into another defeat. Several Rudd supporters resigned, including Bowen and Carr. Once again, they all thought that that was that; there could be no further occasion. The election was too close. If the Labor caucus wanted to march into oblivion, then that was its choice. It was not that Rudd had entirely given up. In May, the US Under Secretary of State, Kurt Campbell, a long-time friend of Rudd, told Bob Carr that Rudd had told him he would strike sometime before September—he was still more hopeful than many on his team.

Once again, Rudd's aspirations were resuscitated by the government. Gillard had emailed Rudd in June 2010 arguing a party could not survive with polling in the mid-30s; she was now faced with far worse standings, in the high 20s or low 30s. But advice given in 2010 was not applied in 2013; she was determined to hang on regardless of the likely size of the defeat. However, the government's position just got worse. If Labor was to return to government, it had to retain all its existing seats and win others to reach a majority. But when the party strategies were developed and lists of target seats considered, not only were there no Liberal seats on the lists, but some of the most marginal Labor ones were not even included. They had already been conceded as losses. That meant the Labor machine had already given up on the prospect of winning and had developed a strategy to save as much of the furniture as it could. Given polling suggested that the party would lose all its seats in Queensland (except possibly Rudd's), a swag in western Sydney, everything in Western Australia and perhaps all but one in Adelaide, the prospects were poor indeed.

The final impetus came from the polls in Victoria, the one state where in comparative terms the polls had held up for Labor. They began to go bad too, suggesting a swing of over 10 per cent, bringing nominally safe seats into play. By contrast, the polls suggested that, under Rudd, the party might even have a chance of winning the election. It was a result no-one quite believed. But for those whose continued parliamentary careers were in doubt, any boost to the party vote, particularly one that improved their prospects, was welcome. A few wanted the change but did not want to be seen to advocate it in public.

So the party began to concentrate even more on issues of survival. The key was Shorten, whose support for Gillard had become undermined by the decline in support. Rudd's supporters began to plan a petition that would garner the signatures necessary to demand a meeting and a vote. Rudd and Shorten met in the back rooms while the annual parliamentary ball boomed on. Rudd's backers demanded that Shorten make a public statement that he had changed his mind and would now support Rudd. Rudd had his condition too: party reform that would never again allow a leader to be rolled by faction chiefs.

Faced by the threat of a petition demanding a leadership vote (a petition whose very existence remains in doubt), Gillard followed her strategy of bringing it on as soon as possible. Her advisers proposed that on the day, she had a 50-50 chance, but that by the next day she would have no chance. When announcing the meeting, she stated that if she lost, she would never again challenge for the leadership and would leave parliament at the next election. She proposed that Rudd should agree to the same conditions. He did so publicly.

Before the meeting was held, Shorten announced his change of position. By then, Rudd was expected to win. He did so, by 56 votes to 45. The improbable had happened. Rudd was only the second prime minister in a hundred years to be granted a second term. But this time, the odds were against him.

22

GOING DOWN FIGHTING

Rudd had less than three months to turn around the Labor Party's fortunes. Half of that time was going to be spent in campaign mode. Although there were suggestions that he call an immediate election, that position ignored the requirement that a number of policy areas needed to be at worst neutralised, and at best turned to advantage.

But the immediate demand was to form a Cabinet. Claims that all of Cabinet would resign and refuse to serve under Rudd had been frequent; it was one of the ploys used to try to prevent defections from the Gillard camp. There was a delay in caucus after Rudd's election as the party prepared for a ballot on the deputy leadership. Rudd used that time to circulate around the room making personal appeals to ministers to stay. He argued the past was the past; the party and the government needed them. The appeal made a number of ministers stop and think. Swan had already told caucus he would not continue when he vacated the deputy prime minister position. Eventually, Garrett, Conroy, Emerson, Ludwig and Combet also chose to make themselves unavailable. Burke offered to resign too, but Rudd persuaded him to stay. Some who had been highly critical, such as Gary Gray, stayed as well; he was needed to assist in the campaign in Western Australia, where it had seemed for a time that Labor would lose every seat. The bulk of the ministers remained, even though some indicated they would not stand as a candidate at the next election. None of the female ministers resigned. Penny Wong and Jacinta Collins were elected the leaders of the party in the Senate; Anthony Albanese became deputy leader.

The decision by many ministers to stay limited the scope for a large reshuffle. The allocation of portfolios was discussed with all the leadership group in the room. Chris Bowen was appointed Treasurer. Kim Carr and Joel Fitzgibbon were returned to Cabinet. Alan Griffin was made secretary to the Cabinet.

In the next six weeks, Cabinet met on a regular basis during the week and had additional meetings over the weekend when controversial items needed consideration. Rudd was scrupulous to ensure that they were run in an open manner: political discussion followed by due process. There were occasional meetings of the ERC as Bowen and Wong sought to oversee a budget strategy. There was no re-creation of the SPBC as part of the Cabinet system. After all, most of the attention was focused on the election. For that, Rudd convened a leadership group consisting of the four party leaders, plus Treasurer Bowen and Bill Shorten. They had meetings, usually hook-ups from around the country, almost every day from the beginning of July.

There were a number of issues that had to be cauterised—issues that were dragging the government down. The first was boat arrivals. Seeking to settle the issue gave Rudd an opportunity to show his international connections. He visited Indonesia to talk to its president about regional solutions. Rudd then proposed a new scheme. New arrivals would be sent to Papua New Guinea (PNG) and, if their papers showed them to be genuine refugees, they could then be settled in PNG. He stated that under no circumstances would any arrivals be settled in Australia. The purpose was to make the prospect for admission to Australia so remote and the alternative so unwelcoming that no further boats would set out.

Rudd took his proposal to Cabinet over one weekend, with meetings on 13 and 14 July. During the second meeting, ministers were spread around the country: Rudd was in Brisbane, others were in Canberra, Sydney, Adelaide and Melbourne. Foreign Minister Bob Carr, experienced in such tasks after ten years as New South Wales premier, described the initiative as a master stoke:

> It was my first cabinet meeting with him in the chair. He was efficient, not wordy. He has electric authenticity, that of an authentic prime minister, as opposed to Gillard's mechanised efficiency, which I had found admirable enough in its own way.

The next day Rudd came back to Cabinet to finalise the details. Carr noted:

> His command of it—this sounds slavish—was extremely thorough. He wrapped it up with the summary at the end; we've got to talk about 'adjusting policy on border security … to take account of changing external circumstances'.

On the Sunday evening, Rudd flew to Port Moresby to negotiate with the government of PNG. A week later, PNG Prime Minister Peter O'Neill returned the favour and flew to Sydney to sign the formal agreement. The rapid visit to PNG, the settling of an agreement and its announcement were designed to signal the effectiveness of Rudd in international affairs. Some questioned whether the harsh stand was consistent with Rudd's parting comments to caucus in 2010, when he entreated his colleagues not to seek to outflank the Opposition on the Right in policy on boat people. But the circumstances were now so grim that there was a need to both discourage more boats and be seen to be in charge. The message was intended to be unequivocal: if you come by boat, you won't be settled in Australia. Over the next few weeks, Labor advocates argued that the flow of boats was already slowing down.

Rudd quickly moved back into G-20 mode. A meeting of G-20 leaders was due to be held in September and, back as Prime Minister, he was quick to make contact with national leaders. He talked to the Chinese President in Mandarin on 14 July, and to the Malaysian Prime Minister, the Mexican and Italian presidents, and Russian President Putin on 5 August. Late in July, Rudd flew to Afghanistan to visit the Australian troops there.

The NSC continued to meet as required by international events. After one of these long NSC meetings, Carr diarised: 'I watched Rudd in the National Security Committee with admiration. Rather scary. He was ferocious ploughing through agenda, knowledgeable about every item, totally in charge of his public servants and ministers'.

The second issue was the carbon tax. The tax had from the beginning been intended as a first step towards a carbon trading system where the price would be tied to European levels; these had already collapsed. Rudd decided to speed up the progress. He announced that the carbon tax would be immediately replaced by a trading scheme in which the carbon price per ton would float through market forces. In effect, the proposal was the one that he had wanted from the start and which the Senate had twice rejected. The move gave him the ability to state that the derided carbon tax would be abolished under a new Labor government.

Two other issues had been left incomplete under Gillard: the funding of schools following the Gonski *Better Schools* report and the disability support scheme. The key questions in both cases were how many state governments were prepared to sign up to them and what commitments the federal government would have to make to gain their signatures. Rudd held meetings with state premiers in Hobart, Brisbane, Perth and Sydney. Tasmania quickly signed on to the schools program, in early July; Victoria followed in August. By then, only Western Australia and Queensland had not signed, so there was an argument that the majority of Australians could benefit from the additional funding. The symbolism was the most important concern. Labor needed to protect its reputation as the more trusted party for delivering on education and social services. The actual funding would only gradually cut in over the next five years, and the impact would be even further away. But that is the nature of federal commitments in education: it is about funding. Issues such as curriculum design can be influenced through the power of the purse.

Party reform, however, was the one area where Rudd was completely committed to change. It had been a condition of his return. He had insisted that those who jumped on his bandwagon be prepared to back his intention that never again would a Labor prime minister be so abruptly removed from office. His strategy was to introduce a scheme by which the party membership had a part in choosing the leader. There was nothing novel about such a scheme in international terms. The Canadian party leaders had been elected by party convention since 1925. In Britain, the Conservative Party MPs had a series of votes to reduce the number of candidates to two members of parliament, then held a vote of the party membership to decide between them. The British Labour Party leader was chosen by a system that gave a third of the votes each to the parliamentary party, the affiliated unions and the party membership. In 2010, the parliamentary party preferred David Miliband, but the unions backed Ed Miliband, who won by a narrow margin. So it was not unknown for a leader to win even if the majority of those sitting behind him in parliament had not voted for him. All sorts of permutations were possible; the most radical would see the leader elected exclusively by the party membership. The key issue was that a caucus could not remove and replace a prime minister in one motion. Even if they could in theory vote a prime minister out, that would only initiate a leadership election that would take time and which the deposed leader could contest.

There were several alternative schemes, but two key questions: How could a sitting prime minister be removed, and who should be permitted to vote and in what proportions? The issues had been discussed within the party. Chris Bowen had suggested one proposal in a book that had just been published.

The first issue was whether the caucus could initiate a review of the leadership by moving a vote of no confidence in the prime minister. There had always been reluctance to have no means of shifting a leader who was not listening to anyone. But Rudd wanted a threshold that was tougher than half the caucus. In his view, it should be hard to succeed. The final proposal was that, in government, a leadership election could only be initiated if 75 per cent of the caucus voted in favour; the target in Opposition was later set at 60 per cent.

The balance of the ballot was even more variable. Should unions be granted a vote, as they were in the UK? Should party members choose between a slate of candidates or merely be given a choice between the last two standing? Should members alone be responsible for electing the party leader? There was seen to be logic in the position that a leader could not be entirely imposed on the members of caucus. Besides, if it were to be implemented immediately, any proposal needed the support of the caucus. In his book, Bowen had proposed a 50/50 division between party members and caucus, which had been the upshot of many discussions. What was noticeable was that the unions were not included at all.

Several people argued that there was no rush to make changes, that they could be held over until a National Conference after the election. Rudd insisted; the changes had to be completed while the momentum was there as part of his return. Any delay would remove the sense of urgency and allow the defenders of the status quo to reorganise.

A meeting of the ministry was held and after a morning's debate it was agreed to support a proposal to the caucus. A month's notice was required for caucus to discuss rule changes, which was done at a special meeting held at the Balmain Town Hall. Stephen Conroy, labelled by his former mentor, Robert Ray, as a 'factional Dalek' (a sobriquet in which he took a perverse pride), complained that the changes would give too much power to the Prime Minister. As a factional leader, he did not say that there would be an equivalent reduction in the power of factions to dictate. Despite this and other complaints, Rudd won his reforms. Afterwards, the party held a public meeting at Balmain's Unity Hall, the same place in which the Labor Party had been created back in 1891. There had been no time to convene a special national conference. It was there that union objections would have been most likely heard. In practice, the later success of the post-election leadership ballot and the farce in the WA Senate re-election might have muted those complaints too.

In two moves, in 2007 and 2013, Rudd had changed the form of the Labor Party. In the first, he had 'modernised' the party by taking over for the prime minister the right to select ministers. It may not have made a great deal of difference in the final selection, and on his return in 2013 he consulted with his leadership group to determine the shape of the ministry and the allocation of portfolios. But the power to elect had been removed. Whether that change had brought about a more subservient Cabinet, with ministers scared to oppose the Prime Minister, is a matter of debate. Strong ministers do not fear for their position. However, it was a useful excuse to defend ministers who had not stood up to the perceived centralisation of power in the Rudd government, and who had not voiced their concerns about the way that the government or Cabinet was run.

Now Rudd had also democratised the right to select the leader, taking it from the caucus alone and incorporating the party members. In both cases, the preferences of the leader were endorsed by the caucus; in neither case did the caucus really have an option as it would have required a rebuff, either to a potential prime minister on the rise or to the person to whom they had turned as their only hope of survival. If these changes are retained, future Labor prime ministers (if there are any) may be grateful for the innovations.

With the principal issues cleared as best the party could, the remaining choice was when to call the election. It had long been expected in September; that had been Gillard's choice back in February. There was no reason to wait, and besides, a delay would require the recalling of parliament. There was some speculation that Rudd might delay the election until late September so that he could attend the G-20 meeting earlier that month, thus stressing again his standing in international affairs. But it was not really an option for a prime minister to be absent during an election campaign, and he would anyway be limited in what he could do by caretaker conventions. On 4 August, Rudd announced the election date: 7 September.

There were two interlocking party committees. There was the leadership group: Rudd, Albanese, Wong, Collins, Bowen and Shorten. And in Melbourne there was the party machinery under national secretary George Wright. A link between the two was Penny Wong, but otherwise the relationship was tenuous. Wright had planned a campaign around Gillard; he had even run a simulation in June involving 150 people, including senior members from Gillard's PMO and from other ministers' offices. When Rudd was returned to the leadership, Wright lost a third of his team who had been ministerial staff. There was residual suspicion between the two camps, even after Wright joined the leader's group on the road for a time and after Mark Butler was installed as an additional adviser to Rudd.

The leadership group hook-ups continued on a regular basis and were sometimes extensive. On 13 July, the discussion went for three and a half hours. One observer said: 'Kevin displayed a prodigious knowledge of the policy areas he wanted pursued, including the seven-point plan for the economy. I could almost hear the groans from the others as he painstakingly took us through the points ... again'.

The election campaign was very different from that of 2007. Instead of a buoyant Kevin07, Labor was shackled with a difficult grind. There were a number of problems from the beginning. The Labor Party was heavily outspent; raising money in a losing cause is never easy. Second, parts of the press were dedicated to the removal of the government. The News Limited headlines were designed to denigrate and to ridicule. Third, the Labor Party itself had provided the material for the headlines. The statements made by the party's leaders during the leadership contest in 2012 could readily be resuscitated by the Opposition. At the time, the comments were meant to be so damning that Rudd would never again be a credible leader, because the Opposition could use the free character assessments of his colleagues. Now the worst possible eventuality had occurred. The party had returned to Rudd for survival and all those comments could be used against him and the party. The attacks failed to destroy his leadership, but they undermined his credibility.

The freshness of 2007 could not be re-invented. After Rudd had cauterised the unfinished business, there was little to promise in the fraught economic climate. Those issues that did emerge were often ridiculed in the media, seen as thought bubbles that had just occurred to Rudd as he was about to speak. In practice, the proposals had often been considered by the leader's group; they were the elected politicians.

At times, Rudd took his belief in the leader's discretion to the limits. One proposal was to establish a special economic zone in northern Australia and provide tax incentives for companies to locate there. The leadership group had signed off on the proposal. The campaign committee was surprised when Rudd then went even further and proposed to slash company tax and create a concessional tax zone. Indeed, Bruce Hawker notes, these were all part of the problem that Rudd won the leadership so late that 'we didn't have the time to prepare the policies we need to excite the electorate (and the media). His move to beef up the NT tax policy was a response to this problem'.

A second proposal was to move the principal fleet of Australian ships from Sydney to ports in the north. This had often been discussed as a logical step; given that all the potential threats were going to come from the north, it made sense to have the fleet two days steaming distance nearer any problems. But the suggestion came as a surprise and had extensive jobs implications for Sydney. Then that impact was lost: the New South Wales premier and treasurer arranged to ambush Rudd while he was out walking to complain that they should have been consulted. The meeting, not the idea, was the principal item on the news.

The press, particularly the Murdoch media, were relentlessly aggressive. It began on the day that the election was called. 'Kick this mob out', was the *Daily Telegraph* headline. When Peter Beattie was announced as a candidate for the Queensland seat of Forde, *The Courier-Mail* led with 'Bring on the Clown'. After the first leaders' debate, the *Daily Telegraph* ignored the content and instead claimed that Rudd had been rude to a make-up girl. He had been about to go on stage and was concentrating on the issues he would speak about; he barely responded in the two minutes she spent providing the final touch-up. That, not what he said during the debate, made the headlines. It was a trivialisation of political debate in a coverage designed to undermine.

To some observers, the campaign became concentrated on two people: Rudd and his adviser Hawker. The daily hook-ups of the leadership group went unobserved; what impact the members of the committee had is impossible to estimate. There are claims that Rudd and Hawker 'hijacked' the campaign and ran it from the front line, lacking trust in campaign headquarters. Speeches were written and rewritten, strategies reworked. Meetings of the leadership group were tense because the members were dissatisfied with the work of central headquarters. Hawker's own campaign diary only accentuates the impression that all the ideas came from the one source. The doomed, even silly, plan to parachute former Queensland premier Beattie, a long-time critic of Rudd, into a seat that needed to be won was one of Hawker's less clever brainwaves. The lack of trust all round was evident when leaks from the party's HQ spoke of the unreasonable expectations and demands made of the team on the road. They gave a picture of a campaign in chaos.

As the support in the polls declined, and as there were a limited number of issues to run, it was hard to maintain a positive mien. The theme of 'Building the Future' was difficult to sell. The constant pressure could become depressing. Hawker recalled on 14 August:

> Yesterday I went around to Kevin's room and gave him a pep talk. I told him he can win this election with strong, positive, inspirational performances—the sort of thing for which the Australian public respects him. I said the media is picking up on his demeanour and they are saying it's not like him. I said he can win if he shows himself at his most optimistic, intelligent and charismatic. 'So, no pressure', he said with a wry smile.

At several stages, others too commented that Rudd had fallen far short of his 2007 style. Peter Hartcher suggested he should slow down and campaign thematically and positively; he should leave the negative comments to others. Wright and Butler wanted him to get more rest and focus on the message of 'jobs versus cuts'.

The lowest point of the campaign occurred on 29 August when Rudd led a press conference to attack the Opposition's costing of their policies. In every election there is a search to prove the opponent's figures wrong, to find one mistake in a document in order to cast doubt on the credibility of the whole thing. On this occasion, flanked by his Treasurer, Chris Bowen, and his Minister of Finance, Penny Wong, Rudd argued that a costing of the policies by Treasury and the Department of Finance had found a gap of $10 billion in the Opposition's calculations, and that consequently they would not be able to deliver on the promises they had made. That was routine. As long as the work is done outside the caretaker period, there is nothing unusual in governments asking their departments to test whether the Opposition's alternative policies actually cost what their proponents claim they do. All governments do it.

What followed was not usual. The secretaries of Treasury and the Department of Finance convened a press conference to argue that their figures could not be properly used in that way. They had been done some months before and the outcomes could vary depending on what assumptions were inserted into the model. In one respect, regarding how the costings could vary, the differences might have been minor. The occasion, however, was not. Two senior officials were saying that their ministers, in company with the Prime Minister, were verballing them, using their calculations to make a claim about the Opposition's figures that were not legitimate. Given the high standing of the expert and non-partisan officials and the regard in which their departments were held, the result was devastating for the government. Its argument that the electors should be suspicious of the Opposition because they were being tricky in the presentation of their estimates rebounded on them. If there was ever a chance that the government could present itself as the better economic manager, building on Rudd's leadership as the country survived the GFC, then this press conference destroyed it.

In the midst of the campaign, international affairs again intervened. In Syria, the regime had been accused of using poison gas to devastate areas held by the rebels. There was debate about how the West should respond, and whether Australia should back President Obama if he chose to bomb the facilities that developed the gas. Rudd convened a meeting of the NSC: summoned 'on a Saturday night!', Carr grumbled. However, he noted that Rudd

> entered the National Security Committee room somewhat late: slightly red-eyed, pallid and pudgy but, once again, getting the meeting underway, he demonstrates ease and competence as Prime Minister. What's the threshold? What was the evidence of chemical weapon use? Is this *assessment* as opposed to *raw intelligence*? Why would the Assad regime do this when they are winning on the ground and a UN inspection team has just entered? All the surgically precise questions to put. He's seeking a telephone interview with Obama and has secured one with [French President François] Hollande.

Rudd asked Carr to stay in Canberra overnight so that he could attend the press conference in the Prime Minister's courtyard the next day. Afterwards, they talked in his office, Rudd drinking tea, Carr hot water. Rudd bemoaned the way that a few people ran the country: the Murdoch media, the heads of Rio and BHP, and perhaps those of the big banks. He considered whether he should make the Murdoch bias an issue. Carr wrote that he did not say so, but the opportunity had passed at the beginning of the campaign. By now, he reflected, 'it was too late. "Let us sit upon the ground and tell sad stories of the death of kings." Kevin's Richard II moment'.

Syria was to emerge again as a topic on 31 August. Carr was about to fly off to represent Australia at the G-20. Rudd convened an NSC meeting with ministers around the country. According to Carr:

> It was as serious a discussion as I've ever had at cabinet level: what is the legal basis for a military strike in the absence of a Security Council decision? That's the theme. But one week before polling day, with the polls and the media unanimous that we are to be badly routed, the meeting has more than a touch of Admiral Doenitz about it.

Perhaps Rudd felt more relaxed talking about foreign affairs when domestic ones were going so badly astray. He insisted that such things should be taken seriously.

These meetings of high intent reflected the strange world in which Rudd had to operate. He had good days during the campaign. He performed well in the debates, but got little credit; after one debate, the *Courier-Mail*'s headline was Abbott's quip: 'Does this guy ever shut up?' He was relaxed and comfortable responding to questions for an episode of the ABC's *Q&A*, although a sharp retort to a parson who condemned gay marriage was the principal point of coverage. At the formal launch of the campaign, a week before the vote, he seemed to regather his pizzazz and was well on top of his material. Why, observers asked, couldn't he perform like this all the time? That was because mostly the zip was missing; the freshness and the enthusiasm of 2007 were no longer there. The campaign looked a struggle, and it was.

When Rudd first returned to the leadership, there was a moment when the impossible seemed possible. In the second quarter of 2013, Labor polling was telling the party that it could be reduced to thirty seats. Queensland, Western Australia and South Australia were going to return one Labor Member each, Tasmania and the Northern Territory none. Western Sydney would be Liberal heartland. Not a single poll had shown Labor winning the formerly safe seats of McMahon (Chris Bowen) or Werriwa (Laurie Ferguson). Such a bad result would decapitate the party, removing the next generation of leaders. The awful results in the Queensland and New South Wales elections had shown that devastation to that extreme was possible. But the polls bounced on Rudd's return to the prime ministership. In one Sydney seat, the support jumped from 39 to 50 per cent overnight, from a sure loss to a chance of winning. In July the party was ahead in several seats it needed to win to stay in government.

That was always unlikely to last, however, even if there had been a good campaign. By the time of the election, the issue was whether Rudd would ameliorate the level of the defeat. Rudd's own standing declined during the campaign. He began the campaign with a positive rating of 46 per cent and a negative one of 45 per cent; he was ahead. By 5 September, the figures had fallen to 34 per cent and 56 per cent respectively, a much weaker position.

Nor had the Opposition provided the ammunition that the government had wanted. The campaign was designed around the hope that distrust of Tony Abbott would translate into votes. Labor's tactics were thus to raise suspicions about what he might do: jobs or cuts? Abbott remained disciplined and on message. There were a few key issues defined by sharp slogans: stop the boats, axe the taxes. He stood firm on his one potential vulnerability, his expensive maternity leave scheme, despite the disquiet within his own party. Labor could talk about the government cuts, but the government had largely lost the capacity to control that agenda after its consistent but unfulfilled promises to bring in a surplus. Indeed, Bowen's challenge in his few weeks as Treasurer was to provide an aura of economic credibility. The polls suggested that Abbott may not have been popular or liked, but his tightly controlled campaigning meant that he was not as big an issue as Labor had hoped.

By election day, no-one thought Labor could win. The defeat was complete, though not as bad as had been feared three months earlier. In Queensland, a couple of seats were narrowly lost, but Moreton, Rankin and Lilley were retained; none of the Labor candidates had been in Rudd's camp and they now owed him the change in their fortunes—not a debt that the member for Lilley, Wayne Swan, is likely to acknowledge. In Western Australia, all of Labor's seats were retained—not that there were many of them in the first place. Western Sydney was not a disaster; the swing was limited and the next generation of leaders from that area was saved. National secretary George Wright told the Press Club that while polling had suggested thirty Labor seats before Rudd's recall, the party had won fifty-five. That implied twenty-five seats had been saved by the change of leadership. It was, Wright said, a 'solid loss. A bitter disappointment. But as one commentator wrote, we pulled off a Dunkirk—suffering a major defeat but managing to escape with our army intact. We live to fight another day'.

On election night, Rudd conceded with a rather rambling reminiscence of his political career. In an aside that he admitted was not prime ministerial, he taunted his direct opponent, who had run a long and committed campaign for the seat; it was a moment when the brawler within surfaced again. He then announced that he would stand down from the party leadership.

All that was left were the last rites from the party. It did not take long. On election night, the member for Blaxland, Jason Clare, had already argued that Rudd should stand down. A few days later, former minister Craig Emerson demanded that he leave parliament too. These demands led to responses from Rudd supporters that he be permitted to go in his own time, that he had just been elected for Griffith and should not immediately bail out and create a by-election.

Rudd did not respond. He waited. The party became involved in a leadership election. For the first time, the members had a vote, as Bill

Shorten and Anthony Albanese stood. The process was a success as members flocked to participate in meetings where they could listen to the views of the two candidates. The very process of electing a leader meant that Rudd's insistence that the change be made in July was justified. The commitment had been made before the need for a party election was clear. It will make it harder for the party to reverse the process and take the vote away from members in the future. The history of enfranchisement is one of continual expansion, not sudden restrictions. Albanese won a majority of the members' votes, but not by a large enough margin to counterbalance the caucus support for Shorten.

The leader elected, the reform of party procedures apparently consolidated, Rudd quietly arose in the House on the evening of 13 November to announce that he was resigning his seat and leaving Australian politics. The announcement took most MPs by surprise. He had kept the occasion to himself.

NOTES

Preface

p. xiii, 'When regimes are deposed': Lindsay Tanner, *Politics with Purpose*, Scribe Publications, Melbourne, 2012, p. 343.

1   A Queensland Boy

p. 3 'It also provided a flip side': Michael Wesley, 'Mandate of Heaven', *Griffith Review*, vol. 21, 2008, p. 181.

p. 4 'One was that of a young convict girl': Robert Macklin, *Kevin Rudd: The Biography*, Penguin, Melbourne, 2007, pp. 1–12.

p. 8 'Initially Kevin and Greg shared a room': ibid., p. 21.

p. 8 'Malcolm joined the army': ibid., p. 20.

p. 13 'Sometimes after school': ibid., p. 41.

p. 14 'Ron Derrick, said': Ron Derrick, 'Kevin Rudd as a Kid', *The Sunshine Coast Daily*, 24 November 2007.

p. 15 'She later described the process': Fae Barber, *Insiders*, Australian Broadcasting Commission, 23 November 2008.

p. 16 'fascinated by the interplay': Peter Costello, *The Costello Memoirs*, Melbourne University Publishing, Melbourne, 2008, p. 22.

p. 16 'Whitlam wrote back': Macklin, p. 43.

p. 17 'Kevin lapped it up': Fiona Neucom (nee Callander), 'Kevin Rudd as a Kid', *The Sunshine Coast Daily*, 24 November 2007.

2   Calligraphy and Christianity

p. 21 'He moved further south to Sydney': Macklin, pp. 44–6.

p. 23 'courteous, willing to work and with a happy disposition': Frank Freckleton, cited in Nicholas Stuart, *Kevin Rudd: An Unauthorised Biography*, Scribe Publications, Melbourne, 2007, p. 46.

p. 33 'was very surprised and impressed': Macklin, p. 55.

p. 33 'Over the next year': Kevin Rudd, Human Rights in China: The Case of Wei Jingsheng, BA (Hons), Australian National University, Canberra, 1980.

3   Diplomat to China

p. 36 'Ah, the universal wisdom': Macklin, p. 64.

p. 36 'We arrived at Stockholm': ibid.

p. 37 'He wrote with elegance': Roger Brown, cited in Macklin, p. 66.

p. 39 'Kevin recalls': H McDonald and M Toy, 'Rudd's Long March to Asia's Heart', *Sydney Morning Herald*, 28 April 2007.

p. 41 'maintained contact with them in a very sensible, non-risk type of way': ibid.

p. 44 'Once, when asked to brief Prime Minister Bob Hawke': ibid.

p. 44 'China and Australia are currently experiencing fantastic simultaneous orgasms': ibid.

p. 45 'it was pretty evident to me that Kevin was the clueiest person': Linda Jaivin, cited in McDonald and Toy.

p. 45 'In 2003, Greg Sheridan wrote': Greg Sheridan, 'The Music Stops, but Sure-footed Rudd Will Dance to the End', *The Australian*, 2 December 2003.

4   Politics in Queensland

p. 50 'We were going to have a run-through': Wayne Goss, cited in Macklin, p. 83.

p. 53 'An edited account of the election': Rosemary Whip and Colin A Hughes (eds), *Political Crossroads: The 1989 Queensland Election*, University of Queensland Press, St Lucia, Queensland, 1991.

p. 53 'So Tom Burns, the voice': Macklin, p. 86.

p. 54 'to set broad objectives': Glyn Davis, *A Government of Routines: Executive Coordination in an Australian State*, Macmillan, Melbourne, 1995, p. 38.

p. 54 'So Goss wanted "good coordination"': ibid., p. 39.

p. 55 'He argued that leaders' offices': Kevin Rudd, 'Decision Making in Queensland', in Glyn Davis (ed.), *Public Sector Reform under the Goss Government,* Royal Institute of Public Administration (RIPA)/Centre for Australian Public Sector Management (CAPSM), Brisbane, 1993, p. 44.

p. 56 'So Rudd standardised all advice': Glyn Davis, *A Government of Routines,* p. 83.

p. 56 'Goss doesn't see himself as the ringmaster': ibid., p. 37.

p. 57 'During the first term there was suspicion': ibid., p. 42.

p. 60 'can be defined as the consistent, codified and publicly articulated response': ibid.

p. 60 'seek co-ordination by testing': Kevin Rudd, 'Problems of Policy Coordination: the Role of Queensland's Office of the Cabinet', in Davis, *Public Sector Reform,* p. 70.

p. 65 'At his instigation': Joanne Scott, Ross Lawrie, Bronwyn Stevens and Patrick Weller, *The Engine Room of Government: The Queensland Premier's Department 1859–2001,* University of Queensland Press, St Lucia, Queensland, 2001.

p. 65 'the development of a comprehensive understanding': ibid., p. 409.

p. 65 'Queensland was given': ibid., p. 410.

p. 65 'Rudd chaired the': ibid.

p. 65 'Nevertheless a common': ibid.

p. 67 'It is breaking no confidence to say that Rudd is frequently a brilliant contributor to the dialogue': Sheridan, 'The Music Stops'.

5   A Political Initiation: from Candidate to Backbencher

p. 73 'would arrange introductions to mayors': McDonald and Toy.

p. 73 'I don't think it enters his head': Macklin, p. 103.

p. 76 'Dear Peter, You probably don't know me': Kevin Rudd, 'Costello must Emerge from Republican Closet', *The Australian,* 22 January 1999.

p. 80 'Rudd is not a short term': Michelle Grattan, 'ALP's Odd Couple Break the Bland Mould', *Sydney Morning Herald,* 8 June 2001.

p. 80 'In June 2001 he wrote to Rudd': Laurie Brereton to Kevin Rudd, letter, 1 June 2001.

p. 80 'complete absence of liaison': Grattan, 'ALP's Odd Couple'.

p. 81 'that you didn't raise any of the concerns': Kevin Rudd to Laurie Brereton, letter, 4 June 2001.
p. 82 'No, you're pretty good on policy': Michael Duffy, 'Never Mind Policy, Watch the Nuances', *Courier-Mail*, 6 June 2001.
p. 82 'He argued that Rudd had failed to take account': Laurie Brereton to Kevin Rudd, letter, 1 June 2001.
p. 83 'Mark Latham is often a thoughtful': Grattan, 'ALP's Odd Couple'.
p. 83 'The erudite Rudd': ibid.
p. 83 'Mark is a bright bloke': ibid.
p. 84 'Their styles, not their background': ibid.
p. 84 'Your friend and colleague': Kevin Rudd to Laurie Brereton, 4 June 2001.

6 Stalking Downer, Surviving Latham

p. 88 'All this sounds like': 'Gee, the Region has Changed, but Don't Call Us', *The Australian*, 9 January 2002.
p. 89 'He concluded that the role': ibid.
p. 89 'In one of his first appearances': *Insiders*, 'Bali Conference Flawed without Pakistan', Australian Broadcasting Commission, 24 February 2002.
p. 90 'When Rudd returned': *Insiders*, 'Rudd Asks US to Make Case against Iraq', Australian Broadcasting Commission, 1 September 2002.
p. 90 'On *Lateline* on 24 September': *Lateline*, 'Labor to Decide Position on Iraq Attack', Australian Broadcasting Commission, 24 September 2002.
p. 91 'Of course, he argued': House of Representatives, *Official Hansard*, no. 1, 4 February 2003, p. 10 669.
p. 92 'I've never given a commitment': 'Rudd Wants Top Job but after Poll', *The Australian*, 24 May 2003.
p. 93 'He might be regarded as pushy': 'Labor's Ambitious Diplomat', *Courier-Mail*, 26 April 2003.
p. 93 'Ironically, the story about the mates': Dennis Atkins, 'Labor Mates', *Courier-Mail*, 14 June 2003.
p. 93 'Matt Price, as entertaining as ever': Matt Price, 'Rudd Mentioned in Dispatches, Flaws and All', *The Australian*, 27 November 2003.
p. 94 'I think Kevin Rudd wants to run': Paul Kelly, *Insiders*, Australian Broadcasting Commission, 30 November 2003.

NOTES

p. 95 'Over the next year, Latham diarised': Mark Latham, *The Latham Diaries,* Melbourne University Press, Melbourne, 2005.

p. 96 'In March Rudd appeared': Annabel Crabb, *Losing It: The Inside Story of the Labor Party in Opposition,* Pan Macmillan Australia, Sydney, 2005, pp. 201–4.

p. 100 'I've got a field marshal's': Christine Jackman, *Inside Kevin07: The People, the Plan, the Prize,* Melbourne University Press, Melbourne, 2008, p. 14.

7 Winning the Leadership

p. 104 'A detailed report': 'Faith, Politics and Values: Report to the Shadow Executive', internal document.

p. 106 '*Sunrise* continued to be important': *Sunrise* compilation featuring Kevin Rudd, Parliamentary Library.

p. 107 'He is making himself an inevitability': Peter Hartcher, 'Man on the Move', *The Age* (*Good Weekend*), 5 November 2005.

p. 107 'I seriously don't give': ibid.

p. 117 'His key phrase, much repeated': Jackman, pp. 75–6.

8 Models, Ideas and Beliefs

p. 118 'Faith in Politics': Kevin Rudd, 'Howard's Brutopia', *The Monthly*, no. 18, November 2006.

p. 120 'politics is about power': Kevin Rudd, First Speech to Parliament, 11 November 1998.

p. 122 'This capital must be husbanded': ibid.

p. 122 'For social democrats': Kevin Rudd, 'Inserting a New Dialectic: Governance', *Globalisation: Australian Impacts,* UNSW Press, 2001.

p. 123 'Rudd's ideas were eventually': Kevin Rudd, 'Faith in Politics', *The Monthly*, no. 17, October 2006.

p. 123 'The second paper he wrote': Rudd, 'Howard's Brutopia'.

p. 123 'Working within a comprehensive framework': ibid.

p. 125 'the article a month earlier': Rudd, 'Faith in Politics'.

p. 125 'Gospel is both a spiritual and a social Gospel': ibid.

9 To Victory

p. 129 'making sure that we': *The 7.30 Report,* Australian Broadcasting Commission, 4 December 2006.

p. 134 'The outer shell of': Hartcher, 'Man on the Move'.
p. 136 'We know all about': Laurie Oakes, 'Strip Mining', *The Bulletin,* 24 August 2007, p. 15.
p. 137 'freaking out to find': ibid.
p. 137 'A Labor frontbencher was startled': ibid.
p. 137 'When Downer was asked': Michelle Grattan, 'Strip Club Visits: Rudd Regrets, Whitlam Regales', *The Age,* 21 August 2007.
p. 137 'His office responded that': Mark Metherell, 'A Kiss and Make up as Rudd's Halo Slips', *Sydney Morning Herald,* 20 August 2007.
p. 140 'The most striking image': Jackman, p. 159.
p. 143 'He will demand the': Christopher Hammer, 'Inside Fortress Rudd', *The Bulletin,* 27 November 2007.

10 Taking Over

p. 152 'a brave decision to': Robert Ray, cited in Peter Hartcher, *To the Bitter End,* Allen & Unwin, St Leonards, New South Wales, 2009, p. 147.
p. 158 'I sat down with the Prime Minister': John Faulkner, Senate Estimates Committee, CPD *Senate,* 26 May 2008.
p. 158 'He talked to the secretaries': Kevin Rudd, Address to Heads of Agencies and Members of Senior Executive Service, Great Hall, Parliament House, Canberra, 30 April 2008.
p. 159 'The phrases he used': Michelle Grattan and Paul Austin with Simon Mann, 'Three Amigos from the Sunshine State', *The Age,* 9 February 2008.

11 Reaching Out

p. 161 'As Rudd put it at one Community Cabinet': Transcript of author's attendance at Community Cabinet meeting in Beenleigh, Queensland, 28 June 2009.
p. 163 'The voice to be heard in parliament': Apology to Australia's Indigenous People, House of Representatives, *Official Hansard,* no. 1, 13 February 2008.

12 Punching above Our Weight

p. 175 'Whether he sits down with a tea lady': Tony Walker, 'Rudd's New World Order', *Weekend Australian Financial Review,* 26–27 September 2009, p. 19.

p. 177 'A true friend is': Kevin Rudd, 'A Conversation with China's Youth on the Future', transcript of speech at Peking University, 9 April 2008.

p. 179 'I look forward to a free-flowing and open discussion': Kevin Rudd, Address at Shangri-La Dialogue, Singapore, 29 May 2009.

p. 180 'In fact I believe this is potentially dangerous': ibid.

p. 181 'political will exercised through ministerial forums': Kevin Rudd, Address to the United Nations, General Assembly, New York, 25 September 2008.

p. 182 'Australia is also a strong believer': Kevin Rudd, Address at Shangri-La Dialogue.

p. 183 'Rudd presented to parliament what he described as': Kevin Rudd, Address to Parliament, CPD HR, 4 December 2008.

13 Facing the Global Crises

p. 198 'He also wrote an essay': Kevin Rudd, 'The Global Financial Crisis', *The Monthly*, no. 42, February 2009.

p. 203 'Rudd explained what the': Kevin Rudd, 'Pain on the Road to Recovery', *Sydney Morning Herald*, 25 July 2009.

15 A Time for Questions

p. 223 'So, just to go back to the other part': Kevin Rudd, Press Conference, Parliament House, 19 June 2009.

p. 225 'It's clear that Rudd': Bernard Keane, 'Rudd, a PM with "four-in-the-morning courage"', *Crikey*, 26 June 2008, http://www.crikey.com.au/2009/06/26/rudd-a-pm-with-%e2%80%9cfour-o%e2%80%99clock-in-the-morning-courage%e2%80%9d/, accessed 30 June 2008.

16 Playing on the International Stage

p. 242 'the biggest innovation in global politics': Greg Sheridan, 'Rudd Role Vital to G20 Emergence', *The Weekend Australian*, 7–8 November 2009.

17 Resetting Priorities: Climate Change

p. 249 'final report in May 2007': Peter Shergold, *Prime Ministerial Task Group on Emissions Trading—Final Report,* May 2007, http://pandora.nla.gov.au/pan/79623/20080117-2207/dpmc.gov.au/emissions/index.html, accessed 28 November 2009.

p. 249 'An interim report was issued': Ross Garnaut, *The Garnaut Climate Change Review*, 30 September 2008, http://www.garnautreview.org.au/index.htm, accessed 28 November 2008.

p. 250 'and the Stern Report': Nicholas Stern, *Stern Review on the Economics of Climate Change*, 30 October 2006, http://mudancasclimaticas.cptec.inpe.br/~rmclima/pdfs/destaques/sternreview_report_complete.pdf, accessed 28 November 2008.

p. 252 'the Green Paper was signed off': Australian Government, Department of Climate Change, Green Paper, *Carbon Pollution Scheme Green Paper*, 1 July 2008.

p. 253 'A White Paper was produced': Australian Government, Department of Climate Change, White Paper, *Carbon Pollution Reduction Scheme: Australia's Low Pollution Future*, 15 December 2008.

p. 258 'That single voice is saying': Kevin Rudd, joint press conference with Ban Ki-moon and Lars Rasmussen, Trinidad, 29 November 2009.

p. 260 'the washing away of villages in Tuvalu': Kevin Rudd, 'The Time Has Come for a Grand Bargain between the Past and the Future', speech at COP15 conference Copenhagen, 17 December 2009.

p. 261 'By 11 a.m. on Saturday, a text was agreed': Kevin Rudd, transcript of joint press conference with the Minister for Climate Change, Copenhagen, 19 December 2009.

18 Challenges

p. 268 'an interpretation that Gillard disputes': Philip Chubb, *Power Failure*, Black Inc, Melbourne, 2014, p. 94.

p. 269 'The BER was delivered by state governments': *Report of the Task Force*, chaired by Brad Orgill, reported December 2010.

p. 270 'The home insulation scheme was much smaller': *Review of the Administration of the Home Insulation Scheme*, Allan Hawke, April 2010; *Home Insulation Program*, The Auditor General, Report no. 12, 2010–11; *Findings of Inquest*, Office of the State Coroner, July 2012; Witness statement, Hon Kevin Rudd to the Royal Commission into the Home Insulation Scheme, 14 May 2014.

p. 271 'One of Thatcher's businessmen': cited by Ken Stowe in G Davis and P Weller (eds), *New Ideas, Better Government*, Allen & Unwin, St Leonards, New South Wales, 1996, p. 197.

p. 273 'Let's not try to sugar-coat this': *The 7.30 Report*, Australian Broadcasting Commission, 25 February 2010.

p. 274 'We are taking a whacking': *Insiders*, Australian Broadcasting Commission, 1 March 2010.

p. 276 'Rudd was all smiles': Peter Hartcher, 'Why Rudd Needs to Slow Down', *Sydney Morning Herald*, 17 August 2013.

p. 278 'Alternative ways had been considered': Chubb, pp. 104–5.

p. 278 'But the belief it was just routine': Lenore Taylor, 'ETS off the Agenda until Late the Next Term', *Sydney Morning Herald*, 27 April 2010.

p. 279 'Taylor suggested putting climate change': 'Decision that Shattered Faith in PM', *Sydney Morning Herald*, 5 June 2010.

p. 281 'Swan's office later argued that it never said': Jim Chalmers, *Glory Daze*, Melbourne University Press, Melbourne, 2013, p. 159.

p. 282 'You've spent the best part of two years': *The 7.30 Report*, Australian Broadcasting Commission, 12 May 2010.

19 The Coup

p. 287 'If Kevin had been able to buy himself': McClelland quoted in Maxine McKew, *Tales from the Political Trenches*, Melbourne University Press, 2011, p. 187.

p. 288 'After a walk on the beach': David Marr, 'Power Trip', *Quarterly Essay*, no. 38, 2010, pp. 85–6.

p. 290 'It was reported that Arbib rang Feeny': Laurie Oakes, 'The Real Story of a Bloody Downfall', *Daily Telegraph*, 30 October 2010.

p. 291 'he stated to the *Financial Review* that Rudd would lead': 'Labor 100 Per Cent behind Rudd: Swan', *Australian Financial Review*, 14 June 2010.

p. 292 'Martin Ferguson says he was approached': Peter Hartcher, 'The Faceless Men at Work', *Sydney Morning Herald*, 18 November 2013.

p. 292 'McClelland was shown polling': McKew, p. 187.

p. 292 'To state the obvious': Troy Bramston, *Rudd, Gillard and Beyond*, Penguin Books, Melbourne, 2014, p. 5.

p. 292 'The next day Gillard had a meeting': Hartcher, 'The Faceless Men at Work'.

p. 293 'Crean was shown some': Aaron Patrick, *Downfall: How the Labor Party Ripped Itself Apart*, ABC Books, Sydney, 2013, p. 30.

p. 293 'When the challenge was on': Patrick, p. 40.

p. 293 'In *The Sydney Morning Herald*': Peter Hartcher and Philip Cooray, 'Rudd Secret Polling on His Leadership', *Sydney Morning Herald*, 23 June 2010.

p. 293 'Indeed, in 2012, Dennis Shanahan': Dennis Shanahan, 'When It Comes to the Rudd Coup, Gillard's Word Can be Believed', *The Australian*, 19 February 2012.

p. 295 'By one account, she also said': Rhys Muldoon, 'A Coup by Any Other Name', *The Monthly*, March 2012.

p. 295 'When she rang, it was not as if': Bramston, p. 25.

p. 297 'Hartcher claims Swan had been appalled': Hartcher, 'The Faceless Men at Work'.

p. 297 'So he told the caucus he would not stand': McKew, p. 168.

20 How Rudd Governed: For Better or Worse

This chapter is based on interviews with ministers, senior officials and staffers, on the prime ministers' schedules, and on observation.

p. 300 'Captain Chaos': The title of an article written by John Lyons for *The Australian*, 21 June 2008.

p. 303 'Bruce Hawker identified the characteristic trait': Bruce Hawker, *The Rudd Rebellion*, Melbourne University Publishing, Melbourne, 2013, p. 116.

p. 326 'Bob Carr, writing only about': Bob Carr, *Diary of a Foreign Minister*, University of New South Wales Press, Sydney, 2014.

21 Limbo

p. 339 'According to a Fairfax Nielsen pollster': Peter Hartcher, 'The Rise and Fall of Gillard', *Sydney Morning Herald*, 18 November 2013.

p. 343 'In September 2011, polls suggested': Philip Cooray, 'Rudd Surges as the People's Choice', *Sydney Morning Herald*, 12 September 2011.

p. 345 'Look, I am not surprised that': *Four Corners*, 'The Comeback Kid', Australian Broadcasting Commission, 13 February 2012.

p. 346 'I've reflected a lot on that': Sky News, *Australian Agenda*, 19 February 2012.

p. 347 'In *The Australian*, Shanahan wrote': Shanahan, 'When It Comes to the Rudd Coup, Gillard's Word Can be Believed'.

p. 348 'violent condemnations from ministers', various articles *Sydney Morning Herald* and *The Australian*, 22–24 February 2012.

p. 350 'His chief of staff writes that': Chalmers, p. 31.

p. 352 'Bob Carr thought the proposals insane': Carr, p. 304.

p. 353 'It was not that Rudd had entirely': ibid., p. 364.

22 Going down Fighting

p. 358 'Foreign Minister Bob Carr, experienced in such tasks': Carr, pp. 415, 416, 419.

p. 359 'He talked to the Chinese president': Hawker, p. 86.

p. 359 'I watched Rudd': Carr, p. 419.

p. 361 'Chris Bowen had suggested one proposal': Chris Bowen, *Hearts and Minds: A Blueprint for Modern Labor*, Melbourne University Press, Melbourne, 2013, pp. 116–19.

p. 363 'When Rudd was returned': Bramston, p. 49.

p. 364 'Kevin displayed a prodigious knowledge': Hawker, p. 94.

p. 364 'The election campaign was very different': for accounts, see Pamela Williams, 'How Kevin Rudd's Campaign Unravelled', *Australian Financial Review*, 9 September 2013; Deborah Snow, 'A Lost Week', *The Age*, 9 September 2013; Hawker for a general account.

p. 365 'we didn't have the time to prepare': ibid., p. 156.

p. 366 'There are claims that Rudd and Hawker': Bramston, p. 42.

p. 366 'Yesterday I went around': Hawker, p. 152.

p. 366 'Peter Hartcher suggested he should': Hartcher, 'Why Rudd Needs to Slow Down'.

p. 366 'Wright and Butler wanted him': Bramston, pp. 49–50.

p. 368 'on a Saturday night': Carr, pp. 447, 449.

p. 369 'It was as serious a discussion': ibid., p. 456.

p. 369 'In the second quarter': Bramston, p. 45; George Wright, Address to the National Press Club, 20 October 2013.

p. 370 'The polls bounced on Rudd's return': Bramston, p. 57.

p. 371 'A solid loss': Wright, Address to the National Press Club; see also Jonathan Swan, Bianca Hall and Rick Feneley, 'Rudd Saved Labor, Leaked Polling Shows', *The Age*, 22 September 2013.

ACKNOWLEDGEMENTS

I would like to thank the former prime minister, Kevin Rudd, for the cooperation that made this book possible, and members of his family, Thérèse Rein, Jessica and Nick Rudd, and Loree, Malcolm and Greg Rudd, for allowing me to talk to them about the private life of the extended Rudd family.

In the Prime Minister's Office, Alister Jordan and his colleagues were hospitable and relaxed about an academic sitting around the office and dropping in to talk on a number of occasions. They facilitated access where possible and never made me feel like an intruder; that made the research so much easier. In particular, Katie Nguyen assisted with the arrangements, organised interviews and in general smoothed my path in a way that really helped. None of this assistance was accompanied by any attempt to tell me what I could or could not write.

I conducted extensive interviews with Rudd's colleagues; they included ministers, public servants, ministerial staff and journalists. The arrangement was always that I could use all the material, but if I wanted to attribute a comment, I would get clearance for the text. If the speakers wanted to remain anonymous, they could. Some comments are therefore attributed, others are not. Where they are not,

Acknowledgements

I have indicated the arena from which the speaker has come. I would like to thank all those who assisted in this way in the research.

Several people have read drafts of one, more or all chapters, of one or both versions of this book. They include Glyn Davis, John Faulkner, Haig Patapan, Xu Yi-chong, Jack Corbett and some participants whom I asked to check the factual accuracy of what I describe in particular chapters. I would like to thank them all for their comments and assistance. None of them are responsible for the final form of the book.

Loree Rudd helped us identify photographs of the early Rudd years and we are grateful for that access to the family albums. We thank Michael Jones of Auspic for assistance in identifying suitable photographs. At Melbourne University Press, Louise Adler provided constant support. Foong Ling Kong, Helen Koehne and Gillian Hutchison were meticulous in their editing, and patient in dealing with ever-changing text in 2010. Colette Vella took on the role of editor in 2014, and assisted the process of rewriting with cheerful enthusiasm and encouragement. Paul Smitz edited the text, old and new, with skill and expedition. My thanks to all of them.

At Griffith University, Tracee McPate provided support in travel and the daily organisation of the research. Paula Cowan and May McPhail have been wonderful research assistants: careful, persistent and inventive. Even while the future of the enterprise may have seemed to be in doubt, they continued to collect information, so it was all there when I needed it in 2014. May also collected a bank of photographs from which we could draw. I am grateful for their faith and support. The book could not have been completed without their assistance.

Patrick Weller
Griffith University, Brisbane
May 2014

INDEX

AALD *see* Australian-American Leadership Dialogue
Abbott, Tony 152, 226, 254–5, 262, 268, 276, 370
ABC Radio 612 Brisbane 101
ABC TV *see* 7.30 *Report*; *Four Corners*; *Insiders*; *Lateline*
Abu Ghraib prison 114
Aceh 116
administrative arrangements for government 171, 173
Advanced Economies Forum 237
advertisements (campaign) 158, 159, 166–7
Afghanistan
  Australian casualties 293
  Rudd visits Australian troops 183, 359
  in Rudd's address to UN 211
  war 103, 109, 158, 211
Africa, and climate change 259
Age (newspaper) 203
AIG insurance company 190
Airports Act 1996 91
Albanese, Anthony
  at SPBC financial crisis meeting 191
  chairs Tactics Committee 207, 216
  competence 332
  compliments Mark Arbib 115
  as deputy leader, 357
  in leadership contest 372
  as member of leadership group 363
  on Rudd government 295
  support for Kim Beazley 136
  support for Rudd 350
  works with Rudd 157–8
Albright, Madeleine 277
Allan, Col 163
ANZAC service in Vietnam 162
Apex Clubs 18
apology to Stolen Generations 188, 190–4, 205, 298
Arbib, Mark
  lack of experience of governing 290
  on removal of Rudd from leadership 290
  Rudd seeks support from 114–16
  Rudd's manifesto for 130, 132, 147, 158
  on Rudd's success 165
Argentina 234, 241
Armitage, Richard 81, 114, 205
Asia, Australian engagement with 106, 149, 202
Asia Watch journal 30
Asia-Pacific Economic Cooperation (APEC) 146, 147

Index

role in regional cooperation 202, 207–8
Rudd's use of Mandarin 206
Singapore meeting 2009 258
Sydney meeting 2007 165, 166
Asia-Pacific region
  community advocated by Rudd 208, 209
  included in G-20 228
  US presence 212
'Asian Languages and Australia's Economic Future' report 79–80
ASIO 56, 210
'The Atavism of Social Justice' (Hayek) 148
Atkins, Dennis 70, 75, 78, 110
Auditor General 221, 281
Australia
  at UN Climate Change Conference at Copenhagen 256, 259
  in G-20 229, 241
  middle power diplomacy 200–1
  role as US 'deputy sheriff' 106, 108, 200
Australia China Consultancies 87–8
Australian Chamber of Commerce and Industry 210
Australian economy
  boom period 158, 185
  debt following GFC 202, 203, 218
  fiscal stimulus packages 194, 196, 197, 200–1, 218
  impact of GFC 191, 192, 193, 200, 202, 204, 219
  need for stimulus 193, 202
  Rudd briefed on when elected 176–7
  Rudd campaigns on 155, 160
Australian education system 79, 80
  see also education; education revolution
Australian Export Awards (2008) 212

Australian Federal Police 283
Australian film festival in Stockholm 47
Australian Financial Review 92
Australian Labor Party National Conference 344
Australian National Training Authority 182
Australian National University (ANU) 23, 24, 28, 65, 152
Australian (newspaper)
  on George W Bush's rumoured ignorance about G-20 211, 231
  on leadership crisis 347
  Matt Price makes fun of Rudd 111
  Rudd writes for 92, 93, 106
  seeks comment from Rudd on Scores nightclub incident 163
Australian Prime Minister's Working Papers 236
Australian Public Service *see* public service
Australian Secret Intelligence Service (ASIS) 56, 57
Australian troops 183, 211, 359
Australian Wheat Board (AWB) 124, 127–9, 200
Australian Workers Union (AWU) 64, 136, 178, 179
Australian-American Leadership Dialogue (AALD)
  Bob Zoellick at 81, 183
  established by Phil Scanlan 80–1, 208
  Kurt Campbell at 241–2
  Larry Smarr at 159
  Richard Armitage at 114
  Rudd's links 93, 204

babushka dolls, Rudd likens public policy to 160, 244
Bachelet, Michelle 206

Baker, Anthony 191
Bali Conference on Climate Change
  (2007) 182, 248
Ban Ki-moon 183, 256, 258
Bangladesh 256, 259
banks 191, 192, 194
Barber, Fae 14, 15
Barber family 16
Barber, Harry 28, 30–1
Barnett, Colin 281
Barrett, Chris 191
Beale, Roger 79
Bear Stearns 189, 211
Beattie, Peter 86, 188, 365, 366
Beazley, Kim
  attends AALD 81
  cancels Rudd's 1995 East Timor trip
    95
  chairs Tactics Committee 123
  challenges Mark Latham's leadership
    117
  challenges Simon Crean's leadership
    110–11
  David Epstein works with 159
  Department of Homeland Security
    proposal 173
  friendship with John Faulkner 175
  leadership challenged by Rudd
    115–16, 122, 130, 134–6, 157
  muddles Rove McManus with Karl
    Rove 133
  relationship with Mark Arbib 115,
    116, 132
  Rudd on his leadership 109, 112
  Rudd seeks a position in his
    Department of Defence 62
  and Rudd's row with Laurie
    Brereton 98, 101
  union support 156
  Wayne Swan works with 63
Beijing
  Australian journalists 57
  David Irvine's diplomatic posting
    55–6
  economic transition 52
  Rudd's diplomatic posting 48–51,
    206
  Tiananmen demonstrations 66
  see also China
Bennett, Christine 275
Berlusconi, Silvio 238, 239
Bethege, Eberhard 141
Bevis, Arch 136
BHP Billiton 282
Bin Laden, Osama 167
Bjelke Peterson, Joh 60
Blair, Tony 107, 188
blogs 188, 197
boat people 105, 246, 292, 357–9
Boland, Adam 118
Bolkus, Nick 81
Bolt, Robert 138–9
Bomana war cemetery 125
Bonhoeffer, Dietrich 29–30, 118, 138,
  140–3, 150–2
border protection 292
Botswana 277
Bowen, Chris 132–3, 135, 136, 350,
  353, 357, 361, 363, 367, 370
Boxall, Peter 180
Bracks, Steve 321, 344
Brazil 229, 230, 234, 261
Brereton, Laurie 94–5, 96–7, 98, 100–1
Bretton Woods system 211
briefing processes for government
  185–8
'Bringing Them Home' report (1997)
  190–1
Brisbane 3, 4, 9, 10, 11
Brisbane Airports Corporation 91
Brisbane floods 351
Britain 205, 227, 256, 259
British Cabinet 330, 338
British Labour Party 360

broadband network 159, 245, 246
Brown, Gordon
  at Copenhagen Conference 257
  at G-20 summit, Washington 233, 234
  'fast start' fund 358
  Rudd's discussions with 204, 228, 237, 258, 259
  in Rudd's tweets 199
  split with Tony Blair 188
Brumby, John 276
Buchan, John 9, 18
budgets
  2008 189, 200
  2009 281
  deficits 201–2, 203, 218
  surpluses 201, 203
Buna (New Guinea) 4, 125
Burgmann College, ANU 23, 24, 26, 27, 28
Burke, Brian 161
Burke, Tony 179, 347, 356–7
Burns, Tom 67, 70, 72, 78
Bush, George (snr) 81
Bush, George W (jr)
  convenor of Washington G-20 meeting 233
  Mark Latham's comments on 109
  policy on Taiwan 93
  Rudd's meetings with 166, 205
  speculation about his ignorance of G-20 211, 231
  wars on Afghanistan and Iraq 103, 107
business community, relations with Rudd government 293
Butler, Mark 364, 366
Byrne, Anthony 168

Cabinet Committees 327–31
Cabinet Handbook (Goss government) 68
Cabinet process 283, 325–7, 338
Cabinet Secretary 175–6
Callander, Bob 17–18, 18, 18–19, 20, 21
Callander, Fiona 14, 17, 27
Callander family 15, 17
calligraphy 31
Cameron, Ross 101
campaign advertising 158, 159, 166–7
Campbell, Ian 161–2
Campbell, Kurt 205, 241–2, 353
Canada 227, 228, 229, 241
Canberra Times 92
Canning Vale Community Cabinet 188–9
Canterbury Hospital 22
cap and trade system 252, 253
Captain Chaos 300
car dealers 192, 196, 220, 223
carbon emissions 252
carbon markets 239
Carbon Pollution Reduction Scheme (CPRS) 327
carbon pricing, deferral of 278–80
carbon tax 262, 359
carbon trading 206
The Cardinal (Moran) 321
Carr, Bob 165, 352, 358, 359, 368
Carr, Kim 133, 134, 136, 292–3, 350, 353, 357
Casey, Richard 342
Cassidy, Barrie 274
Catholic faith 7–8, 9, 23, 25, 138
caucus committees 96, 97, 98
caucus meetings 208
CCC (Copenhagen Commitment Circle) 256
Centre for Independent Studies (CIS) 147, 148
'Certain Maritime Incident' 175
Chalmers, Jim 191
Chaney, Richard 81

Channel 7 118, 119
  see also Sunrise program
Charlton, Andrew 314
  during GFC 191
  fake Ozcar email sent in his name 220–1, 223, 281
  as Rudd's 'sherpa' for G-20 summits 233
Charter Letters 184, 185
Charter for Sustainable Economic Activity (Germany) 238
The Chaser (comedy troupe) 165
Cheeseman, Darren 345
Cheney, Dick 205
'Children Overboard' incident 174–5, 180
Chile 206, 277
China
  at G-20 228, 229, 230, 241
  at Pacific Island Forum 210
  at UN Climate Change Conference at Copenhagen 256, 259, 261
  Australia China Consultancies 87–8
  as a big polluter 251, 255
  diplomatic life 48–59
  and GFC 190, 191, 230
  Hu Jintao as President 234
  human rights 43–4, 58
  importance to Australia's national security 182
  Joel Fitzgibbon's trips 219
  not represented at G-7 227
  Ross Garnaut as ambassador 249
  Rudd government issues with 248
  Rudd's 2006 delegation to 134
  Rudd's first visit to as Prime Minister 205, 206–7
  Rudd's interest 16, 24, 27
  Rudd's writing on 92, 93
  see also Beijing
China Daily (newspaper) 234

Chinese Nationalist Party (KMT, Kuomintang) 41, 42
Chinese studies 27, 30–1
Chinese University 48
Christian philosophy 138, 140–3, 150–4
Christian Socialists 149
'The Church and the Jewish Question' (Bonhoeffer) 140
CIS (Centre for Independent Studies) 147, 148
Citizen's Assembly 339
Citizens Electoral Council 189
citizenship test 164
Clare, Jason 371
clean-coal technology 356
climate change
  Bali Conference on Climate change (2007) 182
  competes with GFC for significance 206
  divisions over policy 297
  financial package 241
  G-8 meeting discussions 238
  impact on poor countries 153, 259
  Pittsburgh G-20 discussions 240
  policy difficulties 292
  Rudd government signature policy 176, 245
  Rudd's action on 248, 250, 262
  Rudd's addresses on 149, 211
  Rudd's campaigns on 155, 156, 160
  Rudd's discussions in China 134
  UN Climate Change Conference at Copenhagen (2009) 238, 241, 248, 253, 254–62
  UN meetings 239
Climate Change Committee (CCC) 206, 209, 250, 251, 283, 327
Clinton, Bill 204, 239
Clinton, Hillary 205, 260
Clinton Global Initiative 208

Index

COAG *see* Council of Australian Governments
Coaldrake, Peter
  background and education 61
  comments on Rudd 76
  in Goss government 62, 69, 70, 72, 77
Coalition of the Willing 103, 109, 200, 205
codes of conduct for ministerial staff 176
Cole, Terence 127, 128
Cole Inquiry 128
Collins, Jacinta 357, 363
Combet, Greg 179, 274, 356
Committee for Economic Affairs 133
Committee for Foreign Affairs 92
Commonwealth Heads of Government (CHOGM) 358
communications technology 323
Community Cabinets 188–90, 212
computers, for secondary school children 160
Confessing Church seminary 140
Conroy, Stephen 110, 136, 348, 351–2, 356, 362
Conservative Party (UK) 360
conservative politics, and Christianity 151–2
control, by prime ministers 310–12
convicts 4
Coombs, Nugget 186
Coordination Committee 329, 330
Copenhagen Commitment Circle (CCC) 255
corruption, in Queensland 60, 64
The Cost of Discipleship (Bonhoeffer) 138, 140
Costello, Peter
  at university 16
  challenges Rudd about Brian Burke 161

desire to be Prime Minister 158
  discordant relations with John Howard 188
  parliamentary performances 217
  Rudd compares with Friedrich A Hayek 146
  Rudd's open letter to 92
Council of Australian Governments (COAG)
  agreements with states on health and hospital reform 277
  change and reform policies 245
  and former Special Premiers Conferences 78
  negotiation on Asian studies in schools 79–80
  report on health and hospital reform 246
  role of Victoria 321
  Rudd chairs 247
  Rudd's first meeting with as Prime Minister 183
  successes 208
Country Life 7
Country Party 17, 157
Courier Mail (newspaper) 61, 66, 92, 110, 111, 365, 369
Crean, Frank 205
Crean, Simon
  at Question Time 217
  concern over performance of Gillard government 352
  insistence Rudd challenge for leadership 352, 353
  as Labor Party leader 103, 107, 109, 130
  leadership challenged by Kim Beazley 110–11, 287
  public criticism of Rudd 347
  sacking by Gillard 353
  support for Julia Gillard as Labor Party leader 136

Crean, Simon (cont.)
   support for Rudd return 352
   on use of SPBC over Cabinet 283, 329
credit schemes 192
Criminal Justice Commission 77
cross-folio issues 322

Daily Telegraph (newspaper) 135, 365
Danger Man (nickname for Laurie Brereton) 94
Davis, Glyn
   in Goss government 69–70, 78, 84
   holidays with Rudd in Sicily 120–1
   Rudd involves in 2020 Summit 194–5, 196
   on Rudd's approach to policy 73
   Rudd's first meeting 65–6
   speculation over post with PM&C 181
De Bruyn, Joe 136
De Lacy, Keith 70, 78
De LaSalle Catholic School, Scarborough 11
Deakin, Alfred 311
Dean, William 191
debating societies 19
Declaration of Human Rights (UN) 208
Defence White Paper (2008) 211–12
Democratic Labor Party 17, 157, 174
Dempster, Quentin 64
Deng Xiaoping 42, 44, 52, 53
Denmark 256, 257, 258
Department of Climate Change 248
Department of Finance 367
Department of Foreign Affairs (DFA) 45–6, 55, 105
Department of Foreign Affairs and Trade (DFAT) (formerly DFA)
   concern over Rudd's regional cooperation initiatives 210

   Dick Woolcott heads 208
   Michael L'Estrange heads 180
   Rudd criticises 107
   Rudd's career in 58, 62, 86, 92
   Rudd's idealisation of 202–3
   work standards 72
Department of Homeland Security proposal 173, 212
Department of Prime Minister and Cabinet (PM&C)
   advisory role 320, 308
   advisory system 321–2
   centralisation of policy-making 322–3
   David Tune in 232
   'Dorothy Dixers' for Question Time 216
   during GFC 196
   during transition to Rudd government 171, 172–3, 176, 179
   investigation into fake Ozcar email 222, 223, 281
   Office of National Security 183
   plans Canning Vale Community Cabinet 188
   as Prime Minister's surrogate 325
   relationship with prime minister 309
   Rudd's demand for rolling policy dialogue 323
   Secretary 181, 249, 321–2
   support provided 324
Department of Treasury
   costing of Opposition's policies 367
   during GFC 194, 195, 196
   economic forecasting 193
   investigation into faked Ozcar email 222, 223, 281
departmental secretaries
   appointment 180–1
   at Community Cabinets 188, 189, 190

Index

portfolio meetings 184
Rudd addresses 186
in Task Group on Emissions Trading 249
Derrick, Ron 14, 20
Deutsche Christen 140
DeVere, Margaret *see* Rudd (née DeVere), Margaret
diplomatic life 46–59, 301
disability support scheme 360
disloyalty, in Rudd government ministry 180
Doha round 211, 235, 240
Donate to the World Food Program 165
'Dorothy Dixers' ('Dorothies') 216, 217
double dissolution 267–8
Downer, Alexander
  asked about strip clubs 163
  during 2007 election campaign 165–6
  as Foreign Minister 342
  links with AALD 93
  makes fun of Labor party 96
  management of DFAT 56, 86, 92, 203
  relationship with Rudd 105–6, 128, 129, 145, 163
Dr Death (nickname for Rudd) 72
drama 15
Dreyfus, Mark 191
drought-relief taskforce, Queensland 77

e-democracy 99–100
East Asian Summit 208, 248
East Timor 94, 95, 183, 339
economic management 166, 167, 310
economic policy, as key policy area 244–5
economic taskforce 208, 211

economy *see* Australian economy
education 156, 158, 177, 352, 359–60
education revolution 160, 174, 245, 269
  see also Australian education system
Edwards, Graham 161
elections *see* federal elections
Electoral and Administrative Review Committee 77
Electrical Trades Union 84
Elliot, Justine 13
email
  fake Ozcar email 220–6
  use by Rudd to communicate with public 197
Emerson, Craig 89, 110, 356, 371
emissions trading scheme (ETS) 249, 250, 262, 267, 327, 334
English studies 15
environment policy 177
Epstein, David
  at SPBC financial crisis meeting 191
  as PMO's chief of staff 159, 314, 317
  role in transition arrangements for Rudd government 172
  on Rudd's campaign team 166
Ethiopia 256, 258, 259
Eumundi, Qld 5, 6, 23
Eumundi advertisement 158
Eumundi Primary School 10
Eumundi state school 6
Europe and G-20 235, 238, 241
European Commission (EC) 228, 234
European Community (EC) 206, 256
European Union (EU) 147, 205, 210, 256
Evangelical Union 28, 29
Evans, Gareth 56, 94, 95, 209
Expenditure Review Committee (ERC) 189, 327, 330, 339

factions
  concessions to 177
  impact when selecting ministers
    157, 169, 178, 179
  Left 84, 115, 174, 178, 207
  New South Wales Right 114–15,
    116, 132
  Old Guard 83, 84, 87
  and poll results 290
  Right 174, 178, 207
  role 115
  and Rudd 136, 156, 286
  Victorian Left 116, 133
  and Wayne Goss 136
Fair Work bill 211
'Faith in Politics' (Rudd) 138
Faith, Values and Politics Group 123,
  149
fake Ozcar email 220–6
Family First 123, 152, 250
family values, social democratic views
  on 148, 149
Fannie Mae 190
farming 5–6, 7, 8, 9
Faulkner, John
  advice on composition of Cabinet
    285–6
  comments on Rudd's portfolio
    meetings 184–5
  as Defence Minister 338
  and fake Ozcar email 222
  handling of Joel Fitzgibbon
    controversy 219
  Labor campaign report 344
  meeting with Rudd and Gillard
    on performance of government
    294–5
  on need for early 2010 election
    268
  resignation from Ministry 337–8
  supports Rudd's challenge to Kim
    Beazley's leadership 136

  works with Rudd in Opposition
    157, 166, 167, 170, 172
  works with Rudd as Prime Minister
    174–6, 178, 181
federal elections
  1996 84–5, 89
  1998 94, 101
  2001 101–2, 105, 174
  2004 114, 149
  2007 122, 130, 155, 166–9, 177
  2010 267–9
  2013 363, 371
Federal Reserve 127
Feeney, David 286
Fejo, Nanna Nungala 191
Ferguson, Laurie 370
Ferguson, Martin 281, 292
Fielding, Steve 250
finance companies 196
financial institutions 194
  see also international financial
    institutions
financial markets 199
financial regulation 235, 237, 240,
  241
Financial Review 291
Financial Stability Board (FSB) 238,
  241
Financial Stability Forum 211, 231
Financial Times 234
Firbank Grammar School 26
First Home Owners Grant 197
fiscal stimulus
  in Australia 194, 196, 197, 200–1,
    218
  exit strategies 240, 241
  global 234, 237, 238, 241
Fisher, Andrew 89, 136, 149
Fitzgerald report 60, 62, 64–5, 68, 77
Fitzgerald, Tony 60, 64
Fitzgibbon, Joel 217, 218–19, 357
Flanagan, William 47

INDEX

Flossenburg concentration camp 138, 141
Ford dealerships 197
Forde electorate 365
Foreign Affairs journal 229, 234
foreign policy 108–9, 146, 200, 202, 205, 342
Forrest, Andrew 282
Fortescue Metals 282
Four Corners (ABC TV) 60, 344
France 227, 231, 235, 241, 258
Fraser, Malcolm 22, 311, 312, 329, 330, 298–9
Freckleton, Frank 23
Freckleton family 22, 23
Freddie Mac 190
free markets 147, 199
free trade 146
freedom of information 176, 327
French Communist Party 53–4
Friday All Stars (*Sunrise* nickname for Rudd and Hockey) 118
friends of the Chair in Copenhagen 256, 259, 261, 333
Fuel Watch 218
Fukushima nuclear power station 342
Fussell, Lieutenant Michael 211

G-7 227–8, 230, 231, 238, 241
G-8 237–8, 255
G-10 227
G-20
　Australia represented at 202, 211
　and climate change 261
　development and future 228–35, 240–3
　multilateral diplomacy 200
G-20 summits 363
　London, April 2009 234–5, 255
　Pittsburgh, September 2009 237, 238, 239–41, 248
　September 2013 359

　Washington, November 2008 233–4
Gallop, Geoff 161
Garnaut, Ross 55, 249
Garrett, Peter 24, 157, 273, 356
Gartrell, Tim 123, 124, 134
Geelong Grammar 28
General Theory (Keynes) 196
Georges, George 18
Germany 227
GFC *see* Global Financial Crisis
Gillard government, performance 343, 350–1, 352, 353–4
Gillard, Julia
　accusations about fake Ozcar email 224
　as Acting Prime Minister 332
　on age pension 338
　announces 2013 election 351
　at Question Time 209, 216, 217
　attends funeral of Matt Price 180
　on border control issue 292
　calls 2010 election 338
　calls for leadership ballot 352–3, 354
　daily meetings with Rudd 283–4
　as deputy prime minister 332
　disinterest in foreign affairs 341
　draft victory speech 344–5
　during GFC 195
　on dysfunctional Rudd government 348
　as Education Minister 332
　education reform 332
　election as Labor leader 298, 344
　enters parliament 89
　friendship with Mark Latham 133
　on Government Staffing Panel 185
　as a Labor star 188
　leadership aspirations 291
　leadership style 336
　meeting with Rudd over performance of government 294

395

Gillard, Julia (cont.)
   opposition to early 2010 election on climate change 268
   on parental leave scheme 338
   positioning for leadership 288
   as potential leader 116–17
   'real' Julia 340
   reconciliation meeting with Rudd 340
   request for leadership ballot 295
   on Rudd as Foreign Minister 347
   as Rudd's deputy in government 136, 173–4, 177, 178
   as Rudd's deputy in Opposition 92, 157
   on Scores nightclub incident 163
   SPBC membership 327
   supports Rudd in challenging Kim Beazley's leadership 134–5
   on Tactics Committee 207
   tour of Western Sydney 352
'Global Economic Recovery – An International Framework for Toxic Asset Management (IFTAM)' (working paper) 236
'The Global Financial Crisis' (2009) (Rudd) 198–9
Global Financial Crisis (GFC)
   Australia's survival of 335
   car dealerships affected by 220
   competes with climate change 206
   and G-20 230, 238, 248
   impact on 2020 Summit 196–7
   and International Monetary Fund 190, 211
   recedes 246
   Rudd's articles about 234
   Rudd's daily economic briefings 205
   Wayne Swan as Treasurer 189
globalisation 146
GM dealerships 197

goat, given to John Howard by Rudd 165
Gonski report 352, 359
goods and services tax (GST) 89
Gorbachev, Mikhail 58
Gore, Al 237
Gorton, John 298–9, 347
Goss, Wayne
   in campaign to oust National Party government 65, 66–7
   comments on Queensland electors 85
   diagnosed with a brain tumour 86–7
   elected as Labor Party leader 61
   media links 92
   as Queensland Premier 67–71, 73, 74, 75, 82
   Rudd works with 62–3, 76, 77, 89, 314–15
   seeks Commonwealth funding 80
   triumvirate with Rudd and Wayne Swan 64, 78, 110, 157, 349
government ethics 176
Government Research Unit (GRU) (Goss government) 72
Government Staffing Panel 185
Grace Brothers, Roselands 21
Grant, John 220, 221, 223
Grattan, Michelle 96, 100
Gray, Gary 179, 357
Great Depression 192
Great Wall of China 51
Grech, Godwin 220, 221, 223, 224–5
Green Paper on Carbon Pollution Reduction Scheme 251, 252
Green Party 250, 252, 254, 262
Greiner, Nick 73, 78
Griffin, Alan 116, 117, 133, 134, 357
Griffith electorate 83, 84, 87, 89, 101, 371
Griffith University 65, 69, 84, 196
GST (goods and services tax) 89

Index

Gusmao, Xanana 183
Guyana 259
Gympie 3, 4, 8

Hale School 55
Halton, Jane 180
Haneef, Mohamed 164–5
Hansards 12, 91
Hanson, Pauline 106
Hardie, Keir 127, 149
Harper, Stephen 228
Harris, Lachlan 159, 166, 314, 315
Hartcher, Peter 293, 366
Hasluck, Paul 342
Hatoyama, Yukio 209
Hawke, Bob
  advised by Ross Garnaut 249
  briefed by Rudd as a diplomat 54
  discordant relations with Paul Keating 188
  leadership style 311–12, 305
  longevity as leader 287
  loss of leadership 348
  proposes establishment of Special Premiers Conferences 78
  relationship with Keating 299
  supports Kim Beazley's leadership 136
Hawke government 94, 185, 330, 332
Hawker, Bruce 303, 365, 366
Hayden, Bill 58, 63, 64, 342
Hayek, Friedrich A 146, 147, 148, 149
health 156, 177
health and hospital reform plan 164, 245, 246, 275–7, 333–4, 341–2
Henderson, Peter 45–6
Henry, Ken 182, 189, 193, 281
Henry Review 280
Henson, Bill, photograph controversy 218
History of the Reign of Richard III (More) 139

history studies 15
Hitler, Adolf 138, 141
Hockey, Joe
  links with Godwin Grech 224
  potential Liberal Party leader 254
  on *Sunrise* program 118, 124, 125, 162
Holbrooke, Richard 237
home insulation scheme 200, 270–4
Homer 120
Hong Kong 48, 52, 208
Horne, Donald 65
Horta, Ramos 294
hospitals, Rudd visits 276
Howard government
  Alexander Downer in 105
  Asian relations 106
  attacks on Rudd's credibility and integrity 161–3
  criticism from Rudd 92, 93, 97, 144, 149
  economic management 185
  election victories 89, 105
  forced resignations 218
  handling of AWB scandal 127–9
  Michael L'Estrange in 180
  National Security Committee 330
  policy on cap and trade system 252, 253
  role of Cabinet Secretary 175–6
  Rudd seeks to differentiate himself from 155, 160
  Rudd-Gillard alliance to oust 135
  Task Group on Emissions Trading 248–9
  tax cuts during 2007 election campaign 166
  use of public funds to support initiatives 282
Howard, John
  concedes to Rudd 170

Howard, John (cont.)
   contribution to National Portrait Gallery 210
   dominance 332
   firing of departmental secretaries 181
   friendship with George W Bush 205
   longevity in government 122
   mentioned in Rudd's paper 'What I stand for' 131
   relationship with Peter Costello 188
   resigns 173
   Rudd compares with Friedrich A Hayek 146
   Rudd's birthday gift 164
   Rudd's wish to 'play with his mind' 215
   similar beliefs to Rudd on hospital funding 164
   spending promises in 2007 election campaign 168
   televised debate with Rudd 167
   testifies at Cole Inquiry 129
   time management 312–13
   trails in polls 158
   use of National Security Committee 329
   in Washington on September 11 107
'Howard's Brutopia: The Battle for Ideas in Australian Politics' (Rudd) 147, 149
Howes, Paul 296
Hu Jintao 126, 206, 234, 237
Hughes, Billy 311, 322
human rights, in China 43–4, 58
Human Rights Commission 190–1
Humphreys, Ben 83

Iceland 192
'incomings' (questions from Opposition) 216–17
Independents 174, 254
India
   at UN Climate Change Conference at Copenhagen 261
   as a big polluter 255
   and international forums 208, 227, 228, 229, 230
Indigenous policy 191
Indonesia
   on G-20 229, 241
   invasion of East Timor in 1975 94
   refugees 246
   Rudd visits 95–6
   Rudd writes on 92
   Rudd's contacts 205
   Rudd's meetings with President 182–3, 208, 234, 237
   visit by President 277
Indonesian House of Representatives, visit by Speaker 211
Indonesian language 80
industry policy 245
infrastructure, stimulus spending on 197, 198, 200, 201
Infrastructure Australia 189
Insiders (ABC TV) 106, 111–12, 274–5
insulation scheme 200, 270–4
interest rate cuts 189, 192
International Climate Change Committee 250
international credit system 192
International Crisis Group 209
international diplomacy 310
international financial institutions (IFIs) 190, 231, 234, 239, 241
   see also financial institutions
International Monetary Fund (IMF)
   and GFC 190, 211
   predictions on world economy 194, 203, 239
   reform 236, 237, 241
   role in G-20 233, 234

Rudd's involvement with 231–20, 238, 240, 277
internet 197
Interschool Christian fellowship 15
investment tax breaks, for small business 201
Iraq
  Australian Wheat Board scandal 124, 127
  Rudd visits 183
  war 103, 107, 109, 158, 200, 205
Irish government 292
Irvine, David 55–7
Italy 227, 235

Jaivin, Linda 57
Jakarta 56, 92, 95
Japan 210, 227, 238, 241, 342
Japanese language 80
Jaycees public-speaking competition 14
Jews, Nazi attacks on 140, 153
John Grant Motors 223
The Joke (police corruption in Queensland) 64
Jones, Norma 84
Jordan, Alister
  at SPBC financial crisis meeting 191
  background and education 103
  contacting of backbenchers 293–4
  and fake Ozcar email 221
  polling of backbenchers 347
  on Rudd's campaign team 166
  as Rudd's chief of staff 159, 205, 314, 315, 317
  supports Rudd's challenge to Kim Beazley's leadership 116, 124, 132, 135, 136
Joyce, Barnaby 250, 253–4

Kaohsiung Incident 42
Karzai, Hamid 183

Keating government 89, 94, 167, 174, 185
Keating, Paul
  challenges to Hawke's leadership 348, 350
  leadership style 312
  parliamentary performances 217
  prime ministerial style 185
  relations with Suharto 95
  relationship with Hawke 188, 299
  time management 312
'Keep Kevin' posters 101–2
Kelly, – (Mr) (teacher at Eumundi state school) 6
Kelly, – (Mrs) (teacher at Eumundi state school) 6
Kelly, Mike 179
Kelly, Paul 111–12
Kemp, David 81
Kevin Rudd Foreign Language Award 91
Kevin07 promotion 166–7, 197, 207, 213, 364
Keynes, John Maynard 196
Kiribati 255, 260
Kirribilli House 194, 198, 211, 268, 326
Kissinger, Henry 236, 239
Koch, David 118
Kokoda Trail 124–5
Korea 118, 229, 234, 237, 238, 241
Korean language 80
KPMG 88
Kuomintang (Chinese Nationalist Party, KMT) 41, 42
Kyoto Protocol 191, 248, 255, 260

labour markets 146, 149
Lake Burley Griffin 29
L'Aquila G-8 summit 237–8, 241, 255
Lateline (ABC TV) 107–8, 113–14, 118, 124, 126, 168, 296

Latham, Mark
  book published by 146
  comments on George W Bush 109
  conflicts with Rudd 99–101
  elected 89
  friendship with Julia Gillard 133
  leads in polls 158
  office managed by George Thompson 159
  resignation 130
  seeks party leadership 110, 111–12
  'sharpens' Labor policy on troops in Iraq 113, 114
leaders' debates (National Press Club), Rudd vs Abbott 276
leaders' debates (televised)
  Rudd vs Abbott 365, 369
  Rudd vs John Howard 167
'Leaders must act together to solve the crisis' (Rudd) 234
leaks to media 279–80, 338–9
Lehman Brothers 190, 211, 230
L'Estrange, Michael 180
'lettuce run' 52
Lewis, C S 29
Lewis, Duncan 182, 283
Lewis, Steve 221, 223
liberal capitalism 199
Liberal Party
  coalition with National Party 60
  disagreement over climate change bill 250, 253–4
  John Buchan in 9, 18
  leadership struggles 218
  Rudd lambasts 203
liberation theology 152
Libyan crisis 342
Lilley electorate 371
'Little Children are Sacred' report 164
Lodge (prime ministerial residence)
  Andrew Charlton visits 224
  Cabinet meetings 326
  Christmas reception 208
  Glyn Davis visits 194
  meetings scheduled by Fraser 314
  Rudd in 157, 173
  Terry Moran visits 182
  London G-20 summit 234–5, 255
Love Letters from Cell 92 (Bonhoeffer) 141
Ludwig, Bill 136, 356
Ludwig, Joe 179

Mabo case 76
McCain, John 205
McClelland, Doug 286–7
McDougall, Graeme 89
Macfarlane, Ian 77, 254
Machinery of Government (MOG) Committee (Goss government) 70
McKew, Maxine 111, 179
Macklin, Jenny 136, 164, 184, 191, 332
McLeay, Leo 93, 112
McMahon electorate 370
McMahon, William 342
McManus, Rove 133
maiden speech 143–6, 200, 207
Major Economies Forum 255
major reforms 311
'Making Government Work' (paper) 66
Maldives 259, 260
Man for All Seasons (Bolt) 138–9, 142
Mandarin language
  Rudd's fluency 55, 66, 126, 166, 206–7
  taught in Australian schools 80
Marist Brothers, Ashgrove 9, 10, 10–11, 289
market systems 153
markets, social democratic views on 144, 145, 146, 149
Marr, David 288–90

Index

Martin, Stephen 95
Masons 7
Mater Hospital, Brisbane 9, 11
media 197, 202, 316, 317, 322, 351, 364, 365
media regulation 351, 352
Medicare 271
Meles Zenawi 258, 259, 261
Melham, Daryl 178
members of parliament, pay and entitlements 286
Memorandum on the International Financial System 231
Menzies, Robert 18, 46, 311, 342
Merkel, Angela 228, 238, 258
Mexico 228, 229, 241, 256, 259, 261
Mickel, John 70
middle power diplomacy 210, 211
Miliband, David 237, 360
Millennium Development Goals 211, 237
Milne, Glen 163
Minchin, Nick 24, 250, 254
Ming tombs 51
mining industry, campaign against mining tax 282–3, 293
mining tax 280–3, 341
minister Question time 207
ministerial policy 245–6
ministers
   individual standing 332
   involvement with SPBC 328–9, 330–1
   and PMO 317–19
   Question Time 209, 216, 217
   and SPBC 191
   'spin' GFC 202
Mitchell, Chris 211
Le Monde 234
The Monthly 150, 198–9, 234
'Moonlight State' (*Four Corners*) 60
Moore Wilton, Max 322

Moral Sentiment (Smith) 121
Moran, Terry 182, 321–2
More, Thomas 16, 138–40, 141–3, 152
Moreton electorate 371
mortgage brokers 197
Mrdak, Mike 323
multilateral diplomacy 200, 235
Mumbai terrorist attack 205
Mural Hall, Parliament House 205
Murdoch, Rupert 239
Murdoch Press 364, 365, 368
Muspratt, Beryl 15

NAB (National Australia Bank) 205
Nambour 3–4, 5, 11, 12, 17, 18
Nambour High School 13, 63, 196, 301
Nambour state school 13
nation-building schemes 190
National Asian Languages/Studies Strategy for Australian Schools 80
National Australia Bank (NAB) 205
National Broadband Network 159, 245, 246
National Health and Hospitals Reform Commission 275
National Party
   domination of Queensland politics 60
   opposes emissions trading scheme 250, 253–4, 254
   Queensland Labor Party's campaign to oust 62, 64, 65, 66–7
National Portrait Gallery 209–10
national security
   decision-making 310
   Department of Homeland Security proposal 173
   Labor Party lags 160
   policy 244–5
   Rudd campaigns on 155, 161, 166
   Rudd initiates APEC forum 207–8

National Security Committee (NSC) 211, 283, 310, 327, 329, 359, 368, 369
National Security Statement (Security White Paper) (2008) 211, 212–13
National Trade Strategy 79
native title cases 76–7
NATO 342
Nazi regime 138, 140, 141
Nelson, Brendan 194, 218, 253
neo-liberalism 147–8, 198–9
Nepal 259
Netherlands 235
New Guinea 124–5
New York Times 237
Nicklin, Frank 17
North Africa 125
North Korea 92, 93, 118
Northern Rock Bank 189
Northern Territory 164
Norway 47, 256, 259
'Not a Happy Vegemite' (YouTube video) 345–6
nuclear non-proliferation 209
nuclear weapons 211

Oakes, Laurie 41, 339
Oakshort, Michael 147
Obama, Barack
  at G-20 235, 238, 240
  at UN Climate Change Conference at Copenhagen 259, 261
  briefed on CHOGM 258
  discussions with Rudd 205, 228, 236, 277
  response to Syrian gas attack 368
  Rudd sends report on nuclear non-proliferation 209
O'Brien, Chris 197
O'Brien, Kerry 155, 282
Oceanic Viking 246
Odyssey (Homer) 120
Office of National Assessments, London 59
Office of National Security 132, 283
O'Neill, Peter 358
Opposition syndrome 334–5
Ozcar scheme 196, 220–6
  see also Utegate
ozone depletion 47

Pacific Forum 202
Pacific Islands 210, 255, 260, 261
Pacific Islands Forum (PIF) 180, 210, 255
Paddington Hotel 21
'Pain on the Road to Recovery' (Rudd) 203
Pakistan 277
Palestine 125
Papua New Guinea 56, 183, 357–8
parable of the talents 152–3
Parkinson, George 4
Parliament House (New) 62, 204
parliamentary performance styles 217
parliamentary secretaries 179
Paterson, Mark 180
Peacock, Andrew 330, 342
Pearson, Noel 77, 194
People's Liberation Army (PLA) 49
permits (cap and trade system) 252, 253
Petraeus, General David 183
Philip, Pradeep 191
PIF *see* Pacific Islands Forum
'pillars' of foreign policy 202
Pittsburgh G-20 summit 238, 239–41
PM&C *see* Department of Prime Minister and Cabinet
police corruption in Queensland 60, 64
Policy Coordination Division (Goss government) 73
policy-making 244–5, 322–3

political economy cycle, definition 199
political management 333
Political Strategy Group 234
poll figures 158–9, 164, 168
pollution, world's biggest polluters 251, 255
poor countries 241, 259
portfolio meetings 184
poster campaign of 1978 and 1979 (Shanghai) 43
Press Gallery Ball 220
press regulation 351, 352
Price, Matt 111, 180
Price, Roger 116, 132, 207, 286
prime ministers
  arrival at Parliament House 204–5
  contingent nature of job 300–1
  decision-making 310–12
  dominance 332–6
  portfolio 176
  prerogatives 171–2, 173
  relationship with PM&C 309
  relationship with PMO 309
  relationship with public 212–13
  resources to provide advice and assistance 308
  right to select ministers 362–3
  role 183–4, 184, 213–14
  rules for election and removal 360–3
  schedules 312–14
Prime Minister's Office (PMO)
  advisory role 315, 319–20, 308
  chiefs of staff 314–15
  criticisms of 310, 320–1
  experience of staff 315
  investigates fake Ozcar scheme email 220, 221
  Joel Fitzgibbon controversy 218–19
  as link with ministers and their offices 317–19
  in Opposition mode 317
  physical layout 308–9
  as prime minister's surrogate 325
  prioritising Rudd's schedule 314
  relationship with prime minister 309
  release of YouTube video of Rudd 345–6
  scheduling of daily meetings between Rudd, Gillard and Swan 283–4
  strategy to eliminate Rudd from office 346–7
Progressive Governance Summit 206
public policy 160, 244
public sector, risk management 271–2
Public Sector Management Commission (PSMC) 69, 70, 72, 77
public service
  Rudd's disappointment with 72, 185–6, 194, 202–3
  Westminster 181
public speaking 14

Q&A (ABC TV) 369
Quarterly Essay 288
Queensland Institute of Technology (QIT) 61, 63
Queensland Labor Party 64, 65, 66–7, 72
Queensland Office of Cabinet 73, 77, 78, 79, 84
Queensland public service 72
Queensland University of Technology (formerly Queensland Institute of Technology) (QUT) 64
Question Time
  briefs for Rudd 197
  Goss government ministers' behaviour 67–8
  procedures 215–17
  Rudd addresses 161, 205, 220

Question Time (cont.)
  Tactics Committee questions 123, 207
Quihuangdao 51
Quinlan, Garry 315

Rankin electorate 371
Rasmussen, Lars Lokke 258, 259
Ray, Robert
  advice on composition of Cabinet 285–6
  on Conroy as 'factional Dalek' 362
  John Faulkner works with 174
  role in Senate inquiry into 'Children Overboard' incident 175
  Rudd works with 117, 157, 167, 172, 178–9
  support for Rudd in challenging Kim Beazley's leadership 136
Readings Bookshop, Carlton 212
recession 202, 292–3
Reconciliation Action Plan (National Australia Bank) 205
Reed, Bruce 81, 205
reform policies 245
refugees 246, 339
regional engagement 207, 211
regional resettlement for asylum seekers 357–8
regulation of financial institutions 190, 229, 235, 237, 240, 241
regulation of financial markets 198, 199
Rein, John 26
Rein, Thérèse
  1996 campaign 84, 85
  attends opening of National Portrait Gallery 209
  birth and childhood 26–7
  comments on Harry Barber 29
  comments on Rudd's calligraphy studies 31
  diplomatic wife 48, 50
  mentioned by Rudd on *Sunrise* 118
  relationship with Rudd 25–7, 27–8, 46
  walks Kokoda Trail 124
  Work Directions Australia business 87, 162–3
  work in public service 41
religious vote 123
'Renewing the IMF: A Practical Resourcing and Reform Plan to Deal with the Crisis' (working paper) 236
Reserve Bank 191, 192
Resource Super Profits Tax (RSPT) 260–2
Richardson, Dennis 210, 227
Richardson, Graham 115
Rio Tinto 282
risk management, in public sector 271–2
Rove (TV program) 197
Rove, Karl 133
Roxon, Nicola 89, 247, 275, 348–9
Rudd, Bert
  birth and early life 3–4
  death 9–10, 162
  employment 7, 18
  life insurance policy 12
  marriage 4–5, 8
  political preferences 17, 157
  relationship with Rudd 7, 8
'Rudd bikes' 91
Rudd, Greg
  at Rudd's fortieth birthday party 86
  comments on Rudd's political life 59, 63
  education 9, 10
  relationship with Rudd 5, 8
  religious beliefs 9, 23
Rudd, Jessica 48, 50, 101, 166

Index

Rudd, Kevin
  agreement to stand down 295
  as backbencher 337, 351, 298
  birth and childhood 5–12
  campaigning for 2010 election 338, 339–41
  challenge to Gillard's leadership 347, 350
  character
    ability to mix with public 168
    ambitiousness 57
    attitudes toward studying 43
    disciplined 62, 63
    drive and determination 299, 301, 335
    need for information and data 203–4, 302–4, 314, 315
    need to be in control 307
    nerdiness 126, 305
    persuasiveness 259–60, 335
    political ruthlessness 335
    self-belief 299, 301, 335
    tidiness 8
    values personal contact 204, 305–6
  Christian faith 143, 149–54, 302
  Catholic origins 7, 23–4
    explored in early years 22–5, 29–30
  declines to challenge for leadership 352–3
  determination to regain leadership 342–55
  education
    primary 6, 10
    secondary 12–19
    university 24, 25, 30–1, 48, 142
  employment in early life 21–2, 41
  fiscal conservatism 161, 169, 185
  as Foreign Minister in Gillard government 340, 341–2, 343, 346, 347
  health problems 5, 83, 222, 225, 338
  interests 9, 14–16, 19, 24–5, 28
  leadership style 335–6, 336
  leaks to media 338–9
  marriage 46
  policy interests 333–4, 335–6
  political instincts 305
  as Prime Minister (2007–2010)
    ability to connect with people 305–6
    ambitious policy agenda 306–8
    Cabinet style 326
    coup against his leadership 296–7
    decision-making 310–12
    loss of leadership 297–8
    need to understand issues and underpinning logic 302–4
    party reform 362
    philosophy of governing 308
    popularity with electorate 285, 286, 287
    standing in Labor Party 285–7, 335
    treatment of staff 72, 75–6, 320, 324, 303–4
    work habits 301, 302
  as Prime Minister (2013)
    attack on Opposition's policy costings 367
    Cabinet style 326
    election campaign 363–8
    formation of Cabinet 356
    party reform 360–3
    policy agenda 357–63, 365
    popularity with electorate 279, 280, 282, 370
    speech conceding election defeat 371
    standing down as leader 371
    time management 313–14
  reconciliation meeting with Gillard 340
  regaining of leadership 355
  relations with media 316
  resignation as Foreign Minister 347

405

Rudd, Kevin (cont.)
    resignation from seat of Griffith 372
    use of Queensland country
        vernacular 156
    writing
        in *Australian* 92, 93, 106
        in *Foreign Affairs* 229
        on GFC 198–9, 203
        manifesto of beliefs 130–2, 147, 158
        in *The Monthly* 147, 150, 234
Rudd, Loree
    at Rudd's Nambour home 12, 20
    comments on Rudd's work ethic 88
    convent life 11
    education 8–9, 13
    relationship with Rudd 5, 6–7
    visited by Rudd as a student 41
    visits Bert Rudd in hospital 10
Rudd, Malcolm 5, 8, 9, 10
Rudd (née DeVere), Margaret
    birth and early life 4
    Catholicism 7
    death 20
    ill health 20
    impact of Bert Rudd's death 10–12
    marriage 4–5, 8
    nursing career 10–11, 12
    political preferences 17, 157
    relationship with George Parkinson 125
    religious faith 23, 150
Rudd, Nick 56, 101, 124–5
Rudd, Thomas 4
Russia 208, 237
Ryckmans, Pierre 33, 34, 43, 44

Sachs, Jeffrey 237, 239
St Thomas More Forum 150
Salad Days (musical) 213
Sarkozy, Nicolas 233, 240, 258
SAS soldiers 219
Saudi Arabia 241

Scanlan, Phil 80–1, 208
Scarborough, Qld 11
schedules, of prime ministers 312–14
Schlesinger, Arthur Jr 199
school building and maintenance
    programs 200, 201, 202
Scores nightclub incident 20, 163
Scowcroft, Brent 81
Second World War (1939-45) 4, 9
Secord, Walt 159
'secret politicians business' 326
security *see* national security
Security Council (United Nations) 207, 211
Security White Paper (National
    Security Statement) (2008) 211, 212–13
Selangor Hospital 4, 12
Senior Committee in National
    Security (SCNS) 283
September 11 attacks 101, 103, 105, 109
services housing 200
7.30 Report (ABC TV) 64, 118, 124, 155, 163, 252, 273, 282
Shanahan, Dennis 347, 293
Shangri-la dialogue (2009) 208–9
share farms 10, 157
Shergold, Peter
    heads Task Group on Emissions
        Trading 249
    report on a cap and trade system 252
    resigns from PM&C 181, 182
    works with Rudd in government 171, 179, 180
Sheridan, Greg 57–8, 81
Sherry, Nick 294
Shop and Allied Workers Union 136
Shop, Distributive and Allied
    Employees Association (SDA) 178, 179

Index

Shorten, Bill 99, 115, 179
  election as Labor leader 371–2
  lack of experience governing 290
  meetings with Rudd over leadership 354
  as part of leadership group under Rudd 357, 363
  support for Rudd's return to leadership 355
Sicily 120–1
signature policies 245, 246, 310, 332
signature reforms 31
Singapore 183, 208, 209
Skills Australia 189
Sky News 346, 296
Slipper, Peter 101, 118
small business 201
Smarr, Larry 159
Smith, Adam 16, 100, 121
Smith, Ric 212
Smith, Stephen 110, 122, 136, 340
Smith, Warwick 81
social democracy 198, 199
social democrats 146, 147, 148
'sofa' government 330
Somare, Michael 183
Soros, George 239
South Africa 229, 239, 261
South Korea 118, 229, 277
Soviet gas pipeline 47
Spain 235, 277
Special Premiers Conferences 78
'spin' 202, 316
state assistance as a government principle 153
state governments see Council of Australian Governments 183
Stephenson, Michael 71
Stern, Nicholas 250
Stern Report 250
Stiglitz, Joe 237
Stockholm 46–7

Strategic Priorities and Budget Committee (SPBC)
  deferral of plan to price carbon 277–8
  during GFC 191, 194, 200
  importance 327
  involvement of ministers 328–9, 330–1
  meetings 283, 329–30
  members 327
  number of issues dealt with 283
  powers 327–8
  process 329–30
  role 310, 327, 310
  and Rudd 208
Strong, Sustainable and Balanced Growth framework 240
Sturgess, Gary 73, 78
sub-prime crisis in United States 189
Sugden, Fiona 13
Suharto 95
Summer Palace 51
Summers, Larry 206
Sunrise (TV program) 101, 117, 118–19, 124–6, 162, 305
  see also Channel 7
superannuation policy 245, 351
superpower, Australia as 210
Swan, Wayne
  at Nambour High School 13, 15
  at Question Time 216, 217
  background and education 63–4
  book published by 146
  in campaign to oust National Party government 65
  contemporary of John Faulkner 175
  criticism of Rudd 349
  daily meetings with Rudd 283–4
  develops confidence as Treasurer 188
  during GFC 191, 195, 196
  and fake Ozcar scheme email 220, 221, 224

Swan, Wayne (cont.)
   as member of Climate Change Committee 252, 327
   negotiations with states and mining companies regarding mining tax 281, 282
   retention of his seat in 2013 election 371
   returns to Parliament in 1998 89
   SPBC membership 327
   support for Kim Beazley as leader 110, 122, 136
   support for Rudd as leader 291, 297
   on Tactics Committee 207
   tax reform 332
   triumvirate with Wayne Goss and Rudd 78
   works with Rudd 109, 157, 177, 178, 189, 190
   writing on 1989 Queensland election 67
Sweden 46–8
Sydney Morning Herald 203, 279, 293
Sydney Opera House 205
Syria 368

Tactics Committee 123, 207, 208, 216, 209
Taipei 42–3
Taiwan 41–3, 92, 93
talents, parable of 152–3
Taliban 103
Tampa affair 101
Tanner, Lindsay
   ambitiousness 89
   book published by 146
   competence 332
   on deferral of carbon pricing 278
   during GFC 195
   retirement from politics 337
   SPBC membership 327
   works with Rudd 157, 177, 178

Tansuo journal 44
Task Group on Emissions Trading 249
tax on carbon 262
tax reform 334
taxpayers, stimulus spending on 200, 201
Taylor, Lenore 278–9, 280, 343
technology, Rudd's use 187, 188, 197, 199
telecommunications policy 246
terrorism 205, 211
Thailand 277
theatre 15, 19
Thompson, George 159, 185
three 'pillars' of foreign policy 202
Tiananmen demonstrations 66
time management 312–14
Tintin 301
toxic assets 234, 236
trade affairs 123
transition arrangements for Rudd government 171, 172, 173
Tune, David 232, 323
Turkey 229, 241
Turnbull, Malcolm
   beliefs about climate change 253, 254, 262
   and fake Ozcar scheme email 220–6
Tuvalu 255, 260
24-hour media cycle 317
2020 Summit 188, 194–7
Twitter 188, 197–9

unions 156, 164, 178
United Nations (UN)
   Australian mission 128
   Ban Ki-moon as Secretary General 183, 205
   Climate Change Conference at Copenhagen (2009) 238, 241, 253, 254–62, 267, 306
   climate change meetings 239
   Declaration of Human Rights 208

membership 149
resolutions 108
Rudd addresses 190, 211, 230
Security Council 207, 211, 341
United States
  as a big polluter 251, 255
  and climate change financing for Africa 259, 260
  Copenhagen Commitment Circle seeks to engage 256
  Dennis Richardson as ambassador 210
  economic uncertainty in 2008 211
  Framework for Strong, Sustainable and Balanced Recovery 240
  on G-7 227
  on G-20 235, 241, 242
  impact of Global Financial Crisis 230
  importance to Australia's national security 284
  Rudd seeks to involve in Asia-Pacific community 208
  Rudd's first visit to as Prime Minister 205
United States alliance
  Laurie Brereton's scepticism 94
  as a 'pillar' of foreign policy 108, 109, 146, 149, 202
  reaffirmed by National Security Statement 211
  reaffirmed in Defence White Paper 212
  Rudd's commitment 161, 200, 205
United States 'deputy sheriff,' Australia's role as 106, 108, 200
Unity Hall, Balmain 362
universities, stimulus spending on 200
University of Berlin 140
University of Melbourne 181–2
University of Queensland 19, 21, 63, 104

University of Western Australia 55
Uranquinty, NSW 4, 9
Utegate 225, 226
  see also Ozcar scheme
Utopia 16, 140
Utzon, Jørn 205

Vaile, Mark 129
Valley of Death period of GFC 193, 197
Victorian Premier's Department 249, 321
Vietnam 8, 259
Vietnam ANZAC service 162
Volker, Paul 127

Wade, Mary 4
Washington G-20 summit 233–4
Washington Post 52
Watt, Ian 179
Wealth of Nations (Smith) 16
weapons of mass destruction (WMD) 107–8
website (Rudd's) 197
Wei Jingsheng 43–4
Wen Jinbao 259, 261
Werriwa electorate 370
Wesley, Michael 196
West Timor 95
Western Australian Crime Commission 161
Western Ring Road, Melbourne 212
Westminster system 180, 181, 186, 202
Wheat Board *see* Australian Wheat Board
White Paper on Carbon Pollution Reduction Scheme 253
Whitlam, Gough 16, 17, 95
Whitlam government 22, 185
whole-of-government responses 322
Wilson, Harold 334
Wirajuda, Hassan 107

Wolfensohn, Jim 236
Wombye, Queensland 17
Wong, Penny
  at Bali Conference on Climate
    Change (2007) 182
  competence 332
  on deferral of carbon pricing plan
    278
  in emissions trading scheme
    negotiations 252, 254
  as Finance Minister 367
  heads Department of Climate
    Change 306
  as member of CCC 327
  as member of leadership group 363
  as Senate leader 357
  works with Rudd 172, 184
Woolcott, Birgit 208
Woolcott, Dick 81, 208
Work Choices 159, 173, 211, 245
'working families' 159
workplace relations 155
World Bank
  aid for Pacific Islands 210
  change to governance arrangements
    241
  during Global Financial Crisis 190,
    203, 238
  Jim Wolfensohn at 236
  role in G-7 227–8
  role in G-20 233, 234
  Rudd's first meeting as Prime
    Minister 183
  Rudd's links 205
World Vision gift-in-kind program
  165
Wright, George 363–4, 366, 371

Xi Jinping 291

Yandina Creek 5, 14
Young Labor meetings 18
Young, Mick 63
Yudhoyono, Susilo Bambang 182–3,
  208

Zoellick, Bob
  in AALD 81, 183
  comments on G-20 228, 232, 235
  President of World Bank 183,
    205–6, 228

CITY LIBRARY